Prosody in Syntactic Encoding

Linguistische Arbeiten

Edited by
Klaus von Heusinger, Agnes Jäger,
Gereon Müller, Ingo Plag,
Elisabeth Stark and Richard Wiese

Volume 573

Prosody in Syntactic Encoding

Edited by
Gerrit Kentner and Joost Kremers

DE GRUYTER

ISBN 978-3-11-099211-3
e-ISBN (PDF) 978-3-11-065053-2
e-ISBN (EPUB) 978-3-11-065141-6
ISSN 0344-6727

Library of Congress Control Number: 2020938896

Bibliographic information published by the Deutsche Nationalbibliothek
The Deutsche Nationalbibliothek lists this publication in the Deutsche Nationalbibliografie;
detailed bibliographic data are available on the Internet at http://dnb.dnb.de.

© 2022 Walter de Gruyter GmbH, Berlin/Boston
This volume is text- and page-identical with the hardback published in 2020.
Typesetting: le-tex publishing services GmbH, Leipzig
Printing and binding: CPI books GmbH, Leck

www.degruyter.com

Contents

Gerrit Kentner and Joost Kremers
Prosody in syntactic encoding —— 1

Arto Anttila, Timothy Dozat, Daniel Galbraith, and Naomi Shapiro
Sentence stress in presidential speeches —— 17

Tina Bögel
**German case ambiguities at the interface:
Production and comprehension** —— 51

Miriam Butt, Farhat Jabeen, and Tina Bögel
**Ambiguity resolution via the syntax-prosody interface:
The case of *kya* 'what' in Urdu/Hindi** —— 85

Katy Carlson
Focus structure affects comparatives: Experimental and corpus work —— 119

Marta Wierzba
The ordering of interface mapping rules in German object fronting —— 159

Johannes Heim and Martina Wiltschko
Interaction at the syntax–prosody interface —— 189

E Jamieson
Syntacticizing intonation? Tag questions in Glasgow Scots —— 219

Hisao Tokizaki and Jiro Inaba
A prosodic constraint on prenominal modification —— 245

Volker Struckmeier
**Cartography cannot express scrambling restrictions –
but interface-driven relational approaches can** —— 265

Joost Kremers
Head movement as a syntax-phonology interface phenomenon —— 303

Index —— 331

Gerrit Kentner and Joost Kremers
Prosody in syntactic encoding

1 Introduction

Prosody and syntax are fundamental components of linguistic form. The term prosody refers to those properties of the speech signal that are not reducible to the individual phones but to their grouping into phonological units of higher order, such as syllables, metrical feet, phonological words or prosodic phrases (Nespor & Vogel 2007; Selkirk 1984). The smaller prosodic units are necessary and inherent parts of the larger ones, i.e. every prosodic phrase consists of at least one phonological word which in turn consists of at least one metrical foot which in turn consists of at least one syllable. Therefore, with prosody, the sound string is not merely a linear sequence but it is endowed with hierarchical structure, i.e. another dimension of phonological organization. The audible reflex of this multi-layered organization is the rhythm, the phrasing, and the intonation of an utterance.

Like the sound units, the meaningful building blocks of language (the morphemes) are organized in hierarchical fashion: words consist of morphemes and are grouped into phrases, according to the rules of (morpho)syntax.

Whether the kind of hierarchical organization in phonology is comparable to the one in syntax is a contentious issue. To be sure, whatever the respective organizing principles, the structures are necessarily compatible. This is because phonology and syntax together are tasked with the form of language, albeit on different layers: Phonology is primarily responsible for the subsymbolic layer on which the sound units (which may bring about a difference in meaning but are themselves devoid of meaning) are put together, and syntax is responsible for the symbolic layer on which morphemes are arranged.

In spite of these similarities, however, the phonological and syntactic modes of hierarchical organization employ ontologically different vocabularies. For example, while the notion of *size* matters for the organization of prosody (smaller units, e.g. syllables, are grouped into larger ones, e.g. metrical feet), embedding in syntax does not make reference to size. Conversely, morphosyntactic concepts like the distinction between arguments and adjuncts are alien to the phonology.

The syntax-phonology interface is responsible for fusing these different structures to evolve into a coherent *Gestalt* of linguistic form. It is commonly assumed that prosody takes its cue from, and therefore reflects, syntactic structure (for a recent review, see Bennett & Elfner (2019)). The prosodic rendering of syntactic structure, however, is imperfect and limited, as prosody is affected by other conditions as well, e.g. discourse-related and paralinguistic ones. What is more, prosody leads a life of its own, i.e. it is subject to inherently *prosodic* well-formedness conditions; chief among those are the constraints formulated in the Strict Layer Hypothesis (Selkirk 1984), or the preference for rhythmic alternation of stressed and unstressed syllables, or for balanced phrasing. It has been suggested that, under certain circumstances, syntax is malleable at the will of such prosodic well-formedness conditions. This is most obvious in metered poetry; poets may violate syntactic rules in order to make the word sequence fit the predetermined arrangement of metrical feet (Fitzgerald 2007; Kiparsky 1975; Youmans 1983). To a lesser degree, this is true for rhetoric registers as well (Bolinger 1957 and Anttila, this volume); crucially, even in normal language use, prosodic influences on syntax have been shown (see Sect. 3 and Anttila (2016) for a review), though they appear to be rather limited in scope (Kentner & Franz 2019).

At first sight, these reciprocal influences defy the traditional prerequisite that syntax be "phonology-free": syntax operates on morphosyntactic structures without any awareness of the phonological structures onto which they are mapped. This assumption is in fact one of the main arguments in favor of so-called sequential grammar models, such as the derivational models developed within generative grammar.

Similarly, phonologists generally assume that phonology is syntax-free. For example, Scheer (2008, p. 146) refers to the principle of *Indirect Reference*: "according to which phonology cannot directly access morpho-syntactic structure and hence may not mention morpho-syntactic categories in the structural description of rules (or in constraints)", see Bermúdez-Otero (2012) for a similar point.

However, it is becoming increasingly clear that there are phenomena that violate these principles. Faced with apparently reciprocal influences of syntax and prosody, some phonologists suggest certain aspects of prosody to be beyond the realm of phonology proper. For example, Scheer (2012) considers intonation to be syntactic in nature as it shows signs of recursion, a property that is considered to be at the heart of syntax. Some syntacticians happily co-opt prosodic phenomena into their representations: With the rising interest in, and development of, discourse-related left-peripheral projections in syntax (Rizzi 1997), researchers have incorporated *intonational morphemes* into the syntactic spine to signify notions such as focus.

On the other hand, recent years have seen widespread acknowledgement of the assumption that word order, a core aspect of sentence structure, is not solely the business of syntax but subject to phonological constraints as well (Bennett et al. 2016; Agbayani & Golston 2016; Kentner & Franz 2019).

In sum, in the current discourse on the syntax-phonology interface, we observe a shifting definition of whether certain properties of linguistic form are phonological in nature or whether they are considered to be of syntactic essence (cf. Bermúdez-Otero & Honeybone 2006). The contributions in this volume take different stances regarding this question, and they bring to bear a variety of phenomena in evaluating this issue.

Before summarizing the contributions in this volume, we briefly review the two sides of the coin, as it were; namely, on the one hand, syntactic influences on prosody, and conversely, prosodic effects on sentence structure.

2 Syntax affecting prosody

The syntactic constituent structure is, to some extent, reflected in prosodic phrasing. In languages such as English or German, if a syntactic phrase boundary corresponds with a prosodic boundary, it is usually the right edge of the phrase that is prosodically marked: Intonational boundaries are signalled by final lengthening (a slowdown in speech rate towards the end of prosodic phrases), boundary tones (rising or falling pitch towards the end of a prosodic phrase) or pauses; usually, such intonational phrase boundaries correspond with the edges of major syntactic constituents. This is certainly true for boundaries of sentences (1b), but also for parentheticals such as in (2), which are prosodically detached from the clause they appear in.

(1) a. Martin heiratet Maria nicht. Féry (1993)
   Martin marries Maria not
   'Martin does not marry Maria.'

   b. Martin heiratet. Maria nicht.
   Martin marries Maria not
   'Martin is getting married. Maria [is] not.'

(2) In Pakistan, Tuesday, which is a weekday, is, Jane said, a holiday.
   Selkirk (1984)

However, while the distribution of intonational boundaries is not arbitrary (cf. the impermissible phrasing in (3c)), it is variable: both the phrasings in (3a) and (3b) are licit. As the prosodic integration of the PP *from London* into its host NP in (3a) shows, not all major syntactic phrases necessarily correspond to prosodic phrases.

(3) a. Jill Smith from London # took part in the march.
   b. Jill Smith # from London # took part in the march.
   c. *Jill Smith from # London took part in the march.

Whether or not a syntactic phrase has a prosodic analogue is determined by various factors. According to Watson & Gibson (2004), the production of prosodic boundaries depends both on syntactic structure and on the constituents' size. Specifically, Watson & Gibson (2004) observe that prosodic boundaries are often set after long constituents, providing the speaker with time for recovery, and – to a far lesser extent (Kentner 2007) – before long constituents to give the speaker planning time. Therefore, a prosodic break is very likely to occur before the conjunction *and* in (4a) but far less likely at the same syntactic position in (4b).

(4) a. The guest list includes Benedict Timothy Cumberbatch and Daniel John Higginbotham.
   b. The guest list includes Ben and Daniel.

Notably, if the conjuncts in (4b) are not separated by a clear prosodic phrase break before *and*, the conjunction is preferably cliticized to the preceding monosyllabic name *Ben*, effectively forming a trochaic foot that straddles a syntactic phrase boundary (Lahiri & Plank 2010).

The likelihood of observing a prosodic boundary at the edge of a syntactic boundary is also dependent on the depth of the constituent's embedding. Consider the potential phrase boundary before the *because*-clause in (5). A prosodic phrase boundary is likely to be stronger (or, put differently: more likely to be present) in (5a) compared to (5b). This is because in (5b) the *because*-clause is embedded under the sentence-initial concessive clause which in turn is embedded under the following main clause. Evidently, in (5b) the syntactically higher boundary between the concessive and the main clause needs to be marked more clearly by a prosodic phrase break than the lower boundary before *because*, while at the same time producing a coherent intonation for the whole sentence.

(5) a. Jane was late because she had run into a friend; she still managed to catch the bus.
   b. Although Jane was late because she had run into a friend, she still managed to catch the bus.

In line with this observation, studies by Wagner (2005) and Kentner & Féry (2013) on various string-identical structures involving coordinated names reveal a prosodic reflex of syntactic depth of embedding. The prosodic boundary after the name *Willi* in (6a) is more pronounced compared to (6b), in which *Willi* is embedded within a larger constituent which in turn is closed off by a stronger intonational break after the name *Mila*. Because of the strong prosodic break after *Mila* in (6b), the two structures in (6) are clearly disambiguated by prosodic means.

(6) a. (Nino and Willi) or Mila or Suse
    b. ((Nino and Willi) or Mila) or Suse

Interestingly however, as shown by Kentner & Féry (2013), while the left branching structures in (6) are marked by significantly distinct prosodic phrasings, the prosodic difference between the right-branching counterparts (7) is minuscule and the prosodic renderings of (7a) and (7b) hardly discernible. That is, whether or not syntactic depth of embedding is reflected in prosodic phrasing crucially hinges on the branching direction.[1]

(7) a. Nino or Willi or (Mila and Suse)
    b. Nino or (Willi or (Mila and Suse))

Like prosodic phrasing, prosodic prominence can be affected by syntax. For example, while lexical arguments usually bear sentence stress, their heads do not, or at least not necessarily (Gussenhoven 1983; Truckenbrodt 2006). As a case in point, consider the phrase *in Berlin* in (8): When serving as a prepositional object (8a) it receives nuclear accent and the verb may remain unaccented; as a locative adjunct (8b), *Berlin* bears prenuclear or secondary accent, with the main accent falling on the verb. Truckenbrodt (2006) attributes this difference in accentuation to the workings of the syntax-phonology interface constraint STRESSXP that requires every lexical XP to bear stress. This constraint is sensitive to the different syntactic associations of the phrase *in Berlin* in (8a) and (8b): the object *in Berlin* (8a) is considered an inherent part of the VP; therefore, stress on *Berlin* satisfies STRESSXP for the VP and the prepositional object at the same time. In (8b), *in Berlin* is adjoined to the VP. Stress on the adjunct alone however, would not satisfy

---

[1] There is reason to doubt that the correspondence between syntactic constituent structure and prosodic phrasing is universal. A comparable study on coordinated names in Hindi failed to show effects of syntactic embedding on prosodic phrasing (Féry & Kentner 2010); another study by Féry & Schubö (2010) shows syntactic effects on prosodic phrasing in center embedded relative clauses in German, but fails to find them in equivalent structures in Hindi. Apparently, languages differ with respect to the plasticity of their prosodic structures, with Hindi displaying rather rigid prosodic phrasing that is less responsive to syntactic or pragmatic givens when compared to intonation languages like German or English (Féry 2016).

STRESSXP for the core projection of the intransitive verb. Therefore, main stress on the verb is called for in (8b).

(8) a. Peter hat sich in BERLIN verliebt.
Peter has himself in Berlin fallen-in-love
'Peter has fallen in love with Berlin.'

b. Peter hat sich in Berlin VERLIEBT.
Peter has himself in Berlin fallen-in-love
'Peter has fallen in love in Berlin.'

The minimal pair (9) by Bresnan (1971) works in a similar way. In (9a), *plans* is the direct object to the verb *leave*; hence, with stress on *plans*, STRESSXP is satisfied for the entire VP and the verb remains unstressed, as in (8a) above. In (9b), on the other hand, *to leave* is the argument to the noun *plans* and hence needs to receive prominence.

(9) a. George has PLANS to leave.

b. George has plans to LEAVE.

Another case of prosodic prominence reflecting syntactic structure is represented by expressions with focus-sensitive particles like *only* (10).

(10) a. Brian only touched the CHALICE [... but not the altar].

b. Brian only TOUCHED the chalice [... but did not drink from it].

The accentual difference is due to the different foci in (10a) (focus on *chalice*) and (10b) (focus on *touched*), with *only* associated with the respective domain of focus (skipping the verb in the case of (10a)).

Similarly, as shown by Selkirk (2002); Féry & Hartmann (2005), and Kentner et al. (2008), elliptical sentences like (11b) are prosodically distinct from string-identical non-elliptical counterparts (11a). Again, this difference is related to focus, as the verb *fixing* in the second conjunct in (11b) is contrasted to the verb *riding* in the first conjunct, hence the contrastive focus on *fixing* that is marked by accentuation.

(11) a. Nina is RIDING and Ian is fixing a BIKE.

b. Nina is RIDING a bike and Ian is FIXING a bike.

Whether information structural notions such as topic or focus are to be directly represented as dedicated heads in the syntactic representation (Rizzi 1997;

Frey 2004), or whether they only indirectly interact with syntax and hence need to be modelled independently (Fanselow 2007), is debatable (see, e.g. the contributions by Struckmeyer and Wierzba, this volume). Nevertheless, the examples clearly show that different syntactic associations (focus-related or otherwise) may have consequences for the pattern of prosodic prominences.

3 Prosody affecting syntax

Syntactic phenomena in which phonology appears to play a role are also well-known. For example, Zec & Inkelas (1990) discuss three phenomena, among which the well-known Heavy-NP Shift phenomenon in English, where a "heavy" NP undergoes movement to the right:

(12) a. *Mark showed to John {some pictures}$_{p\text{-phr}}$.

b. Mark showed to John {some pictures}$_{p\text{-phr}}$ {from his beloved city}$_{p\text{-phr}}$.

One of the factors that appears to play a role in allowing the NP to shift is its phonological structure. If the NP consists of at least two phonological phrases, shifting is possible, provided the NP also constitutes new information (cf. Arnold et al. 2000). An NP that consists of a single phonological phrase cannot shift, even if it is new information.

Similarly, Samek-Lodovici (2005) discusses Italian examples in which the syntactic structure appears to adapt itself in order to meet a prosodic requirement:

(13) context: *What happened?*

[Gianni ha RISO]$_F$
Gianni has laughed

(14) context: *Who laughed?*

a. *GIANNI$_F$ ha riso
 Gianni has laughed

b. Ha riso GIANNI$_F$
 has laughed Gianni

In (13), the entire clause is new information (focus), answering the question *What happened?* In (14), the verb *laughed* is mentioned in the question, so when it appears in the answer, it is not in focus. Instead, only the subject *Gianni* is in focus. In English, it is possible to indicate this by emphasising the subject (cf. *JOHN laughed*). In Italian, this option is not available. In order to mark subject focus, the syntactic structure must be changed. The trigger for this change, however, is not syntactic but prosodic, as Féry (2013) argues: the focused element *Gianni* must be right-aligned with an intonational phrase (IntP).[2]

If the proposed phonological (or prosodic) analysis for such phenomena is on the right track, several important questions are raised. Foremost, interactions between syntax and phonology of this type are difficult, if not impossible, to account for in standard models of grammar. A common assumption in many generative approaches is that the grammar is sequential. Syntax operates on morphosyntactic heads void of phonological content and without prosodic constituency. Only when syntax completes a structure is it handed over to the phonological component. At this point, the syntactic structure is fixed and cannot be altered anymore.

One analysis that has been proposed is to have syntax generate multiple structures simultaneously and have phonology filter out those structures that violate some phonological or prosodic constraint. One such proposal is made by Büring (2013), who calls this a *Try-and-Filter* approach. A similar proposal is the so-called *distributed deletion* account (e.g., Fanselow & Çavar 2002), which exploits Chomsky's (1993) *copy theory of movement*. Chomsky argues that a moved element does not leave behind a trace in the traditional sense, but a copy of itself, so that the syntactic structure contains multiple copies of any moved element. Chomsky simply assumes that it is always the highest copy that is pronounced, while all other copies are by definition silent. Fanselow & Çavar argue that under certain circumstances, the phonological component has the option to spell out a lower copy.

However, such proposals cannot escape the fact that they need some point in the derivation in which syntactic and phonological information is available simultaneously. For example, in Samek-Lodovici's focus example above in (13) / (14), it is the element that carries the focus feature that must be right-aligned with the IntP boundary. This focus feature is not a phonological feature, however, and the element that carries it is a syntactic constituent.

Note that we cannot argue that what is actually being aligned is a prosodic constituent that has some phonologically visible property (e.g., sentence stress) that corresponds to the focus feature. As Féry (2010) points out, languages generally do not have a single phonological correlate of focus (apart from alignment).

---

[2] Other phenomena not discussed here include subject drop in English (Weir 2012), *wh*-movement or lack thereof (Richards 2010). See also Erteschik-Shir & Rochman (2010) for further discussion.

For example, in languages like German, the focused constituent often carries sentence stress, but it does not always do so. Alignment applies nonetheless.[3]

The sequential approach therefore runs into a fundamental problem: in order to account for phonology-to-syntax interaction effects, the grammar needs access to syntactic and phonological information *at the same time*. In a sequential model, this inevitably requires making detailed information from one module available in another, or, alternatively, setting up an additional module that has access to both kinds of information. In some approaches, this is the role ascribed to the PF component of grammar (e.g., Kandybowicz 2007).

One possible solution may be to adopt Chomsky's (2001) proposal that the derivation proceeds *cyclically*: at certain steps in the derivation, the structure built up so far is evaluated by phonology and the result passed back to syntax. If the cycles are small enough, the grammar may be able to deal with the phenomena under discussion, although it is an open question how exactly this would work. Another solution could be to adopt a parallel model (Culicover & Jackendoff 2005; Sadock 2012, 1992), since such a model makes the fundamental assumption that the relevant syntactic and phonological information is available simultaneously, albeit to different modules. Here, too, the question is how exactly such a system would work, however, since it is not clear how violations of phonological constraints can be fed back to syntax in a parallel model.

Another question that is raised by the idea that phonology can affect syntax concerns the types of phonological information that has the ability to trigger syntactic effects. Zec & Inkelas (1990) argue that this should be limited to prosodic structure, i.e., requirements on prosodic structure can trigger syntactic reordering, but other phonological information cannot.

While it is true that there do not seem to be languages with syntactic rules of the type "Front a word if it starts with [b]", it is not entirely certain that segmental structure is completely irrelevant for syntax. For example, Golston (1995) points to effects such as the one illustrated in (15):

(15) a. The video of "Macbeth" / The "Macbeth" video

   b. The video of "The Dead" / *The "The Dead" video

Golston does note that *The "The Dead" video* is only ruled out because there is an alternative structure that has the same semantics and does not have a se-

---

[3] Note, however, that Kügler & Féry (2017) show that even deaccented foci have some residual accent. It is an open question whether this residual accent would suffice for alignment to be prosodic in nature.

quence of *the the*. Similar structures in German are not ruled out because there is no syntactic alternative:

(16) a. die, die die Blumen gekauft haben
 those who the flowers bought have
 'those who have bought the flowers'

 b. dass das das Problem ist
 that this the problem is
 'that this is the problem'

These facts suggests that syntax overrules phonology, at least when it comes to phonological constraints involving segments, but the question is still very much open, especially considering the fact that in the English example, the two *the*'s are morphosyntactically identical, while the three *die*'s and the three *das(s)*'s in the German examples are not, suggesting that a purely morphosyntactic analysis may not be infeasible.

4 Outline of this book

The contributions in this volume bring to bear various kinds of evidence in evaluating the role of prosody in syntactic encoding; the theoretical models that guide both the research questions and the interpretation of the data are equally diverse. Therefore, the reader will not find a unique and coherent answer to the question what role prosody has to play in sentence formation. Rather, the variety of answers presented here reflect the different stances the authors take regarding what the terms prosody and syntax entail. At the same time, they hint at how far-reaching the question of prosody-syntax interactions is for the study of linguistic form.

Arto Anttila, Timothy Dozat, Daniel Galbraith, and Naomi Shapiro examine the prosody and syntax of presidential speeches. Even though this rhetoric genre consists – to a large extent – of scripted speech, the authors make a general point regarding the sources of prosodic prominence and its relation to syntax. Specifically, they argue that sentential prominences are, on the one hand, directly related to surface syntactic structure and, on the other hand, to the informativity of a given word within its context. The analysis of the speeches reveals that syntax and informativity independently contribute to perceived sentence stress. Moreover, the data suggest that speakers preferably place the more informative words in positions that receive prominence by virtue of their syntactic status.

Tina Bögel presents a formal model within the framework of Lexical Functional Grammar (LFG) that is concerned with the role of prosody in the resolution of syntactic ambiguities in sentence comprehension. This model assumes a close relationship between syntactic and prosodic constituent structure, such that, e.g. syntactic XPs are mapped onto prosodic phrases in sentence production. By way of a comprehension experiment, Bögel shows how such a close association may be exploited by listeners when parsing ambiguous word strings in German. The special feature of Bögel's LFG architecture is its ability to model both the syntax-prosody mapping in production as well as the prosody-syntax mapping in comprehension while otherwise maintaining strict modularity in linguistic representation.

Bögel's ideas on the syntax-phonology interface also feature prominently in the chapter by **Miriam Butt, Farhat Jabeen, and Tina Bögel**. This time, the LFG architecture is used to model the prosodic rendering of the ambiguous word *kya* in Hindi/Urdu which differs depending on its syntactic status. In a production experiment, the authors establish that this ambiguous word remains accentless when serving as a polar question particle; as wh-word in (potentially string-identical) constituent questions, *kya* bears prosodic prominence. Listeners are shown to be sensitive to this prosodic difference. According to the model presented, the prosodic difference between the polar and wh-reading of *kya* is not due to lexical differences but to syntactic constituent structure. Within the LFG interface architecture, this structure is annotated with prosodic information requiring accentuation of *kya* in the case of the wh-questions and prohibiting accentuation in polar questions.

The experiments and corpus studies reported in the contribution by **Katy Carlson** are concerned with the interpretation of elliptic sentences and the role of accentuation for the syntactic association of a remnant like *Wally* in sentences like (17), which may be interpreted as subject (... *than Wally respected Kenny*) or object (... *than Theo respected Wally*).

(17)   Theo respected Kenny more than Wally.

The results of a comprehension experiment reveal a general preference for object interpretations (i.e. with *Kenny* and *Wally* being the contrasted grammatical objects) but this preference is modulated by accentuation: When the subject (*Theo*) and the remnant (*Wally*) are prosodically contrasted with both bearing accent, the likelihood of the subject reading is significantly increased. Interestingly, a corpus study reveals that bare NP ellipses as in (17) serve as contrasted subjects in 80% of the cases, which is at odds with the strong preference for object remnants found in the comprehension experiment. Carlson ascribes these conflicting results to different strategies in comprehension versus production.

Marta Wierzba discusses the syntactic and prosodic makeup of noncanonical, object initial orders in German under different information structural conditions. Based on the observation that "object-initial sentences can have a broad focus interpretation under the condition that sentence stress falls on the object and the subject is either a definite pronoun or a given DP" Wierzba proposes a serial architecture of the syntax-phonology interface and the role of information structure in it. This model predicts that focus may impinge on the syntactic makeup of sentences and also determines sentence stress; givenness, on the other hand, does not affect the syntactic structure, and its effect on prosody is limited to conditioning accent types and pitch excursion and does not touch upon the prosodic phrasing and the presence of accents.

Johannes Heim and Martina Wiltschko analyse the sentence-peripheral particle *eh* in Canadian English (as in *You have a new dog, eh?*) and argue that it is used to manage the Common Ground. In addition, they discuss specific sentence-final intonation patterns and argue that these have the same function as the various instances of *eh* in managing the Common Ground. Based on this shared function, Heim and Wiltschko argue that sentence-final intonation should be represented in the syntactic structure, adding a third functional layer to the clause above the CP and TP layers.

The proposal made by Heim and Wiltschko is taken up in **E Jamieson**'s analysis of the sentence-final questions tag *-int* in Glasgow Scots. Due to the posited meaning for intonation and the nature of *-int*, this particle is predicted not to be compatible with rising intonation. Jamieson presents an experiment to test this hypothesis, the results of which suggest that the hypothesis is wrong. This, in turn, leads Jamieson to argue that intonation should not be represented in syntax, because its (un)acceptability is not as sharply delineated as one would expect for a syntactically represented property.

Hisao Tokizaki and Jiro Inaba look at complex prenominal modifiers across languages, e.g., English *a [sleeping on the sofa] baby* vs. German *ein [in München wohnhafter] Künstler* ('an in Munich living artist'). Tokizaki and Inaba argue that the grammaticality facts can be accounted for by a prosodic constraint, without needing to assume something like an adjacency requirement or a head-finality constraint. Essentially, a prosodic break between the prenominal modifier and the head is not allowed. The approach can be extended to languages such as Russian, which do allow structures such as *[gotovyi na vse] student* 'ready for all student', and to phrasal compounds such as *connect-the-dots puzzle*. These are correctly predicted to be grammatical due to the differences in prosodic phrasing compared with the ungrammatical English structure **a sleeping on the sofa baby*.

In his paper on scrambling in German, **Volker Struckmeier** argues against a cartographic approach, in which scrambling targets specific functional heads in the clause and focused constituents cannot scramble. On the basis of two experiments, Struckmeier shows that focused constituents do have the ability to scramble in German, provided the resulting structure transparently represents focus or if the resulting outcome is prosodically inconspicuous. Based on his data, Struckmeier argues that restrictions on scrambling should be formulated in terms of relations between constituents.

Joost Kremers discusses the topic of head movement in minimalist theories, which, as has been pointed out before, actually comprises two very different operations: head substitution and head adjunction. Head adjunction is thought to be the operation that builds complex word forms in syntax, but it is problematic from a theoretical perspective for various reasons. Kremers argues that these problems can be resolved if head adjunction is treated as an operation that is essentially phonological: the phonological form onto which a syntactic head is mapped essentially determines its position. Unlike previous attempts to treat head adjunction as a phonological operation, Kremers argues that there is no need to add a phonological diacritic to syntactic heads or syntactic information to the phonological representation.

5 Concluding remarks

The present volume is a collection of works from different linguistic camps that have been presented at the eponymous workshop on "Prosody in Syntactic Encoding" on the occasion of the 2017 annual meeting of the German Linguistic Society (Deutsche Gesellschaft für Sprachwissenschaft, DGfS) in Saarbrücken. We thank the group of reviewers for their assessment and their valuable suggestions for improvement of the contributions.

References

Agbayani, Brian and Chris Golston (2016). Phonological constituents and their movement in Latin. *Phonology*, 33(1):1–42. doi:10.1017/S0952675716000026.

Alexiadou, Artemis, ed. (2002). *Theoretical approaches to universals*. Amsterdam / Philadelphia: John Benjamins.

Anttila, Arto (2016). Phonological effects on syntactic variation. *Annual Review of Linguistics*, 2:115–137. doi:10.1146/annurev-linguistics-011415-040845.

Arnold, Jennifer, Tom Wasow, Anthony Losongco, and Ryan Ginstrom (2000). Heaviness vs. newness: The effects of structural complexity and discourse status on constituent ordering. *Language*, 76(1):28–55.

Bennett, Ryan and Emily Elfner (2019). The syntax-prosody interface. *Annual Review of Linguistics*, 5:151–171. doi:10.1146/annurev-linguistics-011718-012503.

Bennett, Ryan, Emily Elfner, and James McCloskey (2016). Lightest to the right: An apparently anomalous displacement in Irish. *Linguistic Inquiry*, 47(2):169–234. doi:10.1162/LING_a_00209.

Bermúdez-Otero, Ricardo (2012). The architecture of grammar and the division of labour in exponence. In Trommer, Jochen, ed., *The morphology and phonology of exponence*, pp. 8–83. Oxford University Press.

Bermúdez-Otero, Ricardo and Patrick Honeybone (2006). Phonology and syntax: A shifting relationship. *Lingua*, 116(5):543–561.

Bolinger, Dwight L. (1957). Maneuvering for stress and intonation. *College Composition And Communication*, 8(4):234–238. doi:10.2307/354910.

Bresnan, Joan W (1971). Sentence stress and syntactic transformations. *Language*, 47(2):257–281.

Büring, Daniel (2013). Syntax and prosody, syntax and meaning. In den Dikken (2013), pp. 860–896.

Chomsky, Noam (1993). A minimalist program for linguistic theory. In Hale & Keyser (1993), pp. 1–52.

Chomsky, Noam (2001). Derivation By Phase. In Kenstowicz (2001).

Culicover, Peter and Ray Jackendoff (2005). *Simpler syntax*. Oxford: Oxford University Press.

den Dikken, Marcel, ed. (2013). *The Cambridge handbook of generative syntax*. Cambridge: Cambridge University Press.

Erteschik-Shir, Nomi and Lisa Rochman (2010). *The sound patterns of syntax*. Oxford: Oxford University Press.

Fanselow, Gisbert (2007). The restricted access of information structure to syntax: A minority report. In Féry, Caroline, Gisbert Fanselow, and Manfred Krifka, eds, *The notions of information structure*, pp. 205–220. University of Potsdam.

Fanselow, Gisbert and Damir Çavar (2002). Distributed deletion. In Alexiadou (2002), pp. 65–107.

Féry, Caroline (1993). *German intonational patterns*. Tübingen: Niemeyer.

Féry, Caroline (2010). Informationsstruktur: Begriffe und grammatische Korrelate. In Tanaka, Shin, ed., *Linguisten-Band 9 der Japanischen Gesellschaft für Germanisten*. Japanische Gesellschaft für Germanisten.

Féry, Caroline (2013). Focus as prosodic alignment. *Natural Language and Linguistic Theory*, 31:683–734.

Féry, Caroline (2016). *Intonation and prosodic structure*. Cambridge, UK: Cambridge University Press.

Féry, Caroline and Katharina Hartmann (2005). The focus and prosodic structure of German right node raising and gapping. *The Linguistic Review*, 22(1):69–116.

Féry, Caroline and Gerrit Kentner (2010). The prosody of embedded coordinations in German and Hindi. In *Proceedings of Speech Prosody*, Chicago.

Féry, Caroline and Fabian Schubö (2010). Hierarchical prosodic structures in the intonation of center-embedded relative clauses. *The Linguistic Review*, 27(3):293–317.

Fitzgerald, Colleen M. (2007). An optimality treatment of syntactic inversions in English verse. *Language Sciences*, 29(2):203–217. doi:10.1016/j.langsci.2006.12.020.

Frey, Werner (2004). A medical topic position for German. *Linguistische Berichte*, 198:153–190.

Golston, Chris (1995). Syntax outranks phonology: Evidence from Ancient Greek. *Phonology*, 12(03):343–368. doi:10.1017/S0952675700002554.

Gussenhoven, Carlos (1983). Focus, mode and the nucleus. *Journal of Linguistics*, 19(2):377–417.

Haegeman, Liliane, ed. (1997). *Elements of grammar*. Dordrecht: Kluwer.

Hale, Kenneth and Samuel Jay Keyser, eds (1993). *The view from building 20: Essays in linguistics in honor of Sylvain Bromberger*. vol. 24 of *Current Studies in Linguistics*. Cambridge, MA: The MIT Press.

Hartmann, Jutta, Veronika Hegedűs, and Henk van Riemsdijk, eds (2008). *Sounds of silence: Empty elements in syntax and phonology*. Amsterdam: Elsevier.

Inkelas, Sharon and Draga Zec, eds (1990). *The phonology-syntax connection*. Chicago: University of Chicago Press.

Kandybowicz, Jason (2007). Fusion and PF architecture. *University of Pennsylvania Working Papers in Linguistics*, 13(1):85–98.

Kenstowicz, Michael (2001). *Ken Hale: A life in language*. Cambridge, MA: The MIT Press.

Kentner, Gerrit (2007). Length, ordering preference and intonational phrasing: Evidence from pauses. In *Proceedings of Interspeech 2007*, Antwerp.

Kentner, Gerrit and Isabelle Franz (2019). No evidence for prosodic effects on the syntactic encoding of complement clauses in German. *Glossa: a journal of general linguistics*, 4(1):1–29.

Kentner, Gerrit and Caroline Féry (2013). A new approach to prosodic grouping. *The Linguistic Review*, 30(2):277–311.

Kentner, Gerrit, Caroline Féry, and Kai Alter (2008). Prosody in speech production and perception: The case of right node raising in English. In Steube, Anita, ed., *The discourse potential of underspecified structure*, pp. 207–223. Berlin: Mouton de Gruyter.

Kiparsky, Paul (1975). Stress, syntax, and meter. *Language*, 51(3):576–616. doi:10.2307/412889.

Kügler, Frank and Caroline Féry (2017). Postfocal downstep in German. *Language and Speech*, 60(2):260–288.

Lahiri, Aditi and Frans Plank (2010). Phonological phrasing in Germanic: The judgement of history, confirmed through experiment. *Transactions of the Philological Society*, 108(3):370–398.

Nespor, Marina and Irene Vogel (2007). *Prosodic phonology*. Berlin: De Gruyter.

Richards, Norvin (2010). *Uttering trees*. Cambridge, MA: MIT Press.

Rizzi, Luigi (1997). The fine structure of the left periphery. In Haegeman (1997), pp. 281–337.

Sadock, Jerrold M. (1992). *Autolexical syntax*. Chicago: University of Chicago Press.

Sadock, Jerrold M. (2012). *The modular architecture of grammar*. Cambridge: Cambridge University Press.

Samek-Lodovici, Vieri (2005). Prosody-syntax interaction in the expression of focus. *Natural Language and Linguistic Theory*, 23:687–755.

Scheer, Tobias (2008). Why the prosodic hierarchy is a diacritic and why the interface must be direct. In Hartmann et al. (2008), pp. 145–192.

Scheer, Tobias (2012). How phonological is intonation? In *Jahrestagung der deutschen Gesellschaft für Sprachwissenschaft (DGfS)*, Frankfurt.

Selkirk, Elisabeth (1984). *Phonology and syntax*. Cambridge, MA: MIT Press.
Selkirk, Elisabeth (2002). Contrastive FOCUS vs. presentational focus: Prosodic evidence from right node raising in English. In *Proceedings of the First International Speech Prosody Conference*, pp. 643–646. Université de Provence.
Truckenbrodt, Hubert (2006). Phrasal stress. In Brown, Keith, ed., *The encyclopedia of languages and linguistics*, vol. 9, pp. 572–579. Amsterdam: Elsevier: 2 edn.
Wagner, Michael (2005). *Prosody and recursion*. Phd thesis, MIT, Cambridge, Massachusetts.
Watson, Duane and Ted Gibson (2004). The relationship between intonational phrasing and syntactic structure in language production. *Language and Cognitive Processes*, 19(6):713–755.
Weir, Andrew (2012). Left-edge deletion in English and subject omission in diaries. *English Language and Linguistics*, 16(1):105–129. doi:10.1017/S136067431100030X.
Youmans, Gilbert (1983). Generative tests for generative meter. *Language*, 59(1):67–92. doi:10.2307/414061.
Zec, Draga and Sharon Inkelas (1990). Prosodically constrained syntax. In Inkelas & Zec (1990), pp. 365–378.

Arto Anttila, Timothy Dozat, Daniel Galbraith,
and Naomi Shapiro
Sentence stress in presidential speeches

Abstract: Sentential prominence is not represented in writing, it is hard to measure phonetically, and it is highly variable, yet it undoubtedly exists. Here we report preliminary findings from our study of sentential prominence in the inaugural addresses of six U.S. presidents. We confirm the familiar hypothesis that sentential prominence has two sources (Jespersen 1920): it is partly MECHANICAL and depends on syntax (Chomsky & Halle 1968, Liberman & Prince 1977, Cinque 1993) and partly MEANINGFUL in that it highlights informative material (Bolinger 1972). Both contribute independently to perceived prominence. Pursuing the view that sentential prominence is a matter of STRESS, we provide evidence for the linguistic reality of the Nuclear Stress Rule (Chomsky & Halle 1968) as well as the view that information coincides with stress peaks in good prose (Bolinger 1957). We also observe that part of speech matters to sentence stress: noun and adjective stresses are loud and mechanical; verb and function word stresses are soft and meaningful. We suggest that this may explain why parts of speech differ in word phonology as well.

1 Introduction

Sentential prominence is a complex and fascinating topic: it is not represented in writing, it is hard to measure by phonometric methods, and it is highly variable, yet it undoubtedly exists.[1] Consider the following excerpt from Jimmy Carter's inaugural address (January 20, 1977, sentence 3), transcribed by a native speaker of English:

---

[1] This research was partially funded by the Office of the Vice-Provost for Undergraduate Education (VPUE) at Stanford University and by the Roberta Bowman Denning Initiative Committee, H&S Dean's Office, as part of the project *Prose Rhythm and Linguistic Theory* (Arto Anttila, PI). Our work was inspired by the project *The sound of text*, partially funded by the VPUE and carried out in collaboration with Joshua Falk and Ryan Heuser in the summers of 2010 and 2011. We are deeply indebted to Alex Wade for his help with the dataframe construction. This paper has benefited from presentations at the Stanford Phonology Workshop (March 3, 2017), the 39th Annual Meeting of the Deutsche Gesellschaft für Sprachwissenschaft (DGfS), Workshop on *Prosody in Syntactic Encoding*, Saarland University, Saarbrücken (March 10, 2017), and the Archbishop Mitty High School Linguistics Club (April 6, 2017). We thank the audiences for helpful feedback.

https://doi.org/10.1515/9783110650532-002

(1) We mùst adjùst to chánging TIMES and stìll hóld to unchánging PRINCIPLES.

The transcriber heard four degrees of prominence: primary (capitalized), secondary (acute accent), tertiary (grave accent), and none (unmarked). The same utterance can be heard slightly differently by different speakers. Here's another transcriber:

(2) We mùst adjúst to chànging TIMES and stìll hóld to unchànging príncipes.

The two transcribers differ by one step on the words *adjust, changing, unchanging,* and *principles*. However, the essential shape of the perceived prominence contour remains the same. This becomes evident if we convert the accents to numbers, marking higher level of prominence with a higher number (primary = 3, secondary = 2, tertiary = 1, none = 0). Anticipating our conclusion, we will call such prominences STRESSES.

(3) a. 0 1 1 0 2 3 0 1 2 0 2 3   transcriber (1)
    b. 0 1 2 0 1 3 0 1 2 0 1 2   transcriber (2)

Stress is a matter of relative, not absolute prominence, and numerical differences can be irrelevant. Consider the opening phrase *My fellow citizens* from Barack Obama's first inaugural address (January 20, 2009, sentence 1) transcribed 1 2 3 by the first transcriber and 0 1 2 by the second. The numbers differ for each word, but both transcribers heard the same steadily rising contour.

Why are sentences stressed the way they are? Linguistic tradition holds that there are two kinds of sentence stress (Jespersen 1920: 212–222). First, there is MEANINGFUL stress, sometimes called "semantic" or "psychological" stress (Jespersen's *Wertdruck, Neuheitsdruck, Gegensatzdruck*). Meaningful stress is illustrated in (4):

(4) In the Gilmore Girls universe, Luke and Lorelai seemed inevitable. He served the coffee; she needed the coffee. (Correction: NEEDED the coffee.)[2]

In particular, we thank Jared Bernstein, Canaan Breiss, Joan Bresnan, Uriel Cohen Priva, Vivienne Fong, Penny Eckert, Isabelle Franz, Bruce Hayes, Ryan Heuser, Larry Hyman, Gerrit Kentner, Paul Kiparsky, Mark Liberman, Geoffrey Pullum, Nathan Sanders, Madeline Snigaroff, Benjamin Storme, Meghan Sumner, and Simon Todd. Special thanks to Carlos Gussenhoven for his helpful written comments and corrections. Finally, we thank the Department of Statistics Consulting Services at Stanford University for their advice. We are responsible for any errors.

[2] *Entertainment Weekly*, November 17, 2016, http://www.ew.com/article/2016/11/17/gilmore-girls-luke-originally-woman

Under one natural reading, *needed* is contrastively stressed (as opposed to *served*) and NEEDED receives an additional dose of emphatic stress as indicated by the capitalization in the original. Both stresses are individually meaningful.

There is also MECHANICAL STRESS, sometimes called "physiological" stress (Jespersen's *rhythmischer Druck, Einheitsdruck*). Mechanical stress is illustrated in (5) with an example from Ladd 1996: 166:

(5) Q: How much did they pay you for participating in the experiment?
    A: Five francs.

In the answer, "*francs* is almost entirely predictable if the conversation takes place in a country where the unit of currency is the franc; *five* is the information of interest. Yet the accent is on *francs*." (Ladd 1996: 166). The stress on *francs* is thus not meaningful, but assigned mechanically to the rightmost content word of the sentence.

We first show that both kinds of stresses are real. The evidence is consistent with the view that sentence stress is assigned based on syntax (Chomsky & Halle 1968, Liberman & Prince 1977, Cinque 1993) and that information seeks out stress peaks, especially in good prose (Bolinger 1957). We then present evidence that sentence stress impacts different parts of speech differently: noun and adjective stresses are loud and mechanical; verb and function word stresses are soft and meaningful. We suggest that this may explain why parts of speech differ in word phonology as well (Smith 2011).

Our assumption that sentential prominence is a matter of stress is controversial and requires a comment. Theories of sentential prominence differ on two key questions:

(6) a. Are sentential prominences metrical (stresses) or tonal (pitch accents)?
    b. Do sentential prominences reflect syntax directly or indirectly?

In this paper, we take the view that sentential prominence is a metrical phenomenon: the prominences are genuine stresses, parallel to word stresses (see, e.g., Hayes 1995, Ch. 2). We further assume that sentence stress is assigned directly to words based on the surface syntactic structure. This view may strike some readers as quaint and others as wrong. It most closely resembles the SPE theory of phrasal stress (Chomsky & Halle 1968) and its immediate descendants, such as Liberman & Prince 1977 and Cinque 1993. It is therefore good to briefly motivate our theoretical choices before turning to the empirical part of the study.

Our first assumption, that sentential prominence is a matter of stress, implies that degrees of prominence involve degrees of stress: some words are stronger than others and some words are weaker than others. This is the Infinite Stress

View (ISV), so named by Gussenhoven (2011: 2779), that is rejected by many of today's researchers, including Gussenhoven (1991, 2011, 2015), who instead advocates the Pitch Accent View (PAV), under which "nuclear stress" is a pitch accent, i.e., a tone or a tone complex, left behind when its neighbors are deaccented. Crucially, pitch accent removal is categorical and there is no notion of gradient prominence, implying that apparent primary, secondary, tertiary, etc., stresses are not representable at the sentence level, and any impressions to the contrary must have some other explanation. Gussenhoven further notes that "[t]oday, there are probably no linguists who adhere to the ISV in its original form" (Gussenhoven 2011: 2779). Our analysis builds on the ISV and provides new evidence for it.

Our second assumption, that sentence stress is assigned to words based on surface syntax, as in, e.g., Kaisse 1985, glosses over three decades of work on the prosodic hierarchy; for overviews, see, e.g., Inkelas & Zec 1990, 1995; Truckenbrodt 2007; Selkirk 1995, 2011; and Nespor & Vogel 2007; among others. These theories assume that there exists a hierarchical prosodic structure – essentially an imperfect phonological reflection of syntax – that plays a role in phrasing and prominence. In our analysis, the prosodic hierarchy plays no role.

Why go back to these earlier theories of sentence stress? Our reasons were first and foremost practical. Over the past decades the computational infrastructure for linguistics has taken enormous strides forward. It is now easy to take a large amount of text, parse it syntactically, apply sentence stress rules to the resulting trees, and compare the predicted stress contours to human judgments. This seemed like an interesting project, especially as it had to the best of our knowledge never been attempted before. The Nuclear Stress Rule (NSR) and Compound Stress Rule (CSR) of Chomsky & Halle (1968) are simple rules: given the syntax, implementing them is a programming task. Pitch accent theories (e.g., Gussenhoven 1983; Ladd 1996) are less straightforward to test, mainly because they often rely on notions like accentuation domains that are harder to operationalize. Similar reasons kept us from adopting the prosodic hierarchy.[3]

Practical reasons aside, systematically testing a theoretical claim, even an incorrect one, is a useful mode of investigation. Applying a theory to a significant amount of data often brings up unexpected evidence that speaks to important theoretical questions. Indeed, we believe that our results provide a new argument for the gradience of sentence stress, and hence for the Infinite Stress View, against the Pitch Accent View.

---

[3] Bellik, Bellik & Kalivoda (2017) develop software for generating and evaluating prosodic hierarchy candidate sets based on syntactic trees using violable constraints. Their experiments illustrate that small differences in constraint definitions can have significant consequences for the analysis.

The paper is structured as follows. Section 2 lays out the empirical procedure and explains our stress model. Section 3 shows that both meaningful and mechanical stress matter to perceived stress. Section 4 discusses stress differences among parts of speech. Section 5 concludes the paper.

2 Procedure

Why are sentences stressed the way they are? We approached this question by taking the following steps:

(7) a. Find a scripted speech, with a transcription, audio, and video.
   b. Assign mechanical stress to the text by a computer.
   c. Annotate the text for informativity by a computer.
   d. Collect perceived stress judgments from native speakers.
   e. Try to predict perceived stress from mechanical stress and informativity.

Our data consist of the first inaugural addresses of six presidents: Carter (1977), Reagan (1981), Bush Sr., (1989), Clinton (1993), Bush Jr. (2001), and Obama (2009), available from the American Presidency Project (Peters & Woolley 1999–2018) in script, audio, and video. The work involved annotating the speeches for mechanical stress, informativity, and perceived stress. For mechanical stress, we used the METRICALTREE software written by Timothy Dozat that implements a version of Liberman & Prince's (1977) stress algorithm in conjunction with a syntactic analysis by the Stanford Parser (Klein & Manning 2003; Chen & Manning 2014; Manning et al. 2014).[4] For informativity, we used bigram informativity (e.g., Pan & Hirschberg 2000, Piantadosi et al. 2011, Cohen Priva 2012, 2015). Both aspects of the analysis will be explained below. Finally, the perceived stress judgments were collected with the web application METRICGOLD developed by Naomi Shapiro concurrently with the annotation process.[5] The result was a spreadsheet of about 11,500 words annotated for several syntactic and phonological variables, crucially mechanical stress, informativity, and perceived stress. We then used statistical tools to evaluate to what extent perceived stress is determined by phonology, syntax, and informativity.

---

[4] The source code for MetricalTree is freely available at https://github.com/tdozat/Metrics.
[5] The source code for MetricGold is freely available at https://github.com/tsnaomi/metric-gold.

Inaugural addresses are a very specific genre: the delivery is slow and fluent, most likely well rehearsed, and the text has benefited from the skills of professional speechwriters. However, we have no particular reason to believe that the underlying stress contours would be any different from those of ordinary English. Rather, it seems that oratorical prose maximizes the use of natural prosodic resources in ordinary speech, highlighting properties that are hard to detect in rapid conversation. Like the speech of radio announcers, which is characterized by "natural but controlled style, combining the advantages of both read speech and spontaneous speech" (Hasegawa-Johnson et al. 2005), oratorical prose turns out to be a rich source of evidence for the study of sentence prosody.

2.1 The mechanical stress model

In classical generative phonology (Chomsky & Halle 1968, henceforth *SPE*), stress is a feature that takes numerical values: [1 stress], [2 stress],..., [n stress]. Content words start out with [1 stress] assigned by word stress rules, while function words have no word stress. Sentence stress rules apply cyclically to syntactic constituents, starting from the innermost constituent, assigning [1 stress] to a designated word and reducing stress elsewhere by one (stress subordination). The sentence stress rules are stated below:

(8) **The Nuclear Stress Rule (NSR):** Assign [1 stress] to the rightmost vowel bearing the feature [1 stress]. Applies to phrases (NP, VP, AP, S).

(9) **The Compound Stress Rule (CSR):** Skip over the rightmost word and assign [1 stress] to the rightmost remaining [1 stress] vowel; if there is no [1 stress] to the left of the rightmost word, then try again without skipping the word. Applies to words (N, A, V).

The NSR and CSR are illustrated below by the famous sentence *John's blackboard eraser was stolen* (Chomsky & Halle 1968: 15–24). The parentheses indicate syntactic constituents. Each cycle is represented as a row. The outcome is the stress contour 3 2 5 4 1. Compared to the perceived stress numbers in our earlier examples, the predicted stress numbers are inverted, with the consequence that they are readily translatable into ordinary English: 1 = primary stress, 2 = secondary stress, 3 = tertiary stress, etc.

(10) [[[John's] [[[black] [board]] [eraser]]] [was stolen]]
      1   1   1   1   1
              [1   2]   Cycle 1
              [1   3   2]   Cycle 2
       [2   1   4   3]   Cycle 3
       [3   2   5   4   1]   Cycle 4

In Liberman & Prince's (1977) revision of the SPE stress theory, the two stress rules are defined on local syntactic trees as follows: in a configuration [A B], if the constituent is a phrase, B is strong (= NSR); if the constituent is a word, B is strong iff it branches (= CSR).[6] Our program METRICALTREE essentially implements Liberman & Prince's (1977) sentence stress rules building on the phrase structures provided by the Stanford Parser (Klein & Manning 2003; Chen & Manning 2014; Manning et al. 2014), with a number of modifications to be discussed shortly.

In the SPE theory, words come labeled as either stressed (content words) or unstressed (function words). Our mechanical stress model adopts a more finegrained three-way taxonomy: words can be stressed, unstressed, or stress-ambiguous. For earlier proposals along the same lines, see, e.g., Hirschberg 1993 and Shih 2014. We considered all words lexically stressed except for those listed in (11). These special words were identified as unstressed or stress-ambiguous by three sometimes overlapping criteria: (a) word form, (b) part of speech, and (c) syntactic dependency. This taxonomy is a working hypothesis that we expect to revisit in future work (Snigaroff 2017). For the meaning of the part of speech and dependency labels, see Appendix A.

(11) Lexically unstressed and stress-ambiguous words (first approximation)
       UNSTRESSED   STRESS-AMBIGUOUS
    a. it   this, that, these, those
    b. CC, PRP$, TO, UH, DT   MD, IN, PRP, WP$, PDT, WDT, WP, WRB
    c. det, expl, cc, mark   cop, neg, aux, auxpass

Positing a stress-ambiguous category reflects our uncertainty about the presence vs. absence of lexical stress on some function words. However, it also serves a deeper purpose in making the realistic prediction that sentence stress is variable.

---

[6] Under Cinque's (1993) reformulation, stress falls on the most deeply embedded phrase, i.e., to the right of V in VO languages and to the left of V in OV languages. More generally, complements win over heads and specifiers, and in the absence of complements, heads wins over specifiers. Cinque's proposal is an improvement in terms of cross-linguistic coverage, but does not affect our discussion as we are only concerned with English at the moment.

Consider the following sentence from Ronald Reagan's first inaugural address (January 20, 1981, sentence 63):

(12) I do not believe in a fate that will fall on us no matter what we do.

By our taxonomy, this sentence has nine stress-ambiguous words. Since the sentence stress rules presuppose that words are either lexically stressed or unstressed, such words must be first disambiguated before the sentence stress rules can apply. Assuming that the actual stress values of ambiguous words are independent of each other, the sentence has 2^9 = 512 stress paths, each one potentially resulting in a distinct sentence stress contour.[7] Instead of examining the 512 readings individually we opted for three basic stress models described in (13).

(13) Model 1: Ambiguous words are stressed.
      Model 2: Ambiguous monosyllables are unstressed, polysyllables stressed.
      Model 3: Ambiguous words are unstressed.

In addition, we constructed an "ensemble model" that takes the mean of the three basic models. Our model thus diverges from SPE in permitting lexical stress ambiguity. As a result, we have the beginnings of an explanation for why sentence stress is variable. The stress rules (NSR, CSR) are invariant; variation comes from lexical stress ambiguity in certain common function words.

2.2 Information-theoretic variables

According to the information-theoretic view, sentence accent is a matter of information, not of structure: what is informative is accented, what is uninformative is unaccented.[8] This is the general idea behind what Ladd (1996: 163–166) calls Focus-to-Accent theories, either structure-based (e.g., Ladd 1980; Gussenhoven 1983) or highlighting-based (Bolinger 1972, 1985). The latter is illustrated in the following quote:

> "In phrases like bóoks to write, wórk to do, clóthes to wear, fóod to eat, léssons to learn, gróceries to get – as they occur in most contexts – the verb is highly predictable: food is to

---

[7] The unambiguously stressed words are believe, fate, fall, on, matter, do; the unambiguously unstressed words are a, no. All other words are stress-ambiguous.
[8] The terminological shift from "sentence stress" to "sentence accent" reflects research tradition. In this paper, we assume that sentence-level prominences are genuine stresses, analogous to word stresses, accompanied by an overlay of pitch accents (see, e.g., Hayes 1995, Ch. 2).

eat, clothes are to wear, work is to do, lessons are to learn. Less predictable verbs are less likely to be de-accented – where one has *léssons to learn*, one will probably have *pàssages to mémorize*." (Bolinger 1972: 634)

Information content has been found to be a good predictor of perceived prominence in earlier work, see, e.g., Pan & McKeown 1999. Cole et al. (2010: 435) call this EXPECTATION-DRIVEN PROMINENCE: "[T]he listener may judge prominence based on information status alone, rather than judging the acoustic form directly. In this sense, the listener's judgment of word prominence is driven by their expectation based on prior experience of the word." According to Pan & Hirschberg (2000: 239–240), "of all the collocation measures we investigated, bigram word predictability has the strongest correlation with pitch accent assignment."

We operationalized a word's information content using its BIGRAM INFORMATIVITY, the word's average predictability across the entire corpus of inaugural addresses beginning with Roosevelt 1933. This informativity measure is an extension of conditional probability. Conditional probability is a measure of local predictability, in that it estimates the probability of an event based on its immediate context. In particular, the conditional probability of a word w is the probability of seeing w in a specific context or corpus c:

(14) $P(w|c)$

For instance, if we take Barack Obama's 2013 address as our scope, we might be interested in the probability of seeing the word *Americans* in his address:

(15) $P(Americans|\text{Barack Obama's 2013 address})$

We approximate (15) by limiting the scope of the context to the tokens directly preceding w, such as estimating the probability of seeing *Americans* following the word *fellow*. This probability is calculated by taking the number of times we see the phrase *fellow Americans* in Barack Obama's address and dividing it by the number of times we see the word *fellow*. Specifically, this produces a bigram probability, since *fellow Americans* is two words in length.

(16) $P(Americans|fellow) = \frac{\text{count}(fellow\ Americans)}{\text{count}(fellow)}$

The informativity of a word w is the average predictability of w across contexts (cf. Piantadosi et al. 2011, Cohen Priva 2012, 2015). It is measured as the weighted average of the negative log probability of seeing w given every context c that w follows in a corpus. These probabilites are weighted by the conditional probabilities of seeing c given w. Let C be the set of contexts in which w appears:

(17) Informativity(w) = $-\sum_{c \in C} P(c|w) \log_2 P(w|c)$

Tying this to our previous example, the word *Americans* appears 4 times in Barack Obama's 2013 address: twice after the word *fellow*, once after *of*, and once after *as*. In addition, *fellow* appears 3 times in total, *of* 69 times, and *as* 12 times. Therefore, the bigram informativity of the word *Americans* in the 2013 speech is 2.7159, as shown in (18). Likewise, the bigram informativity of *Americans* across the entire inaugural corpus is 5.4126.

(18) Informativity(*Americans*) = $-\frac{2}{4} \log_2 \frac{2}{3} - \frac{1}{4} \log_2 \frac{1}{69} - \frac{1}{4} \log_2 \frac{1}{12}$ = 2.7159

Intuitively, words vary in their informativity. For instance, we might expect prepositions to be generally less informative than nouns and verbs. Consider the informativity of the words *Americans*, *confronting*, and *of*, given the entire inaugural corpus:[9]

(19) Informativity(*of*) = 1.7024
Informativity(*Americans*) = 5.4126
Informativity(*confronting*) = 6.0549

In Bolinger's view, meaningful stress is about informativity. How are mechanical stress and meaningful stress related? Bolinger proposes that there is a natural alignment between the two:

> "The recipe for reconciling the two functions is simple: the writer should make them coincide as nearly as he can by maneuvering the semantic heavy stress into the position of the mechanical loud stress; that is, toward the end." (Bolinger 1957: 235)

Bolinger then makes the interesting suggestion that choices among syntactic variants, such as actives and passives, may be driven by sentence stress:

> "To circumvent the arbitrariness of grammar, the writer may now choose between parallel structures differing only in sentence order. He picks the one that allows him to get his stress at the end. If he defines Canada as *the place where Canadian bacon was invented*, he miscues his reader, for he wants the stress on *bacon* (and can easily put it there if he says it aloud), but his order suggests that it falls on *invented*. A parallel structure, *the place where they invented Canadian bacon*, avoids the trap." (Bolinger 1957: 236)

---

9 An anonymous reviewer asks why we calculated bigram informativity based on the inaugural corpus instead of larger corpora. We suspect that the vocabulary of inaugural addresses may be rather specific to this genre, so using the same genre for calculating frequency-based measures seems appropriate.

In other words, meaningful stress and mechanical stress preferably coincide: information seeks out stress peaks, especially in good prose. We call this hypothesis STRESS-INFORMATION ALIGNMENT; for relevant discussion, see, e.g., Calhoun 2010 and Cohen Priva 2012. Note that Bolinger says "writer", not "speaker", so one would expect his theory to hold particularly well in a scripted genre like the inaugural speech corpus. A plausible alternative to Stress-Information Alignment is COMMUNICATIVE DYNAMISM, a hypothesis that goes back to the Prague School (see, e.g., Firbas 1971), according to which information typically piles up towards the end of the sentence. We will return to both theories shortly.[10]

2.3 Collecting perceived stress judgments

We define perceived stress as syllable prominence intuitively felt by a native speaker. This view is succinctly stated in the following quote:

> "what makes a syllable accented is for the large part the work of the perceiver, generating his internal accent pattern on the basis of a strategy by which he assigns structures to the utterances. These structures, however, are not fabrications of the mind only, for they can be related to sound cues." (van Katwijk 1974: 5, cited in Baart 1987: 4)

Native speakers usually find it easy to tap, hum, exaggerate, or otherwise highlight the "rhythm" of a sentence they hear. Our goal was to make maximal use of this native speaker ability to interpret prosody. In interpreting prominence contours, a native speaker is in the position to draw upon rich resources, not only the familiar objective phonetic cues, such as pitch, amplitude, and duration that are in principle available to anyone, but also the speaker's overall knowledge of the language. One way to make such intuitions explicit is through gestures, for example, by tapping out the rhythm of the sentence. In fact, the presidents themselves often involuntarily annotate the text they are delivering by head nods and hand gestures. In our annotation practice, we considered the cues in roughly the following order. For a more detailed explanation, see Appendix B.

(20) a. native speaker intuitions
      b. embodied cues, e.g., tapping (annotator), nodding (president)
      c. explicit phonetic cues

---

[10] Yet another hypothesis is UNIFORM INFORMATION DENSITY (Levy & Jaeger 2007; Jaeger 2010), which proposes, roughly, that information strives to be evenly spread across the time it takes to utter a sentence. At this level of generality, this theory flatly contradicts the other two.

A key question is the choice of a transcription system. The alternatives include the popular ToBI (Silverman et al. 1992; Veilleux et al. 2006), RaP (Rhytm and Pitch, Dilley & Brown 2005), and RPT (Rapid Prosody Transcription, Cole et al. 2017). The matter is effectively decided by our hypothesis: since our goal is to verify the NSR/CSR, which predicts gradient stress contours, the optimal annotation system must allow for similar gradience. ToBI only allows for the binary prominence distinction pitch-accented vs. unaccented and does not describe metrical prominence; RaP allows for the three-way distinction non-prominent, prominent but not pitch-accented, and prominent and pitch-accented (Breen et al. 2012: 284); finally, RPT uses the binary distinction prominent vs. not-prominent. The binarity assumption seems normal in computational work (see, e.g., Pan et al. 2002; Nenkova et al. 2007).

To achieve the level of granularity appropriate for verifying the NSR/CSR we chose to transcribe the data directly in terms of metrical grids (Prince 1983). This involves taking an utterance of a suitable length and marking the words with grid columns of different heights that translate into whole numbers ranging from 0 (non-prominent) to 8 (highly prominent). In practice, the annotators limited themselves to a scale from 0 to 6. The annotation method is described in more detail in Appendix B. Stress judgments were collected from two native speaker annotators using the web application METRICGOLD developed concurrently with the annotation process with the help of the annotators. The annotators were native speakers of two varieties of English: Irish and American (West). Both had completed coursework in phonology and took part in weekly project meetings, but did the actual annotation work independently of each other. The meetings took place over the summer of 2016 and resulted in the informal protocol summarized in Appendix B. The resulting data frame contains approximately 11,500 words coded for perceived stress as well as for various phonological, syntactic, and frequency variables.

Any transcription is to some extent subjective and there is always variation across transcribers. However, in our view, such variation is not noise, but data. This is not simply making a virtue out of necessity, but has a serious scientific rationale. Assuming that prominence is largely the work of the perceiver, it is possible that two native speakers with different linguistic experience genuinely differ in their interpretation of the same prominence contour.[11] Variation in the stress annotation thus does not necessarily mean that at least one of the annotators must

---

[11] This opens up the interesting possibility of using the stress annotation to study, not just the grammar of the president being transcribed, but also the grammar of the annotator doing the transcription.

be wrong. It may mean that the annotators have subtly different grammars and consequently interpret the same signal differently. Moreover, eliminating variation across annotators by "harmonizing" the discrepancies is a procedure fraught with difficulties (see, e.g., Ernestus & Baayen 2011). For these reasons, we took no explicit steps to eliminate variation from our stress transcriptions, beyond the loose guidelines outlined above. Even with this freedom, the interannotator reliability turned out good (Cronbach's alpha = 0.85).

3 Both mechanical and meaningful stress matter

The goal of this section is twofold. First, we visualize the key relationships between perceived stress and other variables to help the reader intuitively appreciate the systematic patterns in the data. Based on earlier linguistic literature we have a fairly good sense of what to expect and the first order of business is to confirm these expectations. Second, we present regression models that support the composite nature of perceived stress: both meaningful stress and mechanical stress are real.

We start by focusing on four major syntactic categories, namely nouns, adjectives, verbs, and function words, trimming the data down from 11,641 to 10,982 words. The obvious first thing to look at is the relationship between mechanical and perceived stress. The scatterplots in (21) visualize the relationship between the "ensemble model", i.e., the mean of the three basic mechanical stress models, and perceived stress, with data from both annotators pooled.[12]

---

[12] These scatterplots were drawn using the xylowess.fnc convenience function from the languageR package with the default smoother added (Baayen 2008: 40, Baayen 2013).

(21) Mechanical stress vs. preceived stress by president

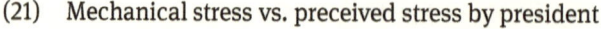

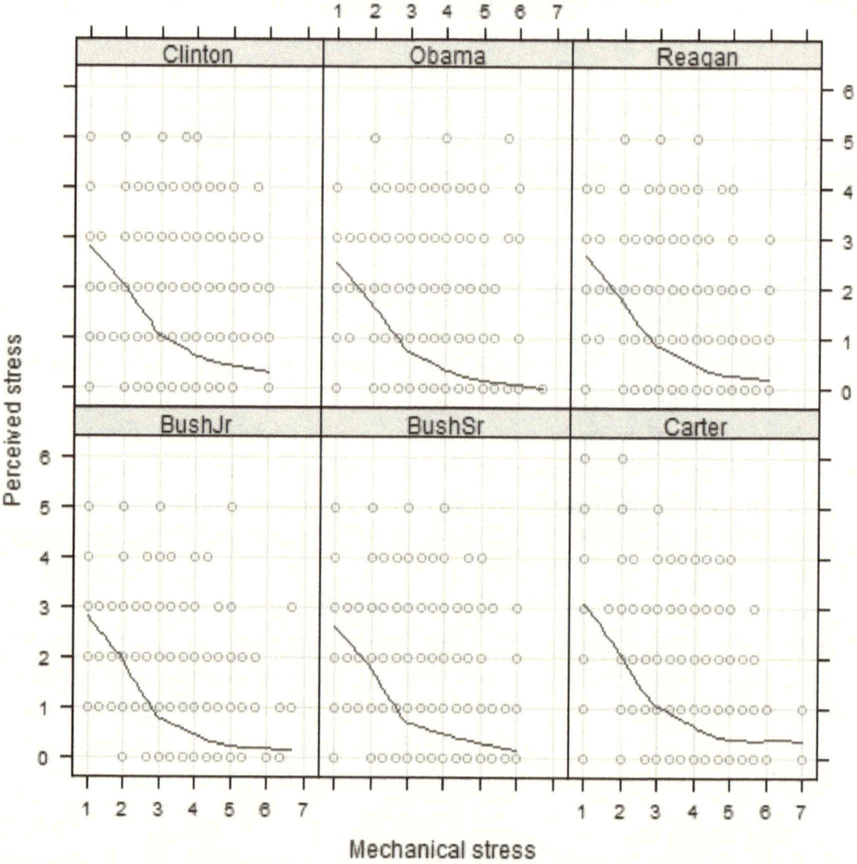

Recall that mechanical stress follows the SPE convention: 1 = primary stress, 2 = secondary stress, etc., where a lower number stands for more stress. Perceived stress inverts this order: 0 = no stress, 1 = one degree of stress, 2 = two degrees of stress, etc., where a lower number stands for less stress. We would thus expect a negative correlation between mechanical and perceived stress and this is indeed what we see (Spearman's $\rho = -0.4957$, $p < 2.2e-16$). One is immediately struck by the shape of the curve: the relationship is nearly one-to-one at the loud end of the spectrum where primary stress is heard as 3, secondary stress as 2, and tertiary stress as 1, but as soon as we go below tertiary stress the graph starts to flatten out. This is what we might expect: the theory predicts quaternary, quinary, senary, and septenary stresses with no problem, but to the human ear such distinctions become increasingly hard to hear.[13]

The obvious next thing is to examine the relationship between informativity and perceived stress. One would expect more informative words to have more stress, i.e., the correlation should be positive. Again, this turns out to be so (ρ = 0.6034, $p < 2.2\text{e-}16$). The scatterplots in (22) visualize the relationship between bigram informativity and perceived stress, with data from both annotators pooled.

(22) Bigram informativity vs. perceived stress by president

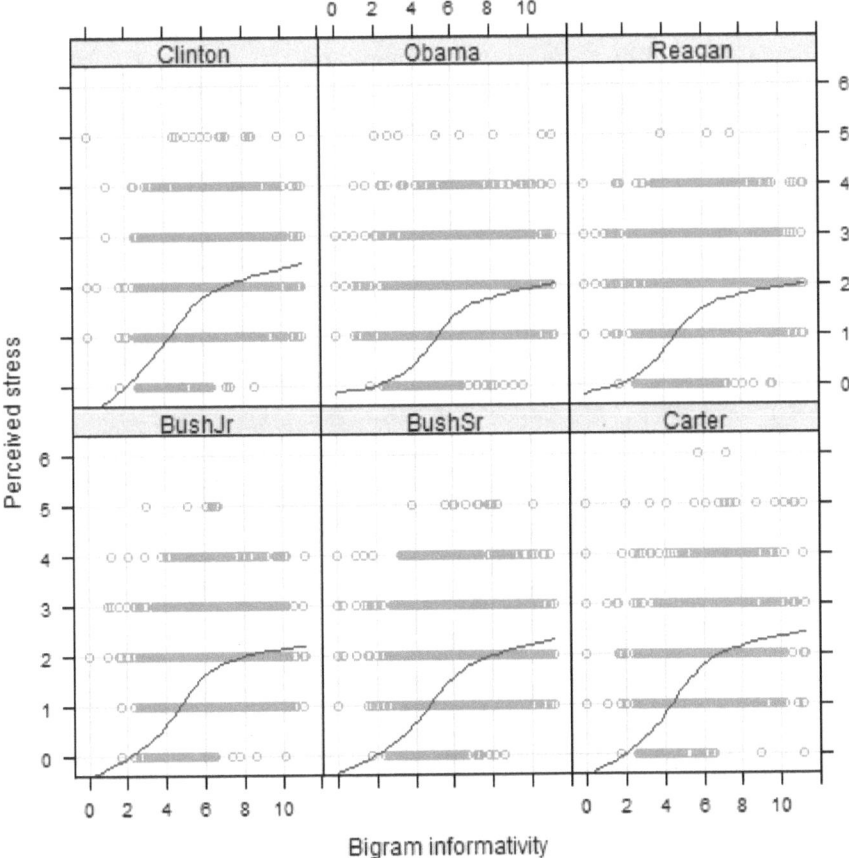

---

[13] A reviewer notes that the six individual presidents seem to behave very similarly and wonders if there are any differences among them. While we are not aware of any systematic differences this question clearly deserves more exploration. President and annotator will be included as random effects in our final model.

We now turn to Stress-Information Alignment. Recall Bolinger's (1957) suggestion that meaningfulness and mechanical stress ideally coincide in good prose. Let us start by checking whether bigram informativity and mechanical stress are correlated. One would expect a negative correlation because our mechanical stress model follows the SPE numerology: the larger the stress number, the weaker the stress. Indeed, we find a strong negative correlation ($\rho = -0.4341$, $p < 2.2\text{e-}16$), which is consistent with Bolinger's (1957) hypothesis.

(23) Mechanical stress vs. bigram informativity by president

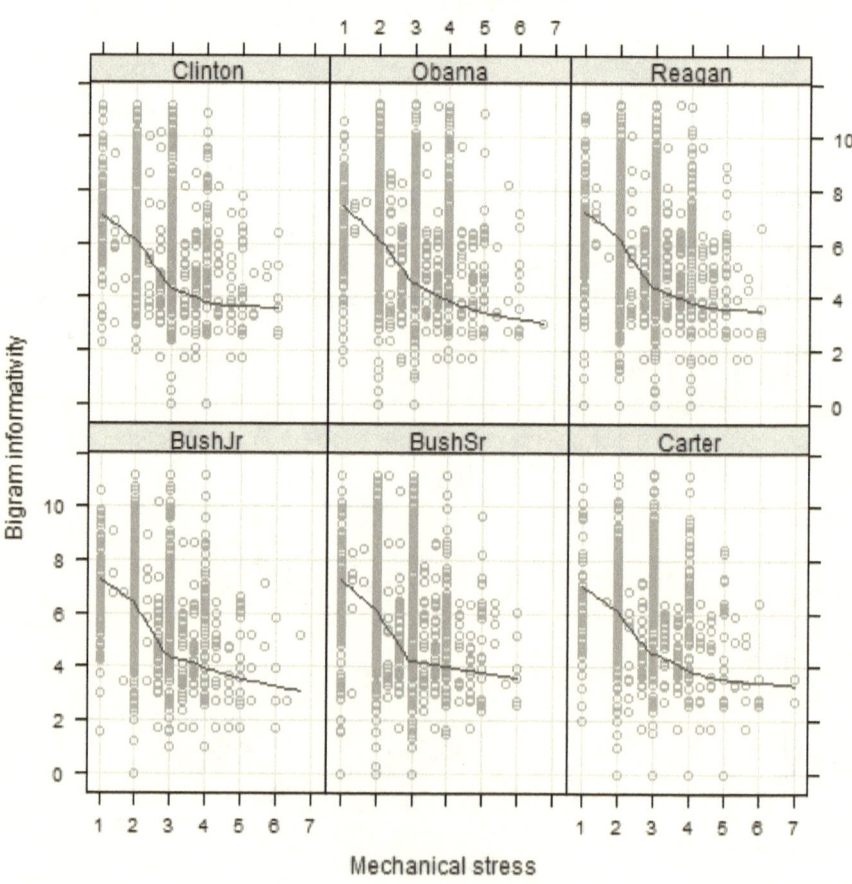

An alternative to Bolinger's Stress-Information Alignment hypothesis is Communicative Dynamism which predicts that information should pile up towards the end of the sentence. The scatterplots in (24) visualize the relationship between a word's linear position in the sentence and bigram informativity. Since sentences vary greatly in length we normalized word position by sentence length, so that every word falls on a scale between 0 (beginning) and 1 (end). Communicative Dynamism predicts that we should find a positive correlation and that is indeed what we do find ($\rho = 0.0621$, $p < 2.2\text{e-}16$). However, this correlation is much weaker than the correlation between mechanical stress and bigram informativity pictured above.

(24) Word position (normalized) vs. bigram informativity by president

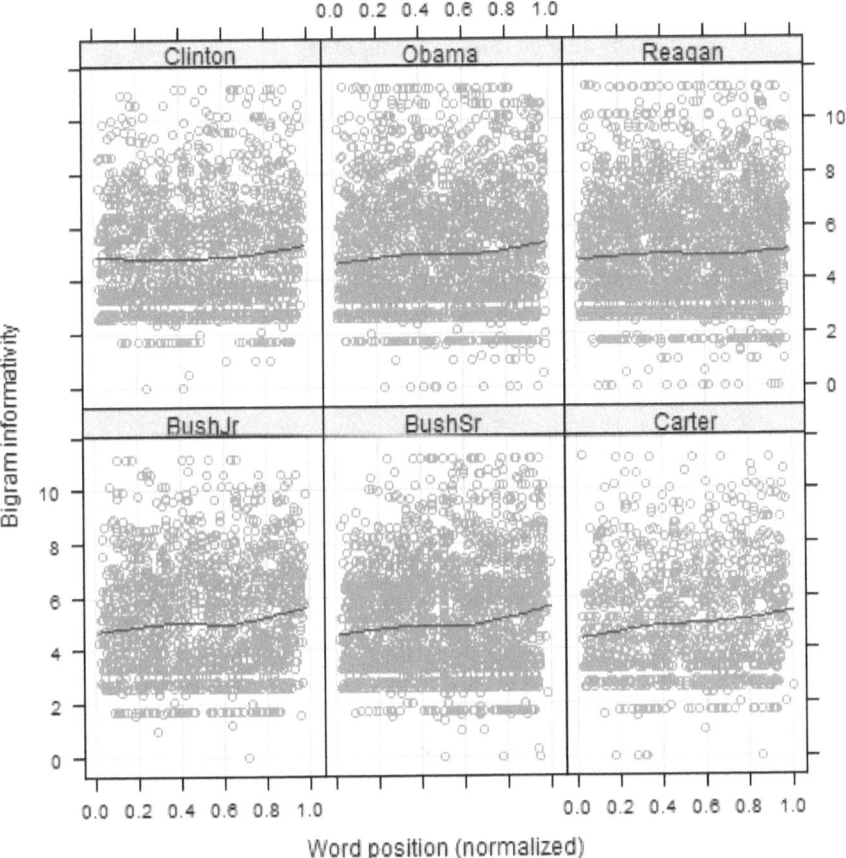

Do all three predictors (bigram informativity, mechanical stress, word position) independently contribute to perceived stress? In order to find out, we fitted a linear regression model to the data. The model is summarized in (25). The response variable is perceived stress on a scale from 0 to 6, log transformed.[14]

(25) A linear regression model of perceived stress (logged)

	Estimate	Std. Error	t value	$Pr(>|t|)$
(Intercept)	1.163686	0.039481	29.47	< 2e-16 ***
bigram informativity	0.215886	0.003171	68.07	< 2e-16 ***
mechanical stress	−0.366282	0.007644	−47.92	< 2e-16 ***
word position	0.032694	0.025341	1.29	0.197

Signif. codes: 0 '***' 0.001 '**' 0.01 '*' 0.05 '.' 0.1 ' ' 1
Residual standard error: 0.9417 on 21901 degrees of freedom
  (59 observations deleted due to missingness)
Multiple R-squared: 0.3633, Adjusted R-squared: 0.3632
F-statistic: 4165 on 3 and 21901 DF, p-value: < 2.2e-16

Only bigram informativity and mechanical stress come out significant, both in the expected direction. In order to get a sense of each predictor's relative importance we calculated the contribution of each predictor using the relaimpo package (Grömping 2006). All four methods point at bigram informativity (info) as being the most important predictor, followed by mechanical stress (NSR), followed by the word's normalized position in the sentence (wpos).

---

14 The 59 observations deleted due to missingness are of two kinds: (i) the contractions 'll, 'm, 're, 's, 've were not assigned a mechanical stress value by MetricalTree; (ii) one of the annotators declined to give a perceived stress value for the word *4-year*.

(26) The relative importance of predictors for perceived stress (logged)

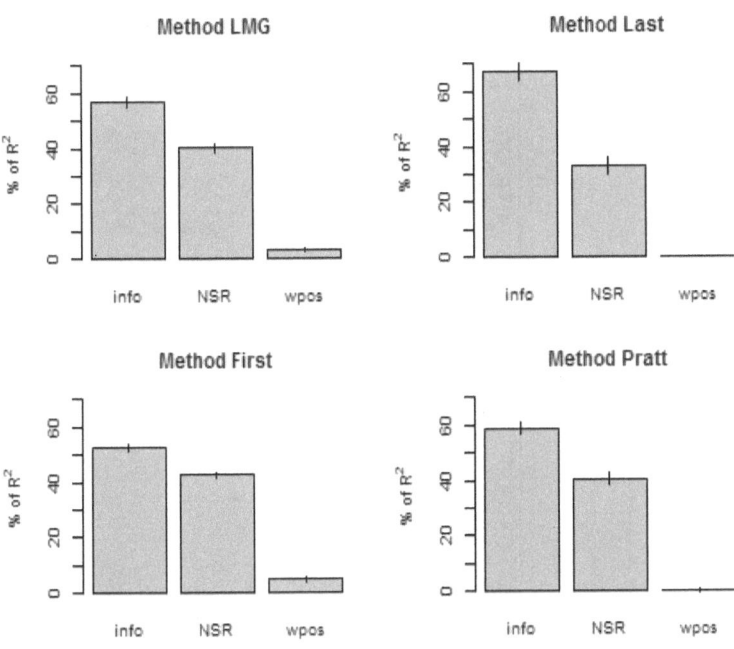

$R^2 = 36.33\%$, metrics are normalized to sum 100%.

We conclude that both meaningful stress and mechanical stress are real and both contribute to perceived stress. In particular, the evidence supports the reality of the Nuclear Stress Rule (Chomsky, Halle & Lukoff 1956; Chomsky & Halle 1968; Liberman & Prince 1977; Cinque 1993) as an independent source of stress.

There remain a number of additional structural predictors that one can expect to influence stress perception. In the next section we will consider one such predictor: PART OF SPEECH. While the general picture will not change with the addition of the part-of-speech variable, the linguistic plot will thicken.

4 Part of speech effects

It is well known that parts of speech differ in degree of stress (see, e.g., Altenberg 1987; Hirschberg 1993; German et al. 2006). The boxplot in (27) shows the level of perceived stress by part of speech, with data from both annotators pooled. The bottom and top of the box are the 25th and the 75th percentiles; the black band is the median.

(27) Perceived stress vs. part of speech

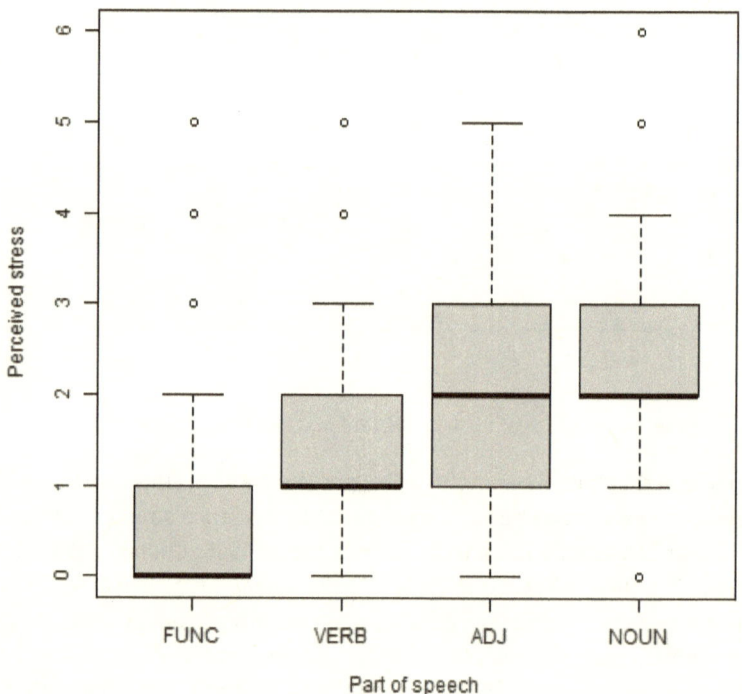

What we see here is a stress hierarchy FUNC < VERB < ADJ < NOUN. Function words are soft, nouns are loud. Adding part of speech into our model shows that NOUN is a good predictor of perceived stress just as FUNC and VERB are good predictors of its absence.

(28) A linear regression model of perceived stress (logged)

	Estimate	Std. Error	t value	$\Pr(>|t|)$
(Intercept)	1.335652	0.046119	28.961	< 2e-16 ***
bigram informativity	0.123341	0.003421	36.052	< 2e-16 ***
mechanical stress	-0.125354	0.008629	-14.527	< 2e-16 ***
category FUNC	-0.976762	0.026459	-36.916	< 2e-16 ***
category NOUN	0.198743	0.024628	8.070	7.41e-16 ***
category VERB	-0.403530	0.025801	-15.640	< 2e-16 ***
word position	0.196662	0.024064	8.173	3.18e-16 ***

Signif. codes: 0 '***' 0.001 '**' 0.01 '*' 0.05 '.' 0.1 ' ' 1
Residual standard error: 0.8734 on 21898 degrees of freedom
 (59 observations deleted due to missingness)
Multiple R-squared: 0.4523,   Adjusted R-squared: 0.4521
F-statistic: 3014 on 6 and 21898 DF, *p*-value: < 2.2e-16

All the predictors (bigram informativity, mechanical stress, part of speech, word position) are independently significant in the expected direction. The dependence of stress on syntactic category has been stated in various ways by earlier researchers. Arguments are more "accentable" than predicates (Schmerling 1976; Gussenhoven 1992; Ladd 1996: 187–193); content words are more accentable than function words; nouns are more accentable than other content words; and indefinite nouns are more accentable than definite nouns (Ladd 1980: 84–92). Fine-grained language-specific "accentability hierarchies" have been proposed; for a summary, see Baart 1987: 56–57. Pan & Hirschberg (2000: 237) note that "[i]n general, nouns, especially head nouns, are very likely to be accented", while Pan et al. (2002) report that "[v]erbs, which are content words, are not accented, according to the POS-pitch accent model."

The stress hierarchy FUNC < VERB < ADJ < NOUN bears an uncanny resemblance to hierarchies independently discovered in word phonology. In many languages, verbs, adjectives, and nouns exhibit different phonological behavior. In an overview article, Smith (2011: 2439) employs the term *"phonological privilege* [...] understood to mean the ability to support a greater array of phonological contrasts, whether this is manifested as a larger number of underlying distinctions, more variety in surface patterns, or a greater resistance to assimilation or other phonological processes." Intuitively, nouns are phonologically more resilient than adjectives which are more resilient than verbs. Smith concludes with the following statement:

> "Many, although perhaps not all, cases are consistent with a universal scale of phonological privilege, N > A > V. Furthermore, the overwhelming majority of cases involve prosodic and suprasegmental phenomena [...]" (Smith 2011: 2459).

Could the similarity between "accentability" in sentence phonology and "privilege" in word phonology be an accident? That seems unlikely.[15] We would like to put forward the hypothesis that word-level privilege scales reflect sentence-level accentability scales, synchronically or diachronically. This is based on the following reasoning. For syntactic reasons, nuclear stress typically falls on nouns because they are arguments and avoids verbs because they are predicates. We also know that stress inhibits phonetic reduction. Therefore, words that are typically stressed, i.e., nouns, become resistant to reduction and are better able to support contrasts, whereas words that are typically unstressed, i.e., verbs, are more susceptible to reduction and tend to lose contrasts. In this way, word phonology ultimately depends on sentence phonology. Note that this explanation makes sense only if sentential prominence is stress: stress-based segmental effects are common, whereas tone-based segmental effects are virtually unknown (see, e.g., Hyman & Schuh 1974: 108). This view is also in general agreement with the position of Kelly & Bock (1988) and Kentner (2012) who argue based on experimental evidence that word stress can be sensitive to sentence stress.

Smith's privilege scale is strikingly manifested in word length. The boxplot in (29) visualizes word length by part of speech in the inaugural address corpus. We measured word length in terms of the number of phonological segments based on the CMU pronouncing dictionary (Weide 1998).

---

15 The hierarchy N > A > V where adjectives are sandwiched between nouns and verbs is also familiar from other contexts. Richard Wiese (p.c.) points out that adjectives have often been described as partly noun-like, with both grouped together under the category "nominal", and partly verb-like, as in the case of predicate adjectives.

(29) Number of segments vs. part of speech

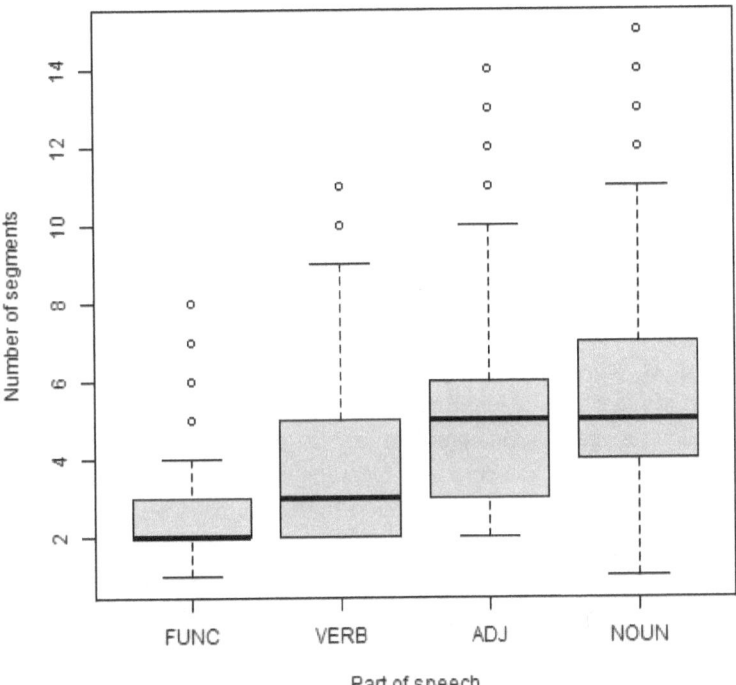

What we see here is a length hierarchy FUNC < VERB < ADJ < NOUN. Function words are short, nouns are long. The obvious parallel between the stress hierarchy in (27) and the length hierarchy in (29) strongly suggests that the two are related. An anonymous reviewer points out that the NSR was developed for English and might apply fairly straightforwardly to other SVO languages with similar prosodic systems. One such language for which we have suitable corpora available is Finnish, an SVO language with a phrasal stress system much like in English, although different in terms of intonation (Sadeniemi 1949: 78–100; Iivonen et al. 1987: 219–250; Vilkuna 1998). In the *Aamulehti 1999* newspaper corpus (Aamulehti 1999) the mean lengths of verbs, adjectives, and nouns are neatly arranged along Smith's privilege hierarchy: verbs are shortest, nouns are longest. It remains to be seen to what extent the parallel holds up cross-linguistically. An anonymous reviewer asks what the predictions are for languages without lexical stress, tone languages, verb-final languages, and languages without clear sentence stress. Languages without lexical stress cannot have an NSR that refers to word stress, but they might well have other ways to classify words for the purposes of phrasal stress. Tone languages could have an NSR to the extent they also have lexical stress (Hyman 2006). Verb-final languages with lexical stress, such as German, seem to behave largely as predicted by the NSR suitably generalized, see, e.g., Cinque 1993; Wiese 1996, Sect. 8.5.1; and Wagner 2005, and one would thus expect a similar word length effect. As for languages without clear sentence stress, one would have to know the details.

The evidence suggests that a word's typical sentence prosody is somehow crystallized in its lexical representation.[16] This might explain the success of ACCENT RATIO as a measure of accentability (Nenkova et al. 2007). The intuition is that people simply memorize how likely a word is to be accented and do this separately for each word. Nenkova et al. (2007) define accent ratio as equal to the estimated probability of a word being accented if this probability is significantly different from 0.5 and equal to 0.5 otherwise. This predictor alone turns out to perform about as well as five other predictors together (unigram and bigram probability, part of speech, word length, and word position in the utterance) and generalizes well across genres. One predictor not included in the Nenkova et al. (2007) models is the NSR/CSR. It would be interesting to see to what extent the NSR/CSR can explain accent ratio, but we will leave that for future work.

Our final model of perceived stress that includes word length as a predictor is summarized in (30). This is a linear mixed model that uses the R packages lme4 (Bates et al. 2014) and lmerTest (Kuznetsova et al. 2016). The dependent variable is perceived stress (logged); the fixed effects are bigram informativity, mechanical stress, word length (logged), part of speech, and word position. President and annotator were included in the model as random effects. All the fixed effects are independently highly significant in the expected direction.

(30) A mixed effects linear regression model of perceived stress (logged)
Formula: perception ~ info + NSR + nseg.log + category + wpos +
(1 | president) + (1 | annotator)
Data: presidents.data.words.navf.final
Random effects:

Groups	Name	Variance	Std.Dev.
president	(Intercept)	0.01199	0.1095
annotator	(Intercept)	0.04476	0.2116
Residual		0.71199	0.8438

Number of obs: 21830, groups: president, 6; annotator, 2

---

[16] There is segmental evidence that nouns are more exhaustively footed than verbs in Finnish (Anttila 2006). Adams (2014) argues that low-frequency adjectives are more completely prosodified than high-frequency adjectives in English.

Fixed effects:

	Estimate	Std. Error	df	t value	Pr(> |t|)	
(Intercept)	7.926e-01	1.640e-01	1.000e+00	4.833	0.0737	.
bigram informativity (info)	1.056e-01	3.451e-03	2.182e+04	30.594	< 2e-16	***
mechanical stress (NSR)	-8.785e-02	8.502e-03	2.182e+04	-10.333	< 2e-16	***
word length (nseg.log)	3.676e-01	1.578e-02	2.182e+04	23.304	< 2e-16	***
category FUNC	-8.012e-01	2.664e-02	2.182e+04	-30.069	< 2e-16	***
category NOUN	1.705e-01	2.403e-02	2.182e+04	7.096	1.33e-12	***
category VERB	-3.003e-01	2.541e-02	2.182e+04	-11.817	< 2e-16	***
word position (wpos)	2.246e-01	2.332e-02	2.182e+04	9.629	< 2e-16	***

Signif. codes: 0 '***' 0.001 '**' 0.01 '*' 0.05 '.' 0.1 ' ' 1

We conclude with a final remark on parts of speech. Our final regression model shows that bigram informativity matters to perceived stress, but interestingly, this effect seems to be entirely driven by verbs and function words. The scatterplots in (31) show the level of perceived stress as a function of bigram informativity, with the data grouped by part of speech.

(31) Perceived stress vs. bigram informativity by part of speech

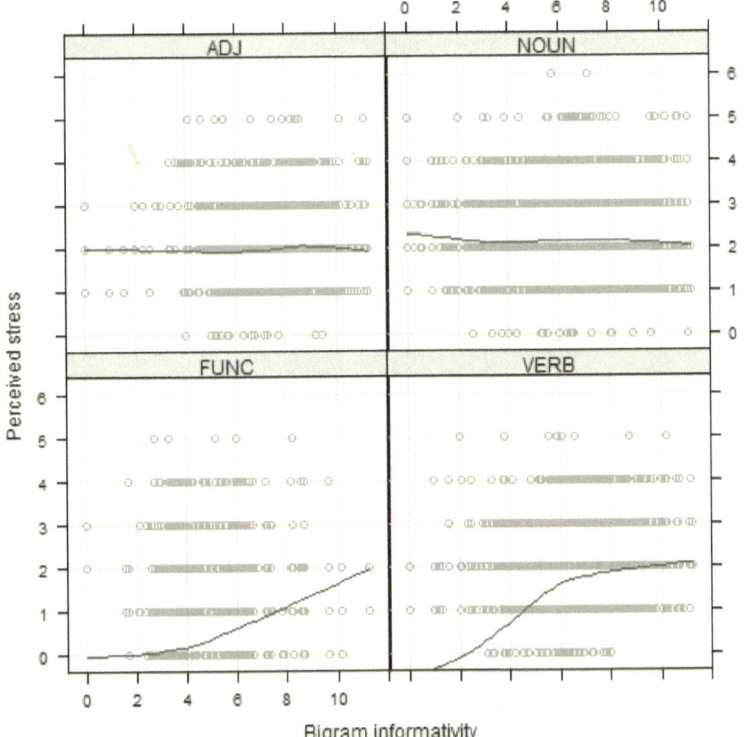

A clear two-way split among parts of speech is immediately apparent. There is no correlation between perceived stress and bigram informativity in nouns (ρ = −0.0116, p = 0.3851) or adjectives (ρ = 0.0415, p = 0.08522), but a strong positive correlation emerges in verbs (ρ = 0.4810, p < 2.2e-16) and function words (ρ = 0.3810, p ≤ 2.2e-16). We can summarize this finding as follows: noun and adjective stresses are loud and mechanical; verb and function word stresses are soft and meaningful.[17]

These observations are consistent with Bolinger's remark about verbs. Recall that Bolinger argues that stress differences are a matter of informativity, in particular "[l]ess predictable verbs are less likely to be de-accented – where one has *léssons to learn*, one will probably have *pàssages to mémorize*" (Bolinger 1972: 634). Some of Bolinger's key examples are repeated in (32).

(32) a. I have léssons to learn.
I have pàssages to mémorize.
b. I have a póint to make.
I have a pòint to émphasize.

Although the facts are beyond dispute, our results suggest an alternative explanation. A fact not commented on by Bolinger is that *memorize* and *emphasize* are simply longer words than *learn* and *make*. Our final regression model shows that word length matters to perceived stress. Could it be that the stress Bolinger is hearing depends, not on informativity, but on word length? Since the two are correlated it may be hard to tell, but the explanations are entirely different and the possibility of a length effect cannot be ruled out. We also note that the correlation between perceived stress and word length is strongest precisely in verbs (ρ = 0.4957, p < 2.2e-16), where length is measured in terms of the number of segments (logged). The upshot is that a simple phonological variable such as word length may partially undermine explanations based on informativity.

5 Summary

The results presented here are preliminary. One area where improvement is clearly needed is our mechanical stress model, in particular our lexical stress taxonomy

---

[17] A related observation is made by Cole et al. (2010: 438) who note that frequency matters for prominence in function words, but less in content words: "for most content words factors other than word frequency play a larger role in prominence perception than they do for function words."

which is a first approximation. An initial study has been conducted to evaluate the quality of the model (Snigaroff 2017), but the results were not used in the present paper.

We offer three main results. First, we have seen new evidence that syntax plays an important role in sentence accentuation. While earlier studies have approximated mechanical stress in various ways (see, e.g., Calhoun 2010), we explicitly combined stress rules with syntax and compared the predicted stress contours to the perceived stress contours. Second, we observed that noun and adjective stresses are loud and mechanical whereas verb and function word stresses are soft and meaningful. The gradience that emerges from the transcriptions suggests that binary classification schemes are insufficient, posing a problem for a pure pitch accent view, which assumes that the grid, i.e., a gradient representation of sentential prominence, does not exist (see, e.g., Gussenhoven 2015). Third, we speculated that sentence stress may explain part-of-speech effects in word phonology. For example, nouns tend to be resistant to reduction and better able to support lexical contrasts than verbs because nouns are typically sustained by higher levels of sentence stress. If that is correct, word phonology is not a self-contained system and cannot be completely understood without first understanding sentence phonology.

Appendix A: Lexical stress annotation

Our mechanical stress model relies on the output of the Stanford Parser (Klein & Manning 2003; Chen & Manning 2014; Manning et al. 2014). The Stanford Dependency Parser (Chen & Manning 2014) follows the Stanford Dependency labeling scheme, where the label a word is assigned is dictated both by the lexical properties of the word and by the role that word plays in the sentence. In this Appendix we describe the labels used by the metrical parser in addition to some prototypical examples of their intended usage. While there is some overlap between the part-of-speech and dependency labels, we found both types of annotations were needed for best performance.

We marked words as unstressed and stress-ambiguous based on the part-of-speech and dependency labels listed below. The following words override part-of-speech tags and dependency labels: *it* (unstressed), *this, that, these, those* (stress-ambiguous). In addition to labels and informal descriptions, we include representative examples. For the part-of-speech tags we also give the number of matching words in our corpus of 11,641 words. All other words were labeled as lexically stressed.

(33) Unstressed part-of-speech labels

CC	coordinating conjunction (*and, but, nor, or, so, yet*)	639
PRP$	possessive pronoun (*my, your, his, her, its, their*)	445
TO	*to*	352
UH	interjection (*yes, well, amen*)	7
DT	determiner (*a, all, an, another, any, both, each, every, many, neither, no, some, that, the, these, this, those*)	1,174

(34) Stress-ambiguous part-of-speech labels

MD	modal (*can, could, may, might, must, shall, will, would, need, should, 'll, can't*)	276
IN	preposition, subordinating conjunction (*about, above, across, after, against, alongside, among, around, as, at, because, before, beneath, between, beyond, but, by, during, except, for, from, if, in, into, lest, like, of, off, on, out, outside, over, since, so, than, that, though, through, throughout, 'til, toward, under, unless, until, up, upon, whether, while, with, within, without*)	1,309
PRP	personal pronoun (*he, himself, I, it, itself, me, myself, one, ours, ourselves, she, thee, them, themselves, they, us, we, you, your*)	762
PDT	predeterminer (*all, such*)	10
WDT	wh-determiner (*that, which, whatever*)	78
WP	wh-pronoun (*what, who, whom, whoever*)	94
WRB	wh-adverb (*how, when, where, why, whenever, wherever*)	60

(35) Unstressed dependency labels

det	determiner (*a, an, the, this, that, these, those, every, each*)
expl	expletive (*there*)
cc	coordinating conjunction (*and, or, but, yet, as, nor*)
mark	complementizer or similar introducing a subordinate clause or phrase (*that, if, whether, to, because, in, of, than, as, for, upon, though, while, since*)

(36) Stress-ambiguous dependency labels

cop	copula (*be, am, is, are, were, was, been, being*)
neg	negation (*no, not, never, n't*)
aux	auxiliary (*have, has, must, will, can, might, may, do, does, did, should, is, are, were*)
auxpass	passive auxiliary (*been, is, be, was, were, been, are, being*)

Appendix B

The annotators were instructed as follows: "If intuitions are crystal clear, no further confirmation is necessary and the annotator should feel free to move on to the next sentence. If the intuitions are not so clear, there are various ways to make them more explicit: (i) Replay the utterance multiple times in quick succession to hear and feel its rhythm; (ii) While listening, tap out the utterance rhythm. Most people find it easier to tap on stressed syllables than on unstressed syllables; (iii) Humming along, i.e., substituting a syllable like *ma* for each syllable of the utterance, may also help one. This is called "reiterant speech" (Liberman & Prince 1977: 250); (iv) Take note of visual cues in the video, such as the speaker's head nods and hand gestures. If none of the above methods helps, the annotator should pay explicit attention to the linguistic cues in the signal. Cues for presence of stress: an abrupt pitch movement on a syllable (rise, fall); longer vowel duration (*this is soooo difficult*); strong aspiration (*This is p[hhh]retty difficult*); selection of the stressed allomorph (*a/ey*), *the/thee*); etc. Cues for absence of stress: vowel reduction (schwa); auxiliary contraction (e.g., *have* → *'ve*); etc."

Data sources

Aamulehti 1999. An electronic document collection of the Finnish language containing 16.6 million words. Gatherers: The Department of General Linguistics, University of Helsinki; The University of Eastern Finland; CSC – IT Center for Science Ltd. Available through the Language Bank of Finland, http://www.kielipankki.fi/. URN: http://urn.fi/urn:nbn:fi:lb-201403268.

Peters, Gerhard and John T. Woolley. 1999–2018. The American Presidency Project, http://www.presidency.ucsb.edu/index.php.

References

Adams, Matthew E. (2014). *The comparative grammaticality of the English comparative*. Ph. D. thesis, Stanford University.

Altenberg, Bengt (1987). *Prosodic patterns in spoken English: Studies in the correlation between prosody and grammar for text-to-speech conversion*. vol. 76. Lund: Studentlitteratur.

Anttila, Arto (2006). Variation and opacity. *Natural Language & Linguistic Theory*, 24(4):893–944.

Baart, Joan (1987). *Focus, syntax, and accent placement*. Ph. D. thesis, University of Leiden.

Baayen, R. H. (2008). *Analyzing linguistic data: A practical introduction to statistics using R*. Cambridge: Cambridge University Press.

Baayen, R. H. (2013). languageR: Data sets and functions with *Analyzing linguistic data: A practical introduction to statistics*, R package version 1.4.1. http://CRAN.R-project.org/package=languageR.

Bates, Douglas, Martin Maechler, Ben Bolker, and Steven Walker (2014). lme4: Linear mixed-effects models using Eigen and S4. R package version 1.1–6. http://CRAN.R-project.org/package=lme4.

Bellik, Jenny, Ozan Bellik, and Nick Kalivoda (2017). SPOT. JavaScript application. https://github.com/syntax-prosody-ot.

Bolinger, Dwight (1985). Two Views of Accent. *Journal of Linguistics*, 21(1):79–123.

Bolinger, Dwight L. (1957). Maneuvering for stress and intonation. *College Composition and Communication*, 8(4):234–238.

Bolinger, Dwight L. (1972). Accent is predictable (if you are a mind reader). *Language*, 48:633–644.

Breen, Mara, Laura C. Dilley, John Kraemer, and Edward Gibson (2012). Inter-transcriber reliability for two systems of prosodic annotation: ToBI (Tones and Break Indices) and RaP (Rhythm and Pitch). *Corpus Linguistics and Linguistic Theory*, 8(2):277–312.

Calhoun, Sasha (2010). How does informativeness affect prosodic prominence? *Language and Cognitive Processes*, 25(7–9):1099–1140.

Chen, Danqi and Christopher Manning (2014). A fast and accurate dependency parser using neural networks. In *EMNLP* 2014.

Chomsky, Noam and Morris Halle (1968). *The sound pattern of English*. New York: Harper and Row.

Chomsky, Noam, Morris Halle, and Fred Lukoff (1956). On accent and juncture in English. In Halle, Morris, Hugh McLean, Horace G. Lunt, and Cornelis H. Van Schooneveld, eds, *For Roman Jakobson: Essays on the occasion of his sixtieth birthday*, pp. 65–80. The Hague: Mouton & Co.

Cinque, Guglielmo (1993). A null-theory of phrase and compound stress. *Linguistic Inquiry*, 24:239–298.

Cohen Priva, Uriel (2012). *Sign and signal: Deriving linguistic generalizations from information utility*. Ph. D. thesis, Stanford University.

Cohen Priva, Uriel (2015). Informativity affects consonant duration and deletion rates. *Laboratory Phonology*, 6(2):243–278.

Cole, Jennifer, Timothy Mahrt, and Joseph Roy (2017). Crowd-sourcing prosodic annotation. *Computer Speech & Language*, 45:300–325.

Cole, Jennifer, Mo Yoonsook, and Mark Hasegawa-Johnson (2010). Signal-based and expectation-based factors in the perception of prosodic prominence. *Laboratory Phonology*, 1(2):425–452.

Dilley, Laura C. and Meredith Brown (2005). The RaP (Rhythm and Pitch) labeling system. Unpublished manuscript, MIT, available at http://web.mit.edu/tedlab/tedlab_website/RaP%20System/RaP_Labeling_Guide_v1.0.pdf. [Accessed July 25, 2018].

Ernestus, Miriam and R. Harald Baayen (2011). Corpora and exemplars in phonology. In Goldsmith, John A., Jason Riggle, and Yu Alan, eds, *The handbook of phonological theory*, pp. 374–400. Malden, MA: Wiley Blackwell: 2nd edn.

Firbas, Jan (1971). On the concept of communicative dynamism in the theory of functional sentence perspective. *Sborník Prací Filosofické Fakulty Brněnské University* (Studia Minora Facultatis Philosophicae Universitatis Brunensis), A-19:135–144.

German, James, Janet Pierrehumbert, and Stefan Kaufmann (2006). Evidence for phonological constraints on nuclear accent placement. *Language*, 82(1):151–168.

Grömping, Ulrike (2006). Relative importance for linear regression in R: the package relaimpo. *Journal of Statistical Software*, 17(1):1–27.

Gussenhoven, Carlos (1983). Focus, mode and the nucleus. *Journal of Linguistics*, 19(2):377–417.

Gussenhoven, Carlos (1991). The English rhythm rule as an accent assignment rule. *Phonology*, 8:1–35.

Gussenhoven, Carlos (1992). Sentence accents and argument structure. In Roca, Iggy M., ed., *Thematic structure: Its role in grammar*, pp. 79–106. Berlin & New York: Foris Publications.

Gussenhoven, Carlos (2011). Sentential prominence in English. In van Oostendorp, Marc, Colin J. Ewen, Elizabeth Hume, and Keren Rice, eds, *The Blackwell companion to phonology*, vol. 2, p. 2778–2806. Malden, MA: Wiley-Blackwell.

Gussenhoven, Carlos (2015). Does phonological prominence exist? *Lingue e linguaggio*, 14(1):7–24.

Hasegawa-Johnson, Mark, Ken Chen, Jennifer Cole, Sarah Borys, Sung-Suk Kim, Aaron Cohen, Tong Zhang, Jeung-Yoon Choi, Heejin Kim, Taejin Yoon, and Sandra Chavarria (2005). Simultaneous recognition of words and prosody in the Boston University radio speech corpus. *Speech Communication*, 46(3–4):418–439.

Hayes, Bruce (1995). *Metrical stress theory: Principles and case studies*. Chicago: Chicago University Press.

Hirschberg, Julia (1993). Pitch accent in context: predicting intonational prominence from text. *Artificial Intelligence*, 63:305–340.

Hyman, Larry M. (2006). Word-prosodic typology. *Phonology*, 23(2):225–257.

Hyman, Larry M. and Russell G. Schuh (1974). Universals of tone rules: evidence from West Africa. *Linguistic Inquiry*, 5(1):81–115.

Iivonen, Antti, Terttu Nevalainen, Reijo Aulanko, and Hannu Kaskinen (1987). *Puheen intonaatio [Speech Intonation]*. Helsinki: Gaudeamus.

Inkelas, Sharon and Draga Zec, eds (1990). *The phonology-syntax connection*. Chicago/London: University of Chicago Press.

Inkelas, Sharon and Draga Zec (1995). Syntax–phonology interface. In Goldsmith, John A., ed., *The handbook of phonological theory*, pp. 535–549. Cambridge, MA: Blackwell.

Jaeger, T. Florian (2010). Redundancy and reduction: Speakers manage syntactic information density. *Cognitive Psychology*, 61(1):23–62.

Jespersen, Otto (1920). *Lehrbuch der Phonetik: Mit 2 Tafeln*. Leipzig und Berlin: B. G. Teubner.

Kaisse Ellen, M. (1985). *Connected speech: The interaction of syntax and phonology*. Orlando, FL: Academic Press.

Kelly, Michael H. and J. Kathryn Bock (1988). Stress in time. *Journal of Experimental Psychology: Human Perception and Performance*, 14(3):389–403.

Kentner, Gerrit (2012). Linguistic rhythm guides parsing decisions in written sentence comprehension. *Cognition*, 123(1):1–20.

Klein, Dan and Christopher D. Manning (2003). Accurate unlexicalized parsing. In *41st Meeting of the Association for Computational Linguistics*, pp. 423–430.

Kuznetsova, Alexandra, Per Bruun Brockhoff, and Rune Haubo Bojesen Christensen (2016). lmerTest: Tests in linear mixed effects models. R package version 2.0-30. http://CRAN.R-project.org/package=lmerTest.

Ladd, D. Robert (1980). *The structure of intonational meaning: Evidende from English*. Bloomington & London: Indiana University Press.

Ladd, D. Robert (1996). *Intonational phonology*. Cambridge: Cambridge University Press.

Levy, Roger P. and T. Florian Jaeger (2007). Speakers optimize information density through syntactic reduction. In Schlökopf, B. and J. Platt & T. Hoffman, eds, *Advances in Neural Information Processing Systems (NIPS)*, vol. 19, pp. 849–856.

Liberman, Mark and Alan Prince (1977). On stress and linguistic rhythm. *Linguistic Inquiry*, 8(2):249–336.

Manning, Christopher D., Mihai Surdeanu, John Bauer, Jenny Finkel, Steven J. Bethard, and David McClosky (2014). The Stanford CoreNLP natural language processing toolkit. In *52nd Annual Meeting of the Association for Computational Linguistics: System Demonstrations*, pp. 55–60.

Nenkova, Ani, Jason Brenier, Anubha Kothari, Sasha Calhoun, Laura Whitton, David Beaver, and Dan Jurafsky (2007). To memorize or to predict: Prominence labeling in conversational speech. In *Human Language Technology Conference of the North American Chapter of the Association of Computational Linguistics*. http://www.aclweb.org/anthology/N07-1002. Also posted at ScholarlyCommons http://repository.upenn.edu/cis_papers/732. [Accessed April 23, 2018].

Nespor, Marina and Irene Vogel (2007). Prosodic phonology: With a new foreword. In *Studies in Generative Grammar*, vol. 28. Berlin/New York: Mouton de Gruyter.

Pan, Shimei and Julia Hirschberg (2000). Modeling local context for pitch accent prediction. In *38th Annual Meeting on Association for Computational Linguistics, Association for Computational Linguistics*, pp. 233–240.

Pan, Shimei, Kathleen McKeown, and Julia Hirschberg (2002). Exploring features from natural language generation for prosody modeling. *Computer Speech & Language*, 16(3–4):457–490.

Pan, Shimei and Kathleen R. McKeown (1999). Word informativeness and automatic pitch accent modeling. In *In 1999 Joint SIGDAT Conference on Empirical Methods in Natural Language Processing and Very Large Corpora*. available at http://www.aclweb.org/anthology/W99-0619.

Piantadosi, Steven T., Harry Tily, and Edward Gibson (2011). Word lengths are optimized for efficient communication. *National Academy of Sciences*, 108(9):3526–3529.

Prince, Alan (1983). Relating to the grid. *Linguistic Inquiry*, 14(1):19–100.

Sadeniemi, Matti (1949). *Metriikkamme perusteet [Fundamentals of Finnish Metrics]*. Helsinki: Suomalaisen Kirjallisuuden Seura.

Schmerling, Susan F. (1976). *Aspects of English sentence stress*. Austin: Texas University Press.

Selkirk, Elisabeth O. (1995). Sentence prosody: Intonation, stress, and phrasing. In Goldsmith, John A., ed., *The handbook of phonological theory*, pp. 550–69. Cambridge, MA: Blackwell.

Selkirk, Elisabeth O. (2011). The syntax–phonology interface. In Goldsmith, John A., Jason Riggle, and Yu Alan, eds, *The handbook of phonological theory*, pp. 435–483. Malden, MA: Wiley Blackwell: 2nd edn.

Shih, Stephanie (2014). *Towards optimal rhythm*. Ph. D. thesis, Stanford University.

Silverman, Kim, Mary Beckman, John Pitrelli, Mari Ostendorf, Colin Wightman, Patti Price, Janet Pierrehumbert, and Julia Hirschberg (1992). ToBI: A standard for labeling English prosody. In *Second international conference on spoken language processing (ICSLP-1992)*, pp. 867–870.

Smith, Jennifer L. (2011). Category-specific effects. In van Oostendorp, Marc, Colin J. Ewen, Elizabeth Hume, and Keren Rice, eds, *The Blackwell companion to phonology*, vol. 4, p. 2439–2463. Malden, MA: Wiley-Blackwell.

Snigaroff, Madeline K. (2017). Evaluating MetricalTree. Ms., Stanford University.

Truckenbrodt, Hubert (2007). The syntax-phonology interface. In de Lacy, Paul, ed., *The Cambridge handbook of phonology*, pp. 435–56. Cambridge: Cambridge University Press.

Veilleux, Nanette, Stefanie Shattuck-Hufnagel, and Alejna Brugos (2006). 6.911 Transcribing Prosodic Structure of Spoken Utterances with ToBI. January IAP 2006. Massachusetts Institute of Technology: MIT Open Course Ware, https://ocw.mit.edu. License: Creative Commons BY-NC-SA.

Vilkuna, Maria (1998). Word order in European Uralic. In Siewierska, Anna, ed., *Constituent order in the languages of Europe*, no. No. 1 in Empirical Approaches to Language Typology 20, pp. 173–233. Berlin/New York: Mouton de Gruyter.

Wagner, Michael (2005). Asymmetries in Prosodic Domain Formation. In Richards, Norvin and Martha McGinnis, eds, *Perspectives on phases* MITWPL 49, pp. 329–367.

Weide, Robert (1998). The Carnegie Mellon pronouncing dictionary [cmudict.0.6]. Technical report, Carnegie Mellon University. ftp://ftp.cs.cmu.edu/project/speech/dict/.

Wiese, Richard (1996). *The phonology of German*. Oxford: Oxford University Press.

Tina Bögel
German case ambiguities at the interface: Production and comprehension

Abstract: This article discusses a new approach to the interface between phonology/prosody and syntax with regard to two perspectives: production and comprehension. The model assumes two transfer processes responsible for the exchange of information at the interface: the *transfer of vocabulary*, which operates at the word-level and below, and the *transfer of structure*, which is concerned with the association of syntactic and prosodic phrasing above the word-level. These transfer processes at the interface are illustrated by means of syntactically ambiguous German genitive/dative case constructions which can be resolved via prosodic phrasing. The relevant prosodic cues for the disambiguation were determined via a production experiment which also showed that the use of acoustic cues is not uniform across speakers. The proposed model allows for a straightforward and elegant resolution of the syntactic ambiguities at the interface to the prosodic module and can furthermore be extended to include speaker variability as well.

1 Introduction

Over the last few decades, several theories on how syntactic and prosodic constituency are related have been proposed, amongst others the *relation-based* approach (Selkirk 1978; Nespor & Vogel 1986), the *edge-based* approach (Selkirk 1986; Chen 1987), and more currently MATCH THEORY (Selkirk 2011, see also Ladd 1986). All of these have been further enhanced by discussions on the recursivity of prosodic constituents (a.o., Ladd 1986; Féry 2010; Elfner 2012), and approaches to reduce overgeneration in form of recursivity, most notably Truckenbrodt (1995, 1999)'s WRAP-constraint, which states that every XP must be 'wrapped' into a phonological phrase, thus allowing nested structures to be dissolved into a single phonological phrase. The approach to the interface between prosody and syntax presented in this paper does not make a claim as to how and which syntactic and prosodic constituents are related. Instead, it offers a formal implementation and shows how information on syntactic and prosodic constituency can be exchanged

---

Note: I would like to thank Gerrit Kentner and Richard Wiese for their close and patient editing, and an anonymous reviewer for her/his valuable comments and suggestions.

at the interface. For demonstration purposes, MATCH THEORY in combination with WRAP is assumed.[1]

It is equally assumed that prosodic phrasing is not only determined by syntactic structure, but by other modules as well, e.g., information structure, in the sense that prosody can be applied to express concepts like focus, topic, and givenness (see, e.g., Féry 1993; Baumann 2006). Furthermore, prosodic phrasing often seems to undergo postsyntactic 'rephrasing' processes to meet well-formedness constraints. Function words in trochaic languages, for example, are often phrased with the previous prosodic word, independent of (and often in opposition to) their syntactic affiliation (a.o., Selkirk 1995; Lahiri & Plank 2010). As a consequence, this interplay between different modules and postsyntactic prosodic rephrasing results in frequent mismatches between syntax and prosody and often makes it difficult to disentangle the individual influences of the different modules on a specific phenomenon.

The idea of grammar as consisting of different modules with their own principles and parameters has been adopted into several frameworks, among them Lexical Functional Grammar (LFG; Kaplan & Bresnan 1985). These modules are assumed to relate *form* (i.e., what is said/perceived) and *meaning* (i.e., what is intended/comprehended), with each module contributing relevant information on, e.g., semantics, syntax, or phonology. An additional important factor with respect to the different modules is the distinction between two perspectives that are essential for the communication between speaker and listener: 1) *production*, which is concerned with the question how the speaker's original intention is transformed into a structured utterance; that is, how meaning is transformed into form. And 2) *comprehension*, which discusses the question as to how information from a concrete speech signal is processed and transformed into syntactic structure (followed by the fundamental 'understanding' of what is being said, i.e., how form is transformed into meaning).

The underlying assumption of the present article is that the different modules of grammar are related in a linear way, as illustrated in Fig. 1. However, it is also clear from phenomena relating semantics/pragmatics/information structure to prosody and vice versa, that the basic linear structure is not sufficient.[2] It is also

---

[1] Note, however, that a) it is likely that different languages may relate prosodic and syntactic constituents differently, and b) MATCH might not be the best choice for German, but it certainly serves for demonstration purposes here. The individual theoretical choice does not affect the formal implementation presented in the paper, as the transfer processes can be adjusted very easily to a number of approaches.

[2] This is indicated by the dotted line in Fig. 1, but is not further pursued here, as it goes far beyond the relationship between syntax and prosody that is the main focus of this paper.

obvious from postlexical phonological rephrasing phenomena that each module should be assumed to have a certain amount of individual generative power. Following models of speech production as they have been proposed by, among others, Jackendoff (2002) and Levelt (1999), the following underlying architecture with respect to the linear order of the different modules of grammar is adopted.

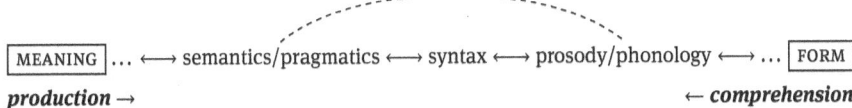

| MEANING | ... ⟷ semantics/pragmatics ⟷ syntax ⟷ prosody/phonology ⟷ ... | FORM |

production → ← *comprehension*

Fig. 1: The underlying linear order of grammar modules

As a consequence of the model proposed in Fig. 1, each interface always has a certain directionality depending on the process: production (i.e., the interface *from* syntax *to* prosody) or comprehension (i.e., the interface *from* prosody *to* syntax, a topic that has received considerably less attention with respect to theories of the interface).

This article focusses solely on the interface between syntax and prosody/phonology and discusses a new account of the interface from both perspectives, comprehension and production, providing a detailed formal implementation of German case ambiguities. Working with spoken data, including speaker variability, the research question is in how far prosodic phrasing can be reliably predicted on the basis of syntactic phrasing and in how far this process is reversible in the sense that prosody influences syntactic phrasing during comprehension. In order to gain insight into these questions and the acoustic realisations of each syntactic structure, genitive or dative, a production experiment was conducted.

As prosody in general rarely influences unambiguous syntactic structures, syntactically fully ambiguous sentences were chosen in order to determine the influence of prosody on syntactic phrasing. In the following example, the verb's optional subcategorization for an object and the syncretism between the feminine forms of the German dative and genitive determiners lead to an ambiguity in the subordinate clause's second NP *der Gräfin*.

(1) Alle waren überrascht dass [der Diener]$_{NP1}$
Everyone was surprised that the.MASC.NOM servant
[der Gräfin]$_{NP2}$ folgte.
the.FEM.GEN/DAT Countess followed
'Everyone was surprised that [the Countess' servant followed // the servant followed the Countess].'

The concrete acoustic cues resulting from experiments are commonly replaced by the abstract notion of a prosodic domain (boundary). However, the question remains as to how far the acoustic cues found in spoken language contribute to the determination of rules and constraints that form the core of the grammar, and how (and if) such naturally occuring and often highly variable data can be integrated into a model of the syntax–prosody interface. Thus, one aim of this paper is to bridge this gap between categorical interpretation and naturally occurring data. It will be shown that the present syntax–prosody interface model can formally integrate both, naturally occuring variability as well as categorical representation, thus allowing for a straightforward analysis of complex ambiguities at the syntax–prosody interface from both perspectives: production and comprehension.

The paper is structured as follows: Section 2 explains German case ambiguities in more detail and describes the possibilities for prosodic phrasing. Section 3 introduces the production experiment and shows the range of varieties found between different speakers. In Sect. 4, the formal implementation of the syntax–prosody interface is described in more detail, followed by Sect. 5 which analyses case ambiguities during production as well as comprehension and offers a solution to speaker variability. Section 6 concludes the paper.

2 The genitive/dative ambiguity

Speakers and listeners can use prosodic information to clarify the meaning of syntactically ambiguous sentences like the subordinate clause given in example (2), where the second NP can either have a dative or a genitive interpretation.

(2) … dass [der Partner]$_{NP1}$ **[der Freundin]$_{NP2}$** zuhörte
 … that the.MASC.NOM partner the.FEM.GEN/DAT friend listened
  … that the friend's partner listened // the partner listened to the friend.

There are two reasons for this particular ambiguity. First, the ambiguity of the second NP in the subordinate clause (*der Freundin*) is based on the syncretism between the feminine dative and genitive form of the determiner (*der*, Table 1).

case	masc	fem	neut
nom	der	die	das
gen	des	*der*	des
dat	dem	*der*	dem
acc	den	die	das

Tab. 1: German determiner system (for the singular)

Second, in addition to the case-related ambiguity with the determiner, the final verb (*zuhörte*) can either be intransitive or transitive, requiring a dative object in the latter case. In combination with the syncretic feminine determiner, the second NP (*der Freundin*) in example (2) can either be interpreted as a dative object of the verb or as a possessor phrase to the first NP *der Partner*, resulting in full ambiguity of the complete subordinate phrase. Crucially, however, in an example with a masculine second NP, the ambiguity is no longer given ((3)). Even though the verb would in principle allow for an ambiguous construction, the masculine dative and genitive determiners are not syncretic. As a consequence, their use clearly disambiguates the second NP as either a dative object ((3a)) or a possessor ((3b)).

(3) a. ... dass [der Partner]$_{NP1}$ **[dem Freund]**$_{NP2}$ zuhörte
... that the.MASC.NOM partner the.MASC.DAT friend listened
(Everyone was surprised) ... that the partner listened to the friend.

b. ... dass [der Partner]$_{NP1}$ **[des Freundes]**$_{NP2}$ zuhörte
... that the.MASC.NOM partner the.MASC.GEN friend listened
(Everyone was surprised) ... that the partner's friend listened.

The full ambiguity in examples like the one in (2) results in two possible syntactic structures (as shown below in Figs. 2 and 3). While the purely syntactic analysis of ambiguous structures leads to multiple representations, a disambiguated structure and with it a singular meaning can be signalled to the listener via the use of different acoustic cues (a.o., Lehiste et al. 1976; Price et al. 1991). These acoustic cues signal prosodic domain boundaries (inter alia), which can be crucial for the disambiguation of syntactic ambiguities. Thus, the question addressed in the present paper is if prosodic information can also be applied to help disambiguate syntactically ambiguous structures like the ones given in (2), and if so, which acoustic cues are associated with which syntactic structure.

Assuming MATCH THEORY (Selkirk 2011) and with it the prosodic hierarchy as discussed in Selkirk (1978), every IP/CP is associated with an intonational phrase (ι), and every morphosyntactic word with a prosodic word (ω). The phonological phrase (φ) is assumed to correspond to an XP consisting of a head and any specifiers or function words included in the XP (albeit further factors, e.g., size, might alter this pattern). Intonationally, phonological phrases contain a pitch accent and an intermediate boundary tone (Frota 2012; Beckman & Pierrehumbert 1986), which is also in line with Truckenbrodt's STRESS-XP, where each phonological phrase contains one main stress placed on the innermost XP in a nested structure (cf. Truckenbrodt 2016).

The following figures show the two possible syntactic structures[3] resulting from fully ambiguous examples as presented in (2), including the predictions made by MATCH and WRAP/STRESS with respect to phonological phrases (where X indicates the nuclear stress of the phonological phrase).

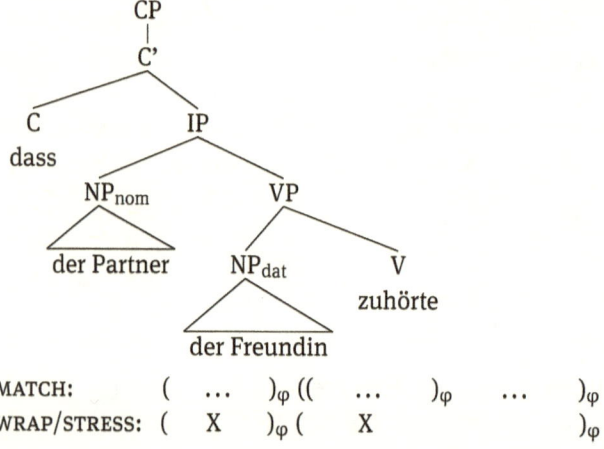

MATCH: (...   )_φ ((...   )_φ   ...   )_φ
WRAP/STRESS: (X   )_φ (X   )_φ

Fig. 2: Syntactic structure depicting the dative (including predictions on prosodic phrasing)

For the dative structure as depicted in Fig. 2, MATCH predicts a separate phonological phrase for *der Partner* and a nested phonological phrase structure for the verb and the object *der Freundin*. WRAP/STRESS then predicts that the object and the verb form one phonological phrase with the dominant stress on the innermost XP (*FREUNdin*).

The structure predicted by MATCH and WRAP/STRESS for the genitive construction differs from the dative structure in that *Der Partner der Freundin* forms one (nested) phonological phrase and the verb *zuhörte* forms a separate one.

A similar prediction is also made by the proximity model assumed in Kentner & Féry (2013), where the syntactic distance between two constituents determines the (gradient) presence of a prosodic boundary. It can thus be concluded that a prosodic boundary can be expected to occur after the first NP *der Partner* in the dative and after the second NP in the genitive.[4]

---

[3] The syntactic structures are modelled according to assumptions currently made in LFG (Dalrymple 2001) and are slightly simplified; see Sect. 4 below for more details.

[4] While these patterns seem to be intuitively right, the boundary between the NP *der Freundin* and the verb *zuhörte* is difficult to verify in both conditions with the data presented here. The reason for this lies in the heterogenous nature of this particular verb group and the nouns of the second NP and will be discussed below in Sect. 3.1.1.

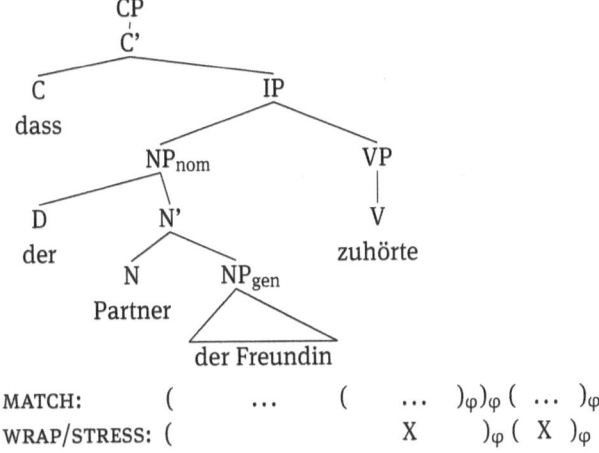

Fig. 3: Syntactic structure depicting the genitive (including predictions on prosodic phrasing)

(4) a. ... dass der Partner)φ(der Freundin ...
    b. ... dass der Partner der Freundin)φ(...

In contrast, in the unambiguous dative example in (3a), the phonological phrase boundary is expected to be placed between the two NPs.

(5) ... dass der Partner)φ(dem Freund ...

This crucial difference between (4) and (5) shows that a certain dominance of syntax over prosody can be assumed. In example (5) it does not matter whether prosodic phrasing is unexpected, that is, whether the phonological phrase boundary is placed somewhere else or is completely missing – under no circumstances can prosody alter the syntactic interpretation of the second NP as a dative object as the form of the determiner (*dem*) only allows for a single interpretation (dative masculine). From the two viewpoints of comprehension and production it can thus be concluded that while for production the placement of a phonological phrase boundary is part of a well-formed sentence, prosodic phrasing is only crucial for syntactic structuring during comprehension in the context of syntactic ambiguities.[5] Phonological phrase boundaries thus *can* determine syntactic phrasing, but *only* if a syntactic ambiguity is given.

---

[5] This does not exclude the impact prosodic indicators might have on meaning interpretation; however, the discussion in this article is reduced to the interface between prosody and syntax and does not include references to, e.g., information structure.

Evidence for a prosodic disambiguation pointing towards a verification of these predictions comes from a production experiment on the impact of different acoustic cues on the interpretation of German sentences with a temporary genitive/dative ambiguity. Gollrad et al. (2010) found f_0, *pause* and *duration* to be relevant cues for the indication of a phonological phrase boundary in a dative construction. In a follow-up perception experiment, they furthermore identified *duration* to be the most important factor for the disambiguation of syntactic structures in language comprehension.

However, in contrast to (2) given above, Gollrad et al. (2010)'s study did not involve completely ambiguous structures. Instead, sentences consisted of three determiner phrases whose relation with each other was disambiguated by a final verb with an unambiguous subcategorization frame. In addition to the incomplete ambiguity, the use of three NPs increased the chance of 'list intonation',[6] which might have distorted the results. Furthermore, Gollrad et al. did not look at the occurence frequency of the different acoustic cues, a topic which is of particular interest to the present paper as it reflects speaker variety and addresses the question as to how 'likely' it is that a speaker indicates a particular interpretation by means of prosody.

3 Experiment

In order to gain insight into the prosodic realization of fully ambiguous sentences with a reduced number of NPs (as described in (2)) and the use of prosody in general across speakers, a further production experiment was conducted. The aim was to determine the respective acoustic cues that contribute to the representation of each case condition and to identify the distribution and frequency of each acoustic cue across all speakers.

3.1 Methods

3.1.1 Stimuli

There are only a handful of verbs in German that allow for an optional dative object.[7] This particular group is very heterogenous with respect to its morphological

---

[6] List intonation refers to the downstepping intonation pattern used if expressing a list, e.g., as in *I bought an apple, a sausage, an orange, and a banana* (see Liberman & Pierrehumbert 1984).
[7] The nine verbs used in the experiment were *widersprechen* 'to object', *zustimmen* 'to agree',

composition, as some are formed with particles (*zu*), or with (lexicalised) prefixes (*ge-*, *wider-*). Furthermore, there are three different stress patterns (with either the 1st, 2nd, or 3rd syllable carrying main lexical stress). These differences are very likely to cause a variety of f_0 patterns and are thus not suitable when trying to establish a phrase boundary between the last NP and the verb by means of a statistical analysis.

There was also a reduced number of choices with respect to the nouns. Each noun used in the experiment followed a trochaic foot pattern and consisted of two syllables plus a determiner across all conditions and sentence types, resulting in the following pattern for the two NPs:

(6)   x   x
    $\underbrace{det\ syll_1\ syll_2}_{NP_1}\ \underbrace{det\ syll_1\ syll_2}_{NP_2}$

For the second NP, only feminine nouns, which were able to form a possessive as well as a subject-object relationship, were chosen. These constraints resulted in nouns with different vowel qualities, both open and closed final codas, and ambisyllabicity. As a consequence, in addition to the heterogenous nature of the verbs, the nouns of the second NP also make it difficult to determine the existence of a phonological phrase boundary after the second NP by means of a statistical analysis. The question whether the predictions made by, e.g., MATCH and WRAP/STRESS concerning the boundary between the second NP and the verb in the genitive, but also the question whether the phonological phrases are recursive (MATCH), or form a single phonological phrase (WRAP) thus has to be left to further research with a carefully controlled data design that is not concerned with syntactic ambiguities.

The experiment in this paper focusses on the presence or absence of a phonological phrase boundary between the two NPs, encoding either a dative or a genitive, respectively. Each stimulus belonged to one of three groups:

1. Three ambiguous and two unambiguous case constructions placed within a larger text, where context disambiguated the ambiguous sentences.
2. Twelve unambiguous structures consisting of two masculine NPs each, whose relation with each other was disambiguated via the respective determiners. Six of these structures were in the dative ((7a)) and six in the genitive condition ((7b)).

---

antworten 'to answer', *gratulieren* 'to congratulate', *fehlen* (intransitive) 'to be absent' / (with dative object) 'to miss (somebody/something)', *zuhören* 'to listen', *folgen* 'to follow', *gehorchen* 'to obey', *helfen* 'to help'.

(7) a. als der Schneider dem Anwalt antwortete
when the.MASC.NOM tailor the.MASC.DAT lawyer answered
'... when the tailor answered the lawyer.'

b. als der Schneider des Anwalts
when the.MASC.NOM tailor the.MASC.GEN lawyer
antwortete
answered
'... when the lawyer's tailor answered.'

Each speaker had to produce a total of six sentences mixed from both conditions and interspersed with fillers.
3. Nine fully ambiguous structures where the first NP was masculine and the second one feminine.[8] All speakers produced these sentences twice, once in the dative, and once in the genitive condition, resulting in a total of 18 sentences. As noted by Allbritton et al. (1996) (see also Snedeker & Trueswell (2003)), subjects will not consistently use phonetic cues to indicate a certain interpretation of syntactically ambiguous sentences. However, if the speakers were made aware of the ambiguity and were asked to pronounce a sentence according to a certain interpretation, the phonetic cues were much more distinct for each condition. In order to ensure clear phonetic cues, the speakers were thus provided with a context that supported one of the two possible interpretations.

3.1.2 Participants

For the experiment, 15 female native speakers of German aged between 20 and 30 were recorded and paid € 4 for their participation.

3.1.3 Procedure

Target sentences (5 sentences in context, 18 ambiguous sentences, 6 unambiguous sentences) and randomly distributed fillers were presented as a slide representation ordered in three successive blocks of sentence types, whereby the ambiguous sentences were split into two parts and grouped around the unambiguous sen-

---

8 All ambiguous sentences are listed in the Appendix.

tences. Participants were asked to read the context silently and to 'mentally understand' the sentence, before producing the sentence as naturally as possible.

Participants were recorded in the soundproof booth of the phonetic laboratory at the University of Konstanz (sampling frequency 44.1 kHz, 16 Bit resolution). Every speaker produced 29 target sentences, resulting in a total of 435 items.

3.1.4 Data analysis

18 of the 435 sentences were discarded because there was no discernable pitch. The remaining files were manually annotated using Praat (Boersma & Weenink 2013). The annotation was conducted syllablewise across the two NPs and included the duration of each syllable, pauses where applicable, and a mean pitch value for each syllable vowel, on the basis of which the difference in pitch between two adjacent syllables was calculated as well.

No difference was found in the pronunciation of ambiguous and unambiguous sentences, therefore both sentence types were included in the statistical analysis. The statistical analysis of the different (non-normalized) phonetic cues was done with a linear mixed effects regression model (LMER, see Baayen et al. (2008) for details) with the two conditions (genitive and dative) as fixed factors, and with subject and item as crossed random factors (adjustment of intercept and slope). Participants were analysed as a group, but also as individuals in order to investigate the frequency of occurrence for each acoustic cue across all speakers.

3.2 Results

The statistical analysis for all speakers showed the following results:
- A significantly steeper drop in F0 between NP1 and NP2 (as measured at the final syllable of NP1 and the determiner of NP2) in the dative as compared to the genitive condition ($\beta = -9.31$, SE = 2.64, $t = -3.53$, $p < 0.01$).
- A pause between the first and the second NP in the dative as compared to the genitive condition: ($\beta = -2.35$, SE = 0.92, $t = -2.55$, $p < 0.05$).
- A significant increase in the duration of the last syllable of the first NP in the dative condition compared to the genitive condition ($\beta = -2.8$, SE = 0.79, $t = -3.58$, $p < 0.01$).

The aim of this experiment, however, was not only to capture the significant phonetic cues indicating a dative or genitive interpretation, but to also consider the less dominant cues which might still be relevant for the calculation of a prosodic phrase boundary if the other indicators are not present, and to examine speaker variability. Therefore, the statistical analysis was applied to individual speakers as well, including phonetic cues that were non-significant in the overall analysis, but were significantly used by at least 20% of the speakers. Particular attention was paid to the fact that the individual cues did not contradict each other.[9]

When tested individually with the lmer model described above for strategies to indicate the dative or the genitive, around 33% of the participants did *not show any* significant prosodic cues. Only 67% of the speakers applied acoustic cues, to a varying extent.[10] In addition to the findings above, two further indicators were found for the genitive: a) a less pronounced difference in the fundamental frequency between the first and the second syllable of the first NP's noun, and b) a drop in fundamental frequency from the second determiner to the first syllable of the second NP's noun. However, there are no significant results identifying a phonological phrase boundary for the genitive construction (no pause, no lengthening of the last syllable, no drop/rise in f_0), neither between the two NPs nor following both NPs. As discussed under 3.1.1., this question has to be left for further research, as the reason for this is most likely the heterogenous nature of the data at that particular sentence position.

The following table gives an overview of all cues found when comparing the dative and genitive condition as calculated above across all speakers, as well as the results for individual speakers.

Tab. 2: Frequency distribution of acoustic cues in the genitive and dative condition

condition	acoustic cue	individ. speakers
dative	pause between NP_1 and NP_2	~40% (6/15)
	longer duration of the last syllable in NP_1	~47% (7/15)
	drop in f_0 between the last syllable of NP_1 and the Det. of NP_2	~40% (6/15)
genitive	smaller rise in f_0 between the two syllables in NP_1	~27% (4/15)
	drop in f_0 between the second Det. and the first syllable of NP_2	~20% (3/15)

The acoustic cues indicating a phonological phrase boundary and thus supporting a dative interpretation are statistically significant across all speakers. Their

---

9 For example, if one subgroup used a rising pattern and another group used a falling pattern on the same syllable in the same condition, this acoustic cue was excluded from the analysis.
10 Note that the data size is greatly diminished for the individual speakers, hence an exact determination of speaker-individual prosodic cues has to be left for further research. With respect to speaker variability, the present paper focusses on a formal representation (and implementation) and takes these initial measurements merely as a basic orientation.

absence, on the other hand, are an indication of a syntactic structure representing a genitive construction. The two acoustic cues listed for the genitive above are not significant for all speakers, but are applied by some of the speakers (27% and 20%, respectively) to indicate a genitive interpretation.

3.3 Discussion

The following figure shows a 'prototypical' instance of the dative stimulus in Praat with four syllables of example (2) (*der Partner der Freundin*). The annotation provides the (non-IPA) reference syllables, a pause (-p-), and a GToBI annotation, indicating High and Low pitch accents and boundary tones (Grice & Baumann 2002).

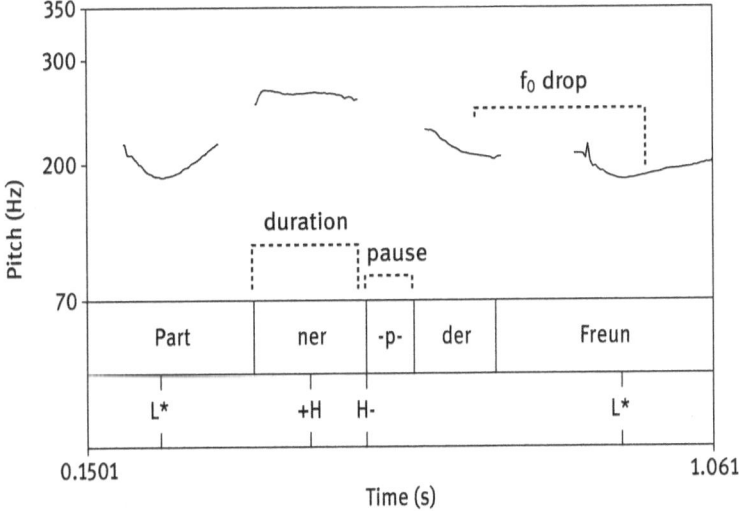

Fig. 4: A 'prototypical' dative

The solid lines in Fig. 4 represent the fundamental frequency as it was calculated by Praat. The dotted lines have been added manually and indicate the three most frequently used acoustic cues for the dative construction: a) the second syllable of the first NP has an increased duration, b) a small pause is inserted between the two NPs, and c) a drop in f_0 can be found between the first and the second NP. Taken together, these acoustic cues indicate the presence of a phonological phrase boundary after the first NP.

The phonological phrase boundary found with the dative signal is not present in the genitive construction (Fig. 5). Furthermore, all of the above mentioned ('dative') indicators are significant for the genitive as well in that they are *not* present.

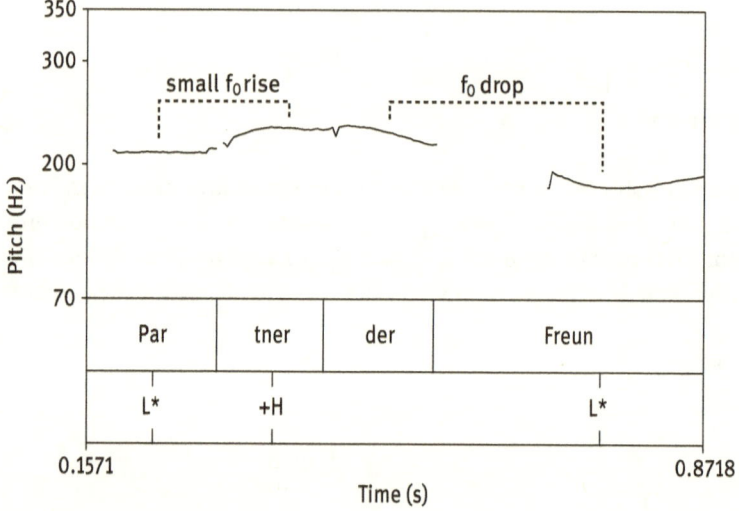

Fig. 5: A 'prototypical' genitive

Acoustic cues in the genitive speech signal are the smaller f_0 rise,[11] and the drop in f_0 from the determiner to the first syllable of the second NP.

While all of the indicators found for the dative are significant if measured for all participants, this is certainly not true for each individual speaker. This applies to an even greater extent to the cues found for the genitive, which are nonsignificant across all speakers, but can be present for the individual speaker. It can be concluded, that participants use different acoustic cues and combinations thereof to indicate a particular case construction – and that a considerable number of them does not use any discernible cues at all. Speaker variability is thus a very important factor when it comes to modelling these constructions and the interplay between syntax and prosody at the interface.

However, even given speaker variety, the experiment confirmed that a certain combination of acoustic cues can be assumed to indicate the presence of a phonological phrase boundary, as predicted in (4), and repeated in (8).

(8) a. ... dass der Partner)$_\varphi$ (der Freundin ...   → *Dative*
    b. ... dass der Partner der Freundin ...   → *Genitive*

---

[11] The rise in f_0 has been compressed to the extent that an L*+H annotation might seem to be uncalled-for. The annotation was left in there because a rise, albeit a small one, is still present.

To conclude, although prosody usually does not determine syntactic structure, syntactic ambiguities can be resolved with reference to prosody. In the following section, this asymmetric relationship between prosody and syntax will be discussed in more detail with reference to the syntax–prosody interface in LFG.

4 The syntax-prosody interface

The modular architecture of LFG distinguishes two syntactic structures. C(onstituent)-structure represents the linear order and the hierarchical organization of words into a syntactic tree (see also Figs. 2 and 3). F(unctional)-structure, on the other hand, encodes the abstract functional organization and the dependency structures of a sentence in terms of an attribute-value matrix; for the interaction with prosody that particular structure is not important and will therefore not be considered any further in this paper.

Apart from these structures representing the syntactic module, there are further modules representing, among others, s(emantic)-structure, i(nformation)-structure, and p(rosodic)-structure. All structures are placed into correspondence with each other via projection functions that relate specific parts of one structure to specific parts of another structure. The projection function ϕ, for example, relates c- and f-structure and determines that the specifier of IP (in c-structure) corresponds to the subject (in f-structure) (see Dalrymple (2001) for a general overview).

Resolving case ambiguities requires the involvement of at least two modules of grammar: syntax and prosody. While the syntactic structures discussed above are well-established, the prosodic module has received considerably less attention (in LFG, but also elsewhere). While over the last decades, some analyses of phenomena have been presented with reference to prosody and phonology in LFG (Butt & King 1998; O'Connor 2004; Mycock 2006; Bögel et al. 2009; Dalrymple & Mycock 2011), all of these approaches are relatively narrow and cannot account for the full complexity found in relation to the form of a sentence, i.e., the spoken utterance. In this paper a new approach to p-structure is introduced, which enables a full interaction between p-structure and other modules of grammar (here: syntax).

The following figure shows the abstract arrangement of modules/structures and projection functions with respect to the prosody–syntax interface, i.e., p-structure and c-structure respectively (see Bögel (2015) for a detailed introduction).

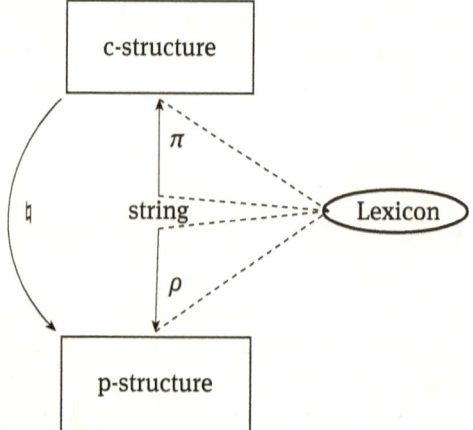

Fig. 6: An abstract representation of the syntax–prosody interface

C-structure is represented by a syntactic tree (Figs. 2 and 3). P-structure is represented via the p-diagram, a compact, syllable-based representation imitating the linear nature of the speech signal over time. For this purpose, each syllable receives a feature vector associating the syllable with a number of attributes, which each assign a specific value to that particular syllable. In the following figure, the NP *der Freundin* ('the (female) friend') is encoded in a p-diagram. Each syllable is assigned a vector (S_n) and a number of attribute-value pairs. The attribute SEGMENTS, for example, associates the value /de^ɐ/ with the syllable representing *der* 'the'.

ATTRIBUTE$_3$	...	...	...	...
ATTRIBUTE$_2$	...	...	...	...
SEGMENTS	...	/de^ɐ/	/fʁɔœn/	/dɪn/
VECTORINDEX	S_3	S_4	S_5	S_6

Fig. 7: The p-diagram: a compact syllable-based model of p-structure

Three levels can be distinguished within the p-diagram, each with a unique set of attributes: The *lexical level* stores lexical information that is associated with each syllable and applies only during production. The *signal level* records information associated with each syllable in the speech signal and occurs only during comprehension. The *interpretation level*, finally, interprets and abstracts away from both the *lexical* and the *signal level* during production and comprehension.

Because of the distinct nature of each level, only specific attributes can be associated with it: While the signal level will naturally contain attributes like DURATION, PAUSE, and FUNDAMENTAL FREQUENCY (f_0), the lexical level is concerned with attributes like LEXICAL STRESS and SEGMENTS.[12] The interpretation level builds on the different values given in the lexical or the signal level and interprets them in terms of PROSODIC PHRASING or GTOBI annotations, e.g., it determines on the basis of the values given for DURATION, PAUSE, and FUNDAMENTAL FREQUENCY if a phonological/intonational phrase boundary is present after a specific syllable, or if a high tone is given on the basis of f_0-movement.

Two levels of information transfer are assumed at the syntax–prosody interface, i.e., between c- and p-structure: the *transfer of vocabulary* and the *transfer of structure*.

4.1 The *transfer of vocabulary*: information exchange at the lexical level

The *transfer of vocabulary* operates at the word-level and below with reference to the string via the projection functions ρ and π (Fig. 6). Each element of the string is related to its associated morphosyntactic and phonological information in the lexicon, projecting this information to the respective structures (c-structure or p-structure).

LFG supports the strong lexicalist hypothesis (Lapointe 1980) and the *principle of lexical integrity* (Bresnan & Mchombo 1995) in that only morphologically complete words can enter the syntactic module. The lexicon in LFG is thus a rich and complex structure whose output consists of fully-fledged wordforms.[13] Each lexical entry has three dimensions: The *concept* which includes all semantic information associated with that particular form,[14] the *s(yntactic)-form* including all morphosyntactic information on, e.g., case, number, or gender, and the *p(honological)-form* which contains all information associated with segmental

---

[12] In fact, the attribute SEGMENTS occurs with both, lexical and signal level. However, while the value represents the underlying segments as they are stored in the mental lexicon at the lexical level (feature bundles, as suggested by Lahiri & Reetz (2002, 2010) and indicated by slashes / /), the SEGMENTS attribute at the signal level encodes the segments as given in the speech signal, including possible variations or coarticulation phenomena (represented by square brackets [ ]).
[13] These wordforms are assumed to be generated dynamically within the lexicon and its associated structures, e.g., lexical phonology and morphology (Kiparsky 1982; Mohanan 1982; Meinzer et al. 2009, a.o.).
[14] The *concept* is not of relevance for the current discussion and will therefore be omitted from depictions of the lexicon following Table 3.

and suprasegmental (word-level) phonology (cf. Levelt et al. 1999). In the following table, the lexical entries for the determiner *der* 'the' and the noun *Freundin* 'friend' are given.[15]

Tab. 3: (Simplified) lexical entries for *der* and *Freundin*

concept	s-form			p-form	
FREUNDIN	N	(↑ PRED)	= 'Freundin'	SEGMENTS	/fʁɔœndin/
		(↑ NUM)	= sg	METRICAL FRAME	('σσ)_ω
		(↑ GEND)	= fem		
DETERMINER	D	(↑ PRED)	= 'der'	SEGMENTS	/deɐ/
		(↑ NUM)	= sg	METRICAL FRAME	σ
		(↑ GEND)	= fem		
		(↑ CASE)	= {gen | dat}		

Besides information on number and gender, the s-form of the determiner *der* also encodes the inherent case ambiguity between genitive and dative within the multidimensional lexicon using the formal disjunction operator {gen | dat}. The p-form entries, on the other hand, provide information on the individual segments associated with that entry, the number of syllables (σ), stress distribution (') among these syllables, and the prosodic domain: a prosodic word (ω) for *Freundin*, but only a syllable for the function word *der* (cf. Selkirk 1995, a.o.). Note that the segments are not associated with the syllable structure of a lexical entry. This is assumed to be a dynamic process which is also determined by preceding and following words and postlexical phonological processes, e.g., resyllabification. A function word without prosodic word status might be prosodically grouped with the preceding prosodic word. If that 'host' is terminated by a consonant and the function word starts with a vowel, a majority of the languages will apply onset maximisation, drawing the final consonant of the host into the onset of the following function word. It is therefore crucial to only associate segments with syllables once the context is given as well (see also Levelt et al. (1999) for a further discussion of the topic).

This strict separation of module-related information within the multi-dimensional lexicon is in line with a modular view of grammar (cf. Fodor (1983), see also Scheer (2011) for an overview, but also fn 2). Each lexical dimension can only

---

15 Note that the lexical entry for *der* is restricted to the feminine form here. Further morphosyntactic information could be included based on the syncretism with the masculine and the plural forms, but was left out for reasons of simplification. It is also worth mentioning that *Freundin* is feminine because of the suffix *-in* (with *Freund* as the masculine form).

be accessed by the related module of language: c-structure can access only information associated with the s-form, and p-structure can only access information stored within the p-form. However, once a lexical dimension (e.g., s-form) is activated, the related dimensions (e.g., p-form) can be accessed as well and the information can be instantiated to the related modules, i.e., c-structure can relate to a specific s-form in the lexicon which activates the associated lexical p-form whose information then becomes available to p-structure and vice versa. The multidimensional lexicon therefore adopts a translatory function at the phonological and morphosyntactic word-level and below, thus enabling the *transfer of vocabulary* between c- and p-structure.

4.2 The *transfer of structure*: information exchange on constituents

The *transfer of structure* directly associates c- and p-structure via the projection function ♮ (Fig. 6) and exchanges information on syntactic and (higher) prosodic constituency, and on intonation (see Butt, Jabeen & Bögel, this volume). The assumptions made here roughly follow Selkirk (2011)'s MATCH THEORY[16] for the higher constituents, in that each IP/CP matches an intonational phrase (ι) and each XP corresponds to a phonological phrase (φ). The prosodic domain information associated with a specific syntactic node by means of an annotation is related to p-structure via the correspondence function ♮. The following figure shows a sample *transfer of structure* between the syntactic CP node and p-structure, relating the CP to an intonational phrase.

The annotations to the CP node can be read as follows: For every terminal node T of the current node * (here referring to each terminal node belonging to the CP), take the corresponding string in p-structure (related via ♮, which associates the CP and its terminal nodes to all syllables of which the terminal nodes consist of in the p-diagram). For the syllable with the lowest index (S_{min}, i.e., the first syllable of the string representing the CP) and the one with the highest index (S_{max}, i.e., the last syllable of the string representing the CP) insert an intonational phrase boundary (ι) as the value of the attribute PROSODIC PHRASING (from hence on shortened to PHRASING).

The *transfer of structure* effectively allows for the formal determination of prosodic phrasing on the basis of syntactic phrasing, relating the CP to an in-

---

[16] The model presented here is not limited to the MATCH approach, but can easily be adjusted to fit other approaches to the interface as well.

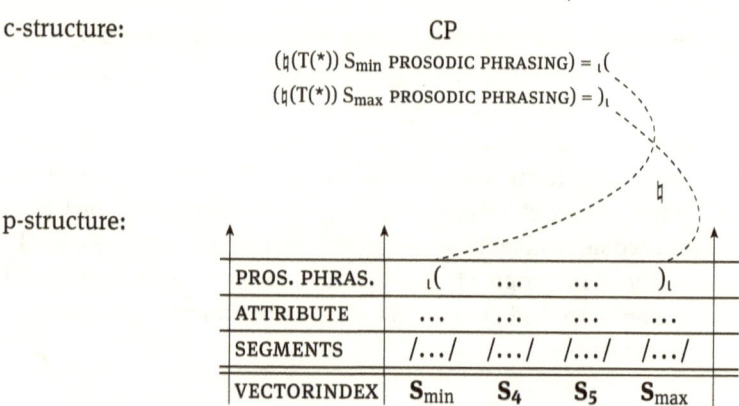

Fig. 8: The *transfer of structure*

tonational phrase that contains all the segmental material corresponding to the terminal nodes underneath the CP.[17] Thus, in contrast to the *transfer of vocabulary*, which operates on the word-level and below, the *transfer of structure* only relates information on higher syntactic and prosodic constituents (XP/φ and above). Taken together, the two transfer processes complement each other and provide for a complete transfer of all necessary information at the interface between syntax and prodody.

5 At the interface: *production* and *comprehension*

Having established the underlying architecture, the following sections will analyse the dative-genitive case ambiguities at the interface in more detail. As mentioned above (Fig. 1), the syntax–prosody interface is assumed to be placed between two reference points: form and meaning. *Production* is the process of cre-

---

[17] This first indication of prosodic phrasing on the basis of syntactic phrasing is taken to only be the initial input to p-structure. The full model assumes generative power within p-structure as well in the sense that prosodic rephrasing may happen purely on the basis of prosodic constraints, e.g., function words may be prosodically grouped with a host. This is also true in the context of recursive prosodic phrasing: MATCH theory implies the creation of recursive prosodic structures as nested syntactic structures are directly reflected in prosodic constituency. However, this initial prosodic structure can be adjusted according to language-specific constraints, e.g., via the application of the WRAP-constraint (Truckenbrodt 1999) in p-structure. As a p-structure internal rearrangement of prosodic units is not relevant for the present analysis, it has been excluded here. The interested reader is referred to Bögel (2015, ch. 4-6) for further reading.

ating speech starting from meaning and assigning it a particular form which the recipient can understand. *Comprehension*, on the other side, takes form as an input and assigns meaning to it. Depending on the type of process, the interface thus has to be interpreted either from syntax to prosody (production) or from prosody to syntax (comprehension), with prosody having a less strong effect on syntactic phrasing[18] compared to syntax' influence on prosody (cf. the discussion in Sect. 2).

5.1 Case in *production*

In a production process, the concept of what the speaker intends to say is first encoded in syntax/c-structure. As was shown in the experiment described above, a significant number of speakers insert a phonological phrase boundary between the two NPs to indicate a dative object interpretation of the second NP. This information on phrasing is related from syntax to p-structure via the *transfer of structure*, as shown in the following model of a complete syntax-to-prosody interface for a dative construction in production.[19]

The *transfer of vocabulary* (ρ) builds up the fundamental structure of the p-diagram by associating each separate morphosyntactic item with its respective p-form via the multidimensional lexicon. The information encoded within the p-form is transferred to the p-diagram syllablewise, projecting lexical phonological information associated with each syllable, e.g., lexical stress or segments. Following the experimental results discussed above, the *transfer of structure* ($\natural$) determines that a phonological phrase boundary is placed between the last syllable of the NP *der Partner* and the first syllable of the NP *der Freundin*, prosodically indicating a dative construction. In addition, following the assumptions made by MATCH, the CP projects an intonational phrase (ι) to p-structure that wraps all phonological material associated with the subordinate clause.

Together, both transfer structures provide an initial input to p-structure. Further prosodic (re-)phrasing and completion of prosodic domains follows according to p-structure-internal constraints (e.g., if there is an intonational phrase boundary, there will also be a phonological phrase boundary according to the *Strict Layer Hypothesis* (Selkirk 1995)). The output of the phonological module will thus consist of a complete underlying phonological/prosodic model of the string. In a further step, this information is then 'transformed' into spoken lan-

---

[18] This is certainly true for German and English, but this might be different in other languages.
[19] For reasons of readability, only the transfer of left intonational and phonological phrase boundaries is depicted via dashed lines. For the same reason, nested prosodic structures were excluded, but could easily be added to the model.

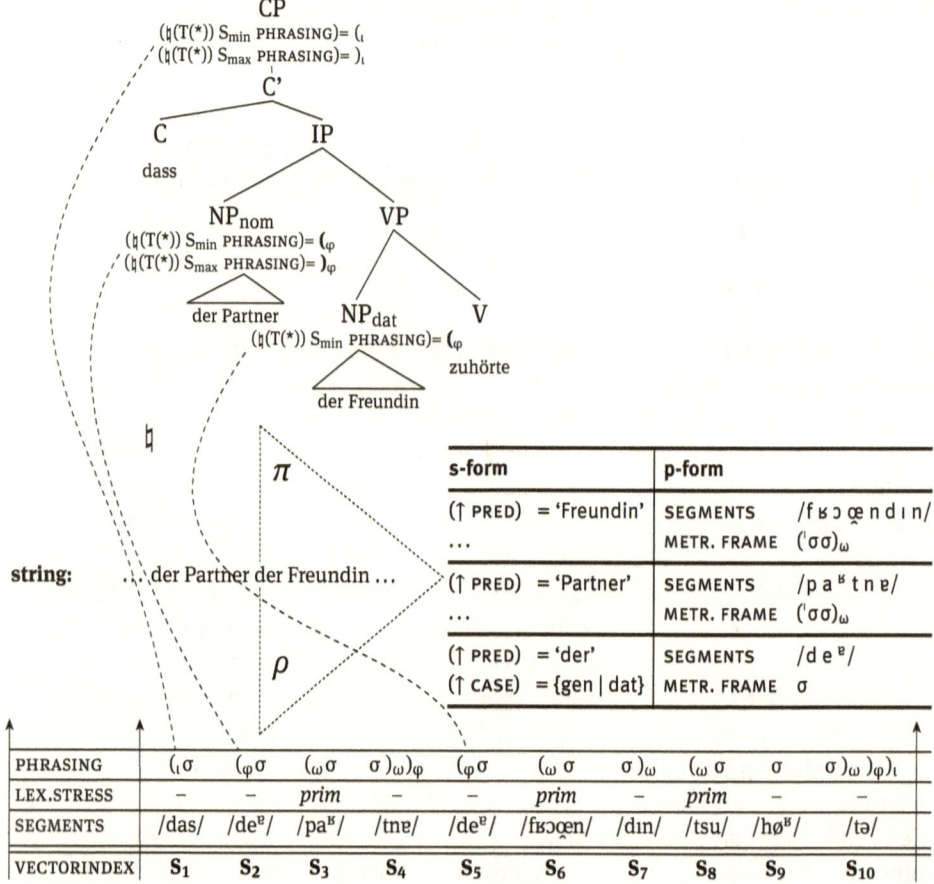

Fig. 9: The production of a dative construction at the syntax–prosody interface

guage via the phonetic module, which would encode concrete acoustic realisations of, e.g., a phrase boundary, or determines coarticulation of the different segments, but is also dependent on nonlinguistic factors like the gender of the speaker. As these considerations go far beyond the production of a dative construction at the syntax-prosody interface, they are not further discussed here. The paper will, however, briefly touch on the phonetics–phonology interface in Sect. 5.2 below.

A genitive in production is very similar to a dative, except that (following the results of the experiment conducted above) there is no transfer of a phonological phrase boundary between the two NPs.

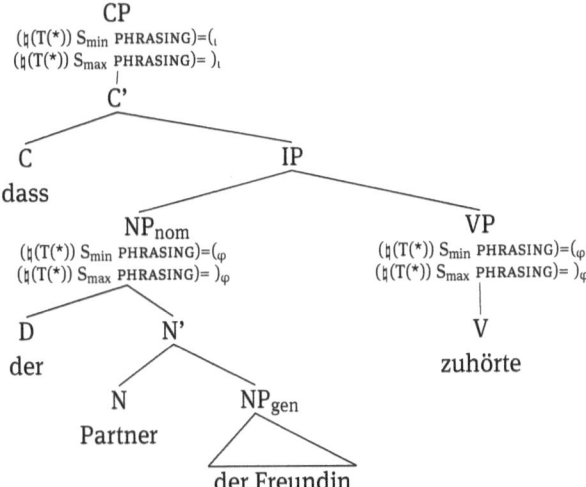

Fig. 10: P-structure annotation in the c-structure relating to a genitive construction

Apart from the missing phonological phrase boundary, the p-diagram and the lexicon of the genitive construction are identical to a dative in production. The interface model proposed here thus allows for a very straightforward and uniform phonological/prosodic description of different syntactic structures, where the difference in prosodic phrasing can be modelled by simply adjusting annotations relating to the *transfer of structure*.

5.2 Case in *comprehension*

As discussed above, the p-diagram during production leaves out explicit phonetic details as it is concerned with the underlying phonological categories, and not with the surface form realisation (even though this can, in principle, be included as well, as part of the phonology-phonetics interface). However, during comprehension, phonetic details are included in the model, in order to show how the results gained through the experiment reported above can inform the phonological categories relevant at the interface. In order to show this distinction between the phonetic and the phonological module, the p-diagram during comprehension is split into two levels, the *signal* level and the *interpretation* level. While information stored in the signal level is taken directly from the speech signal, the interpretation level abstracts away from the concrete data to a more categorical representation. Figure 11 shows the p-diagram of a concrete speech signal of *der Partner der Freundin* representing dative case.

	...	...	...	...	...	...	interpretation
PHRASING	–	–	)φ	(φ	–	–	↓
SEMIT_DIFF	...	–1	6.8	-4.3	-1.9	2.6	
GTOBI	–	L*	+H H-	–	L*	+H	
BREAK_IND	–	–	3	–	–	–	
...	...	...	...	...	...	...	signal
P_DURATION	–	–	0.07	–	–	–	↓
DURATION	0.15	0.25	0.25	0.13	0.31	0.19	
FUND. FREQ.	192	181	269	209	188	218	
SEGMENTS	[deɐ]	[paʁ]	[tnɐ]	[deɐ]	[fʁɔɢen]	[dɪn]	
VECTORINDEX	S_1	S_2	S_3	S_4	S_5	S_6	

Fig. 11: P-diagram for the speech signal of a dative construction.

Figure 11 includes several attributes whose values allow for a prosodic interpretation. At the signal level, the attributes SEGMENTS, DURATION of the syllable, P(AUSE) DURATION[20], and the syllable's mean FUNDAMENTAL FREQUENCY (f_0) value have been included. A further attribute-value pair could be, e.g., INTENSITY. On the basis of these concrete values the interpretation level allows for an abstract representation of the speech signal. For example, on the basis of f_0 values, semitones for each syllable can be calculated. By subtracting a semitone from the following semitone, the differences between these semitones (SEMIT_DIFF) allow for an abstract representation of the pitch, where negative values are associated with a fall and positive values indicate a rise in f_0. The resulting abstract contour representation allows for the interpretation in terms of prosodic phrasing and low and high tones (represented via GToBI, Grice & Baumann (2002)): the strong rise in pitch to the otherwise unstressed second syllable of *partner* and the following drop, for example, are likely to indicate a phonological phrase boundary. Further indicators for such a boundary are pauses and syllable duration. Concrete signal information on pauses can be recoded as break indices (Silverman et al. 1992) (BREAK_IND), indicating the length of a pause after a specific syllable (here: after the first NP). In addition, the relatively long duration of the unstressed second syllable of *partner* (DURATION) also indicates the presence of a phonological phrase domain boundary after the first NP.

---

[20] PAUSE DURATION does not receive an individual vector in the p-diagram because this would make it more difficult for c-structure to 'check', as an individual pause-vector would *not* correspond to a specific element in c-structure.

Taken together, the drop in f_0, the pause, and the syllable duration value clearly indicate a phonological phrase boundary after the first NP, which is consequently encoded as a value of PHRASING. During the *transfer of structure*, this boundary indication is then the sole relevant value for the correct interpretation of ambiguous syntactic phrasing.

As discussed above, the relation between prosodic and syntactic structure is asymmetric in that prosody cannot alter an unambiguous syntactic structure during comprehension, while syntax is much more influential when it comes to prosodic phrasing during production. This difference, however, only applies to the *transfer of structure*. The *transfer of vocabulary* works equally from both sides: During production, c-structure terminal nodes correspond to s-forms, which activate the associated p-forms in the multidimensional lexicon, thus making them available to p-structure. During comprehension, on the other hand, segmental chunks of the signal are matched against the lexicon's p-form (see also McQueen (2005)) and if a match is made, the associated s-form information becomes available to c-structure. While the segmental level is always given during comprehension, prosodic phrasing can be quite erratic.[21] It is therefore necessary to constrain this part of the information transfer in the sense that syntax is independent of prosody, *except* in cases where syntactic phrasing is ambiguous and can be disambiguated via prosody. As a consequence, information on prosodic phrasing is not automatically projected from p-structure to c-structure. Instead, the *transfer of structure* only requests information on prosodic phrasing if syntactic ambiguities are identified. Formally, this is achieved by adding a constraint to the annotation associated with the dative object NP, which effectively prevents the syntactic structure from being parsed unless the required value is present.

(9) $(\natural(T(*))\ S_{min}\ \text{PHRASING}) =_c (\varphi$

which reads as: The value of PHRASING for the first syllable of the phonological string corresponding to the current syntactic node must be equal ($=_c$) to a phonological phrase boundary.[22]

The following figure shows a dative construction in comprehension, where the p-diagram reflects a concrete speech signal at the signal level and its abstract rep-

---

[21] For example, a long pause might just be caused by a distraction of the speaker, or a particular prosodic pattern might only be relevant for information structure, but not syntax.

[22] In principle, the annotation does not have to refer to the PHRASING attribute, but could refer to any attribute-value given in the p-diagram's *interpretation* level. However, it seems that it is mostly prosodic phrasing that is relevant for syntax. For information structure, on the other hand, the relevant information mostly seems to be information on the pitch of a clause (in particular the nature and the distribution of high and low tones, see also Butt et al., same volume).

resentation in prosodic terms at the interpretation level. The NP annotation is not a projection of information *to* p-structure, but a constraint as to what p-structure should look like in order for this syntactic interpretation to be valid.

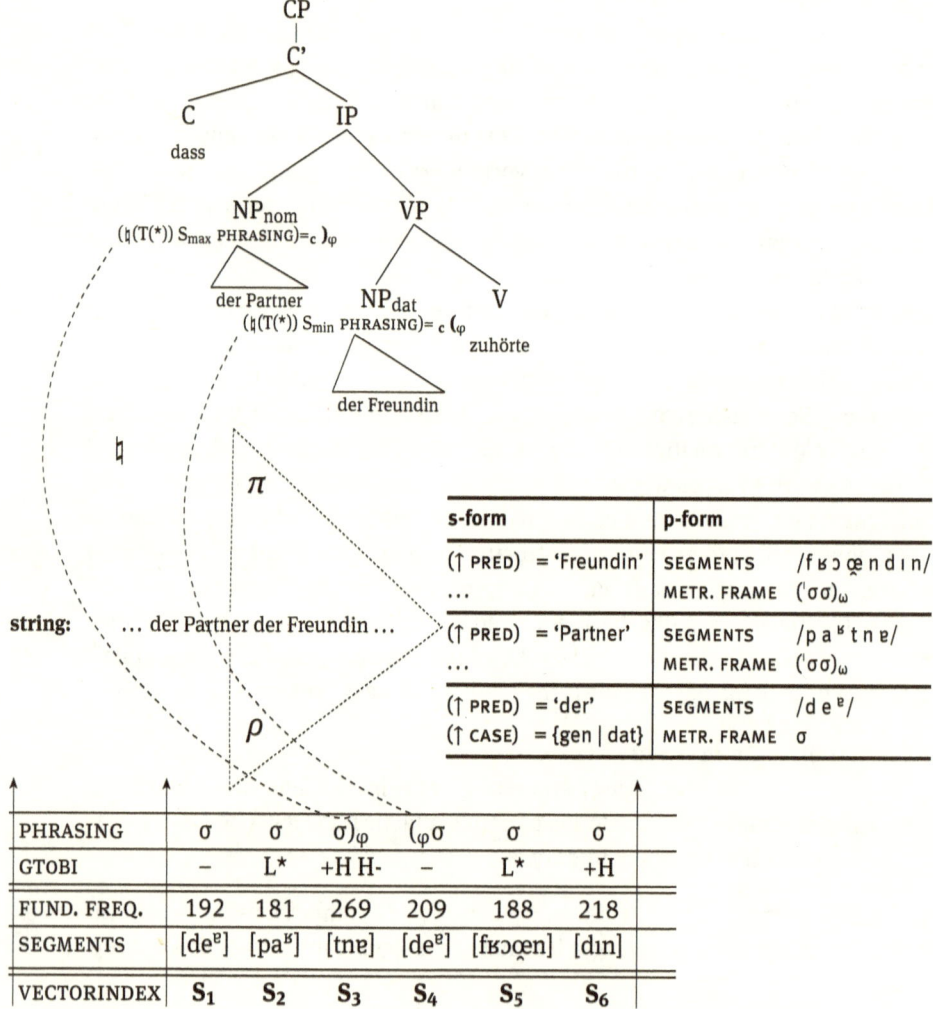

Fig. 12: The comprehension of a dative construction at the prosody–syntax interface

As a result, the syntactic structure relating to the interpretation of the second NP as a dative object can only be parsed if it is preceded by a phonological phrase boundary in p-structure.

The same constraint annotation can be employed with a speech signal indicating a genitive construction, with a constraint annotation to the genitive NP indicating that a phonological phrase boundary *must not* be present preceding the second NP in p-structure ($\neq (_\varphi)$).

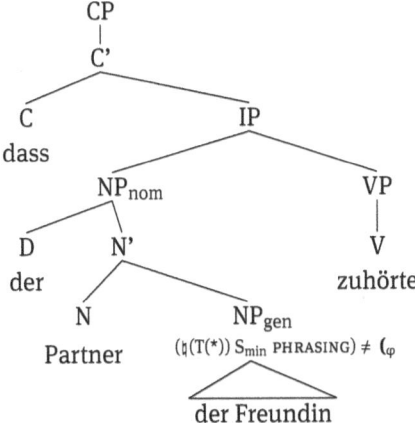

Fig. 13: P-structure annotation in the c-structure relating to a genitive construction

These constraints effectively prevent syntax from trying to interpret every possible prosodic boundary, while at the same time enabling the syntactic constituent to rely on prosody in case of multiple syntactic phrasing options, thus reflecting the asymetric relationship between prosody and syntax.

5.3 Accounting for speaker variability

As described in Sect. 3, speakers show great variability with respect to the realisation of the case structures discussed in this paper. It is therefore essential that constraints (as in (9)) are not strictly implemented as 'hard' constraints, but allow for some flexibility.

To account for speaker variability, OT-like constraints can be implemented in the c-structure rule annotation (originally proposed by Frank et al. (1998) for syntactic preferences, see also Crouch et al. (2017) for an extension). 'OT-like' in this context means that the notion of constraints is not understood as in general Optimality Theory (Prince & Smolensky 2004) or in OT-LFG (Bresnan 2000) in that the underlying assumption is not the existence of a (close to) infinite set of candidates that are analysed according to a set of ranked OT constraints. Instead, the OT-*like* constraints are added to fully-constrained grammars that nevertheless allow for more than one analysis of an input candidate – as it is the case with the dative/genitive ambiguity. The OT-like marks thus rank the different, but syntactically correct analyses of one common input string. On the basis of information coming from other modules or known to the researcher to exist outside of the scope of grammar, e.g., the frequencies across speakers reported above, an OT-like mark can be added to a specific c-structure annotation. In contrast to classic OT rankings, which indicate *dispreference* for certain constructions, the constraints used here can also indicate a *preference*, thus allowing for a constraint that, e.g., expresses the preference for the presence of a prosodic phrase boundary at a certain position.

This system of OT-like constraints allows for the implementation of phenomena, whose analysis cannot be easily divided into 'correct' and 'incorrect', as it is the case with the missing phonological phrase boundaries between the two NPs in a dative construction. That is, in order to account for speaker variability, the constraint that a syntactic dative construction only applies if there is a phonological phrase boundary after the first NP cannot be analysed as a hard constraint, but must be implemented as a soft constraint via OT-like constraints. The following example shows the syntactic rule for the dative including a disjunctive reference to p-structure and a OT-like mark for the member of the disjunction where a phonological phrase boundary is given.

(10) Dative: VP → NP$_{dat}$ V
$\{$ ($\natural$(T(*)) S$_{min}$ PHRASING) =$_c$ (φ
PHPBREAK $\in$ o*
$|$ ($\natural$(T(*)) S$_{min}$ PHRASING) $\neq$ (φ $\}$

The annotation $\natural$(T(*)) in the second conjunct of (10) refers to the (set of) terminal nodes connected with the NP and the projection between c-structure and p-structure as described above. S$_{min}$ PHRASING =$_c$ (φ requires that there is a phonological phrase boundary to the left of that NP.

The OT-like constraint PHPBREAK $\in$ o* indicates that the constraint PHPBREAK is part of the optimality structure (o*), where its nature (preference or dispreference) is defined also with reference to other constraints that are positioned higher or lower. In the following optimalityorder, the positive (+) CONSTRAINT$_1$ is ranked above +PHPBREAK which in turn is ranked above +CONSTRAINT$_2$.

(11) OPTIMALITYORDER   +CONSTRAINT$_1$ +PHPBREAK   +CONSTRAINT$_2$

Coming back to example (10), if the constraint cannot be fulfilled, then the structure is still valid as indicated by the second disjunct which allows for the phonological phrase to be absent ($\neq (_\varphi)$). This means that the dative construction is preferably parsed if a boundary is present, but if that information is not given, then the dative structure is parsed nevertheless. This seems redundant, but given the fact that 30% of the speakers do not indicate a phonological phrase boundary in the dative, it is crucial that the constraint requesting a boundary is not a hard constraint, but rather indicates a 'preferred' structure (but does not discard a dative structure per se). The genitive rule, on the other hand, explicitly excludes the presence of a boundary and is thus parsed along with the unmarked dative in (9), resulting in syntactic ambiguity.[23]

(12) Genitive: $\quad\quad\quad$ NP$_{gen}$
$\quad\quad\quad\quad$ ($\natural$(T(*)) S$_{min}$ PHRASING) $\neq (_\varphi$

The OT-like ranking of constraints allows for a detailed representation of variation and frequency of acoustic cues indicating a particular syntactic construction, as it only indicates a preference when specific information is present, but does not automatically prohibit the rule from firing if the relevant information is *not* present. In a sense, OT-like constraints thus enable the implementation of factors that are part of what is generally considered to be *performance*, for example the frequency of a specific prosodic cue used by a group of speakers. Further possible implementations could include the syntactic preference for a particular syntactic construction, for example a preference for intransitive interpretations as found in Augurzky & Schlesewsky (2010). In that sense, OT-like constraints are the pivot between real-case performance results and the rules and constraints of the 'core' grammar.

6 Conclusion

This article illustrated a new approach to the syntax–prosody interface, distinguishing between two different processes: *production*, where a speaker produces an utterance, going from meaning to form (from syntax to prosody), and *comprehension*, where a speaker's utterance is parsed by the recipient (from form to meaning, thus from prosody to syntax). In doing so, the interface combines three

---

23 As mentioned before, the exact prosodic structure of a genitive construction is left for further research with a homogeneous group of verbs and nouns. If significant prosodic indicators for a genitive interpretation were found for the right edge of the genitive NP, these constraints could be added to the rule in (12), indicating a preference for the genitive structure.

modules of grammar: a) syntax, which represents the linear and the hierarchical structure of the string (c-structure in LFG), b) a multidimensional lexicon which represents lexical phonological and morphosyntactic information of each word, and c) phonology/ prosody (p-structure) in form of the p-diagram, which allows for a compact, syllablewise representation of the speech signal at several levels.

The communication between c-structure and p-structure was defined on the basis of two transfer processes: the *transfer of vocabulary* and the *transfer of structure*. The *transfer of vocabulary* exchanges phonological and morphosyntactic information at the word-level and below via the multidimensional lexicon. Each dimension can only be accessed by the respective associated structure, i.e., information stored within the p(honological)-form is only available to p-structure, while s(yntactic)-form information is associated with syntactic structure. However, once a lexical dimension is activated, other dimensions become available as well. In a sense, the lexicon therefore functions as a kind of translator between lexical phonology and the terminal nodes of syntax.

This lower-level transfer process is complemented by the *transfer of structure* which exchanges information on syntactic and prosodic phrasing. The relationship between prosody and syntax is asymetric in the sense that prosody can disambiguate syntax, but cannot alter an unambiguous syntactic phrase, while syntactic phrasing always has a certain influence on prosody. The correspondence between the modules reflects this asymmetry: the *transfer of structure* always projects information on syntactic phrasing to p-structure during production, but, during comprehension, p-structure only supplies information on prosodic phrasing to syntax if there is a syntactic ambiguity (that is, if syntax requests this information).

This approach to the interface was tested by means of a concrete example: a production study on syntactic ambiguity caused by syncretic case forms in German and its possible disambiguation by means of prosodic phrasing. As was reported in Sect. 3, German speakers can indeed disambiguate dative and genitive case ambiguities by employing prosodic cues. During the *production* of a case structure, syntax therefore projects different phrasing possibilities to p-structure, respectively for the genitive and the dative. During *comprehension*, phonological phrase boundaries are calculated and encoded in p-structure on the basis of the concrete acoustic cues given in the speech signal. This information on prosodic domains hence becomes available at the interface and can be used to disambiguate syntactic phrasing.

However, it was also noted in the production experiment that some acoustic cues indicating a certain syntactic interpretation are more common across speakers in comparison to other cues, and that up to 33% of the speakers do not apply any prosodic phrasing for the disambiguation of syntactic structures. To account for this variability, the paper employs OT-like soft constraints which allow for a syntactic structure to be preferred if a prosodic cue is given. However, if all prosodic indicators are absent from the speech signal, the multiple syntactic structures are nevertheless parsed, resulting in a true (and justified) syntactic ambiguity.

References

Allbritton, David W., Gail McKoon, and Roger Ratcliff (1996). Reliability of prosodic cues for resolving syntactic ambiguity. *Journal of Experimental Psychology: Learning, Memory, and Cognition*, 22(3):714–735.

Augurzky, Petra and Matthias Schlesewsky (2010). Prosodic phrasing and transitivity in head-final sentence comprehension – ERP evidence from German ambiguous DPs. In Yamashita, Hiroko, Yuki Hirose, and Jerome L. Packard, eds, *Processing and Producing Head-Final Structures*, pp. 69–91. Springer.

Baayen, R. Harald, Doug J. Davidson, and Douglas M. Bates (2008). Mixed-effects modeling with crossed random effects for subjects and items. *Journal of Memory and Language*, 59(4):390–412.

Baumann, Stefan (2006). *The intonation of givenness*. No. 508 in Linguistische Arbeiten. Tübingen: Niemeyer.

Beckman, Mary E. and Janet B. Pierrehumbert (1986). Intonational structure in English and Japanese. *Phonology Yearbook*, 3:255–309.

Boersma, Paul and David Weenink (2013). Praat: doing phonetics by computer [Computer program, Version 5.3.56]. available at http://www.praat.org/ [retrieved 15.09.2013].

Bögel, Tina (2015). *The Syntax–Prosody Interface in Lexical Functional Grammar*. PhD thesis, University of Konstanz.

Bögel, Tina, Miriam Butt, Ronald M. Kaplan, Tracy Holloway King, and John T. Maxwell III. (2009). Prosodic phonology in LFG: a new proposal. In *Proceedings of LFG09*. CSLI Publications.

Bresnan, Joan (2000). Optimal syntax. In Dekkers, J., F. van der Leeuw, and J. van de Weijer, eds, *Optimality Theory: Phonology, Syntax, and Acquisition*, pp. 334–385. Oxford: Oxford University Press.

Bresnan, Joan and Sam Mchombo (1995). The lexical integrity principle: evidence from Bantu. *Natural language and Linguistic Theory*, 13(2):181–254.

Butt, Miriam and Tracy Holloway King (1998). Interfacing phonology with LFG. In *Proceedings of LFG98*, Stanford, CA. CSLI Publications.

Chen, Matthew Y. (1987). The syntax of Xiamen tone sandhi. *Phonology Yearbook*, 4:109–149.

Crouch, Richard, Mary Dalrymple, Ronald M. Kaplan, Tracy H. King, John T. Maxwell III, and Paula Newman (2017). *XLE documentation*. Palo Alto, CA: Palo Alto Research Center. Online documentation.

Dalrymple, Mary (2001). *Lexical Functional Grammar*. San Diego [a.o.]: Academic Press.

Dalrymple, Mary and Louise Mycock (2011). The prosody-semantics interface. In *Proceedings of LFG11*, Stanford, CA. CSLI Publications.

Elfner, Emily (2012). *Syntax–Prosody Interactions in Irish*. PhD thesis, University of Massachusetts Amherst.
Féry, Caroline (1993). *German intonational patterns*. No. 285 in Linguistische Arbeiten. Tübingen: Niemeyer.
Féry, Caroline (2010). Recursion in prosodic structure. *Phonological Studies*, 13:51–60.
Fodor, Jerry A. (1983). *The Modularity of Mind*. Cambridge, MA [a.o.]: MIT Press.
Frank, Anette, Tracy Holloway King, Jonas Kuhn, and John T. Maxwell III (1998). Optimality Theory style constraint ranking in large-scale LFG grammars. In *Proceedings of LFG98*, Stanford, CA. CSLI Publications.
Frota, Sónia (2012). Prosodic structure, constituents, and their implementation. In Cohn, A. C., C. Fougeron, and M. K. Huffman, eds, *The Oxford Handbook of Laboratory Phonology*, chapter 11, pp. 255–265. Oxford University Press.
Gollrad, Anja, Esther Sommerfeld, and Frank Kügler (2010). Prosodic cue weighting in disambiguation: case ambiguity in German. In *Proceedings of Speech Prosody*, Chicago.
Grice, Martine and Stefan Baumann (2002). Deutsche Intonation und GToBI. *Linguistische Berichte*, 191:267–298.
Jackendoff, Ray (2002). *Foundations of Language*. New York: Oxford University Press.
Kaplan, Ronald M. and Joan Bresnan (1985). Lexical-Functional Grammar: A Formal System for Grammatical Representation. In *The Mental Representation of Grammatical Relations*, chapter 4, pp. 173–281. Cambridge, MA [a.o.]: MIT Press: 2 edn.
Kentner, Gerrit and Caroline Féry (2013). A new approach to prosodic grouping. *The Linguistic Review*, 30(2):277–311.
Kiparsky, Paul (1982). Lexical morphology and phonology. In *Linguistics in the Morning Calm*, pp. 3–91, Seoul, Korea. Hanshin Publishing Company.
Ladd, D. Robert (1986). Intonational phrasing: the case for recursive prosodic structure. *Phonology Yearbook*, 3:311–340.
Lahiri, Aditi and Frans Plank (2010). Phonological phrasing in Germanic: the judgement of history, confirmed through experiment. *Transactions of the Philological Society*, 108(3):372–398.
Lahiri, Aditi and Henning Reetz (2002). Underspecified recognition. In Gussenhoven, C., N. Werner, and T. Rietveld, eds, *Labphon 7*. Berlin: Mouton.
Lahiri, Aditi and Henning Reetz (2010). Distinctive features: phonological underspecification in representation and processing. *Journal of Phonetics*, 38:44–59.
Lapointe, Steven G. (1980). *A Theory of Grammatical Agreement*. PhD thesis, University of Massachusetts.
Lehiste, Ilse, Joseph P. Olive, and Lynn A. Streeter (1976). Role of duration in disambiguating syntactically ambiguous sentences. *The Journal of the Acoustical Society of America*, 60:1199–1202.
Levelt, Willem J.M. (1999). Models of word production. *Trends in Cognitive Sciences*, 3(6):223–232.
Levelt, Willem J.M., Ardi Roelofs, and Antje S. Meyer (1999). A theory of lexical access in speech production. *Behavioral and Brain Sciences*, 22:1–75.
Liberman, Mark and Janet Pierrehumbert (1984). Intonational invariance under changes in pitch range and length. In Aronoff, M. and R. T. Oehrle, eds, *Language Sound Structure*, chapter 10, pp. 157–233. MIT Press.
McQueen, James M. (2005). Speech perception. In Lamberts, K. and R. L. Goldstone, eds, *Handbook of Cognition*, chapter 11, pp. 255–275. London: SAGE Publications.

Meinzer, Marcus, Aditi Lahiri, Tobias Flaisch, Ronny Hannemann, and Carsten Eulitz (2009). Opaque for the reader but transparent for the brain: Neural signatures of morphological complexity. *Neuropsychologia*, 47:1964–1971.

Mohanan, Karuvannur Puthanveettil (1982). *Lexical Phonology*. PhD thesis, Massachusetts Institute of Technology.

Mycock, Louise (2006). *The Typology of Constituent Questions: A Lexical-Functional Grammar Analysis of 'WH'-Questions*. PhD thesis, University of Manchester.

Nespor, Marina and Irene Vogel (1986). *Prosodic Phonology*. Dordrecht: Foris.

O'Connor, Rob (2004). *Information Structure in Lexical-Functional Grammar: The Discourse-Prosody Correspondence in English and Serbo-Croation*. PhD thesis, University of Manchester.

Price, Patti, Mari Ostendorf, Stefanie Shattuck-Hufnagel, and Cynthia Fong (1991). The use of prosody in syntactic disambiguation. *Journal of the Acoustical Society of America*, 90(6):2956–2970.

Prince, Alan and Paul Smolensky (2004). *Optimality Theory: Constraint Interaction in Generative Grammar*. Oxford, Malden: Blackwell.

Scheer, Tobias (2011). *A Guide to Morphosyntax-Phonology Interface Theories: How Extraphonological Information is Treated in Phonology since Trubetzkoy's Grenzsignale*. Berlin: De Gruyter Mouton.

Selkirk, Elisabeth O. (1978). On prosodic structure and its relation to syntactic structure. In Fretheim, T., ed., *Nordic Prosody II*, pp. 111–140. Tapir.

Selkirk, Elisabeth O. (1986). On derived domains in sentence phonology. *Phonology Yearbook*, 3:371–405.

Selkirk, Elisabeth O. (1995). The prosodic structure of function words. In Beckmann, Jill N., Laura W. Dickey, and Suzanne Urbanczyk, eds, *Papers in Optimality Theory*. University of Massachusetts: Department of Linguistics.

Selkirk, Elisabeth O. (2011). The syntax-phonology interface. In Goldsmith, John A., Jason Riggle, and Alan C. L. Yu, eds, *The Handbook of Phonological Theory*, pp. 435–484. Malden, MA: Blackwell.

Silverman, Kim, Mary Beckman, John Pitrelli, Mari Ostendorf, Colin Wightman, Patti Price, Janet Pierrehumbert, and Julia Hirschberg (1992). ToBI: A standard for labeling English prosody. In *Proceedings of the 1992 International Conference on Spoken Language Processing*, Banff.

Snedeker, Jesse and John Trueswell (2003). Using prosody to avoid ambiguity: Effects of speaker awareness and referential context. *Journal of Memory and Language*, 48(1):103–130.

Truckenbrodt, Hubert (1995). *Phonological phrases: their relation to syntax, focus, and prominence*. PhD thesis, Massachusetts Institute of Technology.

Truckenbrodt, Hubert (1999). On the relation between syntactic phrases and phonological phrases. *Linguistic Inquiry*, 30(2):219–255.

Truckenbrodt, Hubert (2016). Intonation in der Lautsprache: Prosodische Struktur. In Domahs, Ulrike and Beatrice Primus, eds, *Handbuch Laut, Gebärde, Buchstabe*, pp. 106–124. Berlin/Boston: De Gruyter.

Appendix

The following list contains all fully ambiguous structures used in the experiment (Sect. 3):

1. *Das Gericht war daher sehr überrascht, als der Anwalt der Diva widersprach.*
   ... when the diva's lawyer disagreed/the lawyer disagreed with the diva
2. *Um alles mitzubekommen, musste der Fahrer der Dame zuhören.*
   ... the lady's driver had to listen/the driver had to listen to the lady
3. *Alle freuten sich, als der Onkel der Nonne gratulierte.*
   ... when the nun's uncle congratulated/the uncle congratulated the nun
4. *Um rechtzeitig fertig zu werden, musste der Schwager der Tante helfen.*
   ... the aunt's brother-in-law had to help/the brother-in-law had to helpt the aunt
5. *Die Enkel waren daher überrascht, als der Gärtner der Oma zustimmte.*
   ... when the grandma's gardener agreed/the gardener agreed with the grandma
6. *Jeder bemerkte, dass der Partner der Freundin fehlte.*
   ... the friend's partner was missing/the friend missed the partner
7. *Keiner dachte sich etwas dabei, als der Diener der Gräfin folgte.*
   ... when the duchess' servant followed/when the servant followed the duchess
8. *Alle hörten gespannt zu, als der Lehrer der Schwäbin antwortete.*
   ... when the Swabian's teacher answered/the teacher answered the Swabian
9. *Die Anwesenden waren sehr überrascht, dass der Rabe der Heldin gehorchte.*
   ... that the hero's raven obeyed/the raven obeyed the hero

Miriam Butt, Farhat Jabeen, and Tina Bögel
Ambiguity resolution via the syntax-prosody interface: The case of *kya* 'what' in Urdu/Hindi

Abstract: This paper focuses on the prosodic realization of Urdu/Hindi *kya* 'what' in polar and wh-constituent questions. The wh-word *kya* 'what' is polyfunctional in that it is used in wh-constituent questions to mean 'what', but also serves as a marker of polar questions. The distribution of *kya* is relatively free in both types of questions, which can lead to syntactically (and therefore semantically) ambiguous structures involving *kya* 'what'. We show that prosodic information is crucial for the disambiguation of such sentences. We report on a production experiment which establishes that the wh-constituent *kya* is prosodically focused while polar *kya* is accentless. Moreover, the nouns following wh-constituent *kya* have shorter duration as compared with the nouns following polar *kya*, which have longer duration and an LH contour. We show that speakers of Urdu/Hindi are perceptually sensitive to the prosodic properties of wh-constituent and polar *kya* and the following nouns. We take the information established about *kya* 'what' and show how the prosodic differences guide syntactic disambiguation at the prosody-syntax interface, which in turn results in the activation of the appropriate semantic information (polar vs. wh-constituent readings of *kya*). We model our analysis within Lexical–Functional Grammar (LFG) and work with Bögel's framework of the prosody-syntax interface (Bögel 2015, this volume).

Note: We thank the Deutsche Forschungsgemeinschaft (DFG, German Research Foundation) for funding within project BU 1806/9-2 "Information Structure and Questions in Urdu/Hindi" of the FOR2111 "Questions at the Interfaces".
Very many thanks go to Rajesh Bhatt and Veneeta Dayal for the original inspiration and some further discussions, to Ghulam Raza for help with the data, suggestions, general pointers, and interesting discussions and to Doug Arnold, Bettina Braun, Regine Eckardt, Gillian Ramchand, Craige Roberts, Maribel Romero, and Louisa Sadler for helping us to come to grips with the phenomena and to María Biezma for in-depth cooperation. Many thanks go to Habiba who has been our main informant, to the anonymous reviewers, and to Gerrit Kentner for his close and patient editing.

https://doi.org/10.1515/9783110650532-004

1 Introduction

The study of the role of prosody in Urdu/Hindi[1] questions and how it interacts with the syntax and semantics of questions is in its infancy. Our contribution in this paper focuses on the role of prosodic realization of Urdu/Hindi *kya* 'what' in polar and wh-constituent questions.

Polar questions in Urdu/Hindi are string identical to declaratives, as shown in (1). The status of (1) as a declarative vs. a polar question is signaled exclusively via prosodic means (see Sect. 3 for details).

(1) anu=ne   uma=ko   kıtab   d-i   ?/.
     Anu.F=Erg Uma.F=Dat book.F.Sg.Nom give-Perf.F.Sg
     'Did Anu give a/the book to Uma?'   (Polar Question)
     'Anu gave a/the book to Uma.'   (Declarative)

In addition, Urdu/Hindi can optionally use *kya* 'what' in polar questions, as shown in (2). The literature reports that the default placement for this polar *kya* is the clause initial position (Platts 1884; Masica 1991; Montaut 2004) but Bhatt & Dayal (2020) show that it can in fact scramble among all the major constituents of a clause (see Sect. 3 for details).

(2) (kya) anu=ne   uma=ko   kıtab   d-i?
     what   Anu.F=Erg Uma.F=Dat book.F.Sg.Nom give-Perf.F.Sg
     'Did Anu give a/the book to Uma?'   (Polar Question)

This ability to appear in different positions in a clause taken together with similar scrambling possibilities for wh-constituents (see Sect. 4) leads to potential ambiguities with the wh-constituent question use of *kya*. A wh-constituent example is shown in (3), ambiguous cases are illustrated below.[2]

(3) anu=ne   uma=ko   kya   di-ya?
     Anu.F=Erg Uma.F=Dat what give-Perf.M.Sg
     'What did Anu give to Uma?'   (Wh-Constituent Question)

---

[1] Urdu and Hindi are structurally almost identical, but differ in terms of the writing system they employ. Our data is based on Urdu spoken in Pakistan. Where the data and insights apply to both Urdu and Hindi, we use Urdu/Hindi to refer to the language(s).
[2] There is (at least) a third use of *kya* that as been identified in the literature, namely as a scope marker in scope marking constructions (Dayal 1996, 2000).

Ambiguities arise particularly naturally in the preverbal position, which is a syntactic focus position and thus also the default/preferred position for the placement of wh-constituents.[3] We therefore zeroed in on ambiguities in this position and conducted experiments investigating the production and perception of *kya* with regard to examples as in (4). This sentence can be interpreted either as a polar question (4a) or as a wh-constituent question (4b) where *kya* 'what' is part of an NP.

(4) a. ʃahina=ne   naz=ko   kya   [tohfa]   di-ya?
       Shahina.F=Erg Naz.F=Dat   what   present.M.Sg.Nom   give-Perf.M.Sg
       'Did Shahina give a gift to Naz?'

    b. ʃahina=ne   naz=ko   [kya   tohfa]   di-ya?
       Shahina.F=Erg Naz.F=Dat   what   present.M.Sg.Nom   give-Perf.M.Sg
       'What gift did Shahina give to Naz?'

Our investigations show that the wh-constituent *kya* is prosodically characterized by a rising contour while polar *kya* is accentless. Furthermore, the nouns following wh-constituent *kya* are shorter in duration as compared with the nouns following polar *kya*. Our experiments also show that speakers of Urdu/Hindi are perceptually sensitive to the prosodic properties of wh-constituent vs. polar *kya*. We model this effect within Bögel's (2015) prosody-syntax architecture and show how the prosodic information guides syntactic disambiguation, which in turn results in the activation of the appropriate semantic information for polar vs. wh-constituent readings of *kya*.

The paper is structured as follows. Section 2 provides information on Urdu/Hindi intonation. Section 3 discusses the intonation as well as the functions of polar *kya*. Section 4 presents the syntactic and prosodic properties of wh-constituent questions that are relevant for the purposes of this paper. Section 5 discusses the ambiguity that arises due to the distributional properties of polar and wh-constituent *kya* in more detail. We here present a production and a perception experiment focusing on ambiguities at the preverbal position and establish that the prosodic realization of *kya* is crucial for disambigution. This information is then used in Sect. 6 to show how examples as in (4) can be disambiguated via the prosody-syntax architecture developed by Bögel (2015). The analysis is complex in the sense that information coming from the various modules of grammar, namely prosody and syntax, must be integrated. However, the analysis is also simple in that the architecture allows a seamless integration of the information, lay-

---

[3] See Butt et al. (2016, 2017) for details on this.

ing the foundation for work on more complex aspects of question formation in Urdu/Hindi. Section 7 concludes the paper.

2 Basic Intonational Characteristics of Urdu/Hindi

In order to understand how prosody can disambiguate between polar and wh-constituent *kya*, some more general information about the prosody of Urdu/Hindi is in order. In the following sections, we discuss what is known about the basic intonational contour of sentences and the prosodic realization of focus.

2.1 Basic Intonational Patterns

As established early on by Harnsberger (1994), the basic prosodic structure of an Urdu/Hindi clause is a series of LH contours. The precise nature and distribution of these LH contours remains to be established. For example, Harnsberger sees LH contours being associated with content words, but this does not quite hold up as wh-words also receive an LH contour.

Harnsberger (1994, 42) leaves the precise analysis of the LH open. He lists three possibilities: 1) a bitonal pitch accent; 2) an L* pitch accent followed by an H boundary tone; 3) an LH accentual phrase. Our current approach is to follow the analyses in Hayes & Lahiri (1991) and Féry (2010), who work with p(rosodic)-phrases and i(ntonational)-phrases as per the Prosodic Hierarchy (Nespor & Vogel 1986; Selkirk 1995). Féry surveys two Indo-Aryan (Hindi and Bangla) and two Dravidian languages (Tamil and Malayalam) and proposes a new class in the typological space of intonational systems, namely "phrase languages". Phrase languages are characterized by a phrasal accent which determines the prosodic phrasing (rather than pitch accents). In South Asian languages, this phrasal accent is LH, whereby the association of the L and the H with syllables may vary. Hayes & Lahiri (1991) associate an L* with a stressed syllable in Bengali, but this generalization does not quite seem to work for Urdu/Hindi (e.g., Féry 2010 and confirmed by our own work) and remains the subject of further investigation. Similarly, the H is not necessarily associated with the right edge of the p-phrase, but can vary. One factor we have identified as a source of variation is the use of contrastive focus (Jabeen & Braun 2018), whereby the H tends to align with the last syllable of the noun rather than the case marker in case marked NPs that are focused contrastively.

The clause final intonation is determined by the intonational phrase boundary. In declaratives and wh-constituent questions this is generally an L% and in polar questions this is an H%, though we have found some variability in our data (cf. also Moore 1965; Harnsberger 1994; Sect. 3).

An interesting characteristic of Urdu/Hindi declarative intonation is that while sentences show a regular LH f_0 contour on all p-phrases, this does not apply to whatever constituent appears clause-finally (Harnsberger 1994), cf. also Keane (2014) for a similar pattern in Tamil. The clause-final constituent always has a falling intonation. An explanation for this pattern remains to be found.

2.2 Prosody of focus

In terms of prosodic marking of focus, the literature to date has identified differing factors. These include an increased pitch span of the basic LH contour, greater intensity, longer syllable duration within the focused element, and pitch compression after the focused element (Moore 1965; Harnsberger 1994; Dyrud 2001; Patil et al. 2008; Genzel & Kügler 2010; Jabeen et al. 2016; Butt et al. 2016; Jabeen & Braun 2018).

3 Polar Questions

Polar questions in Urdu/Hindi are string identical to the corresponding declarative, as shown in (5) and (6). The difference between question vs. declarative status is signaled via intonation. Declaratives generally have an L% boundary,[4] while a polar question is signaled by an H% boundary (Fig. 1).

(5) (ʃahina=ne   norina=ko   mara)$_{L\%}$
    Shahina.F=Erg Norina.F=Acc hit-Perf.M.Sg
    'Shahina hit Norina.'   (Declarative)

---

[4] Urdu/Hindi also has declaratives with a rising final boundary H% (Patil et al. 2008; Puri 2013). This high boundary tone in declaratives is scaled lower than the high boundary tone in polar questions. Patil et al. report that this final rise in declaratives is not necessarily interpreted as a list intonation by Hindi speakers. More work remains to be done on charting this variation and potential associated differences in interpretation in Urdu/Hindi.

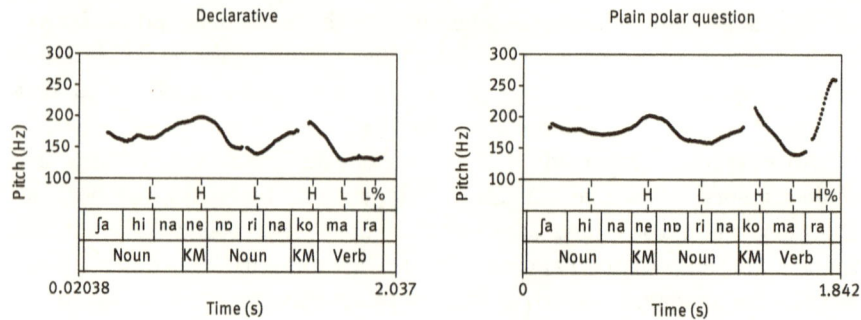

Fig. 1: F₀ contour of a string identical declarative and polar question.

(6) (ʃahina=ne   norina=ko   mara)_H%
    Shahina.F=Erg Norina.F=Acc hit-Perf.M.Sg
    'Did Shahina hit Norina?'   (Polar Question)

Examples (7) and (8) show the prosodic analysis we assume for a typical transitive declarative and its polar question variant.

```
         L    H         L    H      L   L%
(7) ((ʃahina=ne)_P  (norina=ko)_P  (mara)_P)_I
    Shahina.F=Erg Norina.F=Acc hit-Perf.M.Sg
    'Shahina hit Norina.'                        (Declarative)

         L    H         L    H      L   H%
(8) ((ʃahina=ne)_P  (norina=ko)_P  (mara)_P)_I
    Shahina.F=Erg Norina.F=Acc hit-Perf.M.Sg
    'Did Shahina hit Norina?'                    (Polar Question)
```

3.1 Polar *kya* – Distribution and prosody

Polar questions can optionally use *kya* 'what' as shown in (9). This use of *kya* has been dubbed "polar *kya*" by Bhatt & Dayal (2020).

(9) kya ʃahina=ne   norina=ko   mar-a?
    what Shahina.F=Erg Norina.F=Acc hit-Perf.M.Sg
    'Did Shahina hit Norina?'

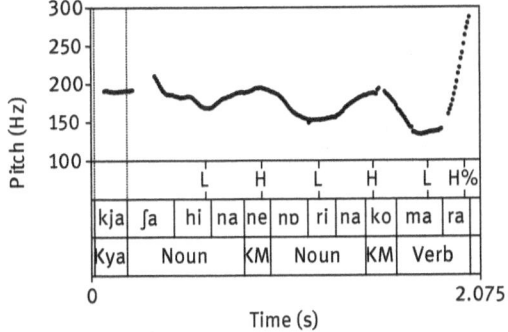

Fig. 2: A polar question with sentence initial *kya*.

Figure 2 shows that, like plain polar questions, a polar question with *kya* ends with a high boundary tone (Harnsberger 1994). Figure 2 also shows that polar *kya* at the sentence initial position is accentless. Harnsberger (1994) has only one example of polar *kya* and he assigns it an LH contour. He reports that polar *kya*, unlike wh-constituent *kya*, is not marked by high F0 register (pitch range). We did not find any instances of polar *kya* with an LH contour in our data but do observe accentless or falling patterns.

The previous, mainly descriptive, literature reports polar *kya* as appearing only clause initially in Urdu/Hindi (Glassman 1977; Platts 1884; Masica 1991; Montaut 2004). However, Bhatt & Dayal (2020) show that polar *kya* can be scrambled among the major constituents of a clause, as illustrated in (10). The prosody of polar *kya* is always flat or falling in any of the possible positions.

(10) (kya) anu=ne   (kya) uma=ko   (kya) kıtab   (%kya)
     what Anu.F=Erg what Uma.F=Dat   what book.F.Sg.Nom   what
     d-i   (kya)?
     give-Perf.F.Sg what
     'Did Anu give a/the book to Uma?'

There is one constraint on polar *kya*: it is dispreferred in the immediately preverbal position. We assume that this dispreference is directly related to the fact that the default position for wh-constituent questions is this immediately preverbal position (see Sect. 4).

3.2 Polar *kya* – Function

Masica (1991) shows that polar 'what' elements or question particles are pervasive in Indo-Aryan and identifies a typological variation by which they either appear clause initially as in Urdu/Hindi or clause finally as in Bangla or Sinhala (for the latter, see Slade 2011). Despite their optionality in Urdu/Hindi, these question particles were generally taken to have a clause typing function (Montaut 2004; Masica 1991; Cheng 1997).

Bhatt & Dayal (2020) adduce several arguments against this analysis. One argument is that it is optional in matrix clauses, a feature not associated with clause typing question markers in general. Another is that it does not fulfill a clause-typing function exactly where it would have been most useful, namely in embedded clauses. Polar *kya* is generally disallowed in embedded interrogative clauses (11a), which is exactly where one would need a question marker as the interrogative status of the embedded clause cannot be signaled via intonation. On the other hand, polar *kya* is allowed in complements of rogative predicates (Lahiri 2002) such as 'wonder' and 'ask' (11b).

(11) a. *anu   jan-ti   hai   [ki   kya   tum   cai
       Anu   know-Impf.F.Sg   be.Pres.3.Sg   that   what   you   tea
       pi-yo-ge?]
       drink-2.Pl-Fut.M.Pl

   Intended: 'Anu knows whether you will drink tea.'   (Non-rogative)

   b. anu   jan-na   cah-ti   hai   [ki   kya   tum   cai
       Anu   know-Inf.M.Sg   want-Impf.F.Sg   be.Pres.3.Sg   that   what   you   tea
       pi-yo-ge?]
       drink-2.Pl-Fut.M.Pl

   'Anu wants to know whether you will drink tea?'   (Rogative)

In previous versions, Bhatt & Dayal (2020) analyzed the word order variation found with *kya* in terms of given vs. new information, whereby all the information to the left of polar *kya* was considered as given and the material to the right as open to question. Their current analysis sees the difference as being between at-issue (to the right) vs. not (to the left). This analysis is illustrated by data as in (12), which shows that it is infelicitous to question/correct material to the left of polar *kya* (not-at-issue) but it is good to question/correct material to the right of polar *kya* (at-issue).

Ambiguity resolution via the syntax-prosody interface: the case of *kya* 'what'

(12) A: anu=ne kya uma=ko tohfa di-ya?
　　　 Anu.F=Erg what Uma.F=Dat present.M.Sg.Nom give-Perf.M.Sg
　　　 'Did Anu give a/the present to Uma?'

　　B: #nahĩ, asım=ne di-ya
　　　 no Asim.M=Erg give-Perf.M.Sg
　　　 'No, Asim did.'

　　C: nahĩ, asım=ko di-ya
　　　 no Asim.M=Dat give-Perf.M.Sg
　　　 'No, to Asim.'

Our own investigation of the prosody of polar *kya* confirms data as in (12) only with respect to a default prosodic structure of a polar question where the entire proposition is in question and the verb is prosodically prominent. However, if another part of the sentence is instead made prominent, that part is available for questioning.

(13) A. **anu=ne**_{Prominent} kya uma=ko tohfa di-ya?
　　　 Anu.F=Erg what Uma.F=Dat present.M.Sg.Nom give-Perf.M.Sg
　　　 'Did ANU give a/the present to Uma?'

　　B. nahĩ, **asım=ne** di-ya
　　　 no Asim.M=Erg give-Perf.M.Sg
　　　 'No, Asim did.'

Reacting to our observation, Bhatt & Dayal (2020) present data as in (14) and posit that prosodic prominence may not license just any element in the clause, but is very likely restricted to the adjacent element to the left of polar *kya*. This issue remains to be investigated at greater depth.

(14) #**ram=ne**_{Prominent} sita=ko kya kal kitab
　　　 Ram.M=Erg Sita.F=Dat what yesterday book.F.Sg.Nom
　　　 d-i tʰ-i ya mina=ne?
　　　 give-Perf.F.Sg be-Past.F.Sg or Mina.F=Erg
　　　 'Had Ram given a/the book to Sita yesterday or had Mina?'

Our current analysis of polar *kya* follows that of Biezma et al. (2018), who propose that polar *kya* is a focus sensitive operator that associates with the focused material. It will either associate with a (left-adjacent) prosodically prominent item in the clause or, by default, with the item to its right. Importantly, when it associates with a prosodically prominent item, it is the item itself that bears the prosodic marking of prominence while polar *kya* remains accentless. As a focus sensitive operator, polar *kya* constrains the set of possible answers viable in the context of an utterance. Assuming that polar questions denote singleton sets as proposed in Biezma & Rawlins (2012) (see also Roberts 1996; Farkas & Bruce 2010) so that a polar question asks about the proffered alternative and conveys that there are other alternatives in the context of utterance, then polar *kya* questions can be understood as further constraining the alternatives to be entertained. Under the Question-Under-Discussion (QUD) approach (Roberts 1996), the polar *kya* is seen as constraining the shape of the QUD. It imposes restrictions on what the question is about and conveys assumptions as to the possible answers to the question. Overall, polar *kya* adds a pragmatic import to polar questions that differentiates these questions from plain information-seeking polar questions.

This analysis is broadly consonant with Syed & Dash (2017), who also see polar question particles in Hindi, Bangla, and Odia as focus sensitive operators, though their analysis relies heavily on syntactic mechanisms, with no recourse to formal pragmatic theories and no integration of prosodic factors. Our analysis is also broadly consonant with the proposal for polar *kya* in Bhatt & Dayal (2020), who see polar *kya* as dividing a clause into information that is at-issue vs. not and locate polar *kya* in a ForceP projection.

We do not pursue the analysis of the syntax-pragmatic interface in this paper, but instead concentrate on the prosody-syntax interface by looking more closely at polar *kya* vs. the wh-constituent version of *kya*.

4 Wh-constituent questions

As already illustrated in (4), the use of *kya* can lead to ambiguity between polar and wh-constituent readings. In this section, we briefly present the centrally relevant prosodic and syntactic properties of wh-questions in Urdu/Hindi.

4.1 Syntax

Urdu/Hindi is traditionally characterized as a wh-in-situ language (Bayer & Cheng 2015). Example (15) shows the wh-phrase *kis=ko* placed in-situ (corresponding constituents shown in italics).

(15) a. sita=ne   dʰyan=se ram=ko   dekʰ-a   tʰ-a
       Sita.F=Erg carefully Ram.M=Acc see-Perf.M.Sg be.Past-M.Sg
       'Sita had looked at Ram carefully'

   b. sita=ne   dʰyan=se kıs=ko   dekʰ-a   tʰ-a?
       Sita.F=Erg carefully who.Obl=Acc see-Perf.M.Sg be.Past-M.Sg
       'Who had Sita looked at carefully?'

However, a closer investigation reveals that the default/preferred position for wh-words is in fact the immediately preverbal position (Féry 2010; Dayal 2017; Butt 2018), as illustrated in (16). This position has also been shown to be the default focus position (Gambhir 1981; Butt & King 1996, 1997; Kidwai 2000). As wh-words are considered to be semantically focused, it stands to reason that their preferred position is immediately preverbal.

(16) a. sita=ne   ram=ko   dekʰ-a   tʰ-a
       Sita.F=Erg Ram.M=Acc see-Perf.M.Sg be.Past-M.Sg
       'Sita had seen Ram.'

   b. ram=ko   kıs=ne   dekʰ-a   tʰ-a?
       Ram.M=Acc who.Obl=Erg see-Perf.M.Sg be.Past-M.Sg
       'Who saw Ram?'

Nevertheless, the immediately preverbal position is only the preferred position for wh-words in constituent questions. Manetta (2012) demonstrates that wh-phrases have the same kind of scrambling possibilities as normal NPs do. Consequently, wh-words can in principle appear anywhere in the clause, as shown in (17).

(17) a. anu=ne   uma=ko   kya di-ya?
       Anu.F=Erg Uma.F=Dat what give-Perf.M.Sg
       'What did Anu give to Uma?'

   b. %kya anu=ne uma=ko di-ya?
   c. anu=ne kya uma=ko di-ya?
   d. anu=ne uma=ko di-ya kya?

As with the distributional possibilities of polar *kya*, there is one position that is dispreferred. In this case it is the clause initial position, which had earlier been identified as the canonical position for polar *kya* (Masica 1991; Montaut 2004).

Overall, the different word orders appear to go hand in hand with differences in interpretation. For example, Butt et al. (2016) investigate constructions as in

(18) where the wh-word appears immediately postverbally within the verbal complex (Bhatt & Dayal 2007; Manetta 2012). They adduce evidence to show that this immediately postverbal position within the verbal complex is a secondary focus position that occurs when the primary focus of the question is placed on the verb.

(18) sita=ne   d^{h}yan=se   [dek^h-a   kıs=ko   t^h-a]?
      Sita.F=Erg   carefully   see-Perf.M.Sg   who.Obl=Acc   be.Past-M.Sg
      'Who had Sita looked at carefully?'

The pragmatic effect of the other word orders remains to be fully investigated.

4.2 Prosody

Figure 3 shows the most typical f_0 contour of a wh-question. The highest f_0 peak in the sentence aligns with the question word *kya* 'what'. F_0 drops on the following noun and the verb to reach a low final boundary tone.

Harnsberger (1994) shows that the prosodic realization of wh-words is similar to that of focus. He reports that the f_0 on the wh-word is upstepped, leading to a raise in register, and that the f_0 on the subsequent phrases is compressed. Butt et al. (2016) corroborate the findings of Harnsberger and show that the preverbal wh-phrases have the highest f_0 maxima in a clause. The boundary tone in wh-questions is typically low (Moore 1965; Harnsberger 1994); however, we have found some variation with respect to this in our data, with high boundary tones also occurring (also see Sengar & Mannell (2012), who exclusively report a high

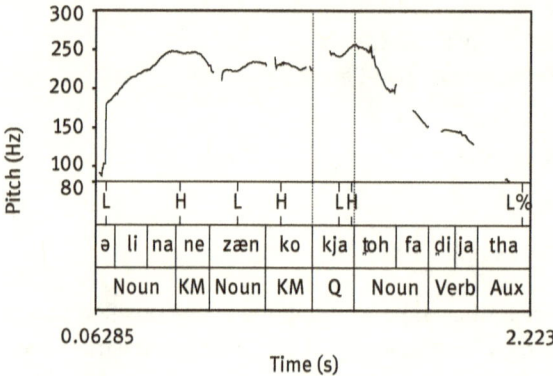

Fig. 3: A wh-question with the wh-word at the preverbal position.

boundary tone for wh-questions). The nature and scope of this variation remain to be thoroughly investigated.

5 Ambiguity resolution via prosodic information

The polyfunctionality of *kya* leads to ambiguous strings, particularly in examples as in (19), repeated here from (4). In these cases *kya* can either be seen as part of a polar question (19a), or it can be interpreted as a wh-word that is part of a nominal phrase (19b).

(19) a. ʃahina=ne naz=ko kya [tohfa] di-ya?
       S.F=Erg N.F=Dat what present.M.Sg.Nom give-Perf.M.Sg
       'Did Shahina give a gift to Naz?'

   b. ʃahina=ne naz=ko [kya tohfa] di-ya?
       S.F=Erg N.F=Dat what present.M.Sg.Nom give-Perf.M.Sg
       'What gift did Shahina give to Naz?'

We maintain that prosodic cues are instrumental for the disambiguation of the examples in (19) and that these cues are centered primarily on the differences in prosody associated with polar *kya* (flat or falling) vs. the constituent *kya*, that bears the basic LH contour. In this section, we demonstrate that the prosodic difference between polar and wh-constituent *kya* is indeed robust by adducing evidence from a production and a perception experiment.

5.1 Production experiment

5.1.1 Materials

We constructed five sets of sentences with *kya* followed by a noun at the preverbal position. Three of the nouns following *kya* were monosyllabic whereas two were bisyllabic. All the target sentences were ditransitive. Each sentence had a wh-constituent as well as a polar reading. Each target sentence was presented in both polar and wh-constituent question contexts. In order to avoid the influence of word order on the production of sentences, the contexts were given in English while the target sentences were presented in the Urdu script. An example sentence with both polar and wh-constituent question contexts is given in (20):

Context for wh-constituent reading:
You want to know what gift was given.

Context for polar reading:
You want to know if Shahina gave Naz a gift.

(20) ʃahina=ne   naz=ko   kya   tohfa   di-ya?
      Shahina.F=Erg Naz.F=Dat what present.M.Sg.Nom   give-Perf.M.Sg
      'What gift did Shahina give to Naz?'
      'Did Shahina give a gift to Naz?'

5.1.2 Participants

Three speakers of Urdu (2 females) were recorded for this experiment. They were all Pakistanis living in Germany. They were multilingual who spoke Urdu as well as English and at least one other regional language from Pakistan.[5]

5.1.3 Data collection

The data was recorded in the phonetics lab in University of Konstanz with a head mounted Shure microphone at the sampling frequency of 44.1KHz. Every target sentence was followed by two declarative sentences functioning as fillers. The target sentences were presented in a slide presentation and the participants controlled the pace of the experiment. The participants were asked to read the context silently and pronounce the target sentence keeping in mind the given context. They were asked to repeat the sentence in case of coughing, laughing, or stuttering. They were all paid a small remuneration for participating in the experiment.

5.1.4 Data analysis

The sentences were analyzed using PRAAT (Boersma & Weenink, 2013, v. 6.0.28). The target sentences were labelled manually to measure the duration of *kya* and the following nouns. The f_0 contour of the question word and the following noun as well as the boundary tone were also labelled. The f_0 values at the local minima and maxima were obtained for the analysis of *kya* and the noun. As the data set is

---

[5] We are aware that their language background influences their language production but Urdu is a lingua franca and it is difficult to find monolingual literate speakers of Urdu even in Pakistan.

small, no regression analysis was conducted. In the following section, we report the results in terms of descriptive statistics.

5.1.5 Results

5.1.5.1 Duration

Our analysis shows that the wh-constituent *kya* has a longer duration than polar *kya*. Additionally, the nouns are longer after polar *kya* than after wh-constituent *kya*. Table 1 shows the average duration of syllables in the target words. This difference in duration is probably correlated with the fact that the noun following the polar *kya* is emphasized (see Sect. 5.1.6).

Tab. 1: Average duration (ms) of polar and wh-constituent *kya* and the following monosyllabic and disyllabic nouns.

	kya	Monosyllabic N	Disyllabic N		
			Total	Syllable 1	Syllable 2
polar *kya*	204	330	408	165	243
wh-constituent *kya*	232	271	370	153	217

5.1.5.2 F₀ contour

Wh-constituent *kya* is produced with an LH contour whereas polar *kya* is always accentless and there is no intonational contour associated with it. However, the results of the analysis of the f_0 contour of nouns following *kya* are less clear cut. The noun after polar *kya* is often, but not always, produced with the LH contour (77%). The f_0 on the noun after the wh-constituent *kya* is mostly compressed (77%). These results indicate a tendency rather than provide an absolute distinction in the f_0 contour of nouns following preverbal polar and wh-constituent *kya*. The general difference between the f_0 contour of the constituent question and polar *kya* is illustrated by Fig. 4, which shows the f_0 contour of the potentially ambiguous examples in (21).

(21) alina=ne zain=ko kya tohfa di-ya t^h-a?
Alina=Erg Zain=Dat what present.M.Sg give-Perf.M.Sg be.Past-M.Sg
Constituent Question: 'What gift did Alina give to Zain?'
Polar Question: 'Did Alina (actually) give a gift to Zain?'

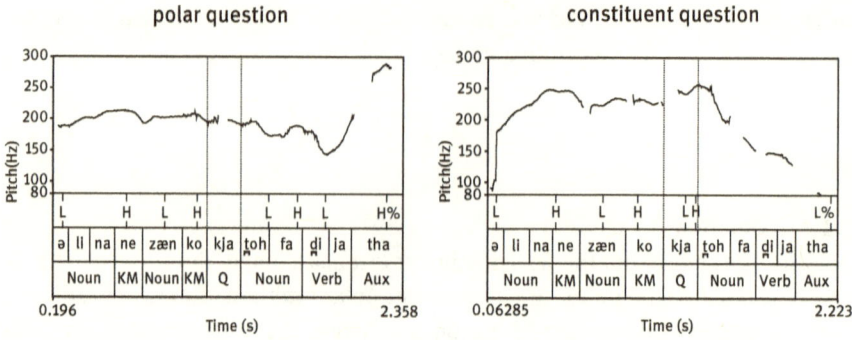

Fig. 4: Polar and wh-constituent readings of *kya*

As noted earlier, there is variability in the realization of the boundary tones so that a proportion of wh-questions were also produced with a high boundary tone, though the pitch excursion does not match the steep rise found in polar questions.

5.1.6 Discussion

The production data reported here shows that there are prosodic differences between wh-constituent and polar *kya*. The wh-constituent *kya* is produced with longer duration and an LH contour while f_0 is compressed on the following noun. This is in line with the findings of Harnsberger (1994) and Butt et al. (2016). Polar *kya*, on the other hand, is produced with shorter duration, is accentless, and the LH contour aligns with the noun following it. Moreover, the nouns following polar *kya* have a longer duration as compared with the nouns after the wh-constituent *kya*. We interpret this difference in their prosody in terms of focus marking. Wh-constituent *kya* is focused as indicated by its longer duration and the LH contour in comparison to its polar variant. Polar *kya* is accentless and it is the following noun that is focused, as shown by its LH contour and longer duration as compared to the noun following wh-constituent *kya*.[7]

5.2 Perception experiment

The production data presented above shows that there are prosodic differences in the production of polar vs. wh-constituent *kya* as well as the following noun. We investigated whether speakers of Urdu are perceptually sensitive to these prosodic differences and whether they have preferences regarding the association of a particular prosodic pattern with *kya* as either a polar or a wh-constituent question.

5.2.1 Materials

In this experiment, we used the same dataset of sentences as the one used in the production experiment. One set of recordings from the production experiment, produced by a female speaker, was used as a stimulus for the perception experiment. This ensured that the participants in the perception experiment were presented with the same prosodic structures as found in the production experiment. As there is variation in the use of boundary tones in polar and wh-questions, we kept the boundary tones consistent across all our target sentences in both the contexts. The contexts were shown in the Urdu script. Each participant was presented with all the target sentences in matching (recorded and presented in the same context) and mismatching (recorded in one and presented in the other) contexts. The prosodic structure of the target sentences was not manipulated. The only manipulated variable was the context.

5.2.2 Procedure

The experiment was carried out via a web-based interface designed specifically for this experiment using Xojo Dev Center (http://www.xojo.com/). The participants were asked to read the context carefully, listen to the target sentence, and rate the naturalness of the sentence in the given context. The rating was based on a five-point Likert scale from 1 (most unnatural) to 5 (most natural) (Likert 1932). The participants controlled the pace of the experiment. They had to play the sentence at least once before rating but could play the target sentence no more than three times. The average time spent on each item was 13 seconds.

5.2.3 Participants

Twenty-seven respondents (4 females) aged between 21 and 30 participated in the experiment. They were all Pakistanis living in Germany. All participants were multilingual and spoke Urdu frequently in their daily life along with English, German, and at least one regional language from Pakistan. They were paid a small remuneration for participating in the experiment.

5.2.4 Data analysis

We used participants' ratings of target sentences in matching and mismatching contexts. For the statistical analysis, we fitted a series of LMER models with ratings as dependent variable and the presented and recorded contexts (polar/wh-question) and their interaction as fixed factors and items and participants as crossed random factors (Baayen et al. 2008).

5.2.5 Results

We found significant interaction between the ratings for recorded and presented contexts (β: 0.84, SE = 0.23, t = 3.6, p < 0.001). The results of participants' ratings are shown in Fig. 5. It shows that *kya* as a wh-constituent question received significantly better ratings than its polar variant (β: 0.62, SE = 0.2, t = 2.1, p = 0.03).

Moreover, the sentences recorded in the wh-constituent context and presented in the polar context were rated as less natural (β: 0.53, SE = 0.1, t = 3.4, p < 0.001) than their counterparts in the matching contexts. Similarly the sentences recorded as polar questions but presented in the wh-constituent context were rated as less natural but the difference between matching and mismatching ratings in the context of polar questions failed to reach significance (β: − 0.31, SE = 0.1, t = −1.8, p = 0.06).

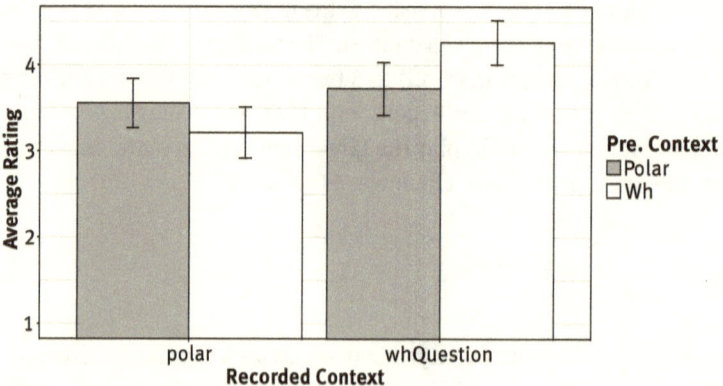

Fig. 5: Mean ratings for preverbal polar and wh- *kya*. The whiskers indicate 95% confidence interval.

5.2.6 Discussion

As the immediately preverbal position is preferred for constituent questions (Gambhir 1981; Butt & King 1997; Kidwai 2000), it stands to reason that *kya* as a constituent question receives better ratings at this position than its polar variant. This is indeed what is found and our results thus further support the existing claims about the distributional preference for polar and wh-constituent *kya* as discussed above (Bhatt & Dayal 2020).

5.3 Interim summary

The findings of our production and perception experiments show that prosodic information can be used to disambiguate between questions with pre-verbal wh-constituent and polar *kya*. We have shown that *kya* as a constituent question has the prosodic structure associated with focus and is followed by f_0 compression, a typical feature of post-focal constituents. On the other hand, polar *kya* is accentless and is followed by a noun with an LH contour. In the following section, we show how this prosodic information can be combined with syntactic structure to disambiguate between wh-constituent and polar *kya* using the framework of Lexical Functional Grammar (Bresnan & Kaplan 1982; Dalrymple 2001).

6 The syntax–prosody interface

Initial LFG proposals for the p(rosodic)-structure were "syntactocentric" (cf. Jackendoff (2002), see Butt & King (1998)), but newer proposals have moved towards seeing prosody as an independent level of representation (Mycock 2013; Dalrymple & Mycock 2011; Dalrymple & Nikolaeva 2011; Bögel 2015), where prosody is taken to interact with morphosyntax, but is not derived from it.

For the analysis of *kya*, we follow the version of the syntax-prosody interface proposed by Bögel (2015). Based on the assumption that *listening* and *speaking* are inherently different processes at the interface between prosody and syntax (and grammar in general), the proposal makes a crucial distinction between *production* and *comprehension*. *Production* refers to the construction of an utterance from MEANING to FORM and *comprehension* refers to the process of understanding an utterance, i.e., from FORM to MEANING. With respect to the interface between syntax and prosody, the former is concerned with the syntax-to-prosody interface, while the latter is concerned with the prosody-to-syntax interface.

- *Production/generation/speaking*:
  from MEANING to FORM (syntax → prosody)
- *Comprehension/perception/listening*:
  from FORM to MEANING (prosody → syntax)

In terms of syntactic analysis, we base ourselves on the approach to Urdu syntax established as part of the Urdu ParGram grammar (Butt & King 2007). The Urdu ParGram grammar uses a flat structure in which all major constituents are allowed to scramble. One of these major constituents is the verbal complex, labeled VC in the c-structure analyses.[6]

In what follows, we focus on the prosody → syntax interface, i.e., we model a process of *comprehension* and show how the respective prosodic information associated with polar and wh-constituent *kya* (as established in the previous sections) can guide syntactic disambiguation, thus supporting the correct semantic interpretation of *kya*. The syntactically ambiguous example in (22) serves as an illustration.

(22) alina=ne zain=ko kya tohfa di-ya t^h-a?
Alina=Erg Zain=Dat what present.M.Sg give-Perf.M.Sg be.Past-M.Sg
Constituent Question: 'What gift did Alina give to Zain?'
Polar Question: 'Did Alina (actually) give a gift to Zain?'

Example (22) allows for two possible interpretations: a) as a constituent question, where *kya* is grouped together with *tohfa* 'gift', and b) as a polar question, where *kya* stands on its own. Following Slade (2011), we analyze *kya* as a Q node within the c-structure and we furthermore assume only one underspecified *kya* 'what' for the polar and the wh-readings.[7] Figure 6 shows the c-structures for both interpretations of *kya*: While *kya* forms an NP together with the associated N in the wh-reading, it remains an independent daughter of S in the polar *kya* interpretation.

---

[6] LFG assumes two syntax-related structures: 1) c(onstituent)-structure, which represents the linear order and hierarchical structure of the constituents (i.e., the syntactic 'tree'), 2) f(unctional)-structure, which encodes predicate-argument relations and functional information.
[7] We could assume two separate lexical and syntactic entities and treat polar and constituent question *kya* as an accidental homophony. However, cross-linguistic evidence shows that there is a general trend for 'what' to be used for other question types and we believe that this is not an accident. We are working on a unified semantic approach to polar and constituent question *what* and we here anticipate that approach by positing just one underlying and underspecified entry for *kya*.

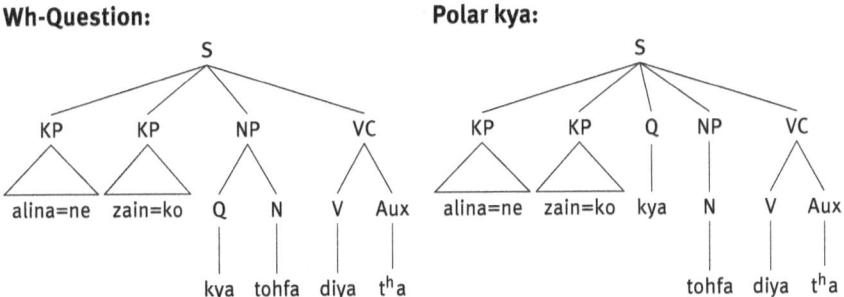

Fig. 6: C-structures for the *wh*-constituent and for *polar kya* questions.

As demonstrated in the previous sections, syntactic ambiguities that arise from the use of *kya* can be resolved via prosodic disambiguation. In the following, we adopt the formal approach to the prosody-syntax interface proposed in Bögel (2015).

6.1 The prosody–syntax interface

Two information transfer processes are assumed at the interface between prosody (p-structure)[8] and syntax (c-structure): The *Transfer of Structure* ($\natural$) relates syntactic and prosodic constituency above the word level and exchanges information on intonational cues. The *Transfer of Vocabulary* (ρ/π), on the other hand, operates on the word level and below by associating the morphosyntactic and phonological form of each item (word) within the lexicon before projecting these onto the respective structures: lexical phonological information is associated with p-structure and lexical morphosyntactic information is associated with c-structure. Figure 7 shows how these transfer processes are integrated into the LFG architecture.[9]

We illustrate how the system works with a concrete example involving the *comprehension* of the utterance shown earlier in (22). In a very first step the acoustic signal corresponding to (22) is received and processed by a hearer. This 'raw'

---

[8] In fact, p-structure represents phonetic, postlexical phonological, and prosodic information. See below for a short explanation and Bögel (2015) for details.
[9] The string represents the linear order of the single lexical items as they are parsed by syntax. Generally, the (syntactic) string is parallel to the linear order of the actual pronunciation; however, there are instances where postlexical phonology/prosody can change the linear order on the basis of phonological constraints, for example *prosodic inversion* (Halpern 1995).

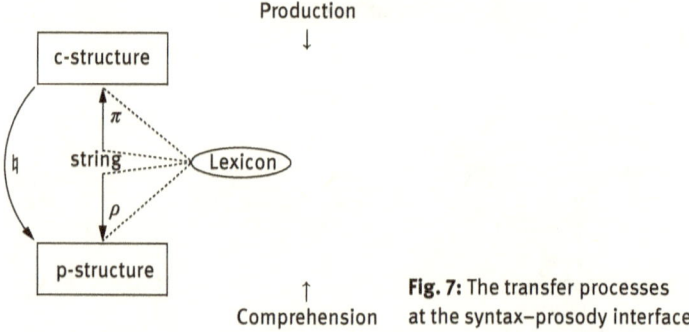

Fig. 7: The transfer processes at the syntax–prosody interface

acoustic information is stored in the *p-diagram*, a syllable-based linear and compact representation of information related to p-structure.

DUR.	0,08	0,16	0,14	0,17	0,28	0,23	0,21	0,20	0,16	0,13	0,11	0,22	SIGNAL
F_0	164	211	239	243	228	229	247	229	162	147	136	(83)	↓
VALUE	[ə]	[li]	[na]	[ne]	[zæn]	[ko]	[kja]	[ṭoh]	[fa]	[di]	[ja]	[tʰa]	
INDEX	S_1	S_2	S_3	S_4	S_5	S_6	S_7	S_8	S_9	S_{10}	S_{11}	S_{12}	...

Fig. 8: Representation of 'raw' acoustic signal information in the p-diagram

In the p-diagram, each syllable receives a vector containing the values for the attributes relevant for the interpretation. For example, the vector for the third syllable (S_3) contains the syllable's duration [DUR = 0,14 s] and its (mean) fundamental frequency [F_0 = 239]. Further possible attributes could be INTENSITY or PAUSE DURATION, for example.

As the speech signal is processed, the phonetic information is identified and used to analyze the speech signal in terms of phonological categories (Fig. 9). For example, f_0 can be interpreted in terms of pitch accents and boundary tones such as H* or L-L%.[10] (PROSODIC) PHRAS(ING), on the other hand, indicates larger prosodic domains on the basis of f_0 or DURATION. Both of these attributes can serve as a reference to the *transfer of structure* as demonstrated below. Since we are mainly concerned with the identification of polar vs. wh-constituent *kya*, the figure only presents the relevant information for the present research question and leaves aside the insertion of further pitch accents, boundary tones, and lower

---

10 In Fig. 9, "ToBI" refers to the system of "Tones and Break Indices" originally devised for English (Silverman et al. 1992).

Phras.	(	...	...	...	...	...	...	...	...	...	)ι	Interpretation
ToBI	...	...	...	...	...	LH	...	...	...	...	...	↓
Dur.	0.08	0.16	0.14	0.17	0.28	0.23	0.21	0.20	0.16	0.13	0.11	0.22	Signal
F₀	164	211	239	243	228	229	247	229	162	147	136	(83)	↓
Value	[ə]	[li]	[na]	[ne]	[zæn]	[ko]	[kja]	[ṭoh]	[fa]	[ḍi]	[ja]	[tʰa]	
Index	S₁	S₂	S₃	S₄	S₅	S₆	S₇	S₈	S₉	S₁₀	S₁₁	S₁₂	...

Fig. 9: Categorical interpretation on the basis of 'raw' information

prosodic domains (e.g., phonological phrase boundaries). Note, however, that all of these could in principle be calculated on the basis of the information encoded under duration, and the difference in f₀ between adjacent syllables.

During the *Transfer of Vocabulary*, (segmental) information coming from the speech signal is matched against the p(honological)-form of a multidimensional lexicon. LFG is committed to the strong lexicalist hypothesis (Lapointe 1980, 8). As a consequence, only fully formed words can enter the syntactic tree (Bresnan & Mchombo 1995; Asudeh et al. 2013) and the lexical 'surface' form contains complete words (albeit these surface forms are assumed to be generated dynamically, following e.g., Kiparsky (1982) and Meinzer et al. (2009)). The lexicon includes several 'dimensions' each associated with a particular module of grammar. The *s(yntactic)-form* encodes morphosyntactic and functional information (on e.g., word category, number, person) and is associated with syntactic structure. The *p(honological)-form*, on the other hand, provides segmental information and metrical structure (e.g., the number of syllables). A third dimension (*concept*) is concerned with meaning, but this is not detailed any further in this paper. Sample lexical entries for the noun *tohfa* 'gift' and the question word *kya* 'what' are provided in Table 2.

When a p-form is identified in the multidimensional lexicon, the associated s-form information also becomes available and can be used as input to c-structure terminal nodes via the π-projection (Kaplan 1987; Asudeh & Toivonen 2009). In a

Tab. 2: Lexical entries for *kya* and *tohfa*

concept	s-form			p-form	
'GIFT'	N	(↑ PRED)	= 'tohfa'	SEGMENTS	/ṭohfa/
		(↑ NUM)	= sg	METRICAL STRUCTURE	σσ
		(↑ GEND)	= masc		
'WHAT'	Q	(↑ INT-FORM)	= kya	SEGMENTS	/kja/
				METRICAL STRUCTURE	σ

sense, the lexicon thus has a translation function between p- and c-structure at the word level, associating information from the speech signal with concrete morphosyntactic items (and vice versa). This clear separation between the phonological and the morphosyntactic form further allows us to maintain LFG's principles of modularity (cf. Fodor 1983; Sadock 1991): Each of the dimensions within the lexicon can only be accessed by the module whose information it encodes. That is, c-structure works with the syntactic forms, semantic structure with the semantic forms, and p-structure with the phonological information.

The *Transfer of Structure* is complementary to the *Transfer of Vocabulary* in that it operates above the word-level and relates c-structure to associated information in p-structure and vice versa. This is the crucial part of the prosody-syntax interface with respect to information that goes beyond the lexicon. The projection ♮ is defined as the inverse projection of π composed with ρ, as shown in (23).[11]

(23) $♮(\equiv \rho(\pi^{-1}))$

Figure 10 shows an abstraction of a typical *transfer of structure*-annotation at the prosody-syntax interface.

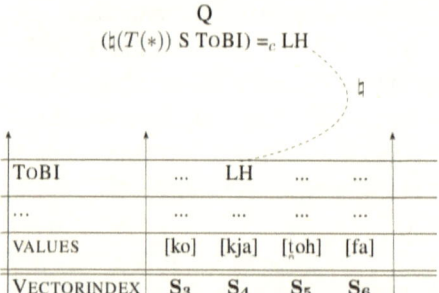

Fig. 10: The *Transfer of Structure*

Q is the terminal node in c-structure that relates to polar or wh-constituent *kya*. This syntactic node is annotated with reference to p-structure (♮). The annotation can be read as follows: For all the terminal nodes (T) of the current node (*), take

---

[11] In the LFG architecture relations between components of grammar are governed by projection functions that map between different structures. For example, the ϕ-projection relates c-structure to f-structure. These functions can be inverted so that the inverse ϕ-projection relates f-structure to c-structure. These inverse functions allow for the inclusion of information from other modules.

the indicated Syllable (S). For the attribute ToBI, this syllable must have ($=_c$) the value LH.[12]

In short, this approach allows for a syntactic construction to 'check' whether a particular value is present in p-structure. Note that the constraining equation $=_c$ is a so-called 'hard constraint'. If the desired value (LH) is not present, this particular syntactic structure will not be parsed.

6.2 Analysis

With the prosody-syntax interface in place, we are now in a position to show how the utterance in (24) (repeated from (22)) can be disambiguated.

(24) alina=ne zain=ko kya   tohfa   di-ya   t^h-a?
     Alina=Erg Zain=Dat what   present.M.Sg   give-Perf.M.Sg   be.Past-M.Sg
     Constituent Question: 'What gift did Alina give to Zain?'
     Polar Question: 'Did Alina (actually) give a gift to Zain?'

6.2.1 Constituent question *kya*

We begin with the wh-constituent reading of *kya*. As shown in Sect. 5, *kya* carries an LH f$_0$ contour. This information is available through p-structure and can be accessed by the *transfer of structure* as in (25).

(25) *kya*: (♮(T(*)) ToBI) $=_c$ LH

The c-structure analysis and the lexicon are repeated in Fig. 11, as is the relevant part of the speech signal represented in the p-diagram. The speech signal contains an LH on vector S7, which represents the segmental string [kja]. The related p-form / k j a / is accessed in the lexicon via the *transfer of vocabulary*. The lexicon then relates the p-form / k j a / to its associated s-form *kya*, which specifies that it is a Q at c-structure. The lexicon otherwise has nothing to say about *kya*. It is completely underspecified as to whether this *kya* signals a wh-constituent or a polar question.

The rules of our grammar allow for two c-structure analyses of the utterance in (23) as shown in Figs. 11 and 12. However, the c-structure in Fig. 11 is only li-

---

[12] T(*) S is in a sense redundant here, because Q is a terminal node and there is only one syllable related with it (*kya*). However, references to prosodic constituency (Bögel, this volume) or to more complex pitch contours often require reference to several terminal nodes/syllables.

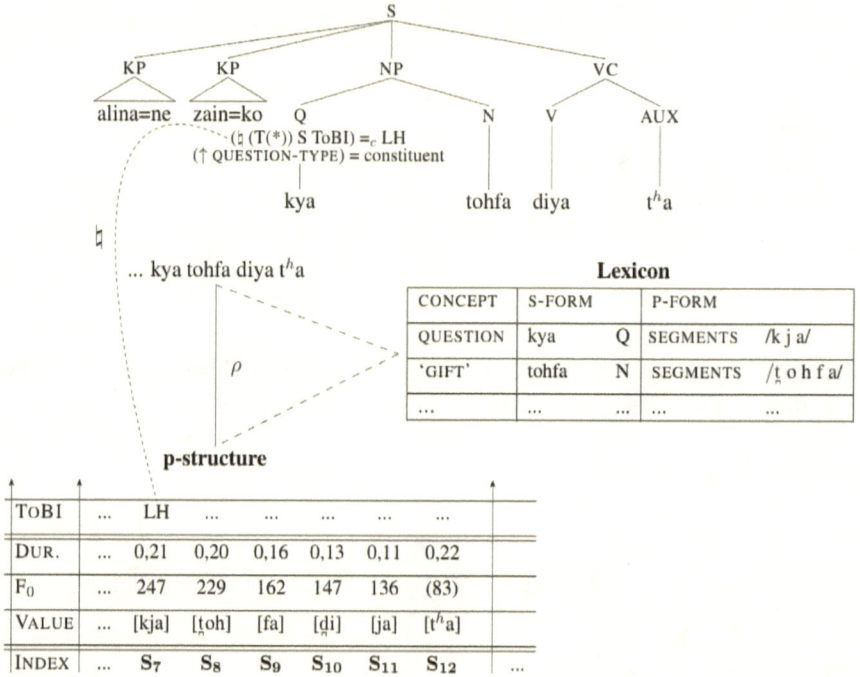

Fig. 11: *kya* as a constituent question

censed if *kya* can be interpreted as a constituent question. In order to be interpreted this way, it needs to be associated with an LH. This is part of the grammatical knowledge of the language and is encoded in our analysis as part of the c-structure annotation on *kya* in Fig. 11, as shown in (26).

(26) NP →   Q   N
              (♮(T(*)) S ToBI) =$_c$ LH
              (↑ QUESTION-TYPE) = constituent

The c-structure annotation on Q in the constituent question interpretation features a constraining equation which ensures that *kya* can only be parsed as a terminal Q node if there is an LH on the corresponding p-form. This is ensured via the *Transfer of Structure*, which relates c-structural and p-structural information via the ♮ projection.

If *kya* is indeed associated with an LH in the speech signal, it can be identified as a constituent question. This information is passed along to the f-structure via the second annotation under Q in (26): an equation assigning the value "constituent" to the feature QUESTION-TYPE.

6.2.2 Polar *kya*

The analysis for polar *kya* is shown in Fig. 12. Here *kya* is analyzed as an immediate daughter of S. Given that all immediate daughters of S can scramble as part of the word order variation exhibited in Urdu/Hindi, the ability of *kya* to scramble can be dealt with via the shuffle operator (Crouch et al. 2017) on a par with the other major constituents of S. The top level S rule is shown in (27), whereby the "," (comma) represents the shuffle operator. The effect is the generation of sentences in which NPs or KPs, the verbal complex and the Q can appear in any order.

(27) S ⟶ (Q), {NP|KP}*, VC.

The round brackets around the Q indicate optionality (polar *kya* is always syntactically optional). The curly brackets in conjunction with the | signals a disjunction. The Kleene * allows for zero or infinitely many occurrences of NPs (bare noun phrases) or KPs (case marked phrases). In practical grammar engineering this will generally be more restricted in number, but the simplified rule in (27) serves to illustrate the main point here, which is that this single rule generates all the possible word orders for main clauses in Urdu. Some sample possible word orders generated by the rule are shown in (28) and these are indeed all legitimate word orders.

(28) a. Q KP NP VC
      b. KP Q NP VC
      c. KP Q NP VC KP
      d. NP VC Q
      e. KP KP VC
      f. ...

Returning to our analysis, the rule in (27) must necessarily be amended via a functional annotation which states that the c-structure analysis in Fig. 12 is actually only possible if *kya* does not carry an LH (≠ LH).

(29) S ⟶   ...   Q   ...
                    (♮(T(*)) S ToBI) ≠ LH
                    (↑ QUESTION-TYPE) = polar

Again, the lexical entry for *kya* has nothing in particular to say with respect to syntax other than that it is a Q. It is the same underspecified entry seen in Fig. 11. The annotations on Q in (29) say two things: 1) this is a polar question; 2) but only if there is no LH on *kya*. The information as to whether the negative constraint on

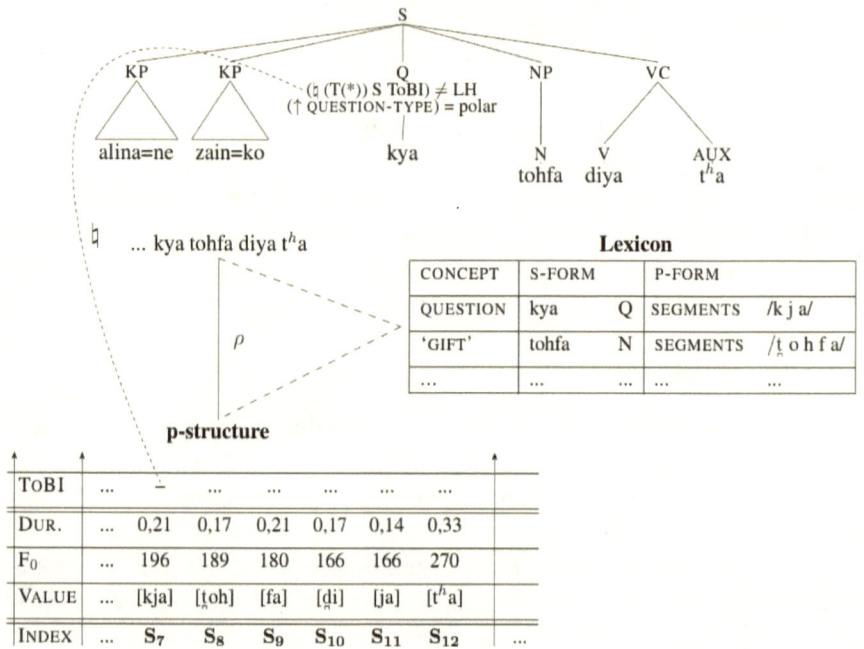

Fig. 12: *kya* as a polar question

Q in (29) is satisfied or not is again determined via the *Transfer of Structure*, which relates prosodic information with syntactic information via the ♮ projection.

Beside the distinct LH contour on *kya*, the production experiment in Sect. 5.1 also showed that the f₀ and the duration of the noun following *kya* change on the basis of its interpretation as a polar or wh-constituent question. In principle, this information could be included at the prosody-syntax interface as well. For example, the longer duration and the typical LH pattern of the noun following polar *kya* indicate a phonological phrase, while the shorter duration and the f₀ compression on the noun following constituent *kya* point towards the noun being phrased with another element. These phrasing patterns can be used to inform syntactic phrasing via the *transfer of structure*;[13] however, the importance of the cues related to the noun from the perspective of perception needs to be left for further research. Furthermore, as polar *kya*, being a focus sensitive operator, takes scope over either the item to its right or a prominent item to its left, an analysis based on the prosody of *kya* itself and not the associated noun is more elegant and effective to help disambiguate between polar and wh-constituent readings.

---

[13] For a concrete example in German, see Bögel, this volume.

Finally, a note on the generalizability of the rules in (26) and (29). The rules are generally applicable, as shown with (27). The wh-constituent rule in (26) is, however, only one possible expansion of the NP. Other expansions allow for the possibility of NPs containing determiners, adjectives, numerals, etc. In the computational Urdu grammar (Butt & King 2007) the NP is quite complex, carefully juggling dependencies and ordering constraints within the NP. The rule in (26) is a subrule within the larger expansion possibilities for an NP.

6.3 Preferences in distribution

In this final analysis section, we address the issue of preferences found with regard to the distribution of polar vs. wh-constituent *kya*. Recall that polar *kya* and wh-constituent *kya* in principle have the distribution of other major constituents in the clause. However, polar *kya* is dispreferred in the immediately preverbal position. We propose that polar *kya* is dispreferred in this position because this is the default position for focus, hence the most natural position for wh-constituent *kya* and hence also an unnatural position for polar *kya* as a focus sensitive operator. Conversely, the reason for the dispreference for the clause initial position by wh-constituent *kya* must be seen as following from distributional preferences for polar *kya*, where the clause initial position has been reported as the default.

These positional (dis)preferences can be modeled very elegantly via the OT-style constraints implemented as part of the XLE grammar development platform for LFG grammars (Frank et al. 1998; Crouch et al. 2017). The OT component implemented within XLE can serve to formulate constraints which disprefer an analysis in which wh-constituent *kya* is placed clause initially and polar *kya* is placed in the immediately preverbal position. The OT-style constraints implemented within XLE can be used in both directions: parsing and generation. Given that Bögel's prosody-syntax architecture takes the needs of comprehension vs. production very seriously, these OT-style constraints are exactly right for our analysis.

7 Conclusion

In this paper, we have presented a prosodic analysis of *kya* 'what' in Urdu. We have shown that ambiguities arise because of the polyfunctionality of *kya* and because of the distributional possibilities of polar and wh-constituent *kya* in the clause. We demonstrate that while *kya* is string identical in polar and wh-constituent questions, the prosodic cues differ quite starkly. With the help of a production experiment, we showed that wh-constituent *kya* has the prosodic realization associated with focus whereas polar *kya* is accentless. Our perception experiment showed that speakers of Urdu are sensitive to the prosodic differences between polar *kya* and wh-constituent *kya* clauses. We posit that prosodic information is crucial for the resolution of syntactic ambiguity and use this information to disambiguate between the two syntactic possibilities. We demonstrate concretely how the relevant prosodic information can be accessed via syntax within the prosody-syntax architecture proposed by Bögel (2015). Bögel's analysis is couched within LFG, which formulates a modular and constraint-based view of syntax. Modules of grammar interact with one another via a complex yet mathematically well defined projection architecture. The modules are characterized by a separate internal logic and concomitant representations, allowing for the specification of prosodic information within a prosodic component that can be accessed freely in the form of targeted requests of information by other parts of the grammar, such as the syntactic modules. Once the syntactic disambiguation has taken place on the basis of prosodic information, the appropriate semantic and pragmatic interpretation (Biezma et al. 2018) can then also be triggered on the basis of the available syntactic information.

References

Asudeh, Ash, Mary Dalrymple, and Ida Toivonen (2013). Constructions with lexical integrity. *Journal of Language Modeling*, 1(1):1–54.

Asudeh, Ash and Ida Toivonen (2009). Lexical-Functional Grammar. In Heine, B. and H. Narrog, eds, *The Oxford Handbook of Linguistic Analysis*, pp. 425–458. Oxford: Oxford University Press.

Baayen, Harold, Doug J. Davidson, and Douglas M. Bates (2008). Mixed-effects modeling with crossed random effects for subjects and items. *Journal of Memory and Language*, 59(4):390–412.

Bayer, Josef and Lisa Lai-Shen Cheng (2015). Wh-in-Situ. In Everaert, M. and H. van Riemsdijk, eds, *The Blackwell Companion to Syntax*. Oxford: Blackwell Publishing.

Bhatt, Rajesh and Veneeta Dayal (2007). Rightward scrambling as rightward movement. *Linguistic Inquiry*, 38(2):287–301.

Bhatt, Rajesh and Veneeta Dayal (2020). Polar question particles. Hindi-Urdu *kya*. *Natural Language and Linguistic Theory*. https://doi.org/10.1007/s11049-020-09464-0.

Biezma, María, Miriam Butt, and Farhat Jabeen (2018). Polar Questions vs. kya Questions in Hindi/Urdu. Paper presented at a workshop on *The grammar and pragmatics of interrogatives and their (special) uses*, GLOW 41, Budapest, 2018.

Biezma, Maria and Kyle Rawlins (2012). Responding to alternative and polar questions. *Linguistics and Philosophy*, 35:361–406.

Boersma, Paul and David Weenink (2013). Praat: doing phonetics by computer [Computer program, Version 5.3.56]. available at http://www.praat.org/ [retrieved 15.09.2013].
Bögel, Tina (2015). *The Syntax-Prosody Interface in Lexical Functional Grammar*. PhD thesis, University of Konstanz.
Bresnan, Joan and Ronald M. Kaplan (1982). Lexical-Functional Grammar: A formal system for grammatical representation. In Bresnan, J., ed., *The Mental Representation of Grammatical Relations*, pp. 173–281. Cambridge, MA: MIT Press.
Bresnan, Joan and Sam Mchombo (1995). The lexical integrity principle: Evidence from Bantu. *Natural Language and Linguistic Theory*, 13(2):181–254.
Butt, Miriam (2018). Word Order Variation in Urdu/Hindi Wh-Constituent Questions. In Butt, M. and T.H. King, eds, *Proceedings of the LFG'18 Conference*, Stanford. CSLI Publications. submitted.
Butt, Miriam, Tina Bögel, and Farhat Jabeen (2017). Polar *kya* and the prosody-syntax-pragmatics Interface. In Butt, M. and T.H. King, eds, *Proceedings of the LFG'17 Conference*, pp. 125–145, Stanford. CSLI Publications.
Butt, Miriam, Farhat Jabeen, and Tina Bögel (2016). Verb Cluster Internal Wh-Phrases in Urdu: Prosody, Syntax and Semantics/Pragmatics. *Linguistic Analysis*, 40(3–4).
Butt, Miriam and Tracy H. King (1996). Structural Topic and Focus without Movement. In Butt, M. and T. H. King, eds, *Proceedings of the First LFG Conference*, Stanford. CSLI Publications.
Butt, Miriam and Tracy Holloway King (1997). Null Elements in Discourse Structure. Written to be part of a volume that never materialized.
Butt, Miriam and Tracy Holloway King (1998). Interfacing Phonology with LFG. In Butt, M. and T. H. King, eds, *Proceedings of the LFG'98 Conference*, Stanford. CSLI Publications.
Butt, Miriam and Tracy Holloway King (2007). Urdu in a parallel grammar development environment. In Takenobu, T. and C.-R. Huang, eds, *Language Resources and Evaluation*, vol. 41, pp. 191–207. Dordrecht: Springer.
Cheng, Lisa (1997). *On the Typology of Wh-Questions*. New York: Garland.
Crouch, Dick, Mary Dalrymple, Ronald M. Kaplan, Tracy Holloway King, John T. Maxwell III, and Paula Newman (2017). *XLE Documentation*. Palo Alto Research Center.
Dalrymple, Mary (2001). *Lexical Functional Grammar*. San Diego [a.o.]: Academic Press.
Dalrymple, Mary and Louise Mycock (2011). The prosody-semantics interface. In Butt, M. and T. H. King, eds, *Proceedings of LFG'11*, Stanford. CSLI Publications.
Dalrymple, Mary and Irina Nikolaeva (2011). *Objects and Information Structure*. Cambridge: Cambridge University Press.
Dayal, Veneeta (1996). *Locality in WH Quantification*. Dordrecht: Kluwer Academic Publishers.
Dayal, Veneeta (2000). Scope Marking: Cross-linguistic variation in indirect dependency. In Lutz, U., G. Müller, and A. von Stechow, eds, *Wh-Scope Marking*, pp. 157–193. Amsterdam: John Benjamins. Volume 37 of *Linguistics Today*.
Dayal, Veneeta (2017). Does Hindi-Urdu have feature driven *wh* movement to Spec vP? *Linguistic Inquiry*, 48(1):159–172.
Dyrud, Lars O. (2001). *Hindi-Urdu: Stress accent or non-stress accent*. Master's thesis, University of North Dakota.
Farkas, Donka and Kim Bruce (2010). On Reacting to Assertions and Polar Questions. *Journal of Semantics*, 27(1):81–118.
Féry, Caroline (2010). The intonation of Indian languages: An areal phenomenon. In Hasnain, I. and S. Chaudhury, eds, *Festschrift for Ramakant Agnihotri*. Akar publishers.

Fodor, Jerry A. (1983). *The Modularity of Mind*. Cambridge, MA: The MIT Press.
Frank, Anette, Tracy Holloway King, Jonas Kuhn, and John Maxwell (1998). Optimality Theory style constraint ranking in large-scale LFG grammars. In Butt, M. and T. H. King, eds, *Proceedings of the LFG'98 Conference*, Stanford. CSLI Publications.
Gambhir, Vijay (1981). *Syntactic Restrictions and Discourse Functions of Word Order in Standard Hindi*. PhD thesis, University of Pennsylvania, Philadelphia.
Genzel, Susanne and Frank Kügler (2010). The prosodic expression of contrast in Hindi. In *Proceedings of 5th International Conference on Speech Prosody*, Chicago.
Glassman, Eugene H. (1977). *Spoken Urdu*. Lahore: Nirali Kitaben.
Halpern, Aaron L. (1995). *On the Placement and Morphology of Clitics*. Stanford: CSLI Publications.
Harnsberger, James D. (1994). Towards an intonational Phonology of Hindi. Master's thesis, University of Florida.
Hayes, Bruce and Aditi Lahiri (1991). Bengali intonational phonology. *Natural Language and Linguistic Theory*, 9:47–96.
Jabeen, Farhat, Tina Bögel, and Miriam Butt (2016). Variable prosodic realization of verb focus in Urdu. In *Proceedings of 8th International Conference on Speech Prosody*, pp. 731–735, Boston, USA.
Jabeen, Farhat and Bettina Braun (2018). Production and Perception of Prosodic Cues in Narrow & Corrective Focus in Urdu/Hindi. In *Proceedings of the 9th International Conference on Speech Prosody*, pp. 30–34.
Jackendoff, Ray (2002). *Foundations of Language*. Oxford: Oxford University Press.
Kaplan, Ronald (1987). Three seductions of computational psycholinguistics. In Whitelock, P., H. Somers, P. Bennett, R. Johnson, and M. McGee Wood, eds, *Linguistic Theory and Computer Applications*, pp. 149–188. London: Academic Press.
Keane, Elinor (2014). The intonational phonology of Tamil. In Jun, S., ed., *Prosodic Typology II: The phonology of intonation and phrasing*, pp. 118–153. Oxford: Oxford University Press.
Kidwai, Ayesha (2000). *XP-adjunction in Universal Grammar: Scrambling and binding in Hindi-Urdu*. Oxford: Oxford University Press.
Kiparsky, Paul (1982). Lexical morphology and phonology. In *Linguistics in the Morning Calm*, pp. 3–91, Seoul, Korea. Hanshin Publishing Company.
Lahiri, Utpal (2002). *Questions and Answers in Embedded Contexts*. Oxford: Oxford University Press.
Lapointe, Steven G. (1980). *A Theory of Grammatical Agreement*. PhD thesis, University of Massachusetts.
Likert, Rensis (1932). A Technique for the Measurement of Attitudes. *Archives of Psychology*, 140:1–55.
Manetta, Emily (2012). Reconsidering Rightward Scrambling: Postverbal Constituents in Hindi-Urdu. *Linguistic Inquiry*, 43(1):43–74.
Masica, Colin (1991). *The Indo-Aryan languages*. Cambridge: Cambridge University Press.
Meinzer, Marcus, Aditi Lahiri, Tobias Flaisch, Ronny Hannemann, and Carsten Eulitz (2009). Opaque for the reader but transparent for the brain: Neural signatures of morphological complexity. *Neuropsychologia*, 47:1964–1971.
Montaut, Annie (2004). *Hindi grammar*. München: Lincom-Europa.
Moore, Robert R. (1965). *A Study of Hindi Intonation*. PhD thesis, University of Michigan.
Mycock, Louise (2013). Discourse Functions of Question Words. In Butt, M. and T.H. King, eds, *Proceedings of the LFG'13 Conference*, Stanford. CSLI Publications.

Nespor, Marina and Irene Vogel (1986). *Prosodic Phonology*. Dordrecht: Foris.
Patil, Umesh, Gerrit Kentner, Anja Gollrad, Frank Kügler, Caroline Féry, and Shravan Vasishth (2008). Focus, word order and intonation in Hindi. *Journal of South Asian Linguistics (JSAL)*, 1(1):55 – 72.
Platts, John T. (1884). *A Dictionary of Urdu, Classical Hindi, and English*. London: W. H. Allen & Co.
Puri, Vandana (2013). *Intonation in Indian English and Hindi late and simultaneous Bilinguals*. PhD thesis, University of Illinois, Urbana Champaign.
Roberts, Craige (1996). Information Structure in Discourse: Towards an Integrated Formal Theory of Pragmatics. Technical report, OSU Working Papers in Linguistics 49, papers in Semantics.
Sadock, Jerrold M. (1991). *Autolexical Syntax: A Theory of Parallel Grammatical Representations*. Chicago: The University of Chicago Press.
Selkirk, Elisabeth (1995). Sentence prosody: Intonation, stress and phrasing. In Goldsmith, J., ed., *The Handbook of Phonological Theory*, pp. 550–569. Oxford: Blackwell.
Sengar, Anuradha and Robert Mannell (2012). A Preliminary study of Hindi intonation. In *Proceedings of the 14th Australasian International Conference on Speech Science and Technology*, Sydney.
Silverman, Kim, Mary Beckman, John Pitrelli, Mari Ostendorf, Colin Wightman, Patti Price, Janet Pierrehumbert, and Julia Hirschberg (1992). TOBI: A standard for labeling English prosody. In *Proceedings of the 1992 International Conference on Spoken Language Processing*, Banff.
Slade, Benjamin (2011). *Formal and Philological Inquiries into the Nature of Interrogatives, Indefinites, Disjunction, and Focus in Sinhala and other Languages*. PhD thesis, University of Illinois at Urbana-Champaign.
Syed, Saurov and Bhamati Dash (2017). A unified account of the yes/no particle in Hindi, Bangla and Odia. In Erlewine, M. Y., ed., *Proceedings of GLOW in Asia XI*, vol. 1, pp. 201–212, Cambridge, MA. MIT Working Papers in Linguistics.

Katy Carlson
Focus structure affects comparatives: Experimental and corpus work

Abstract: Comparative constructions have many possible syntactic continuations, including bare NPs, VP Ellipsis, and full clauses. This project explores their processing and use by examining the frequency of different comparative structures within a set of over 4000 sentences from the Corpus of Contemporary American English (COCA), and by a written and an auditory questionnaire on the interpretation preferences of comparative bare NP ellipsis. The corpus data shows that ellipsis structures are much more frequent than full clauses in comparatives, with bare NP ellipsis most frequent (50% of the data). We suggest that clauses are dispreferred because of the repetition and prosodic deaccenting involved in producing complete clauses compared to structures that retain primarily the contrastive information. Although 80% of bare NP examples in the corpus contrast with the previous clause's subject, ambiguous bare NP remnants are more likely to be interpreted as contrasting with the object in comprehension. Since contrastive accent placement strongly affects the preferred interpretation, as does NP parallelism, we suggest that a default expectation of focus on the last argument accounts for the object bias in processing. Thus both the syntactic structures found in the corpus and the interpretation of ambiguous examples can be tied to different aspects of the focus structure of comparatives.

Note: The author would like to thank Benjamin Lee, Sarah Nelson, Blake Clark, Matthew Porter, Zachary Cole Allen, Katherine Griffitts, Joe Castle, and Torianne Crouch for assistance with the comparative corpus and the setup and running of the experiments, and David Potter for statistics help and discussion of the paper. Portions of this research have been presented at the 2013 AMLaP Conference, the 2016 CUNY Conference, and the 2017 Prosody in Syntactic Encoding session of the Annual Meeting of the German Linguistics Society; we thank the audiences at those conferences for the comments and questions. This work was partially supported by the National Institute of General Medical Sciences of the National Institutes of Health (NIH) [grant number 5P20GM103436-13], and the Eunice Kennedy Shriver National Institute of Child Health & Human Development of the NIH [grant number R15HD072713]. The content is solely the responsibility of the author and does not necessarily represent the official views of the National Institutes of Health.

https://doi.org/10.1515/9783110650532-005

1 Introduction

A comparative sentence using the "more [Adverb] than" frame, as in *more often than* or *more generally than*, can continue in many different ways, as illustrated in (1).

(1) Joan spread butter on her toast more generously than ...

    a. Marie/jam/her bagel.   (NP remnant, subject/object/PP object contrast)
    b. on her bagel.   (PP)
    c. was allowed usually.   (VP)
    d. the other children did.   (VP Ellipsis)
    e. Marie did jam.   (Pseudogapping)
    f. Marie spread butter on her toast.   (full clause)

The great flexibility of this general structure is limited mostly by the number of different phrases the first clause contains to contrast with.[1] Even when expressing the same contrast, though, such as between *Joan* and another subject NP, there are multiple structural options, from a simple bare NP (1a) to VP Ellipsis (1d), Pseudogapping (1e), and full clauses (1f).

This project explored two issues in these types of comparative structures. The first issue was how ambiguous comparative bare NP ellipsis sentences as in (1a) are processed: whether they have a bias in interpretation, how ambiguous they are, and what factors can influence their interpretation. A written questionnaire and an auditory questionnaire found effects of lexical parallelism between NPs and of accent placement on interpretation, along with an overall bias toward the object interpretation. The following corpus study was aimed at finding out whether the object interpretation of bare NP comparatives is also the most frequent, as well as how frequent bare NP ellipsis is compared to other structures. The corpus pulled together over 4000 examples of adjunct comparatives with and without ellipsis, and analyzed their syntactic structures, the contrasts expressed, and parallelism between contrasting NPs. The findings rule out any potential frequency-based explanation for the object bias in processing, since the corpus shows that over 80% of bare NP ellipsis examples express subject

---

[1] Other comparative structures, where the *more (...) than* syntax is located elsewhere in the sentence, may have different properties; see for example subject comparatives such as *More people like pie than cake*, or object comparatives such as *Tina met more people than Susan*. The structures in this project are all what Lechner (2004) calls adjunct comparatives, as in (1), as opposed to subject or object comparatives.

contrast. Additionally, the corpus shows that full clauses are rarely used after the comparative *than* while several types of ellipsis are extremely frequent in this construction.

The question of the frequency of object interpretations arises because a strain of psycholinguistic research uses frequency to explain certain biases. For example, much work on expectations at the verb suggests that comprehenders track the frequency of use of verbs as intransitive vs. transitive, or transitive with an NP object vs. with a CP complement (e.g., theories discussed in MacDonald 2013; MacDonald, Pearlmutter & Seidenberg 1994; Levy 2008, 2013). The frequencies are said to guide comprehenders in their expectations for upcoming material such that more frequent outcomes are easier and faster to process than less frequent ones. On analogy with this line of research, one might speculate that the frequency of particular contrasts in comparative structures could affect what interpretation comprehenders expected. But in this case, it turns out that the relative frequency of object vs. subject interpretations for ambiguous bare NP comparatives in the corpus is in the opposite direction from the interpretation preferences in processing, and thus is not able to explain the preferences.

Overall, this project suggests multiple levels of influence of focus structure on comparatives. The comprehension results show that the position of accent influences interpretation, with accented phrases taken to contrast with a remnant more frequently, as well as showing a general preference for the object interpretation. This bias is explained as the result of default focus, with objects being more likely than subjects to be considered focused and therefore to be used in contrasts, as in other ellipsis structures (e.g., Carlson et al. 2009; Harris & Carlson 2018). The corpus results show that frequency is not an alternative explanation of the object bias, and that bare NP comparative ellipsis is quite frequent. The relative rarity of complete clauses in comparatives (vs. ellipsis structures) is explained as being due to avoidance of long stretches of deaccented and given material. Thus both the structures used in production and the biases in comprehension can be related to focus structure. The rest of the introduction will discuss aspects of focus structure, ellipsis processing, and previous ellipsis corpus work in order to provide background for this project.

1.1 Focus and information structure

Focus and information structure have to do with the different ways that the information in a sentence can contribute to a discourse (Rooth 1992a; Kadmon 2001; Ladd 2008; Roberts 1996; Schwarzschild 1999). A sentence can provide entirely new information, information that contrasts with prior assertions, and information that is already known. Information that is repeated or known is called given, while new and contrastive information is focused (Selkirk 1984; Rooth 1992a).

(2) Jim likes gumdrops.

For a simple sentence like (2), if we've been discussing things that Jim likes, then the subject and verb are given, while the object is new information and focused. If (2) is said in response to the claim that Jim hates gumdrops, on the other hand, then the subject and object are given and the verb would be contrastively focused as a contradiction of *hates*. If we have been wondering who would enjoy the gumdrops that we dislike, then the subject would be focused and new information. As illustrated, the focus structure of a particular string of words can vary greatly depending on its surrounding discourse context.

English speakers tend to arrange information in a sentence so that the subject is given information, a continuing topic, while the predicate contains new information that is added to the discourse (Clark & Havilland 1977; Arnold et al. 2000). This harmonizes with the fact that the main stress in a sentence (also called nuclear stress) is usually on the object or last argument (Chomsky & Halle 1968; Cinque 1993; Selkirk 1984, 1995). Given the variety of possible focus structures for a sentence, there are means of overtly indicating the position of focus for a listener, using prosodic pitch accents, focus particles like *only*, and sentence structures like clefting (Ladd 2008; Pierrehumbert & Hirschberg 1990; Pierrehumbert 1980; Kiss 1998). An interesting finding in prosodic processing research has been that listeners use the overt focus marking in a sentence to decide on its information structure, but they also rely on expectations about common patterns of focus (e.g., Carlson et al. 2009; Harris & Carlson 2018).

In this project, the most relevant type of focus is contrastive focus, since most comparative constructions explicitly contrast information before the comparative morphology/syntax and after. Theories of focus differ on whether contrastive focus is considered to be distinct from focus for new information, also called informational focus (Kiss 1998), or simply one of several possible uses of focus (Rooth 1992a; Schwarzschild 1999). Similarly, prosodic theories differ in whether the pitch accents used to indicate contrastive focus are diffferent prosodic units than the accents used for non-contrastive focus (e.g., Bartels & Kingston 1996; Rump & Collier 1996; Ladd & Morton 1997; Ladd & Schepman 2003; Ito & Speer 2008). In the prosodic theory of Pierrehumbert (1980) and ToBI (Beckman & Elam 1997) assumed here, non-contrastive focus is generally conveyed by an H* accent, expressed as a high F0 target reached within the stressed syllable of an accented word. Contrastive accent is conveyed by a L+H* accent, which is steeper and higher than a simple H* and preceded by a low F0 target.

Consider the sentence in example (1), repeated here:

(3) Joan spread butter on her toast more generously than ...

The ways to continue this sentence can vary in syntactic structure as illustrated in (1), but also in the contrasts which are expressed. The most complete continuation, a full clause, could contain a single contrast with the initial clause (e.g., the subject contrast in *Marie spread butter on her toast*) or could include contrasts with multiple phrases (e.g., *Marie spread jam on her croissant*). Contrasts with single elements in the initial clause could also be expressed by smaller structures, though, such as bare NP remnants (e.g., *Marie/jam/her bagel*), PPs (*on her bagel*), or VP Ellipsis (*Marie did*). Each of these continuations include at least one phrase that is contrastively focused, as it provides an alternative to a specific phrase in the initial clause.

There are also ways to continue the sentence that do not contain direct contrasts with the initial clause, as in *Joan spread butter on her toast more generously than Marie expected [that she would]*, which can occur with or without the material in square brackets. Similarly, the comparative syntax can be followed with an adverb alone (e.g., *more generously than usual*) or another time phrase. In both of these cases, we are not comparing one spreading event with another while swapping out contrasting participants, but comparing the generous spreading event with prior expectations or prior events. Thus the NPs and PPs are not direct alternatives within a similar structure and do not contrast with any specific first-clause constituents.

In the experiments that follow, all examples contain single contrasts with phrases in the initial clause. Thus they contain pairs of NPs that are contrastively focused. The corpus study contains examples like that as well as non-contrastive examples, and explores some of the properties of contrasted phrases.

1.2 Ellipsis processing

This project, which focused on comparative bare NP ellipsis sentences, draws upon earlier work on ellipsis sentences in general and their processing. Primary questions are whether comparative bare NP ellipsis sentences have an object bias and respond to the manipulation of prosodic prominence, which might be expected based on prior results.

Ellipsis sentences have long been a topic of interest in syntax due to their interesting property of having meaning expressed by missing or null structure, as in (4).

(4) Jim likes gumdrops ...
a. and Bill does too. (VP Ellipsis)
b. and Bill, jelly beans. (Gapping)
c. more than Bill. (Comparative bare NP ellipsis)

In each of these examples, a complete initial clause is followed by a clause which elides words or phrases which are identical to contents of the initial clause. In (4a), the meaning is that Bill also likes gumdrops, so the entire VP *[likes gumdrops]* can be considered to be copied in below the auxiliary verb or to be cut from the phonology on identity with the previous VP. In (4b), a gapping example, only the verb *likes* is missing. In (4c), either the VP is missing with no auxiliary verb to mark its lack (if the meaning is that Bill also likes gumdrops), or the subject and verb are missing (if Jim also likes Bill, just less than he likes gumpdrops). Syntactic treatments of ellipsis (e.g., Ross 1967, 1970; Sag 1980; Merchant 2001; Johnson 2001) vary in whether they consider the elided material to be copied from the first clause or deleted in the second.

In ellipsis sentences, the remnants of ellipsis, which are the audible elements in the ellipsis clause like *Bill* and *jelly beans* in (4b), are focused and accented (Kuno 1976; Johnson 2008; Rooth 1992a, 1992b; Sag 1980). Rooth (1992b) points out that the elided portions of the clause would be deaccented if they were pronounced, since they have to be given information. Processing studies following up on this point have found that ambiguous ellipsis structures change in interpretation based on the position of accents or focus particles within the first clause, signaling what upcoming contrast to expect (e.g., Frazier & Clifton 1998; Carlson 2001, 2002, 2013; Carlson & Harris 2018; Harris & Carlson 2018; Carlson et al. 2009; Frazier, Clifton & Carlson 2007; Stolterfoht et al. 2007; Paterson et al. 2007; Hoeks, Redeker & Hendriks 2009). For example, in the sluicing sentence in (5), accenting the first indefinite phrase *some tourist* vs. the later one *someone* affected which NP listeners took the wh-word *who* to contrast with (Frazier & Clifton 1998), with more listeners choosing the accented phrase as the contrast.

(5) Some tourist suspected that the hotelkeeper was hiding someone. Guess who?

Stolterfoht et al. (2007) showed both that the presence and placement of the focus particle *nur* 'only' in German affected the interpretation of bare argument ellipsis sentences as in (6), and also that in the absence of the particle an object bias was present.

(6) Am Dienstag hat (nur) der Direktor (nur) den Schüler getadelt,
on Tuesday has (only) the$_{NOM}$ principal (only) the$_{ACC}$ pupil criticized,
und nicht {der Lehrer/den Lehrer}.
and not the$_{NOM}$/the$_{ACC}$ teacher
"On Tuesday, (only) the principal criticized (only) the pupil, and {the teacher didn't criticize the pupil/the principal didn't criticize the teacher}."

If the focus particle was placed before the earlier NP with the same case as the remnant, then processing either the nominative (subject) or accusative (object) remnant was easy. If the focus particle was not present, error rates were higher and event-related potentials (ERPs) on the remnant phrase *not the teacher* showed additional processing load, especially when the remnant was disambiguated to contrast with the subject instead of the object. Similarly, Carlson et al. (2009) showed that ambiguous English sluicing sentences were sensitive to the position of accent but also had an object bias in interpretation.

Lechner (2004, 2008) claims that both the object and subject interpretations of NP remnants of comparative ellipsis have the same amount of inaudible structure, as does Reinhart (1991), though in a different direction: Lechner suggests complete clausal structures and Reinhart favors simple NPs in both cases. On either theory, structural economy considerations should not affect interpretations (i.e., an object bias based on the object interpretation containing less structure than the subject interpretation). Further, Frazier & Clifton (2001) and Martin & McElree (2008, 2009)[2] have shown that longer structures inside ellipsis do not result in much additional processing difficulty compared to shorter structures, suggesting that whatever mechanism restores structure in ellipsis resolution is cost-free. For all of these reasons, then, any bias in the interpretation of bare NP comparative ellipsis sentences seems unlikely to be based on syntactic economy.

1.3 Previous ellipsis corpus work

There have been several previous corpus studies on ellipsis structures, though none concentrating specifically on comparative ellipsis. Corpus studies like this can show us how common particular structures are compared to others, as in comparatives with more or less ellipsis; unambiguous examples can also show how common particular interpretations of structures are. These frequency counts can

---

[2] Martin & McElree found that some types of complex structures lowered accuracy but not the speed of processing, which they take to argue against copying analyses of ellipsis resolution in favor of direct access in memory.

then be important in deciding whether frequency plays a role in explaining processing biases.

In early work, Hardt (1997) found just under 650 examples of VP Ellipsis within parts of the Wall Street Journal and Brown corpus portions of the Penn Treebank (Marcus et al. 1993) automatically; later hand-annotation led him to conclude that this method had found close to half of the possible VP Ellipsis examples that were present. Bos & Spenader (2011) conducted a later corpus study of VP Ellipsis within all 25 sections of the Wall Street Journal corpus within the Penn Treebank, finding 487 examples (plus some related but distinct ellipsis types). They identified a number of different sub-types of the construction, including VP Ellipsis in comparatives, pseudogapping and comparative sub-deletion, instances of subject-auxiliary inversion, and antecedent-contained deletion. Their most relevant finding is that VP Ellipsis is quite common within comparative and equative structures, making up around 30% of their total examples, though much of the syntactic literature on VP Ellipsis concentrates on its relatively rare use in conjoined structures with *and*.

Miller (2014) conducted a corpus study of pseudogapping sentences with NP object remnants in the Contemporary Corpus of American English (COCA, Davis 2008). He used search strings of auxiliary verbs followed by NPs to find 1415 examples of the structure. His primary finding is that pseudogapping is overwhelmingly more common in comparative structures than non-comparative ones, with 97% of the examples being in comparatives. Many of the comparatives he found used the conjunction *as*, either alone or in phrases like *as much as*, while some used *more than*, *more* [Adverb] *than* or other constructions. His data set thus overlaps with ours in part but also includes non-overlapping structures. He then surveyed the properties of non-comparative pseudogapping vs. comparative pseudogapping, such as the types of subjects and objects. He takes the overall findings to argue against the reducibility of pseudogapping to a sub-type of VP Ellipsis. Hoeksema (2006) examined a smaller corpus of pseudogapping examples (227, including those from Levin 1986), and similarly found that they are more common in comparatives than elsewhere. Pseudogapping examples in comparatives were also rated much higher than non-comparative examples in a short rating study, suggesting marginal grammatical status for non-comparative pseudogapping.

These previous corpus studies overlap to some extent with our corpus study, in that they include examples of VP ellipsis and pseudogapping within comparative structures. But while prior studies were designed to find only ellipsis structures, our study searched for comparative constructions and then looked for the possible presence and type of ellipsis within them. This allows us to compare the frequency not only of different types of ellipsis, but to also compare the frequency of each ellipsis type with complete clauses in the same contexts. Our study is also larger, with over 4000 sentences analyzed and over 2500 sentences with ellipsis. Finally, our study is the only one to concentrate specifically on comparative sentences with and without ellipsis. This makes our corpus study the most directly relevant to the processing studies.

2 Experiment 1

This experiment is a written questionnaire on the interpretation of ambiguous comparative bare NP ellipsis sentences. The main question was what interpretation was preferred for these ambiguous ellipsis sentences. The second issue was whether varying the similarity of NPs in the first clause to the remnant (post-*than*) NP, i.e. lexical parallelism, could affect interpretive preferences. This experiment is based on a similar but smaller study in Carlson (2002).

The idea of varying parallelism came originally from studies of other ellipsis types in Carlson (2002), starting with gapping and replacives. In these other ellipsis sentences, similarities and differences between the NPs that could contrast with each other had substantial effects on interpretation, due in part to the increased comparability of the remnant and a first-clause NP. If ambiguous bare NP comparatives behave like these other ellipsis sentences, then lexical parallelism should influence interpretation. Also, we predict an object bias in interpretation due to a default expectation of focus in object position, as in other ellipsis sentences (e.g., Stolterfoht et al. 2007; Frazier & Clifton 1998; Carlson et al. 2009; Harris & Carlson 2018).

2.1 Method

2.1.1 Materials

The experimental items were 24 comparative bare NP ellipsis sentences as in (7), in three lexical parallelism conditions each.

(7)
a. Theo respected her more than Wally.   (subject parallelism)
b. Theo respected Kenny more than Wally. (neutral parallelism)
c. She respected Theo more than Wally.   (object parallelism)

The sentences were based on the items in a similar experiment in Carlson (2002), with some editing to increase uniformity, plus an additional 6 items to bring up the total number. The parallelism conditions were created by varying properties of the first-clause subject and object, while the final NP remnant was always a proper name like *Wally* in (7). In subject parallelism, the subject was a proper name matching the gender of the remnant, and the object was a different-gender pronoun in half of the items and a definite description in the other half (one item used an indefinite description instead). Most of the definite descriptions were ambiguous in gender (e.g., *the guest, the patient*) though some were likely stereotypically gendered. Object parallelism conditions had the same characteristics, but with the proper name that matched the remnant in object position, and the pronoun or definite description in subject position. Neutral parallelism conditions had three matching-gender proper names. These small featural differences and similarities in NPs are likely to increase the semantic and pragmatic felicity of contrasts between NPs, which could influence comprehension preferences for the ambiguous remnant.

The comparative part of the constructions used *more than*, as in (7), or "more [Adverb] than" with a range of different adverbs. Most of them were among the most common adverbs in this position as determined by the corpus work in Sect. 4. The three adverbs which were not among the top 26 adverbs in American English in this construction were *severely, thoroughly*, and *regularly*. The verbs in the sentences were all transitive ones taking animate NPs as subjects and objects. That allowed the final NP to be a reasonable contrast with both the subject and the object. A full list of the items can be found in Appendix A.

Each sentence was followed by a comprehension question, which was either *What happened?* or *Which is true?* Both of these questions occurred with other item types as well. The answers were complete paraphrases of the meanings of the comparatives, varying by condition as in (8), with the items repeated from (7) and parenthesized labels for clarity:

(8)

a. Theo respected her more than Wally. (subject parallelism)
  i. Theo respected her more than Theo respected Wally. (object answer)
  ii. Theo respected her more than Wally respected her. (subject answer)
b. Theo respected Kenny more than Wally. (neutral parallelism)
  i. Theo respected Kenny more than Theo respected Wally. (object answer)
  ii. Theo respected Kenny more than Wally respected Kenny. (subject answer)
c. She respected Theo more than Wally. (object parallelism)
  i. She respected Theo more than she respected Wally. (object answer)
  ii. She respected Theo more than Wally respected Theo. (subject answer)

The order of the answers was balanced so that object and subject answers appeared first equally often across the experiment.

2.1.2 Participants

A total of 48 participants participated in the experiment. They were paid $3.00 for their participation. They self-reported as native English speakers after completing the study and being assured that they would be paid regardless of their native language. The responses to the 37 unambiguous filler items were examined, and data was dropped from all participants who answered more than 2 of these items incorrectly (those with less than 95% accuracy). Data from one additional participant who missed 2 unambiguous items and failed to answer 1 experimental item was also dropped. This left 41 participants whose data was analyzed.

2.1.3 Procedure

The 24 experimental items were combined with 20 items from an unrelated experiment on verb attachment, 20 items from an unrelated experiment on NP conjunction and relative clauses, 15 fillers with ambiguous pronoun reference, 9 fillers with unambiguous comparatives, 10 fillers with unambiguous conjunction and/or relative clause structures, 10 unambiguous fillers with long final temporal adverbial phrases, and 8 assorted unambiguous fillers for a total of 116 items. These were assembled into 6 questionnaire lists in pseudorandomized orders, with no two consecutive items of the same type and conditions spread throughout the list. The lists rotated through the conditions in a Latin Square design with only one condition of each experimental item present and equal numbers of each condition per list.

Participants were solicited on Amazon Mechanical Turk (AMT) and clicked through to a Qualtrics site for the experiment. They returned to AMT to enter a code provided at the end of the experiment in order to receive payment. A short introduction to the experiment on Qualtrics explained the task they were carrying out, which involved comprehension questions following each sentence.

2.2 Results and discussion

In the written questionnaire, the subject parallelism condition received 65% subject interpretations; the neutral parallelism condition got 33% subject interpretations; and the object parallelism condition, 15% subject interpretations.

The data was analyzed using a linear mixed-effects model with a binomial link function (Bates, Maechler, Bolker & Walker 2015). The dependent variable was the participant response disambiguating the stimuli as an object or subject

Tab. 1: Statistical analysis of experiment 1 results

	Estimate (β)	Std. Error	z value
Intercept	−0.78	0.25	−3.10
subject vs. neutral, object parallelism	3.18	0.26	12.38
neutral vs. subject parallelism	1.27	0.25	5.05

comparative (0 = object comparative response; 1 = subject comparative response). The independent variable was parallelism type (neutral parallelism, subject parallelism, object parallelism), and this three-level factor was helmert coded. The subject parallelism condition (coded as = 0.5) was compared with the mean of the neutral and object parallelism conditions (each coded as = −0.25), included in the model as the fixed effect CompBiasContrastCoding1a. The neutral parallelism condition (coded as = 0.5) was compared with the object parallelism condition (coded as = −0.5), included in the model as the fixed effect CompBiasContrastCoding1b. These two comparisons were each introduced into the model as fixed effects. Additionally, the model included the maximal random effects structure justified by design that would converge (Barr, Levy, Scheepers & Tily 2013): random intercepts by items and by participants and non-correlated random slopes by participants for one of the fixed effects.[3] Comparison of this complete model with models lacking each of the fixed effects revealed significant effects of subject vs. neutral and object parallelism ($\chi^2(1) = 198.48, p < .001$) and of neutral vs. object parallelism ($\chi^2(1) = 20.97, p < .001$). The model results are shown in Table 1.

The differences between lexical parallelism conditions are significant and in the expected directions: subject parallelism was the most likely to favor the subject interpretation and object parallelism was the least. This shows that the variation in the form of NPs did influence interpretation. The overall level of subject interpretations and the fact that neutral parallelism led to under 50% subject interpretations suggests an overall bias toward the object interpretation. Even subject parallelism did not exclusively favor the subject interpretation.

The results show a relatively wide spread of interpretation preferences compared to some ellipsis types, such as gapping in double object sentences (Carlson 2001) or VP Ellipsis with embedded complement clauses (Frazier, Clifton & Carlson 2007). If there were a structural difference between the interpretations, we might have expected a stronger bias in interpretations. The results are thus con-

---

[3] The specific R syntax was (dataModel2 = glmer(dv~ (CompBiasContrastCoding1a + CompBiasContrastCoding1b) + (1 + CompBiasContrastCoding1b||sub) + (1|item), data = dataSet, family="binomial")).

sistent with the syntactic claim (e.g., Lechner 2004, 2008) that comparative bare NP ellipsis involves the same amount of structure for subject and object interpretations. Of course, structural economy may not be an issue in ellipsis sentences anyway, as according to Martin & McElree (2008) and Frazier & Clifton (2001), additional structure within ellipsis does not lead to significant added time or difficulty in processing.

The lexical parallelism manipulation could be seen as a minor difference in some sense, since it only changes lexical features of NPs within a sentence, not the overall sentence structure. On the other hand, it is likely that at least the name vs. pronoun variation in half of the items changed the implicit prosody assigned to sentences, with pronouns more likely to be deaccented than names and therefore less likely to participate in contrasts. Further, all of the lexical parallelism variation affected the semantic comparability of NPs, in the sense that compared items need a certain level of similarity to be appropriate alternatives to each other (Umbach 2004; Zeevat 2004) while not overlapping in identity. The lexical parallelism factor can be seen then as partly a semantic manipulation affecting how reasonable each pair of NPs is as a contrastive pair (and conversely, how unreasonable another pair is). The effectiveness of lexical parallelism in these ambiguous bare NP comparative sentences shows that they pattern with gapping and replacive ellipsis sentences in responding to such manipulations.

As noted earlier, a written questionnaire in Carlson (2002) used slightly modified versions of 18 of the items with the same type of parallelism manipulation. In that experiment, subject parallelism led to 68% subject interpretations, neutral parallelism to 35%, and object parallelism to 18%. The similar results with an entirely different set of participants is reassuring, suggesting that the effect is replicable.

3 Experiment 2

This experiment is an auditory questionnaire on the same sentences as Experiment 1, varying the position of accent on first-clause NPs. This also follows up on a related experiment in Carlson (2002). In this study, the questions are whether contrastive accent placement within the first clause affects interpretation, and how much lexical parallelism still influences preferences. It could be that an overt marker of focus structure like accent placement would outweigh the featural manipulation of NPs, or that both factors could have roughly additive effects on interpretation. Since remnants have to contrast with first-clause NPs, we would expect accenting a specific first-clause NP to increase interpretations where that NP contrasts with the remnant: subject accents should increase subject interpretations, and object accents should increase object interpretations. If true, this would show comparative ellipsis patterning with a number of other ellipsis types (such as gapping, VP Ellipsis, sluicing, replacives) in responding to overt manipulation of focus marking (e.g., Frazier & Clifton 1998; Carlson 2001, 2002, 2013; Carlson et al. 2009; Stolterfoht et al. 2007).

3.1 Method

3.1.1 Materials

The experimental items were recorded versions of 24 bare NP ellipsis sentences as in (9), in three lexical parallelism conditions and two prosodic conditions. The position of contrastive accents is indicated by upper-case letters.

(9)

a. THEO respected her more than WALLY.   (subject parallelism, subject accent)
b. Theo respected HER more than WALLY.   (subject parallelism, object accent)
c. THEO respected Kenny more than WALLY. (neutral parallelism, subject accent)
d. Theo respected KENNY more than WALLY. (neutral parallelism, object accent)
e. SHE respected Theo more than WALLY.   (object parallelism, subject accent)
f. She respected THEO more than WALLY.   (object parallelism, object accent)

The lexical parallelism conditions were exactly the same as described in Experiment 1, since the same sentences were used. The audio recordings varied whether the first-clause subject or object received a contrastive L+H* accent; the remnant phrase was always accented. All sentences were recorded by the author, who is ToBI-trained and experienced in producing prosodic contours, and then analyzed for consistency with the intended prosody. Any recordings that were disfluent or did not adhere to the planned prosody were re-recorded. Acoustic measurements that substantiate the prosodic contours are shown in Table 2.

As seen in Table 2, subject NPs were always longer in duration when contrastively accented than not, and the same for object NPs. Subject NPs were also always higher in F0 when accented than unaccented, and the same is true for objects. Remnant NPs showed less variation in duration and pitch, as they were accented in all conditions as well as being the final words in each sentence. The sentences generally had a small intermediate phrase (ip) boundary on the object, not accompanied by a pause but by a slight slowing of speech and a low F0 consistent with a L- boundary tone.

Tab. 2: Average acoustic measurements of NPs in experiment 2 items (duration in ms, F0 in Hz)

	Subject Dur.	Subject F0 Peak	Object Dur.	Object F0 Peak	Remnant Dur.	Remnant F0 Peak
Subj Par, Subj Accent	393	311	339	179	498	218
Subj Par, Object Accent	305	216	442	269	497	214
Neutral Par, Subj Accent	393	304	377	170	492	217
Neutral Par, Object Accent	320	205	450	266	506	212
Object Par, Subj Accent	369	305	363	169	496	213
Object Par, Object Accent	303	205	445	271	489	211

3.1.2 Participants

A total of 59 subjects participated in the experiment. They were paid $3.12 for their participation. They self-reported as native English speakers after completing the study and being assured that they would be paid regardless of their native language. The responses to 12 unambiguous filler items were examined, and data was dropped from all participants who answered more than 1 of these items incorrectly (those with less than 92% accuracy). Data from 6 other participants, the last ones to complete each list, was also dropped in order to approach equal numbers of participants per list. This left 47 participants whose data was analyzed.

3.1.3 Procedure

The 24 experimental items were combined with 20 items from an unrelated experiment on verb attachment, 20 fillers based on an unrelated experiment on causal interpretation, 15 fillers with ambiguous pronoun reference, 8 fillers demanding sentence completions, and 12 more assorted fillers for a total of 99 items. These were assembled into 12 questionnaire lists in two pseudorandomized orders, with no two consecutive items of the same type. Each list rotated between the conditions in a Latin Square design, with only one condition of each experimental item present and equal numbers of each condition per list.

Participants were solicited on Amazon Mechanical Turk (AMT) and clicked through to a Qualtrics site for the experiment. They returned to AMT to enter a code provided at the end of the experiment.

3.2 Results and discussion

The results of the auditory experiment are shown in Fig. 1, which indicates the percentage of subject interpretations in each condition. The results of the Experiment 1 written questionnaire (labeled Written) are included in the graph for comparison purposes.

The data was analyzed using a linear mixed-effects model with a binomial link function (Bates, Maechler, Bolker & Walker 2015). The dependent variable was the participant response disambiguating the stimuli as an object or subject comparative (0 = object comparative response; 1 = subject comparative response). The independent variables were accent position (Subject vs. Object accent) and parallelism type (neutral parallelism, subject parallelism, object parallelism). The accent position variable was contrast coded (Subject accent = 0.5; Object accent = -0.5) while the parallelism factor was helmert coded. The subject parallelism conditions (coded as = 0.5) were compared with the mean of the neutral and object parallelism conditions (each coded as = –0.25), included in the model as the fixed effect CompBiasContrastCoding1a. The neutral parallelism conditions (coded as = 0.5) were compared with the object parallelism conditions (coded as = –0.5), included in the model as the fixed effect CompBiasContrastCoding1b. These comparisons were each introduced into the model as fixed effects, with interactions between the accent position variable and each of the lexical parallelism variables. Additionally, the model included the maximal random effects structure justified by design that would converge (Barr, Levy, Scheepers & Tily 2013): random in-

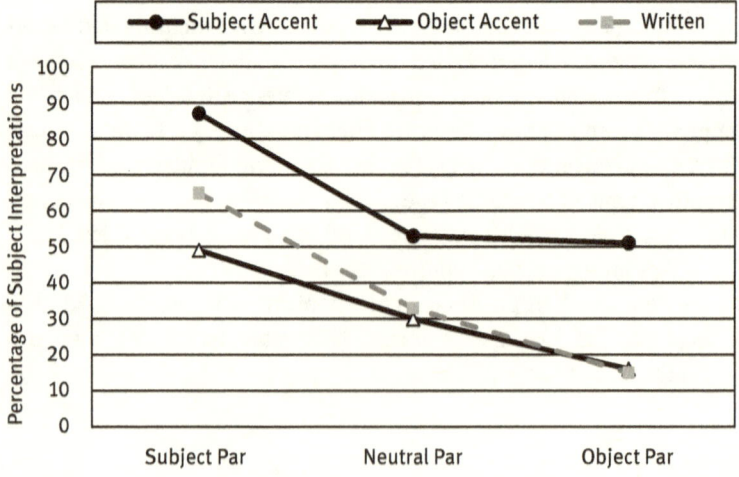

Fig. 1: Results of Experiment 2

Tab. 3: Statistical analysis of experiment 2 results

	Estimate	Std. Error	z value
Intercept	−0.11	0.17	−0.61
subject vs. neutral/object parallelism	2.29	0.22	10.20
neutral vs. object parallelism	0.52	0.18	2.94
accent position	−1.73	0.14	−11.21
accent position x (subject vs. neutral/object parallelism)	0.88	0.44	2.01
accent position x (neutral vs. object parallelism)	−0.85	0.35	−2.43

tercepts by items and by participants.[4] Comparison of this complete model with models lacking each of the fixed effects and the interactions revealed significant effects of subject vs. neutral and object parallelism ($\chi^2(1) = 123.11, p < .001$), of neutral vs. object parallelism ($\chi^2(1) = 8.81, p = .003$), and of accent position ($\chi^2(1) = 146.56, p < .001$). Additionally, the interaction between neutral vs. object parallelism and accent position was significant ($\chi^2(1) = 9.23, p = .002$); the interaction between accent position and subject vs. neutral and object parallelism was also significant ($\chi^2(1) = 4.15, p = .042$). The model results are shown in Table 3.

The position of accent had a significant effect on interpretations, with subject accent leading to at least 20% more subject interpretations in every parallelism condition than object accent. Listeners therefore were more willing to consider the two contrastively accented NPs to be the contrast expressed by the construction than when one NP was unaccented. The lexical parallelism manipulation also continued to affect interpretations, with subject parallelism leading to more subject interpretations than neutral parallelism, and neutral more than object. Similarity between NPs in form and reference increased the likelihood of choosing them as the contrasting pair.

The significant interaction between accent position and neutral vs. object parallelism means that with subject accent, the two parallelism conditions were not very different. With object accent, though, neutral parallelism increased subject interpretations over object parallelism. This suggests that the accent position might be a stronger influence than parallelism, since conflicting parallelism couldn't outweigh the accent position favoring the subject interpretation. The interaction between accent position and subject parallelism vs. the mean of neutral and object parallelism reflects the larger difference between accent conditions

---

[4] The specific R syntax was (dataModel6 = glmer(dv~(CompBiasContrastCoding1a +CompBiasContrastCoding1b) * AccentPositionContrastCoding2 + (1|subject) + (1|item), data = dataSet, family="binomial").

with subject parallelism than elsewhere: there was a 40% boost in subject interpretations with subject accent and subject parallelism, vs. around a 25% subject accent boost for the other parallelism conditions. In general, though, the results show that both accent position and parallelism influenced interpretation.

The object accent results were quite similar to the written questionnaire results from Experiment 1, with the largest difference between them showing up in the subject parallelism condition. This suggests that the object accent pattern was similar to the implicit prosody that readers imposed on the sentences in the written questionnaire. Put another way, the prosodic pattern with focus on the object got essentially the same interpretation results as written sentences in which readers were likely to assume a default focus structure. This suggests that object focus and implicit object accent were generally expected by readers, except in the one condition (subject parallelism) where the form of the NPs made that interpretation somewhat less likely or natural.

As with the written questionnaire, a similar experiment was carried out in Carlson (2002) on a modified set of 18 of these items. In that experiment, the subject interpretation percentages with subject accent were 79% with subject parallelism, 41% with neutral, and 30% with object parallelism; with object accent, the percentages were 56%, 25%, and 8%, respectively. Therefore, both accent placement and lexical parallelism had similar effects in this prior study, again showing that the current effects are replicable.

4 Comparative Corpus construction, results, and analysis

The primary questions that we wished to answer through creating and studying this corpus were: whether bare NP comparative ellipsis is common compared to other possible structures; whether NPs after the comparative *than* have object roles more often than subject roles, or the reverse; whether contrasted NPs within comparatives tend to have similar features (lexical parallelism); and whether subject NPs show up more in disambiguated structures such as VP Ellipsis or full sentences than they do in ambiguous ellipsis structures. Part of the motivation for this study, then, was to contextualize the processing results from Experiments 1–2, in addition to understanding more about the use and form of comparatives in general. If indeed comparative bare NP ellipsis were found to be most common with an object role for the NP, then one could potentially explain the object bias in processing as a consequence of that structure's frequency, or explain the object bias in both frequency and processing as a result of another factor. If, on the other hand, the frequency of object interpretations for bare NP ellipsis were to be equal to that for subjects or less, then the explanation for the object bias in processing would need to come from elsewhere.

4.1 Construction of the corpus

The source for the comparatives corpus was the Contemporary Corpus of American English (COCA) created by Mark Davies (2008-). COCA contains 520 million words of American English from a balanced set of genres, specifically academic, fiction, magazine, news, and spoken genres, with examples drawn from the time period from 1990 to 2015 at the time of extraction. We extracted all sentences using the search string "more [Adverb] than" (e.g., *more often than*) for the 26 most frequent adverbs in that position.

Upon examination, it became clear that the adverbs *so*, *now*, and *even* did not behave like the other adverbs in this environment, forming constructions with different properties,[5] so sentences with those adverbs were removed. We also removed examples with idioms and set phrases that we discovered in the data, such as *more often than not* and *more often than that*. Finally, we found that some authors or speakers produced multiple examples of the construction within a single text; we kept only the first example from a single author for a single adverb. We felt that the particular quirks of a single writer or speaker should not be allowed to skew the results too much, especially for the less common adverbs. Sometimes there were multiple examples from within the same publication on the same date, such as a newspaper or journal issue, but when they seemed to be on different topics they were considered to be from different texts.

After these exclusions, there were 4423 comparative constructions remaining in the extracted corpus. These were hand-coded for the syntactic category of the following constituent, the overall syntactic structure following *than*, the structural role of contrasted Noun Phrases, and properties of the NPs. Ungrammatical or unclassifiable instances (often due to insufficient prior or following context) were removed during this analysis, leaving 4393 analyzed examples. These ex-

---

[5] With *so*, sentences often referred back to a previous adverb elsewhere and the comparative syntax was often preceded by a comma: e.g., *Our front line guys really have the ability to shoot, more so than we'd had in the past*. With *now*, there were fixed expressions like *more now than ever*, and most examples contrasted *now* with a following time phrase: e.g., *I love him more now than when I first met him*. With *even*, many examples were an intensification of a previous *more than* construction, equivalent in meaning to *even more than*: e.g, *More than a college, more even than an educational institution*....

amples contained 23 remaining adverbs, from the most frequent (*often*, with 944 examples) down to the least (*broadly*, with 37). Appendix B shows the full set of adverbs in order by frequency, as well as the raw frequency of the major structures following *than* for each one. The adverbs vary a good deal in how often they appear in comparative constructions, with *often* and the other top 5 adverbs accounting for over half of the examples. A striking feature of the data is the sheer prevalence of NP-only examples, which are the most common structure for all but one adverb (*sharply*, #20).

The particular search phrase that we chose does restrict this data set. There are various types of comparative structures which do not fit this schema and thus are not present in this corpus, including similar structures using *less* instead of *more*. The set excludes any comparatives without an adverb, as in the simple phrases *more than* or *less than*. Other excluded comparatives are those which incorporate nouns (e.g., *more* Xs *than* Ys...), and those which use the morphologically comparative forms of simple adjectives instead of *more* or *less* (e.g., *taller than*, *older than*, etc.). Therefore, it is possible and even likely that there are other sub-types of comparatives which may have different properties than those in this corpus. On the other hand, this data set is relatively robust compared to other ellipsis corpora while remaining of a manageable size for hand-annotation of its properties. The data set also includes some examples in which *more* is modified by an additional degree adverb like *much* or *far*. Bos & Spenader (2011) identified a wide range of patterns of comparative constructions based on their Wall Street Journal corpus, which could be used to extend the current set in future work.

4.2 General syntactic structures and their frequency

The data was initially divided into groups based on the initial syntactic phrase after the comparative *than*. Then we turned to annotating the overall syntactic structure that appeared after the comparative. The table in Appendix B shows an overview of how each adverb behaved in this construction, but in what follows we will concentrate mostly on the full set of comparative examples instead of separating out data by adverb.

There were 10 basic syntactic structures that we found in our corpus. Table 4 shows an example from the corpus for each of the structures we found along with their labels (and abbreviated labels in parentheses). In the ellipsis examples, material in angle brackets is added and crossed out to show what was elided. The NP-only examples are considered to be ellipsis and labeled as bare NPs, and we give examples of both subject and object versions. Structures in Table 4 are listed

Tab. 4: Examples of each labeled post-comparative structure (in order by structure frequency)

Structure Label	Example
Bare NP, subject	These days, even the best movies lose their flavor **more quickly than** matinee Mike and Ikes <del>lose their flavor</del>.
Bare NP, object	In such matters, Victorians of her class used euphemisms **more often than** <del>they used</del> direct language.
Verb Phrase Ellipsis (VPE)	Well, a new study suggests men actually do get sick **more often than** women do <del>get sick</del>.
Clausal Ellipsis	Television changes, but it changes **more slowly than** we think <del>that it changes</del>.
Adverb Phrase (AdvP)	Companies are taking their giving efforts **more seriously than** ever before.
Full Sentence	Most of us buy food much **more often than** we buy clothes.
Prepositional Phrase (PP)	Horrible things seem to happen to children even **more often than** in our own narratives.
VP	Also, Russians use the word Mama **more frequently than** probably is healthy for grown-ups.
Inverted VPE	People with less power typically see the world **more clearly than** do their bosses <del>see the world</del>.
Subordinate Clause (SC)	Edward's heart pounded **more heavily than** when he exercised hard.
Pseudogapping (Pseud.)	Students discussed editing in their responses far **more often than** they did <del>discuss</del> revision.

in order of their overall frequency, with bare NPs also separated out by the function of the NP.

Most of the structures labeled in Table 4 are canonical syntactic categories or well-studied types of ellipsis. A few warrant additional discussion, though.

The structures labeled as Pseudogapping here are only those with remnant NPs following the position of the elided verb, usually objects. Similar examples in which auxiliary verbs preceded an elided verb but the remnants were PPs or AdvPs were classified instead as VP Ellipsis (e.g., *Gerstner also recruited far more aggressively than IBM had <del>recruited</del> in the past*). Johnson (2001, 2009) would classify these as a sub-type of VP Ellipsis, though Levin (1986) distinguishes Pseudogapping as having separate restrictions on it. Miller's (2014) corpus study of Pseudogapping centered on examples with NP remnants for the purposes of searching, but he notes that non-NP remnants are possible as well. Interestingly, the types of examples he searched for were much more frequent in comparative constructions than elsewhere, to the extent that 1368 or 97% of his examples were in comparatives of some type. Bos & Spenader (2011) called these same structures comparative sub-deletion, but then did not distinguish further between them and other pseudogapping examples in further analyses. Due to this inconsistency in labeling, we are treating them as instances of VP Ellipsis instead of Pseudogapping.

Inverted VPE is a category we had not expected to find beforehand, but which emerged as we classified examples which had an auxiliary verb immediately after *than*. Those examples turned out to include both simple VPs as well as these ellipsis examples with an auxiliary verb moved before the subject. Bos & Spenader (2011) also found examples of the inverted VPE structure in their VP Ellipsis corpus, in comparatives as well as after *as, so, neither/nor*, and in tag questions. As they point out, some of these examples would be impossible to reconstruct grammatically with overt material, unlike usual ellipsis structures.

Finally, Clausal Ellipsis is the term we are using for examples in which the material which would contrast with the pre-comparative clause is elided completely, leaving a higher embedding clause. These used a range of embedding verbs such as *think, believe, expect, intend, prefer*, and *admit*. Bos & Spenader (2011) also encountered these structures in their VP Ellipsis corpus study, calling them predicative ellipsis occurring with verbs that aren't auxiliaries or modals. They note that only comparative/equative sentences appear to allow this construction, which is rarely discussed in the ellipsis literature, and suggest further study of the structure.

Figure 2 shows the percentage of all corpus examples that have each labeled structure.

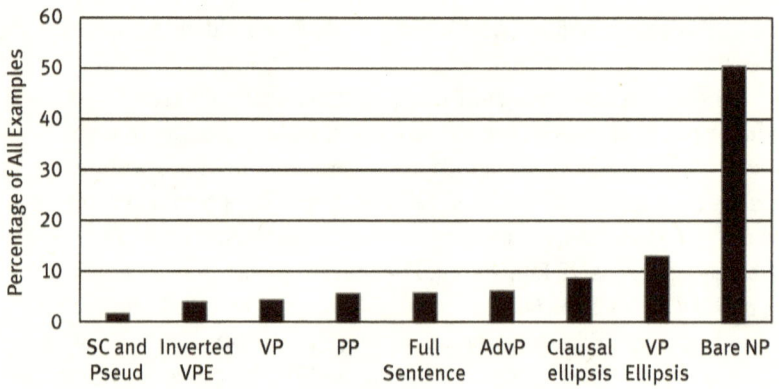

Fig. 2: Syntactic category of constituents after *Than* (N = 4393)

Bare NPs make up half of all examples, and all NP-initial structures (specifically bare NPs, VP Ellipsis, Clausal Ellipsis, full sentences, and Pseudogapping) make up over three-quarters of the data. The graph also illustrates the wide range of possible continuations for comparatives.

There is a marked tendency for NPs to be the first constituent following the comparative *than*. And within the set of examples with NPs first, the greatly preferred option is for the NP to be alone (bare NPs). This preference for the bare NP structure is interesting in light of the fact that all other NP-initial structures are less ambiguous than bare NPs, since they have an auxiliary or main verb present to clarify whether the NP is a subject or object. Further, this data shows that comparative constructions are very likely to produce ellipsis: the top three most common syntactic structures all involve ellipsis, with the most extreme ellipsis type (bare NPs) being overwhelmingly frequent, while full sentences without ellipsis make up a small minority of examples. Looking just at the NP-initial structures ($N = 3466$), which includes the categories of bare NPs, VP Ellipsis, Clausal Ellipsis, full sentences, and Pseudogapping, bare NPs form over 60% of those examples, while less than 10% are full sentences. VP Ellipsis is the second-most common structure in that set, with just under 20% of NP-initial examples.

For all NP-first examples, we categorized the NPs by their sentence role: subjects, objects, adverbials (as in time phrases like *yesterday* or *last week*, which can be arguments of verbs but are usually optional and adverbial), or ambiguous between subject and object roles. NPs in full sentences or in ellipsis structures other than bare NPs were all unambiguous in their roles due to the position of the verb. For the bare NP structures, roles could be confidently assigned in most examples using plausibility, animacy, fit with prior clause verbs, and NP features. A small minority remained ambiguous. Figure 3 illustrates the frequency of NP roles. We should note that the term "object role" is used loosely within this project, to include not only objects of simple verbs but also objects of particle or phrasal verbs (e.g., *work up* X, *call on* X, *make use of* X) and objects of prepositions. NPs with object role are basically any non-subject and non-adverbial predicate NPs.

Overall, about 90% of examples had NPs with subject roles immediately after *than*. If all of the ambiguous examples turned out to be objects, the object examples would still add up to less than 10% of the total number of examples. If the data are restricted to the bare NP examples alone, a total of 2218 items, the sentence roles remain asymmetrical. Over 80% of the bare NP examples have the subject role, around 11% have the object role, with about 2% remaining ambiguous.

One concern regarding the interpretation of this asymmetry in roles could be how often a non-subject role was possible. That is, if sentences tended to be intransitive, then subject roles might be the only ones available for NPs, making it less meaningful or surprising for subjects to dominate. To address this issue,

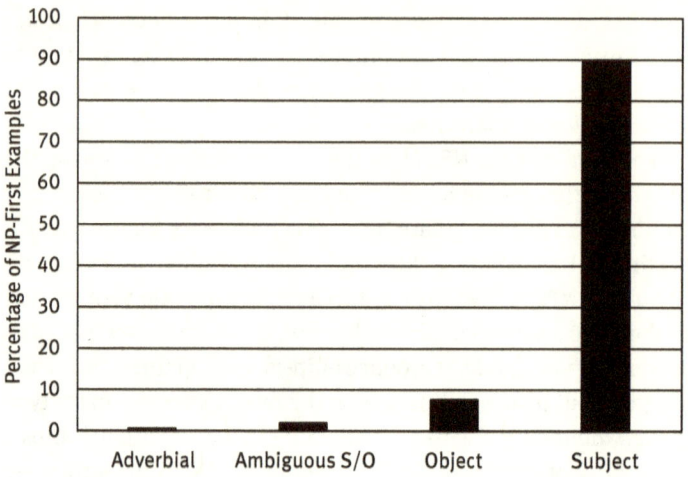

Fig. 3: Role of NP in all NP-first examples (*N* = 3466)

we annotated the availability of other NP roles first for the bare NP subject set (*N* = 1851). First, a number of examples had the comparative expression preposed, either at the start of the sentence or before at least some predicate material, which had the effect of reducing ambiguity by making the subject the only possible role or at least reducing the set of other possibilities. This was true for 111 examples (about 6%). The rest of this set had 829 examples that were intransitive and 912 transitive (with transitive meaning that there was another NP which could contrast, whether it be an actual object or in a PP). So almost half of the set was unambiguous, but the other half of items with subject contrast had actual choices for which NP would contrast. There was no reason to further annotate the set of bare NP object examples, since all of those had to have both a subject and an object or predicate NP. In the set of full sentences (*N* = 248), 67 were intransitive and the rest had multiple NPs to contrast with. Of the 63 sentences with subject contrast, only 13 of them were intransitive with no other choices. Across categories, then, subject roles were the only option in less than half of the sentences, still leaving a large group of sentences with subject contrast when other options were available.

At this point, several of the initial questions that led to the generation of this corpus have been answered. Bare NP comparative ellipsis is indeed quite common, more frequent than other NP-first alternatives. Full sentences in particular are quite rare, by contrast. Bare NP structures with the NP having the subject role are very frequent, far outweighing objects, though both exist. These facts together show that people expressing a comparative structure with the contrast involving an NP in subject role do not commonly disambiguate it, at least not syntactically.

4.3 Analysis of parallelism and contrast

In order to carry out analyses of the contrasts found in different structures as well as NP parallelism, we winnowed down the examples to those with an NP as the first constituent after *than* and a clear subject or object role for that NP. We excluded those with initial adverbial NPs, a few unclassifiable examples, ambiguous examples, and items with clausal ellipsis (because in those cases the subject after *than* was not contrastive with any first-clause NP). This left 2954 examples. Our questions in these analyses were a) what constituent(s) contrasted between the initial clause and the post-*than* material, and b) within NP contrasts, whether the NPs showed parallelism (similar semantic features, contrast markers).

First, we annotated what constituents contrasted between the pre-comparative clause and the post-*than* material. The possible constituent contrasts were subject, object, PP or adverb, and verb, and we also tracked the number of examples with multiple contrasts. The results of this annotation are in Fig. 4, which shows the relative number of instances of specific contrasts in each structure as well as the raw number of instances (items with multiple contrasts, though, are on top of the total number for each structure, because they are also counted as examples of each separate contrast).

In part, some of the results are forecast by the form of the post-*than* material. Bare NP examples can contain only single contrasts with either the subject or the

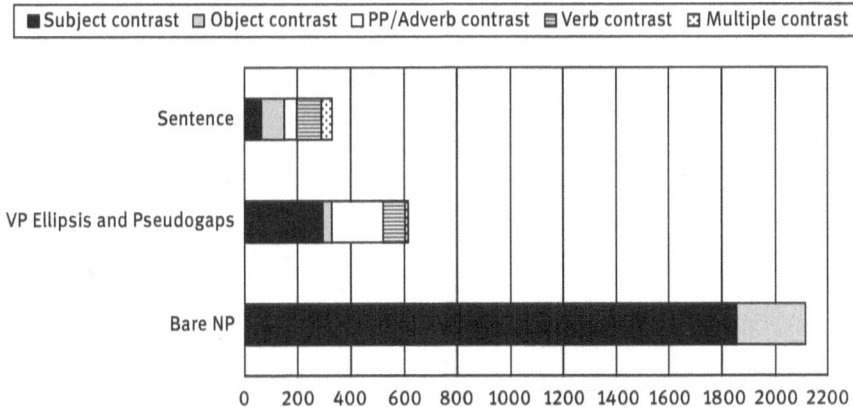

Fig. 4: Position of contrast in unambiguous NP-first examples (*N* = 2954)

object, and obviously the subject is by far the favorite. But we think the comparison between those instances and the complete sentences and other ellipsis types is interesting nonetheless. The VP Ellipsis and Pseudogapping items had the option of contrasting with any of the four constituents we annotated. In the case of verb contrast, these were contrasts with a different auxiliary verb or lack of auxiliary in the prior clause, as in *Breyer could have been questioned more closely than he was*. Object contrasts were present in the Pseudogapping examples but not VP ellipsis (due to our labeling decisions), as in *They portray women more favorably than they do men*, and PP or adverb contrasts in the VP Ellipsis examples. Overall, subject contrasts were the most frequent contrasts within these ellipsis structures at almost 50% of the examples, followed by PP/adverb contrasts (around 30%), and then auxiliary verb contrasts. Multiple contrasts were relatively rare (2%), as in *Mountain lions are able to watch humans a great deal more easily than we can observe them*, even though multiple constituents did appear after *than* which could be contrasted with.

The complete sentences, though, had the most varied repertoire of contrasts. Subject contrasts were not as prevalent in this structure (at about 25%) as either verb or object contrasts (both over 35%). Multiple contrasts were also more frequent in full sentences than in any other structure at around 16% of the sentence examples.

A speaker who wishes to express a subject or object contrast seems most likely to settle on a bare NP structure. Those expressing subject contrasts have VP Ellipsis or Pseudogapping as a distant second choice. For those expressing object contrasts, the full sentence structure is a distant second option. Even those expressing PP or adverbial contrasts, if they want to also include the subject, choose VP Ellipsis over full sentences (and if not including the subject, they go for the simple PP structure: see Fig. 2).

Turning to the parallelism analysis, we focused only on the examples with NPs after *than* which contrasted with NPs in the initial clause. We looked for similarities in form and content between the two contrasting NPs, so any examples missing enough prior context to see the entire earlier NP were eliminated. Some of the exact features tabulated were set up beforehand, while others emerged during the process of examination of the examples. We ended up looking at the prevalence across the different NP-first NP-contrast structures of NPs with the same head noun (whether it was overt or elided because it was the same); NPs with nouns in the same semantic category (e.g., different countries, companies, races); those with antonyms as the head nouns; NPs with similar adjectives on a similar scale (e.g., *large/small, rich/poor*, etc.); and NPs with one of a number of what we are calling contrast markers. Contrast markers included specific determiners, some of which came in pairs (*these/those, this/that, some/other(s), no*);

post-noun modifiers or pronominal forms like *else* (as in *everyone else*), *rest* (as in *the rest*), *other(s)*, and *one(s)*; and a small set of nouns that indicated contrasting sub-groups (e.g., *competitors, peers, predecessors, counterparts*). Examples (10–13) show the annotations applied to particular sentences.

(10) *Gifted persons* learned much more easily than *talented ones*:
same noun (second pronominalized), similar adjective, and contrast marker *one*

(11) *Opal* moved ashore much more quickly than *Andrew*:
same category of noun (names of storms)

(12) *The seeds closest to the tree* died or disappeared much more quickly than *those farther away*: same noun (second one elided), contrast marker *those*

(13) *Sunny mountain slopes* heat up much more rapidly than *shadowy valleys*:
same category of noun (landscape feature), similar adjective

Figure 5 shows the parallelism analysis results for subject contrast NPs across the major structures. The total number of examples in this analysis was 2180 due to elimination of examples that did not have enough prior or following context to fully determine the properties of both NPs. Results are shown as percentages per structure exhibiting each type of parallelism, but the N for each structure is also shown since they differ so widely. The initial part of the graph shows the total

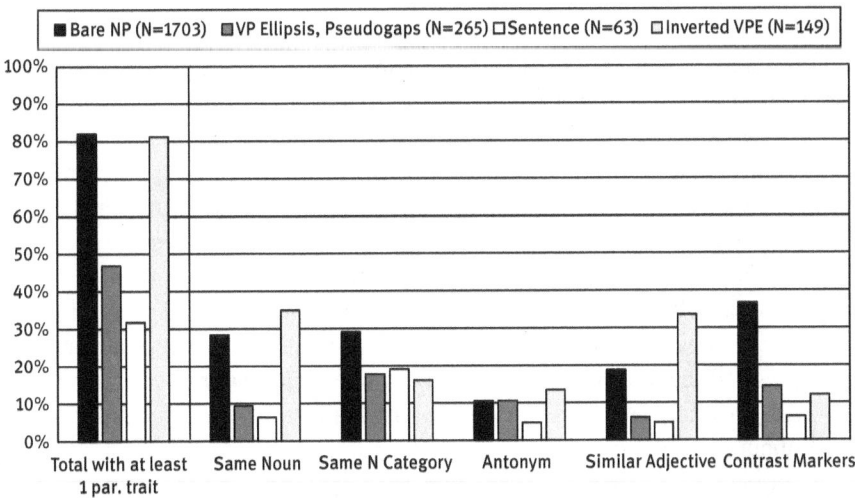

Fig. 5: Parallelism in contrasted subject NPs across structures (N = 2180)

percentage of examples showing any parallelism traits, and the rest shows the rates of the common specific traits.

The bare NP subject group had the most examples overall, and the sentences the least. Interestingly the inverted VP Ellipsis examples and the bare NP examples had the highest rates of parallelism, with slightly over 80% of each structure showing at least one of the annotated traits. Bare NPs were more likely to have the same noun category or contrast markers, while inverted VPE had more same noun and similar adjective types of parallelism. General VP Ellipsis and Pseudogapping examples exhibited parallelism a much lower proportion of the time than these structures, and sentences had very little. Although bare NPs are ambiguous, and thus parallelism could be seen as a strategy to reduce ambiguity, inverted VPE is no more ambiguous than VP Ellipsis in the normal direction or sentences. So the high rate of parallelism in inverted VPE is an issue to consider.

One might wonder whether similar parallelism was seen between non-contrasted subject NPs, in the structural categories where subject NPs could contrast with each other or not. In fact, there was not. Most of the non-contrasted subject NPs in VP Ellipsis, Pseudogapping, and sentences were pronouns, while very few of the contrasted subjects were pronouns. For sentences, 92% of the 185 non-contrastive subjects were pronouns but only 13% of the 63 contrastive subjects were pronominal; for VPE and Pseudogapping, 99% of the 297 examples with non-contrastive subjects used subject pronouns, but 21% of the 294 examples with contrastive subjects had pronouns. Most of the time, therefore, pronouns were not contrastive, and most non-contrastive subjects were expressed with pronouns instead of NPs with the parallelism features we annotated.

Turning to the contrasted objects, we completed a similar annotation of parallel traits and analysis. The number of relevant examples was much smaller, though, so the results (in Fig. 6) could be taken as less definitive.

The set of bare NPs with an object interpretation was 261, and 257 of those had enough material to analyze the object NPs. The Pseudogapping and Sentence examples with contrasted objects were all analyzeable but added up to just about 120 examples. As with the subjects, though, the bare NP structures had the most parallelism, though the other two structures had fairly common parallelism as well. Bare NPs often used the same noun, and had relatively equal proportions of same noun categories, similar adjectives, and contrast markers. Pseudogapping examples had the same noun category and similar adjectives most frequently.

With the analyses in this section, we answered a number of remaining questions about this structure. When subject NPs contrasted, bare NP ellipsis was the most common structure chosen, and bare NP ellipsis was also the most common way to show object contrast. Other structures had more variety in what contrast they expressed, including multiple contrasts in full sentences, but were much less

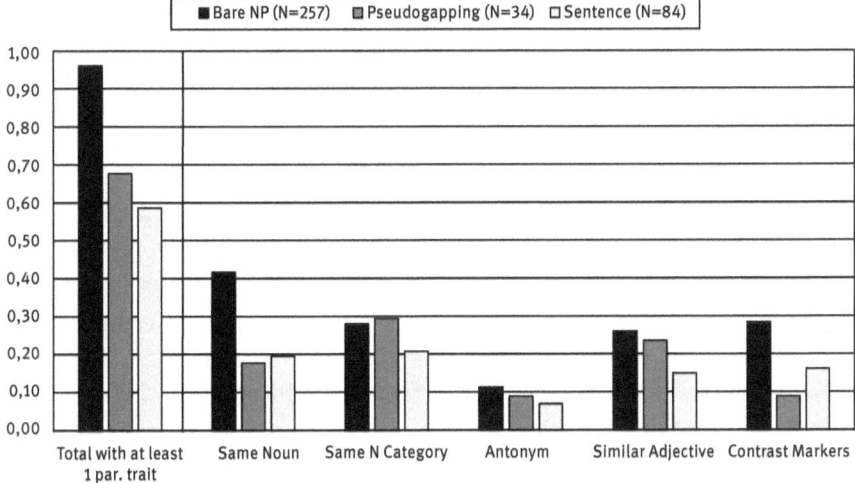

Fig. 6: Parallelism in contrasted object NPs across structures ($N = 378$)

common. Furthermore, contrasted subject NPs quite often showed indicators of parallelism or contrast, especially for bare NP ellipsis and inverted VP Ellipsis; this was less often the case for general VP Ellipsis and full sentences. Within the small set of object contrasts, bare NP ellipsis again showed frequent similarities between the contrasting NPs.

4.4 Corpus conclusions

The corpus research has provided answers to a number of questions about comparative constructions which were raised by the processing work. First, and most obviously, ellipsis is extremely common in comparative constructions (at least those with the adverbs in the particular comparative structure in question). Even beyond that, the most extreme ellipsis, which leaves only bare NPs as remnants, is overwhelmingly frequent. Complete sentences following the comparative machinery are pretty rare. The bare NP ellipsis constructions also are very likely to have a subject role, and almost half of those items did have alternative NPs which could be contrastive. This last result shows a healthy tolerance for ambiguity, since contrast with subject NPs could be unambiguously conveyed by several of the other possible structures (VP Ellipsis or Pseudogapping, Inverted VP Ellipsis, sentences). Mitigating the ambiguity somewhat could be the frequent use of parallelism and contrast markers, in which the remnant NP matches its contrastive partner in features or contains explicit indicators of contrast.

The extremely frequent occurrence of ellipsis in comparatives, we suggest, can be traced to the focus structure of comparatives: since they usually contrast only one phrase or argument, any additional material that appears after *than* is obligatorily deaccented, non-contrastive material. Having whole sentences after *than* leaves a good bit of lexical material that must be deaccented in most cases, and this is awkward, especially when there are multiple types of ellipsis that could be used instead. So complete sentences with deaccented material compete with the multiple possible ellipsis structures to express the intended contrast, and clearly they lose most of the time. Comparative constructions are basically vehicles for expressing a contrast, and lexical material which is extraneous to that contrast tend to be pared away. The other option for which full sentences are available is when there is contrast between multiple phrases, which is also a relatively rare occurrence.

The fact that contrastive subject NPs show parallelism and contrast marking relatively often is interesting, and suggests that the lexical parallelism used in the processing experiments was ecologically valid. The parallelism findings would actually be easier to explain, though, if parallelism was especially frequent only in the bare NPs, and less so in all of the unambiguous other structures. Then it could be seen as a partial redress of the ambiguity introduced by the lack of a verb to show the structural role of the NP in the bare NP ellipsis structures. However, parallelism was also quite common in the inverted VP Ellipsis examples, and less so in the un-inverted VP Ellipsis and full sentence structures. Even there, 30–40% of examples showed some lexical similarity or contrast marking. So the story is not quite so clear, since inverted VP Ellipsis is unambiguous. Perhaps the relative rareness of a post-verb subject in a strict word order language like English accounts for some compensatory parallelism in the inverted examples. That explanation would allow us to suggest that lexical parallelism is seen more commonly in examples which are either more ambiguous or more unusual and complex to parse.

Miller (2014)'s corpus study of pseudogapping ended up capturing a large number of items in comparative constructions, many of which (due to a different type of search string) would not be in this corpus. His data were particularly striking in showing the relative commonality of pseudogapping in comparatives (97% of his data) vs. the relative rarity of this ellipsis type outside of comparatives (less than 50 examples), suggesting that the comparative construction is particularly amenable to ellipsis. This is consistent with our findings and provides some support for the idea that comparative constructions favor ellipsis, which we argue is based on focus structure. Similarly, Bos & Spenader (2011) noted multiple examples of ellipsis types which are only or more frequently found in comparatives. They also point out that, for example, 31% of their total examples of VP Ellipsis were in comparatives, while theoretical papers about VP Ellipsis usually focus on non-comparative VP Ellipsis (and conversely, examples with both *and* and *too* are quite rare, despite those being the canonical examples in theoretical work). They suggested, therefore, that corpus studies may be useful in bringing to light understudied types of ellipsis, and that studying ellipsis-favoring constructions like the comparative may have important implications for the understanding of ellipsis.

5 Conclusions

The two processing experiments show that comparative bare NP ellipsis is an ambiguous structure in which preferences can be significantly influenced by parallelism and overt focus marking. Lexical parallelism between NPs, expressed here as matching in the syntactic and semantic features of remnant and correlate NPs as well as in referent gender, can raise or lower the rate of subject interpretations compared to a neutral condition. In addition, the placement of contrastive accents on the subject or object of the first clause and the remnant NP increases responses where the accented elements are contrasted with each other: subject accent favors subject interpretation and object accent favors object interpretation. The overall level of responses in the neutral parallelism condition and the written conditions suggests that the preferred interpretation of this ellipsis is the object interpretation. This object bias has been found for multiple other ellipsis types (e.g., Stolterfoht et al. 2007; Carlson et al. 2009; Harris & Carlson 2018), and explained as an effect of the default expectation that focus will be on the object in English sentences. So there are two effects in the processing results presented here that relate to focus structure: the effect of overt focus marking using pitch accents on interpretation, and the overall preference for an object interpretation.

One of the initial questions that led to the creation and analysis of the comparative corpus was whether there was a frequency-based motivation for the object bias in comparative ellipsis. This was conclusively ruled out by the examples from COCA, which show quite frequent bare NP ellipsis but very low incidence of object contrast in those or other comparative structures. There is no evidence that processors should expect a bare NP remnant to be an object based on the majority of comparatives that they hear or read. We must look elsewhere for an explanation of the object bias in processing, and our suggestion is that default focus structure is again the answer. Because people expect focus on the object in sentences, a contrast with that object is the most natural interpretation when confronted with a bare NP following the comparative *than*.

In addition to the frequency question for bare NP ellipsis contrast preferences, the comparative corpus analysis also addressed several other questions, including the frequency of elided vs. complete clauses in comparatives, the types of phrases found as comparative remnants, and the prevalence of parallelism between contrasted NPs. We found that ellipsis of several types was not only quite common in comparatives, but far outweighed the use of complete clauses. The most frequent ellipsis type seen by far was bare NP ellipsis, but VP Ellipsis was also relatively common, as were inverted VP Ellipsis and clausal ellipsis under a reporting verb. Most of our analysis looked at examples with NPs at the start of the remnant, but PPs and VPs were also quite possible. Examining NP-initial examples with clear contrasts between NPs, we found that parallelism between the NPs was frequent, especially in bare NP ellipsis and inverted VP ellipsis. Overall, we suggest that the overwhelming preference for ellipsis in comparative constructions is also due to focus structure. Comparatives usually contrast a single phrase with the prior clause, meaning that all additional structure after *than* would be given and deaccented. Long stretches of deaccented material are awkward to produce and thus dispreferred compared to structures which leave only or mostly the contrastive elements.

One might be concerned that focus structure is being used to explain two different things: in processing, it leads to object preferences for ambiguous bare NP ellipsis, but in the corpus, it leads to many bare NPs with a subject role. This is not inconsistent due to the differences between comprehension and production. In processing, readers and listeners are trying to figure out the information structure of a sentence, while the corpus is a record of produced sentences. The writers and speakers of these produced sentences know where the focus is, and so they have no need to assume its presence in a default location. They might well accent contrasted items in their explicit or implicit prosody, and they seem to use parallel features relatively often in contrasting NPs. They tend to omit long stretches of deaccented, given information, even if it leads to ambiguity in the resulting utterance. It so happens that they frequently need to contrast subject NPs, and they usually do so in elided structures. Focus structure does not explain the observation that there are more bare NP ellipsis sentences with subject contrast than object contrast, but it is relevant to the fact that subject contrast is expressed much more often by bare NP ellipsis than by VP ellipsis or full sentences. This point is related to the discussion in Rooth (1992b) on the overlap beween places where people might deaccent information vs. elide it.

In comprehension, on the other hand, readers and listeners do not have the advantage of knowing the information structure ahead of time. Part of their process of interpretation is establishing the focus structure of the sentence, especially in explicitly contrastive constructions like comparatives. Consistent with other research (Carlson et al. 2009; Harris & Carlson 2018; Stolterfoht et al. 2007), the experiments here suggest that the default expectation of focus on the object has a powerful influence on the postulated focus structure, even in the presence of overt signals of focus such as pitch accents. We suspect that a reliance on the default position of focus could arise for many reasons: sometimes listeners miss prosodic cues to focus, sometimes they forget the cues, sometimes speakers provide inconsistent or misleading cues, sometimes speakers don't use helpful prosodic cues, and so on.

References

Arnold, Jennifer E., Thomas Wasow, Anthony Losongco, and Ryan Ginstrom (2000). Heaviness vs. newness: The effects of structural complexity and discourse status on constituent ordering. *Language*, 76:28–55.

Barr, Dale J., Roger Levy, Christoph Scheepers, and Harry J. Tily (2013). Random effects structure for confirmatory hypothesis testing: Keep it maximal. *Journal of Memory and Language*, 68:255–278.

Bartels, Christine and John Kingston (1996). Salient pitch cues in the perception of contrastive focus. In Dickey, Michael Walsh and Sue Tunstall, eds, *UMOP 19: Linguistics in the laboratory*, pp. 1–26. Amherst: GLSA.

Bates, Douglas, Martin Maechler, Ben Bolker, and Steve Walker (2015). Fitting linear mixed-effects models using lme4. *Journal of Statistical Software*, 67:1–48.

Beckman, Mary and Gayle Ayers Elam (1997). *Guidelines for ToBI transcription, version 3*. Columbus: Ohio State University. Retrieved from http://www.ling.ohio-state.edu/~tobi/ame_tobi/. (9 September, 1998).

Dos, Johan and Jennifer Spenader (2011). An annotated corpus for the analysis of VP ellipsis. *Language Resources and Evaluation*, 45:463–494.

Carlson, Katy (2001). The effects of parallelism and prosody on the processing of gapping structures. *Language and Speech*, 44:1–26.

Carlson, Katy (2002). *Parallelism and prosody in the processing of ellipsis sentences*. (Outstanding dissertations in linguistics series). New York: Routledge.

Carlson, Katy (2013). The role of *only* in contrasts in and out of context. *Discourse Processes*, 50:1–27.

Carlson, Katy, Michael W. Dickey, Lyn Frazier, and Charles Clifton, Jr. (2009). Information structure expectations in sentence comprehension. *Quarterly Journal of Experimental Psychology*, 62:114–139.

Carlson, Katy and Jesse A. Harris (2018). Zero-Adjective contrast in much-less ellipsis: the advantage for parallel syntax. *Language, Cognition, and Neuroscience*, 33(1):77–97. doi:10.1080/23273798.2017.1366530.

Chomsky, Noam and Morris Halle (1968). *The sound pattern of English*. New York: Harper & Row.

Cinque, Guglielmo (1993). A null theory of phrase and compound stress. *Linguistic Inquiry*, 24:239–297.

Clark, Herbert H. and Susan E. Haviland (1977). Comprehension and the given-new contract. In Freedle, Roy O., ed., *Discourse production and comprehension*, pp. 1–40. Hillsdale, NJ: Erlbaum.

Davies, Mark (2008–). The Corpus of Contemporary American English: 520 million words, 1990–present. Retrieved from http://corpus.byu.edu/coca/. (28 August, 2015).

Frazier, Lyn and Charles Clifton, Jr. (1998). Comprehension of sluiced constituents. *Language and Cognitive Processes*, 13:499–520.

Frazier, Lyn and Charles Clifton, Jr. (2001). Parsing coordinates and ellipsis: Copy α. *Syntax*, 4(1):1–22.

Frazier, Lyn, Charles Clifton, Jr., and Katy Carlson (2007). Focus and VP Ellipsis. *Language and Speech*, 50:1–21.

Hardt, Daniel (1997). An empirical approach to VP ellipsis. *Computational Linguistics*, 23:525–541.

Harris, Jesse A. and Katy Carlson (2018). Information structure preferences in focus-sensitive ellipsis: How defaults persist. *Language and Speech*, 61(3):480–512. doi:10.1177/0023830917737110.

Hoeks, John C. J., Gisela Redeker, and Petra Hendriks (2009). Fill the gap! Combining pragmatic and prosodic information to make gapping easy. *Journal of Psycholinguistic Research*, 38:221–235.

Hoeksema, Jack (2006). Pseudogapping: its syntactic analysis and cumulative effects on acceptability. *Research on Language and Computation*, 4:335–352.

Ito, Kiwako and Shari R. Speer (2008). Anticipatory effects of intonation: eye movements during instructed visual search. *Journal of Memory and Language*, 58:541–573.

Johnson, Kyle (2001). What VP Ellipsis can do, and what it can't, but not why. In Baltin, Mark and Chris Collins, eds, *The Handbook of Contemporary Syntactic Theory*, pp. 439–479. New York: Blackwell Publishers.

Johnson, Kyle (2008). The view of QR from ellipsis. In Johnson, Kyle, ed., *Topics in Ellipsis*, pp. 69–94. Cambridge: Cambridge University Press.

Johnson, Kyle (2009). Gapping is not (VP) ellipsis. *Linguistic Inquiry*, 40:289–328.

Kadmon, Nirit (2001). *Formal pragmatics: Semantics, pragmatics, presupposition, and focus*. Oxford: Blackwell.

Kiss, Katalin E. (1998). Identificational focus vs. information focus. *Language*, 74:245–273.

Krahmer, Emiel and Marc Swerts (2001). On the alleged existence of contrastive accents. *Speech Communication*, 34:391–405.

Kuno, Susumu (1976). Gapping: a functional analysis. *Linguistic Inquiry*, 7:300–318.

Ladd, D. Robert (2008). *Intonational phonology*. Cambridge: Cambridge University Press: 2nd edn.

Ladd, D. Robert and Rachel Morton (1997). The perception of intonational emphasis: continuous or categorical? *Journal of Phonetics*, 25:313–342.

Ladd, D. Robert and Astrid Schepman (2003). "Sagging transitions" between high pitch accents in English: experimental evidence. *Journal of Phonetics*, 31:81–112.

Lechner, Winfried (2004). *Ellipsis in Comparatives*. Berlin: Mouton de Gruyter.

Lechner, Winfried (2008). On binding scope and ellipsis scope. In Johnson, Kyle, ed., *Topics in Ellipsis*, pp. 154–182. Cambridge: Cambridge University Press.

Levin, Nancy S. (1986). *Main verb ellipsis in spoken English*. (Outstanding dissertations in linguistics series). New York: Garland.

Levy, Roger (2008). Expectation-based syntactic comprehension. *Cognition*, 106:1126–1177.

Levy, Roger (2013). Memory and surprisal in human sentence comprehension. In Roger P. G. van Gompel, ed., *Sentence Processing*, pp. 78–114. Hove: Psychology Press.

MacDonald, Maryellen C. (2013). How language production shapes language form and comprehension. *Frontiers in Psychology*, 4:226. doi:10.3389/fpsyg.2013.00226.

MacDonald, Maryellen C., Neal J. Pearlmutter, and Mark S. Seidenberg (1994). The lexical nature of syntactic ambiguity resolution. *Psychological Review*, 101(4):676–703.

Marcus, Mitchell P., Beatrice Santorini, and Mary Ann Marcinkiewicz (1993). Building a large annotated corpus of English: The Penn Treebank. *Computational Linguistics*, 19:313–330.

Martin, Andrea E. and Brian McElree (2008). A content-addressable pointer mechanism underlies comprehension of verb-phrase ellipsis. *Journal of Memory and Language*, 58:879–906.

Martin, Andrea E. and Brian McElree (2009). Memory operations that support language comprehension: evidence from VP Ellipsis. *Journal of Experimental Psychology: Learning, Memory, and Cognition*, 35:1231–1239.

Merchant, Jason (2001). *The Syntax of Silence: Sluicing, Islands, and the Theory of Ellipsis*. Oxford: Oxford University Press.

Miller, Philip (2014). A corpus study of pseudogapping and its theoretical consequences. In Pinon, Christopher, ed., *Empirical Issues in Syntax and Semantics 10*, pp. 73–90.

Paterson, Kevin B., Simon P. Liversedge, Ruth Filik, Barbara J. Juhasz, Sarah J. White, and Keith Rayner (2007). Focus identification during sentence comprehension: Evidence from eye movements. *The Quarterly Journal of Experimental Psychology*, 60:1423–1445.

Pierrehumbert, Janet and Julia Hirschberg (1990). The meaning of intonation in the interpretation of discourse. In Cohen, Philip R., Jerry Morgan, and Martha E. Pollack, eds, *Intentions in communication*, pp. 271–311. Cambridge, MA: MIT Press.

Pierrehumbert, Janet B. (1980). *The phonetics and phonology of English intonation*. dissertation, MIT, Cambridge, MA.

Reinhart, Tanya (1991). Elliptic conjunctions–non-quantificational LF. In Kasher, Asa, ed., *The Chomskyan Turn*, pp. 360–384. Oxford: Blackwell.

Roberts, Craige (1996/2012). Information structure in discourse: Towards an integrated formal theory of pragmatics. Reprinted in *Semantics and Pragmatics* 6. 1–69.

Rooth, Mats (1992a). A theory of focus interpretation. *Natural Language Semantics*, 1:75–116.

Rooth, Mats (1992b). Ellipsis redundancy and reduction redundancy. In Berman, S. and Arild Hestvik, eds, *Proceedings of the Stuttgarter ellipsis workshop*, Arbeitspapiere des Sonderforschungsbereichs 340, Bericht 29-1992.

Ross, John R. (1967). *Constraints on variables in syntax*. dissertation, MIT, Cambridge, MA.

Ross, John R. (1970). Gapping and the order of constituents. In Bierwisch, Manfred and Karl Erich Heidolph, eds, *Progress in linguistics*, pp. 249–259. The Hague: Mouton.

Rump, H. H. and Rene Collier (1996). Focus conditions and the prominence of pitch-accented syllables. *Language and Speech*, 39:1–17.

Sag, Ivan A. (1980). *Deletion and Logical Form*. New York: Garland Publishing.

Schwarzschild, Roger (1999). Givenness, AvoidF and other constraints on the placement of accent. *Natural Language Semantics*, 7:141–177.

Selkirk, Elisabeth O. (1984). *Phonology and syntax: The relation between sound and structure*. Cambridge, MA: MIT Press.

Selkirk, Elisabeth O. (1995). Sentence prosody: Intonation, stress and phrasing. In Goldsmith, J., ed., *Handbook of Phonological Theory*, pp. 550–569. Oxford: Blackwell.

Stolterfoht, Britta, Angela D. Friederici, Kai Alter, and Anita Steube (2007). Processing focus structure and implicit prosody during reading: Differential ERP effects. *Cognition*, 104:565–590.

Umbach, Carla (2004). On the notion of contrast in information structure and discourse structure. *Journal of Semantics*, 21:155–175.

Zeevat, Henk (2004). Contrastors. *Journal of Semantics*, 21:95–112.

Appendix A

Items in Experiments 1–2, shown in three lexical parallelism conditions: subject parallelism, object parallelism, then neutral parallelism.

1. a. Tasha called him more often than Sonya.
b. He called Tasha more often than Sonya.
c. Tasha called Bella more often than Sonya.

2. a. Louisa punished him more severely than Nina.
b. He punished Louisa more severely than Nina.
c. Louisa punished Alice more severely than Nina.

3. a. Duncan annoyed her more frequently than Oscar.
b. She annoyed Duncan more frequently than Oscar.
c. Duncan annoyed Herb more frequently than Oscar.

4. a. Theo respected her more than Wally.
b. She respected Theo more than Wally.
c. Theo respected Kenny more than Wally.

5. a. Janine impressed the professor more thoroughly than Denise.
b. The professor impressed Jannine more thoroughly than Denise.
c. Janine impressed Eliza more thoroughly than Denise.

6. a. Clementine visited the children more often than Wilma.
b. The children visited Clementine more often than Wilma.
c. Clementine visited Bettina more often than Wilma.

7. a. Pauline assisted the manager more efficiently than Diana.
b. The manager assisted Pauline more efficiently than Diana.
c. Pauline assisted Valerie more efficiently than Diana.

8. a. Portia debated the councilman more effectively than Edwina.
b. The councilman debated Portia more effectively than Edwina.
c. Portia debated Harriet more effectively than Edwina.

9. a. Neil suspected her more than Larry.
b. She suspected Neil more than Larry.
c. Neil suspected Bob more than Larry.

10. a. Betsy tutored him more frequently than Kirsten.
b. He tutored Betsy more frequently than Kirsten.
c. Betsy tutored Lena more frequently than Kirsten.

11. a. Myra tested him more thoroughly than Alicia.
b. He tested Myra more thoroughly than Alicia.
c. Myra tested Ruth more thoroughly than Alicia.

12. a. Leon praised her more readily than George.
b. She praised Leon more readily than George.
c. Leon praised Steve more readily than George.

13. a. Tamara noticed the patient more rapidly than Andrea.
b. The patient noticed Tamara more rapidly than Andrea.
c. Tamara noticed Melinda more rapidly than Andrea.

14. a. Lance recognized an old friend more slowly than Gene.
b. An old friend recognized Lance more slowly than Gene.
c. Lance recognized Fred more slowly than Gene.

15. a. Deirdre saw the doctor more frequently than Barbara.
b. The doctor saw Deirdre more frequently than Barbara.
c. Deidre saw Emma more frequently than Barbara.

16. a. Teddy watched the spy more closely than Donny.
b. The spy watched Teddy more closely than Donny.
c. Teddy watched Robert more closely than Donny.

17. a. Toby entertained the guest more often than Drew.
b. The guest entertained Toby more often than Drew.
c. Toby entertained Richie more often than Drew.

18. a. Leah reassured him more easily than Dora.
b. He reassured Leah more easily than Dora.
c. Leah reassured Helen more easily than Dora.

19. a. Tyler loathed the boss more than Michael.
b. The boss loathed Tyler more than Michael.
c. Tyler loathed Chris more than Michael.

20. a. Kendra texted the intern more often than Jessica
b. The intern texted Kendra more often than Jessica.
c. Kendra texted Maura more often than Jessica.

21. a. Dean interrupted the producer more regularly than Ralph.
b. The producer interrupted Dean more regularly than Ralph.
c. Dean interrupted Tommy more regularly than Ralph.

22. a. Mitch offended her more deeply than Jack.
b. She offended Mitch more deeply than Jack.
c. Mitch offended Robbie more deeply than Jack.

23. a. Janice fooled him more easily than Amy.
b. He fooled Janice more easily than Amy.
c. Janice fooled Madison more easily than Amy.

24. a. Max trusted her more quickly than Jeff.
b. She trusted Max more quickly than Jeff.
c. Max trusted Bill more quickly than Jeff.

Appendix B

Syntactic categories after *than*, by adverb (in order of adverb frequency), plus frequency

	NP only	NP-first ellipsis	AdvP	Aux. Verb	Full sentences	PP	Sub. Clause	VP	Total
1. often	452	234	37	49	100	43	4	25	944
2. quickly	261	161	27	25	37	20	6	34	571
3. slowly	162	68	28	16	17	21	2	18	332
4. frequently	173	52	25	31	9	26	1	9	326
5. rapidly	146	61	12	24	16	31	1	19	310
6. easily	138	64	8	10	15	22	6	6	269
7. effectively	147	38	7	9	4	8	2	2	217
8. clearly	74	34	21	6	7	21	2	0	165
9. closely	65	33	24	10	4	8	0	0	144
10. efficiently	89	25	10	6	3	5	2	2	142
11. strongly	55	28	20	10	5	11	0	1	130
12. seriously	47	47	9	1	14	4	2	0	124
13. readily	68	19	3	7	8	7	1	4	117
14. deeply	46	25	13	3	3	2	1	1	94
15. accurately	59	11	5	4	1	0	0	1	81
16. heavily	47	7	6	3	0	2	2	0	67
17. cheaply	34	8	1	1	5	8	2	1	60
18. aggressively	27	17	7	2	1	4	0	1	59
19. favorably	42	3	0	4	5	0	1	1	56
20. sharply	16	25	7	2	1	4	1	0	56
21. harshly	26	21	1	0	1	1	0	1	51
22. positively	25	3	1	10	2	0	0	0	41
23. broadly	13	9	2	5	2	2	2	2	37

Marta Wierzba
The ordering of interface mapping rules in German object fronting

Abstract: This paper discusses a data set on object-initial sentences in German. It is shown that it can be accounted for under the assumption that prosody-IS mapping rules come into play at different levels of the grammatical model: Some, for example focus-related rules, apply at high levels, where they have access to prosodic and syntactic structure (and potentially even underlying structural representations). Others, in particular givenness-related rules, apply at lower levels, where they can affect phonetic realization, but not prosodic structure.

1 Introduction

Thanks to extensive research in the past decades, we have gained a good understanding of how information structure influences prosody in German. It has been shown that the relation between focus and sentence stress and between givenness and deaccentuation can be successfully modeled in terms of Optimality Theoretical constraints (see e.g. Truckenbrodt 1995; Féry & Samek-Lodovici 2006). Most studies so far, however, have been concerned with canonical subject-initial structures. The investigation of the question how established prosody-IS mapping principles interact with syntactic movement in more complex structures is still at its beginning. In this paper, I will take a look at a type of non-canonical structure and explore what it can tell us about the way in which the mapping principles apply.

In Sect. 2, I will present a data set on German broad-focus object fronting. The data set combines information-structural factors (focus and givenness), syntactic movement, and phonetic effects, and thus provides an interesting basis for the investigation of the interaction between all these components. In this paper, I will primarily discuss the role of givenness, whereas focus is covered in more detail in Wierzba (2017). I will therefore summarize the core idea about focus relatively briefly in Sect. 3: I will argue that focus comes into play at a high level of the grammatical model (at the interface between prosody and syntactic structure,

---

Note: I would like to thank the organizers and participants of the "Prosody in syntactic encoding" workshop at DGfS 39, the anonymous reviewers of this article, and the editor of this series for their helpful comments.

https://doi.org/10.1515/9783110650532-006

including access to traces/lower copies), because it interacts with principles that seem to be sensitive not only to the surface word order, but to underlying syntactic structure. In Sect. 4, I argue that givenness/newness mapping comes into play at the lower levels of intonation and phonetic realization, in line with Féry & Ishihara's (2009) proposal. This is supported by the observation that the possibility to interpret an expression as discourse-new is limited by the phenomenon of postnuclear deaccentuation, which Kügler & Féry (2016) argue to be a phonetic rather than metrical effect. In Sect. 5, I discuss the consequences for the architecture of grammar: I propose that focus and givenness come into play at different grammatical levels. This is illustrated in Fig. 1 and will be motivated in more detail in the remainder of the paper.

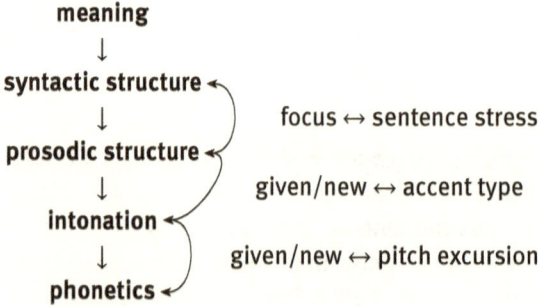

Fig. 1: The influence of information-structural factors at different levels of a serial model of grammar

2 Data set: object fronting in German

Object-initial sentences with sentence stress on the object allow not only for a narrow-focus, but also for a broad-focus interpretation in German, i.e., the interpretation that the whole VP or the whole sentence is focused. This is exemplified for VP focus in (1) (sentence stress is marked by double underlining).

(1) 'What did Maria do in the afternoon?'
     <u>Das Zimmer</u> hat   sie   aufgeräumt.
     the room   has   she   tidied.up
     'She tidied up the room.'

Intuitive judgments supporting this claim have been reported e.g. by Krifka (1998); Höhle (1982), and Büring (1997). It is also supported by experimental evidence. Fanselow et al. (2008) report very similar, high acceptability ratings for object-initial sentences both under broad and narrow focus (6.23 / 6.34 on 1–7 scale; no significant difference reported). Fanselow et al.'s data was obtained from a judgment task with written materials.

Further experimental evidence for the pattern in (1) comes from Féry & Drenhaus (2008), who report results from a judgment task with auditory materials. Again, broad focus was tested in comparison to narrow focus. An example of one of their broad-focus items is shown in (2), where double underlining marks sentence stress, i.e. prosodic prominence at the level of the intonation phrase, and single underlining marks phrasal stress, i.e. prominence at the level of the phonological phrase (the latter is realized by a pitch accent in German; see e.g. Selkirk 2011, 2.3.3). Object-initial sentences with an unaccented pronoun in the subject position, as in (2a), are similarly acceptable in broad (sentence-wide) focus as in narrow object focus (5.8 for broad focus / 5.5 for narrow focus on a 1–6 scale). The authors tested further conditions with other types of subjects and found that this factor influences the acceptability. With an unaccented DP in the subject position, as in (2b), the difference between the two contexts is larger (the authors report a significant interaction between context and subject type), but both values are relatively high on the scale (4.8 for broad focus / 5.8 for narrow focus). Object-initial sentences in which the subject is an accented DP (and therefore carries sentence stress), as in (2c), were judged as unacceptable both under broad focus and narrow object focus (2.2 / 2.0).

(2) 'Why are the neighbors complaining?' (broad-focus context)

 a. Die <u>Miete</u> haben sie wieder mal erhöht.
  the rent have they again once raised

 b. Die <u>Miete</u> hat der Hauswirt wieder mal erhöht.
  the rent has the landlord again once raised

 c. Die <u>Miete</u> hat der <u>Hauswirt</u> wieder mal erhöht.
  'They/The landlord raised the rent once again.'

 Acceptability according to Féry & Drenhaus's (2008) study: a > b ≫ c

The tendency that the acceptability of broad-focus object fronting depends on properties of the subject was also found in experiments with written materials reported in Wierzba & Fanselow (2020). They found that this type of structure is most acceptable when the subject is a definite pronoun or a discourse-given DP and significantly less acceptable when it is a discourse-new DP. Based on experiments with auditory materials, Wierzba (2017) furthermore reports a trend for a cumulative acceptability penalty when more than one discourse-new phrase follows a fronted object.

Taken together, these findings convergingly point towards the following pattern: object-initial sentences can have a broad focus interpretation under the condition that sentence stress falls on the object and the subject is either a definite pronoun or a given DP. This is summarized schematically in (3).[1] The goal of the remainder of the paper will be to provide an interface-based analysis of the pattern (for a different analysis in terms of linearization conditions, see Fanselow & Lenertová 2011).

(3)   a.   ✓ [$\underline{O}$ Aux $S_{pro/given}$ V]$_{focus}$
       b.   ✗ [$\underline{O}$ Aux S_{new} V]$_{focus}$
       c.   ✗ [O Aux $\underline{S}_{new}$ V]$_{focus}$

To give a brief outlook, I will argue that the preference for sentence stress on the sentence-initial object is only seemingly at odds with the default rightward tendency for sentence stress assignment in German – it can be modeled by the same mechanism under the assumption that underlying syntactic structure has to be taken into account. The infelicity of a discourse-new subject can then be considered the result of a conflict between postnuclear deaccentuation and the preference to accent new expressions.

3 Focus mapping as a high-level constraint

I will first consider the position of sentence stress in the data set in (3). What is especially puzzling in this respect is the pattern in (c). The whole sentence is focused, and the subject is the rightmost XP, but it is not acceptable to put sentence stress on the subject. This is surprising because in sentences with canonical word order, there is a rightward tendency for sentence stress assignment: in a

---

[1] A qualification with respect to the generalization: Similar sentences were tested by Wierzba (2017), who did not replicate the clear acceptability difference between sentences of type (2b) and (2c) that Féry & Drenhaus (2008) found. A potential explanation for this deviation is discussed in Wierzba (2017, ch. 5.3 and 5.9): $\underline{O}$VS but not OV$\underline{S}$ in principle allows a broad focus interpretation, but only if there is a (formal or pragmatic) motivation for the object fronting. For the purpose of this paper, the crucial point is that $\underline{O}$VS$_{given}$ is the only one of the structures in (2) for which it has been shown that it can be fully acceptable under broad focus.

sequence of phrases (arguments or adjuncts), it is the rightmost one that preferably receives sentence stress. For example, in a simple subject-initial transitive sentence as in (4), sentence stress typically falls on the object, at least in a broad-focus, all-new context.

(4) 'What's happening?'
Der Hauswirt erhöht die Miete.
the landlord raises the rent
'The landlord is raising the rent.'

If adverbial phrases follow the object, sentence stress falls on the rightmost one:

(5) 'What's happening?'
Der Hauswirt erhöht die Miete ab nächstem Monat um zehn
the landlord raises the rent from next month by ten
Prozent.
percent
'The landlord is raising the rent by ten percent starting next month.'

In this, German behaves similar to English, and the same linear principle can be used to capture the rightward tendency in both languages. An early example of such a principle is Chomsky & Halle's (1968, 90) Nuclear Stress Rule, which states that in a "sequence of heavy stresses" within a constituent, the rightmost one is the heaviest and carries nuclear stress. A more recent implementation of this is found e.g. in Truckenbrodt's (2012, 75) analysis in the form of the Optimality Theoretical (OT; Prince & Smolensky 1993) constraint NSR-I, which states that "the strongest stress in the intonation phrase falls on the rightmost phrasal stress".

An apparent exception to this rightward tendency concerns verb-final transitive sentences in German, in which sentence stress falls on the object rather than the verb, as in (6). This can be explained by the assumption that the VP containing the verb and the object is mapped to a single phonological phrase containing only one instance of phrasal stress (see e.g. Truckenbrodt 1995; Selkirk 2011 for OT implementations of this idea)[2].

---

[2] The unusual preference for leftward stress within the VP is accounted for by a requirement to stress phrases (which enforces stress on an NP object but not on the non-phrasal verb) by Truckenbrodt (1995). Selkirk (2011) implements a similar idea in terms of recursive prosodic phrasing: unlike a verb, an NP object tends to form its own (embedded) phonological phrase, requiring prominence at the phrasal level.

(6) 'What's happening?'
Der Hauswirt hat die Miete erhöht.
the landlord has the rent raised
'The landlord has raised the rent.'

The position of sentence stress is influenced by information structure, in particular by focus. In a sentence with narrow focus on the subject, as in (7), sentence stress falls on the subject. Truckenbrodt (1995) models this in terms of the OT constraint Focus. It requires focused elements to be the most prominent ones within their focus domain, which is defined in terms of alternative semantics (Rooth 1981, 1992). In the question-answer pair in (7), the subject *der Hauswirt* is focused in the answer according to an alternative-semantic approach to focus, because alternative answers to the question would all have the form 'X is raising the rent', with varying subjects. In this case, the whole sentence forms the focus domain, because the alternatives are full sentences/propositions.

(7) 'Who is raising the rent?'
[[Der Hauswirt]focus erhöht die Miete.]focus-domain
the landlord raises the rent
'The landlord is raising the rent.'

This interaction between Focus and NSR-I already shows that focus is an information-structural category that interacts with relatively high levels, i.e. syntactic and prosodic structure (I will make more explicit what I mean by *interaction* below). But how can we account for the non-canonical object-initial data set from Sect. 2? Recall that the puzzling pattern in the data set was (3c), repeated below as (8c). Note that in the case of sentence-wide focus, which we are considering here, the Focus constraint cannot be violated by any positioning of sentence stress, because it merely requires sentence stress to fall anywhere within the whole sentence.

(8) a. ✓ [O Aux S$_{pro/given}$ V]$_{focus}$
 b. ✗ [O Aux S$_{new}$ V]$_{focus}$
 c. ✗ [O Aux S$_{new}$ V]$_{focus}$

In view of the rules that govern the prosodic structure of canonical clauses, two questions arise when we try to make predictions for a broad-focus object-initial clause like (9).[3]

---

[3] Note that the acceptability of (9) depends on prosody, which is left unspecified here. The absence of a judgment diacritic is thus not intended to express that this sentence is well-formed.

(9) *'Why are the neighbors complaining?'*
   [[Die Miete hat der Hauswirt erhöht.]focus]focus-domain
      the rent has the landlord raised
   'The landlord has raised the rent.'

First, does the final verb need to be stressed or not? It does have a complement (the object *die Miete* 'the rent'), and we saw above that in canonical transitive clauses, the presence of a stressed complement exempts the verb from carrying its own pitch accent. In (9), however, the object has been fronted to the left periphery of the clause. Can it still have an effect on the accentuation of the verb if it is not adjacent to it? And second, does the rightward tendency for sentence stress assignment also hold in sentences with non-canonical word order?

As for the first question, previous work on the syntax-prosody interface in German and English suggests that even if the object has undergone syntactic movement and is not adjacent to the verb, it can indeed still have an effect on the verb's prosodic realization. This suggests that taking into account the surface word order is not sufficient to explain the prosodic patterns of sentences involving syntactic movement (Bierwisch 1968; Bresnan 1971, 1972; Selkirk 1995; Legate 2003; Truckenbrodt & Darcy 2010; Korth 2014; Truckenbrodt 2019; but cf. Kahnemuyipour 2009 for a different view).

For example, Bresnan (1971, 1972) argues that a certain generalization concerning the prominence relations within the VP in transitive SVO sentences also holds in object-initial wh-questions: in pragmatically neutral cases, it is preferable to stress the object if it is a lexical phrase, and to stress the verb if the object is an inherently unaccentable functional element like a pronoun.

(10) Functional object → verb stressed; lexical object → verb unstressed.
   a. Helen has <u>written</u> something.   SVO
   b. Helen has written some <u>books</u>.   SVO

(11) Functional object → verb stressed; lexical object → verb unstressed.
   a. What has Helen <u>written</u>?   OSV
   b. What <u>books</u> has Helen written?   OSV

A similar effect is reported to hold in German wh-questions and relative clauses in Truckenbrodt (2012, 86) and Truckenbrodt (2019), respectively. Bierwisch (1968); Truckenbrodt & Darcy (2010), and Korth (2014) report that verb and object influence each other prosodically also when it is the verb that is syntactically dislocated rather than the object (in V2 structures).

This general pattern has been referred to as (prosodic) *reconstruction* (Truckenbrodt & Darcy 2010; Korth 2014;, Wierzba 2017): in analogy to semantic reconstruction, the original position of moved constituents needs to be accessed for the purpose of interface mapping.

In view of these observations, the expectation for an object-initial clause like (9) is that the verb is deaccented. The choice for sentence stress is then between the subject and the object. If sentence stress assignment applies in a surface-oriented way (i.e., based on the linear order in which the sentence is realized), we would expect sentence stress to fall on the subject because it is the rightmost phrase. However, speakers judge this realization as unacceptable. A possible explanation: sentence stress assignment applies under reconstruction. This has been proposed for both English and German (Bresnan 1971; Truckenbrodt 2019).

A formal implementation of prosodic reconstruction based on recent syntactic and prosodic models can be found in Wierzba (2017). The core idea is that lower copies/traces in the syntactic structure are accessible when syntax-prosody mapping takes place, and that they are relevant for the evaluation of constraints like NSR-I.

For German V2 clauses, I follow the standard analysis that they are derived from an underlying verb-final structure by moving the finite verb to C and moving any phrase (e.g., the subject or the object) to SpecCP (Thiersch 1978; den Besten 1989). Under this view, a subject-initial clause like *Maria sang ein Lied* and an object-initial clause like *Ein Lied sang Maria* 'Mary sang a song' are assumed to be derived from the same underlying structure, as shown in (13). What differs is which phrase is fronted to the left periphery.

(12) Maria sang ein Lied.
      Mary sang a song
      'Mary sang a song.'

(13) a. [$_{CP}$ Maria [$_C$ sang] [$_{TP}$ ~~Maria~~ ein Lied ~~sang~~]]
     b. [$_{CP}$ Ein Lied [$_C$ sang] [$_{TP}$ Maria ~~ein Lied sang~~]]

Figure 2 illustrates what is meant by evaluating NSR-I under reconstruction (only sentence stress, marked by double underlining, is considered in this example; phrasal stress and prosodic phrasing will be discussed in more detail in the following sections). In the first tableau, the whole proposition is focused (broad focus, e.g., as an answer to 'What happened?'). In the subject-initial orders (the first two candidates), NSR-I is violated when the subject carries sentence stress, be-

focus: whole proposition	Focus	NSR-I
☞ Maria sang ~~Maria~~ ein Lied ~~sang~~		
Maria sang ~~Maria~~ ein Lied ~~sang~~		*!
☞ Ein Lied sang Maria ~~ein Lied sang~~		
Ein Lied sang Maria ~~ein Lied sang~~		*!

focus: Maria	Focus	NSR-I
Maria sang ~~Maria~~ ein Lied ~~sang~~	*!	
☞ Maria sang ~~Maria~~ ein Lied ~~sang~~		*!
Ein Lied sang Maria ~~ein Lied sang~~	*!	
☞ Ein Lied sang Maria ~~ein Lied sang~~		*!

Fig. 2: Illustration of the interaction between Focus and NSR-I under the assumption that the latter is evaluated under prosodic reconstruction

cause it is not the rightmost (phonological/syntactic)[4] phrase, neither in its surface position nor in its base position. The idea of prosodic reconstruction is that in the object-initial orders (the third and fourth candidates), the NSR-I is also violated when the subject carries sentence stress (just like in the subject-initial candidates), because it is the underlying structure (in which the object follows the subject) that counts for the evaluation. In other words, the violation profile of the subject-initial and object-initial candidates is identical even though the surface word order differs. The lower tableau in Fig. 2 shows the same sentences with narrow focus on the subject (e.g., as an answer to 'Who sang a song?'). Here, the higher-ranked Focus enforces sentence stress on *Maria*, even though it violates NSR-I. Again, under the assumption of prosodic reconstruction, the violation profile stays the same across different surface word orders, because the underlying structures are identical.

If NSR-I was evaluated based on the surface word order, we would expect the fourth rather than the third one of the broad-focus candidates to be optimal. The predictions of an evaluation under prosodic reconstruction are better in line with the data set on object-initial sentences in German, as summarized in (14): it predicts that object-initial broad-focus structures can be acceptable when sentence

---

4 To keep the example simple, I implicitly assume here that a match between syntactic NPs and phonological phrases is ensured by a higher-ranking constraint – in the next section, that constraint and potential violations will be discussed.

stress falls on the object, and cannot be acceptable when sentence stress falls on the subject.

(14)

Predicted by reconstructing NSR-I:	Predicted by surface NSR-I:	Observed:
✓ [O̲ Aux S V]focus	✗ [O̲ Aux S V]focus	✓ [O̲ Aux S_{pro/given} V]focus
		✗ [O̲ Aux S_{new} V]focus
✗ [O Aux S̲ V]focus	✓ [O Aux S̲ V]focus	✗ [O Aux S̲_{new} V]focus

These considerations suggest that the syntax-prosody mapping constraint NSR-I applies at a level at which abstract representations like underlying syntactic structure are accessible, i.e., when the candidates that are evaluated with respect to this constraint contain information about derivational dependecies (e.g., in the form of traces or copies).

FOCUS clearly interacts with NSR-I. By *interaction*, I mean that violations of NSR-I can be licensed by the requirement to satisfy the higher-ranked FOCUS constraint. To model this, both constraints need to be part of the same evaluation step, at a point when the evaluated candidates contain information about prosodic and syntactic structure. In a serial model of grammar, as depicted in Fig. 3 (see e.g. Gussenhoven 2004 for this ordering of levels[5]), the level at which focus comes into play can be considered relatively 'high' or 'early'. If no interaction was observed between the constraints (i.e., if focus could not affect the position of sentence stress), FOCUS could in principle come into play at a later point. The possibility of several sequential evaluation steps, as well as the alternative of a parallel model of grammar, will be discussed in more detail in Sect. 5.

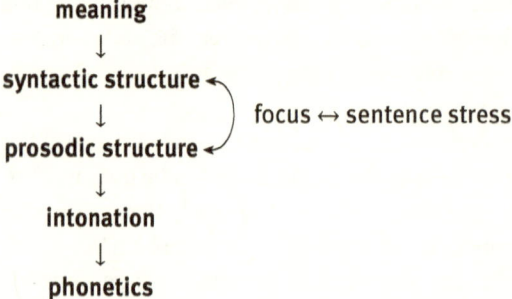

Fig. 3: The influence of focus in a serial model of grammar

---

5 "Prosodic constituents will be constructed on the basis of the morpho-syntactic structure [...]. After the addition of any postlexical tones, adjustments may be made, and the resulting surface representation is delivered to the phonetic implementation." (Gussenhoven 2004, 143).

What still needs to be explained about the object fronting data set in (14) is the role of the subject: object-initial sentences with sentence stress on the object are not always acceptable, only under the condition that the subject is pronominal or discourse-given.

4 Givenness/newness mapping as low-level constraints

Once we adopt the assumption that object-initial structures with broad focus require sentence stress on the object (due to reconstruction for syntax-prosody mapping in interaction with focus, as argued in Sect. 3), it is relatively straight-forward to explain informally why the subject needs to be pronominal or discourse-given: in German, any material following the nuclear accent is deaccented to some extent (a phenomenon referred to as postnuclear/postfocal deaccentuation or compression; see Xu 2011 for a summary of characteristics and a cross-linguistic view on the phenomenon); thus, the subject in OVS will be deaccented. Discourse-new phrases however are preferably realized with a pitch accent. A mismatch between information structure and pronunciation therefore emerges in structures of the form $\underline{O}VS_{new}$ at some level.

When we try to formalize this idea, however, several interesting questions arise, concerning the exact nature of the accenting requirement for new expressions and the status of postnuclear deaccentuation. The object fronting data set suggests that they interact, which presupposes that they are active at the same level. This could be the level of prosodic structure and metrical strength (as was argued above for focus). However, recent empirical findings point towards the view that postnuclear deaccentuation is a phonetic phenomenon; consequently, the accenting requirement for new expressions should also come into play at the phonetic level. Such an approach to givenness has been suggested by Féry & Ishihara (2009). In the following sections, I will propose an explanation for the object fronting data set that is compatible with this approach, and explore the consequences for the architecture of grammar.

4.1 Observations about givenness

In all cases that will be discussed here, if I refer to an expression as '(discourse-) given', I mean that an expression with the same denotation has been mentioned in the preceding discourse. For a more refined semantic definition, see e.g.

Schwarzschild (1999). Crucially, givenness in the sense of being prementioned is orthogonal to the notion of focus in the sense of alternative semantics – it is not the case that given always means unfocused and new always means focused. For example, *tea* in the answer in (15) (from Krifka 2007, 32) is both given and focused, and *in the park* in (15) (from Rochemont 2013, 53) is new, but not focused.

(15) What do you want to drink, tea or coffee?
I want to drink [[tea]$_{given}$]$_{focus}$.

(16) Who did she hug?
She hugged [John]$_{focus}$ [in the park]$_{new}$.

It is a long-standing observation that givenness/newness affects the accentuation of expressions. For English, for example, Brown (2007) presented experimental data showing that discourse-new expressions are usually accented, whereas given ones are usually deaccented. There is also experimental work on German. Baumann & Hadelich (2003); Baumann & Grice (2006), and Röhr & Baumann (2010) report results from a priming, perception, and production study on different degrees of givenness/newness. They found converging evidence for the following realization preferences for phrases in sentence-final position: when they are explicitly discourse-given, they tend to avoid sentence stress. Expressions that are not given in this strict sense, but can be inferred from the context or situation, tend to be either deaccented as well, or to receive an early-peak H+L* accent. New expressions in final position usually carry sentence stress, which is preferably realized in form of a H* pitch accent (see Grice & Baumann 2002 for the GToBI notation for German pitch accent types).

Féry & Kügler (2008) also investigated the effect of givenness/newness on accentuation in German. They analyzed the prosodic properties of the arguments and the verb in transitive and ditransitive sentences. Whereas the studies mentioned above focused on the final argument of a clause and the nuclear pitch accent, Féry & Kügler also analyzed prenuclear accents. They report that the majority of prenuclear phrases, both given and new ones, were realized with rising L*+H pitch accents, and only the magnitude of the pitch excursion differed.

Taken together, the findings indicate that given expressions can be deaccented or marked by a prenuclear accent. This pattern is summarized in (17) (as before, single underlining marks phrasal stress/pitch accents, and double underlining marks the nuclear pitch accent; additionally, italics indicate givenness). New constituents need to carry a pitch accent (be it prenuclear or nuclear). This pattern is summarized in (18).

(17) 'Why is everyone talking about Maria? What happened?'

    a. [*Maria*]_given sang ein Lied.
        Maria   sang a song

    'Maria sang a song.'

    b. [*Maria*]_given sang ein Lied.

    c. #[*Maria*]_given sang ein Lied.

(18) 'What happened?'

    a. Maria sang ein Lied.

    b. # Maria sang ein Lied.

    c. #Maria sang ein Lied.

In sum, there is optionality with respect to prenuclear accents for given expressions, whereas new expressions are accented obligatorily.

4.2 A metrical approach to givenness/newness

Let us first consider what an approach to givenness would look like that locates the effect at the level of prosodic/metrical structure, and under what assumptions it could account for the object fronting data set.

Féry & Samek-Lodovici's (2006) model is an example of such an approach. The authors propose a direct relation between givenness and prosodic structure in the form of the OT constraint DESTRESS-GIVEN (DG), which states that a given expression is prosodically nonprominent. DG is violated if sentence stress falls on a given expression.[6] DG in this form is intended to account for the observation that given expressions seem to avoid sentence stress[7]; it does not predict differences between new and given expressions in the prenuclear domain.

In order to account for the optionality of prenuclear pitch accents on given expressions and the obligatoriness of prenuclear pitch accents on new expressions, it seems necessary to adjust the mechanism that governs the distribution of phrasal stress, and to limit it to discourse-new material.

---

[6] Féry & Samek-Lodovici (2006) do not take DESTRESS-GIVEN to be violated by phrasal stress on a given expression, only by sentence stress; see their example (48).
[7] The assumption that givenness can affect sentence stress has been challenged in some recent work: it has been proposed that this is only possible in combination with focus on the element that the stress is shifted to. See Wagner (2005, 2012); Kadmon & Sevi (2011); Szendrői (2012), and Büring (2015) for discussion.

In Féry & Samek-Lodovici's model, all phrases are subject to the STRESS-XP constraint (adopted from Truckenbrodt 1995, 226). It states that "each lexically headed XP must contain a phrasal stress". (19) shows how it could be adjusted to limit it to new phrases:[8]

(19) STRESS-NEW-XP (SNXP): Each lexically headed discourse-new XP must contain a phrasal stress.

This would amount to locating giveness/newness at a high/early level in the grammatical architecture (similar to focus), because STRESS-NEW-XP affects the prosodic structure of sentences.

Can a model along these lines also account for the part of the object fronting data set that is still unaccounted for? Recall that the open issue is that $\underline{O}VS_{given}$ can be as acceptable as an SVO structure, but $\underline{O}VS_{new}$ cannot.

Let us consider the predictions a model including STRESS-NEW-XP would make for these structures. The upper tableau in Fig. 4 shows a broad-focus, all-new sentence, whereas the lower tableau shows a broad-focus sentence with a given subject.[9]

Candidates a–d in both tableaux have canonical subject-initial order. Candidates a and b illustrate the option that subject and object form separate phonological phrases (φ) within the intonational phrase (ι) and thus each contain phrasal stress. In c and d, there is only one phonological phrase and therefore only one instance of phrasal stress; one of the arguments is deaccented. STRESS-NEW-XP correctly predicts more optionality among the subject-initial candidates in the lower tableau than in the upper one: when *Maria* is given, deaccenting is unproblematic with respect to STRESS-NEW-XP – candidate c is predicted to be as unproblematic as a.

Candidates e–h have object-initial order. Due to the assumption of prosodic reconstruction, which was motivated in Sect. 3, e–h show the same violation profile as a–d. In the upper all-new tableau, only candidate e is unproblematic; in the lower tableau, e and g are both unproblematic.

So far – based only on STRESS-NEW-XP and NSR-I – $\underline{O}VS$ is predicted to be as felicitous as its subject-initial counterpart both with a new subject (candidate e in

---

[8] See Büring's (2015, 560) "condition on prosodic demotion" for a rule with a similar effect in a different framework.
[9] The FOCUS constraint is omitted here; it is not violated in any of the candidates (which all have broad focus). NSR-I is evaluated under prosodic reconstruction, as motivated in Sect. 3. I assume that it is not violated when the whole sentence forms a single prosodic phrase, because it is a constraint on the relative strength of several phrases.

focus: whole proposition, all new		Stress-New-XP	NSR-I
☞ a.	((Maria)_φ (sang ein Lied)_φ)_ι		
b.	((Maria)_φ (sang ein Lied)_φ)_ι		*!
c.	((Maria sang ein Lied)_φ)_ι	*!	
d.	((Maria sang ein Lied)_φ)_ι	*!	
☞ e.	((Ein Lied)_φ (sang Maria)_φ)_ι		
f.	((Ein Lied)_φ (sang Maria)_φ)_ι		*!
g.	((Ein Lied sang Maria)_φ)_ι	*!	
h.	((Ein Lied sang Maria)_φ)_ι	*!	

focus: whole proposition, given: Maria		Stress-New-XP	NSR-I
☞ a.	((*Maria*)_φ (sang ein Lied)_φ)_ι		
b.	((*Maria*)_φ (sang ein Lied)_φ)_ι		*!
☞ c.	((*Maria* sang ein Lied)_φ)_ι		
d.	((*Maria* sang ein Lied)_φ)_ι		*!
☞ e.	((Ein Lied)_φ (sang *Maria*)_φ)_ι		
f.	((Ein Lied)_φ (sang *Maria*)_φ)_ι		*!
☞ g.	((Ein Lied sang *Maria*)_φ)_ι		
h.	((Ein Lied sang *Maria*)_φ)_ι		*!

Fig. 4: OT-based predictions with constraints on prosodic structure. Italics indicate givenness.

the upper tableau) and with a given subject (candidates *e/g* in the lower tableau). Note, however, that candidate *e* represents a structure with phrasal stress in the postnuclear domain.

As discussed above, it is plausible that the missing piece of the explanation has to do with postnuclear deaccentuation. In order to interact with Stress-New-XP, postnuclear deaccentuation would need to be a constraint at the level of prosodic structure, too. In an OT model, this could either be implemented as a restriction within the component that generates the candidates (GEN) such that no candidates could be generated in which the head of the intonation phrase is followed by a further phonological phrase head; or it could be implemented as a constraint (as part of the evaluative component EVAL) which prohibits this kind of structure. Both options would make sure that candidate *e* with an instance of phrasal stress after the sentence stress would be out. Thus, there would be no winning object-initial candidate in the all-new case, but in case the subject is given, there would still be one unproblematic object-initial candidate left: candidate *g* with sentence stress on the object and a deaccented subject. These predictions are in line with the object fronting data set.

4.3 A problem for the metrical approach

As shown above, a metrical approach can make correct predictions for the object fronting data set – under the condition that postnuclear deaccentuation affects prosodic structure and thus amounts to the complete lack of prosodic phrasing and accentuation following the nuclear accent.

A problem for this assumption is posed by empirical findings concerning the postnuclear domain, e.g. in subject-initial clauses with narrow subject focus, as in (20).

(20) 'Who sang a song?'
[Maria]$_{focus}$ [*sang ein Lied*]$_{given}$.

It is clear that there is a difference between the prenuclear and postnuclear domain in German in that fully fledged pitch accents can only be realized in the former. However, it is controversial whether complete deaccentuation or merely a compression of the pitch register takes place following the nuclear accent, and how the prosodic structure of such sentences should best be represented.

As discussed above, one possibility is to assume that postnuclear deaccentuation is essentially a restriction on possible prosodic structures: no further phonological phrase head can follow the head of the intonation phrase. Under this view, the only possible prosodic parse of (20) is one in which the whole clause forms a single phonological phrase with the phonological word *Maria* as its head, which at the same time is the head of the whole intonational phrase.

Another option is to assume that there is a phonological phrase with its own head in the postnuclear domain, but it is not the head of the intonation phrase. The two options are illustrated in (21) (cf. Kügler & Féry 2016, 6 for a similar comparison).

(21) a. (x   )$_\iota$
        (x   )$_\phi$
        Maria   sang   ein Lied

    b. (x   )$_\iota$
        (x)$_\phi$ (x   )$_\phi$
        Maria   sang   ein   Lied

A metrical explanation of the object fronting data set relies on a representation of postnuclear deaccentuation as in (21a). However, Kügler & Féry (2016) have provided evidence in favor of the latter option (21b): in sentences with an early nuclear accent, they found indications of phonological phrases in the postnuclear domain (pitch accents and pitch scaling), even though all material following the nuclear accent is realized with a compressed pitch register. This supports the view that postnuclear deaccentuation does not alter or remove the prosodic structure that is built based on syntactic structure, but it only affects its phonetic realization by compressing the F_0 excursion of postnuclear pitch accents. Wagner & McAuliffe (2017) report similar findings for the postnuclear domain in English.

If we adopt this view, a problem arises for the metrical approach to the object fronting data set that was developed above. Recall that according to STRESS-NEW-XP, a candidate of the form ((object)_φ (verb subject)_φ)_ι is unproblematic. In order to explain that we observe degraded judgments, we would need a postnuclear deaccentuation constraint that penalizes this type of prosodic structure. If, however, postnuclear deaccentuation is not a constraint on prosodic structure, but merely on the phonetic realization, it would not rule out this type of candidate, and it would not explain why it is not accepted by speakers.

4.4 An intonational/phonetic approach to givenness/newness

What seems to be called for is rather a model in which syntax-prosody mapping rules (such as STRESS-XP) outrank constraints concerning givenness, newness, and postnuclear deaccentuation; the latter are not effectless, but they cannot influence the prosodic phrasing. The proposal that givenness does not affect prosodic structure, but only phonetic properties has been put forward by Féry & Ishihara (2009), who suggested that givenness merely compresses the F_0 excursion of pitch accents rather than changing prosodic structure.

How can we explain the object fronting data set under this view? The empirical findings point towards a solution in which the constraints concerning givenness and newness are of a different kind. Instead of establishing a relation between these categories and prosodic structure (by stating which phrases can/must be heads of phonological phrases), it seems more adequate to assume that they are active at a different level, namely the 'lower' levels of intonation or phonetics, as indicated in Fig. 5.

We saw above that there is evidence for intonational preferences in German with respect to given, inferable, and new expressions. Such preferences would need to be modeled in a language-specific way, as languages show different preferences (e.g., Surányi et al. 2012 report a preference for H* accents on topics, which

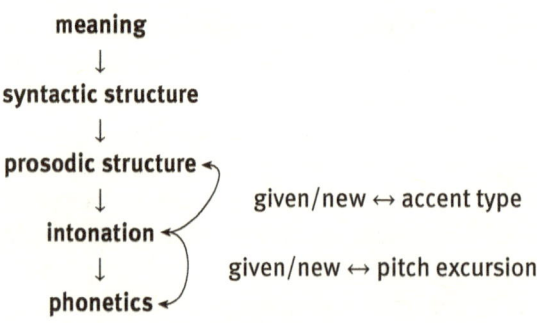

Fig. 5: The influence of givenness in a serial model of grammar

are typically given) and have different accent inventories. The preferences for German, based on the results reported above, are summarized in (22), but I will leave open here what the best technical implementation for these preferences would be. Crucially, such intonational mapping preferences would not make reference to prosodic structure, but rather to tonal events; i.e., they would not influence what constitutes a phonological phrase head, but only the type of accent it receives.

(22) IS-Intonation mapping preferences in German:
  a. Preferred pitch accent type on given expressions (if any): L*+H
  b. Preferred pitch accent type on inferable expressions (if any): L*+H, L+H*
  c. Preferred pitch accent type on new expressions: L*+H, H*

More important for the data set here is the generalization that given expressions can be deaccented, but new expressions cannot. In view of Kügler & Féry's (2016) findings on deaccentuation discussed above, a more precise description is that pitch accents on given expressions can be phonetically compressed, and pitch accents on new expressions cannot. The option to compress given material is also found in other intonational languages (see e.g. Hamlaoui et al. 2018 for Czech and Polish), but it is not universal (see e.g. Nolan & Jónsdóttir 2001; Dehé 2009 for discussion on Icelandic). As for the requirement to express new material with uncompressed accents, it could be modeled in terms of an OT mapping constraint (with a language-specific ranking) between information structure and phonetic realization:

(23) *COMPRESS-NEW (*C-NEW): A pitch accent on new information must not be phonetically compressed.

As for postnuclear deaccentuation, it also seems to be active at the phonetic rather than the metrical level in view of Kügler & Féry's (2016) results. (24) shows a possible OT formulation at the phonetic level:

(24) POSTNUCLEAR COMPRESSION (PNC): Any pitch accent following the head of the intonational phrase is phonetically compressed.

There are cross-linguistic differences with respect to this phenomenon, too. For example, Szendrői (2012) discusses data from Dutch and English showing that the postnuclear domain is not necessarily fully compressed in these languages but can contain (downstepped) pitch accents. (24) allows for cross-linguistic variability in this respect in two ways: PNC could be ranked low in some languages, and/or what counts as 'compressed' in a language might vary in a gradient way.

The latter kind of variability could be implemented in terms of cue constraints that are used to link phonetics and phonology in segmental phonology (Boersma 2009): similar to how languages differ in the phonetic properties of certain phonemes, they might also vary in the relative F_0 excursion that is sufficient to make a pitch accent be perceived as 'uncompressed'. Boersma (2009) models cross-linguistic differences in the perception of vowels using continuous cue constraint families of the form "an auditory F_1 of X Hz should not be perceived as the phonological vowel category Y". An analogous constraint family for modeling compression and its relation to givenness/newness could have the form "an auditory F_0 excursion of X Hz should (not) be perceived as a compressed pitch accent."

In the following figures, I will not try to give concrete phonetic details, but use a more abstract representation. For the sake of brevity, intonational and phonetic properties will be collapsed: I will use the symbol ↓ to represent phonetically compressed pitch accents (of any type). Figure 6 illustrates what exactly this abbreviated notation is intended to represent.

prosodic structure	((Ein Lied)$_\phi$ (sang Maria)$_\phi$)$_\iota$	
intonation + phonetics	H*	↓

prosodic structure	((Ein Lied)$_\phi$ (sang Maria)$_\phi$)$_\iota$	
intonation	H*	H*
phonetic implementation	uncompressed	compressed

Fig. 6: A joint/separated representation of intonation and phonetics

focus: whole proposition, all new	PNC	*C-New
☞ ((Maria)ᵩ (sang ein Lied)ᵩ)ᵢ 　　L*+H　　　　　　H*		
((Ein Lied)ᵩ (sang Maria)ᵩ)ᵢ 　　L*+H　　　　　　H*	*!	
((Ein Lied)ᵩ (sang Maria)ᵩ)ᵢ 　　H*　　　　　　↓		*!

focus: whole proposition, given: Maria	PNC	*C-New
☞ ((*Maria*)ᵩ (sang ein Lied)ᵩ)ᵢ 　　L*+H　　　　　　H*		
((Ein Lied)ᵩ (sang *Maria*)ᵩ)ᵢ 　　L*+H　　　　　　H*	*!	
☞ ((Ein Lied)ᵩ (sang *Maria*)ᵩ)ᵢ 　　H*　　　　　　↓		

Fig. 7: OT-based predictions with intonation-related constraints. Italics indicate givenness.

With this set of phonetic constraints – *C-New and PNC –, the OVS data set can be accounted for. This is illustrated in Fig. 7. Again, only candidates with two phonological phrases and sentence stress on the object are shown here (others would be ruled out by the higher-ranking Foc, NSR-I and Stress-XP; a more complete picture of the involved constraints will be illustrated below).

Under this view, the generalization that OVS_{new} is suboptimal (in comparison to canonical order) results from a clash between two phonetic requirements: the accent on the subject needs to be uncompressed to satisfy *Compress-New, but compressed to satisfy PNC.

A notable property of the model is that OVS_{new} is only predicted to be suboptimal if candidates with different word orders are in the same candidate set. Within the candidates with object-initial order, a realization with a single pitch accent on the object is the best one, even though it violates *C-New. Only a candidate with canonical word order can satisfy all constraints that I am considering here. In contrast, OVS_{given} is equally optimal with respect to these constraints as $S_{given}OV$, which explains why it can be perceived as fully acceptable (under the condition that the same holds for all other constraints that are not explicitly listed here). Thus, the proposed model can only account for the full OVS data set if we allow different word orders to compete with each other.

5 Architecture of grammar

Taking together the conclusions from Sects. 3 and 4, I have now arrived at an interface model in which information structure does not enter at one specific point, but can affect phonological and phonetic processes at different levels. I have argued that due to its effect on sentence stress – which I assume to be governed by a syntax-prosody mapping constraint by default –, focus comes into play (at least) at the level of relatively high-level representations which include both prosodic and syntactic structure; and, based on the observation of reconstruction-like effects, also abstract entities like syntactic copies. Givenness/newness, on the other hand, seems to influence the lower levels of intonational contours and phonetic realization.

5.1 A note on focus

The main question of this section is how these different information-structural mapping rules come together in a unified model. Before I address it, I would like to add a note on focus. As mentioned above, the discussed observations suggest that focus affects *at least* the position of sentence stress. Does it *additionally* have low-level phonetic effects? Féry & Ishihara (2009) argue that not only givenness, but also focus should be thought of as influencing the phonetic realization because of the 'boosting' effect on pitch excursion that narrow focus has. Some phonetic studies making a three-level distinction between broad focus, narrow focus, and contrastive focus suggest that it might be contrast rather than narrow focus that affects the pitch excursion in some languages (e.g., Sityaev & House 2003 on English, Avesani & Vayra 2003 on Florentine Italian); but see Genzel et al. (2015) for the finding that narrow focus differs phonetically from broad focus independently from contrast (in Hungarian), which would mean that focus can have an effect on the phonetic level in addition to the level of prosodic structure. In view of the controversial evidence, I will remain agnostic with respect to the relation between focus and phonetic realization for the purpose of this paper. The following discussion does not hinge on this – the crucial point that I want to address is that information structure can play a role at different levels of grammar, and this is already the case when we assume that focus affects sentence stress and givenness affects phonetic realization.

5.2 Serial model

If we think of the architecture of grammar in terms of a sequence of steps/modules from an abstract representation of meaning, over the building of syntactic and prosodic structure, until the creation of an intonational contour and a phonetic signal, focus mapping is an 'early' process (closer to abstract structures). Since givenness/newness is related to intonational contours and interacts with the phonetic process of postnuclear compression, it is a 'late' process (closer to phonetic form). This can be modeled by several OT components that apply in a certain order. This option is illustrated in Fig. 8. Based on the input (which we can assume to be a proposition along with information-structural annotations), a first set of candidates is generated. Each candidate is a pair of a syntactic and a prosodic structure. In the first evaluation process, syntax-prosody and prosody-IS mapping rules decide which candidate or candidates are optimal (SXP stands for STRESS-XP in the Figure). Based on the winners, a second set of candidates is generated, consisting of pairs of prosodic structure and intonational/phonetic realizations. These candidates are evaluated with respect to a second set of constraints, concerning factors related to the intonational contour and phonetic implementation (recall from the previous section that these could potentially be further disentangled – a third OT component could be added for the phonetic level). The requirement of postnuclear compression comes into play here, as well as the givenness/newness mapping preferences. The winner of this second evaluation step is then the optimal way to realize the initial input. Intonation is represented here as sequences of tonal events. Note that for the ease of illustration, they are displayed below the corresponding prosodic head / boundary, but the actual alignment would be an extra step depending on further intonational and phonetic constraints – see Gussenhoven (2004, ch. 8) for a detailed OT analysis of this step. The advantage of such a serial model is that it allows one to keep the candidates relatively simple (just pairs: syntactic/prosodic structure in the first step, prosody/intonation in the second step), and the different modules of grammar independent from each other.

5.3 Parallel model

The alternative, a parallel model, is exemplified in Fig. 9. The assumption here is that there is only one GEN and one EVAL process. The candidates that are generated have to be more complex than in the serial model: at least triples of syntactic structure, prosodic structure, and intonational contour. The same predictions follow for the chosen example: essentially, $\underline{O}VS_{new}$ is suboptimal because of a

The ordering of interface mapping rules in German object fronting — 181

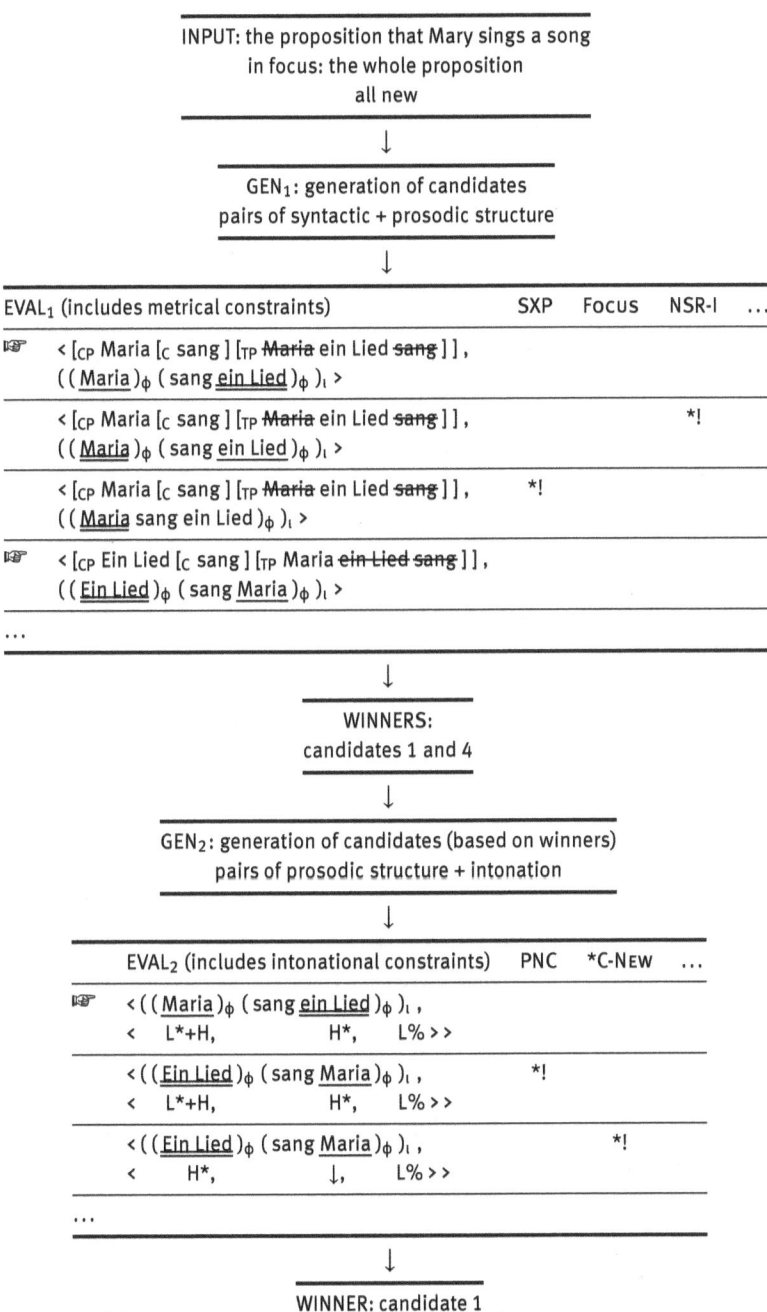

Fig. 8: Illustration of a serial model

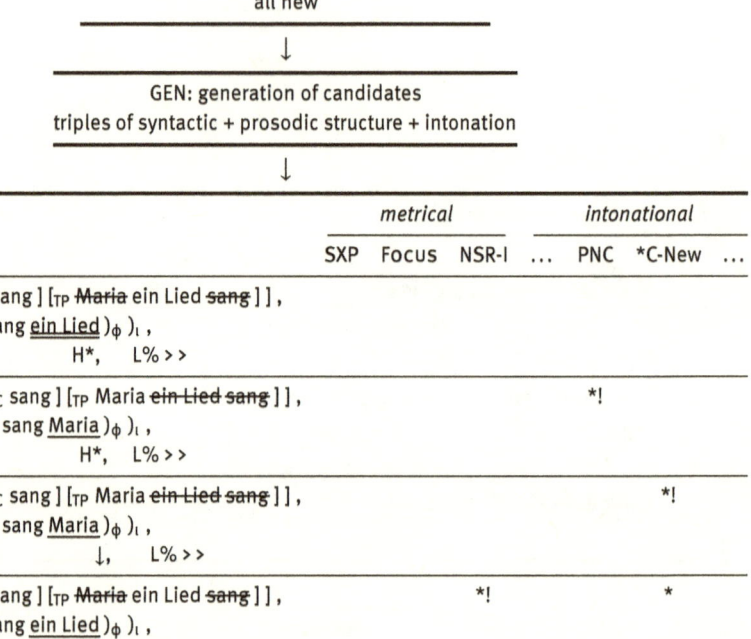

Fig. 9: Illustration of a parallel model

conflict between PNC and *C-New. But in principle, a parallel model is less limited with respect to possible interactions between constraints than a serial model: lower-level constraints could in principle outrank higher ones, which is not possible in the serial model. The parallel model also allows to formulate constraints that require a certain mapping between a high-level representation (say, syntactic structure) and a much lower level (say, intonation), because all information is available in the candidates simultaneously. At the level of segmental phonology, Boersma (2009) convincingly argued that a heavily parallel model is preferable to model both production and perception, because interactions can be found between all levels (between structural, lexical, phonological, phonetic constraints). The same question arises for OT-based models of information structure.

Since the complexity of the candidates and therefore also the number of possible candidates (all possible combinations of prosodic structure, syntactic structure, and intonational contour) is drastically increased in a parallel model as compared to a serial model, robust evidence for an interaction between non-adjacent levels would be needed to support the former.

5.4 Additional data: contrastive topics

I will not try to give a definitive answer here concerning whether there is sufficient evidence supporting a parallel model, but a relevant case in point that is worth further investigation might be a related data set concerning contrastive topics (CTs). Contrastive topics can be defined with reference to discourse strategies (Büring 2003): they signal a particular answering strategy to a broader question. For example, in (25), the speaker decides to answer the question whether Maria tidied up the rooms by dividing it into a series of implicit yes-no-subquestions about each room. In this context, *the living room* and *the bedroom* are contrastive topics.

(25) 'Did Mary tidy up?'
 Das /Wohnzimmer   hat Maria aufgeräumt\...
 the living.room   has Maria tidied.up...
 'Maria tidied up the living room...'
 ...aber das /Schlafzimmer nicht\.
 but   the   bed.room   not
 '...but not the bedroom.

In (25), there is a rising prenuclear accent on the object (marked by /) and a falling nuclear pitch accent on the verb (marked by \), with a high-pitch plateau in between. This intonational pattern is referred to as the hat or bridge contour, which is the intonational correlate of contrastive topics in German (Féry 1993; Jacobs 1997; Büring 1997).

Just like in the case of foci, it is possible that a larger constituent constitutes a contrastive topic. Wierzba (2013, 2017) reports that sentences containing such a 'broad' contrastive topic show reconstruction-like effects which are similar to the broad-focus sentences that were discussed in Sect. 3. For example, (26) shows a sentence in which the speaker contrasts tidying up the room with another activity – the whole VP forms a contrastive topic. This can be felicitously expressed by an object-initial sentence with a rising prenuclear accent on the object.

(26)   'What did Maria do in the afternoon?'
       Das   /Zimmer   hat   Maria   aufgeräumt\...
       the   room   has   Maria   tidied.up...
       'Maria tidied up the room...'
       ...aber /abgewaschen hat sie nicht\.
       '...but she did not clean the dishes.'

In canonical order, the left edge of the hat contour would also be aligned with the object and thus, the left edge of the contrastive topic (the VP). This is illustrated in (27). A possible mapping rule would thus be that contrastive topics are left-aligned with the hat contour.

(27)   'What did Maria do in the afternoon?'
       Maria hat das [/ Zimmer aufgeräumt \ ]$_{CT}$ ...

The observation that a sentence with non-canonical word order like (26) nevertheless shows the same alignment can be captured by the assumption that the contrastive topic mapping rule applies under prosodic reconstruction, in parallel to what I assumed about the sentence stress rule in the case of broad-focus sentences.

If these observations can be shown to be robust, then this would be a case of an intonation-related mapping constraint which needs access to high-level structural information like the underlying position of syntactically displaced constituents. Such a relation between intonational form and high-level structural properties would be easier to represent in a parallel model.

6 Conclusion

Starting from a data set on object-initial sentences in German, I have explored the ordering and interaction of interface mapping rules. I proposed that some information-structural categories, in particular focus, interact with mapping constraints that apply under reconstruction, taking into account underlying syntactic and prosodic structure. Givenness/newness mapping, on the other hand, shows interaction with postnuclear compression in the data set. Following work by Kügler & Féry (2016), I assume that this is a phenomenon that affects the phonetic implementation, but not the prosodic structure. Since this in turn affects whether a phrase in the compressed area can be felicitously interpreted as discourse-new, givenness/newness mapping must consequently also be a low-level process. I have illustrated how the different types of information-structural constraints might come together in a serial or parallel OT model.

The proposal is based on a limited data set, but I hope to have illustrated with the small case study that this type of data, in which different parts of the grammar (syntax, IS, prosody, phonetics) interact in an intricate way, can contribute to answering the following questions explicitly: if OT constraint are used to model the relation between IS and prosody, how are they related to other components of the grammar? Do all of them apply at the same level?

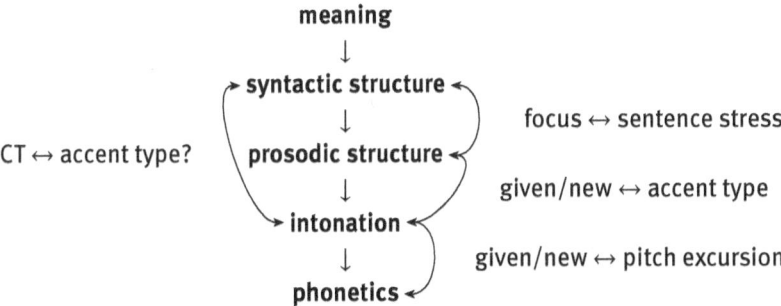

Fig. 10: The influence of information-structural factors at different levels of a serial model of grammar

The answers that I propose are summarized in Fig. 10. Information-structural properties do not influence a single level of the linguistic form, but come into play at several points. If it can be confirmed that there are information-structural effects that require a certain mapping between distant levels, as I tentatively propose for contrastive topics, a parallel model is better suited to model the interactions at the interfaces.

References

Avesani, Cinzia and Mario Vayra (2003). Broad, narrow and contrastive focus in Florentine Italian. In Solé, M. J., D. Recasens, and J. Romero, eds, *Proceedings of ICPhS-15*.

Baumann, Stefan and Martine Grice (2006). The intonation of accessibility. *Journal of Pragmatics*, 38:1636–1657.

Baumann, Stefan and Kerstin Hadelich (2003). Accent type and givenness: An experiment with auditory and visual priming. In *Proceedings of the 15th ICPhS Barcelona*.
Bierwisch, Manfred (1968). Two critical problems in accent rules. *Journal of Linguistics*, 4:173–178.
Boersma, Paul (2009). Cue constraints and their interactions in phonological perception and production. In Boersma, Paul and Silke Hamann, eds, *Phonology in perception*, pp. 55–110.
Bresnan, Joan W. (1971). Sentence stress and syntactic transformations. *Language*, 47:257–281.
Bresnan, Joan W. (1972). Stress and syntax: A reply. *Language*, 48:326–342.
Brown, Gillian (2007). Prosodic structures and the Given/New distinction. In Ladd, D. R. and A. Cutler, eds, *Prosody: Models and measurements*, pp. 67–77. Berlin: Springer.
Büring, Daniel (1997). *The meaning of topic and focus. The 59th Street bridge accent*. London / New York: Routledge.
Büring, Daniel (2003). On D-trees, beans, and B-accents. *Linguistics & Philosophy*, 29(5):511–545.
Büring, Daniel (2015). Unalternative semantics. In D'Antonio, Sarah, Mary Moroney, and Carol Rose Little, eds, *Proceedings of SALT 25*, pp. 550–575. Linguistic Society of America.
Chomsky, Noam and Morris Halle (1968). *The sound pattern of English*. New York: Harper and Row.
Dehé, Nicole (2009). An intonational grammar for Icelandic. *Nordic Journal of Linguistics*, 32:5–34.
den Besten, Hans (1989). *Studies in West Germanic syntax*. PhD thesis, Tilburg University.
Fanselow, Gisbert and Denisa Lenertová (2011). Left peripheral focus: mismatches between syntax and information structure. *Natural Language & Linguistic Theory*, 29:169–209.
Fanselow, Gisbert, Denisa Lenertová, and Thomas Weskott (2008). Studies on the acceptability of object movement to Spec,CP. In Steube, A., ed., *The Discourse Potential of Underspecified Structures*, pp. 413–438. Berlin/New York: de Gruyter.
Féry, Caroline (1993). *German intonational patterns*. Tübingen: Niemeyer.
Féry, Caroline and Heiner Drenhaus (2008). Single prosodic phrase sentences. In Ishihara, S., M. Schmitz, and A. Schwarz, eds, *Working papers of the SFB 632: Interdisciplinary studies in information structure 10*, pp. 1–44. Potsdam.
Féry, Caroline and Shinichiro Ishihara (2009). How focus and givenness shape prosody. In Zimmermann, Malte and Caroline Féry, eds, *Information Structure from Different Perspectives*, pp. 36–63. Oxford University Press.
Féry, Caroline and Frank Kügler (2008). Pitch accent scaling on given, new and focused constituents in German. *Journal of Phonetics*, 36:680–703.
Féry, Caroline and Vieri Samek-Lodovici (2006). Focus projection and prosodic prominence in nested foci. *Language*, 82(1):131–150.
Genzel, Susanne, Shinichiro Ishihara, and Balázs Surányi (2015). The prosodic expression of focus, contrast and givenness: A production study of Hungarian. *Lingua*, 165:183–204.
Grice, M. and S. Baumann (2002). Deutsche Intonation und GToBI. *Linguistische Berichte*, 191:267–298.
Gussenhoven, Carlos (2004). *The phonology of tone and intonation*. Cambridge University Press.

Hamlaoui, Fatima, Marzena Żygis, Jonas Engelmann, and Michael Wagner (2018). Acoustic correlates of focus marking in Czech and Polish. *Language and Speech*, 62:358–377.

Höhle, Tilman (1982). Explikation für 'normale Betonung' und 'normale Worstellung'. In Abraham, W., ed., *Satzglieder im Deutschen*, pp. 75–152. Tübingen.

Jacobs, Joachim (1997). I-Topikalisierung. *Linguistische Berichte*, 168:91–133.

Kadmon, Nirit and Aldo Sevi (2011). Without 'Focus'. In Partee, B. H., M. Glanzberg, and J. Skilters, eds, *Formal semantics and pragmatics. Discourse, context and models. The Baltic International Yearbook of Cognition, Logic and Communication, Vol. 6*, pp. 1–50. Manhattan, KS: New Prairie Press.

Kahnemuyipour, Arsalan (2009). *The syntax of sentential stress*. Oxford University Press.

Korth, Manuela (2014). *Von der Syntax zur Prosodie. Über das strukturelle Verhältnis zweier Komponenten der Grammatik im Deutschen*. Stauffenburg Verlag.

Krifka, Manfred (1998). Scope inversion under the rise-fall pattern in German. *Linguistic Inquiry*, 291:75–112.

Krifka, Manfred (2007). Basic notions of information structure. In Féry, Caroline and Manfred Krifka, eds, *Interdisciplinary studies on information structure 6*, pp. 13–56. Potsdam Universitätsverlag.

Kügler, Frank and Caroline Féry (2016). Post-focal downstep in German. *Language and Speech*, DOI:10.1177/0023830916647204.

Legate, Julie Anne (2003). Some interface properties of the phase. *Linguistic Inquiry*, 34:506–516.

Nolan, Francis and Hildur Jónsdóttir (2001). Accentuation patterns in Icelandic. In van Dommelen, Wim A. and Thorstein Fretheim, eds, *Nordic Prosody: 8th Conference*, pp. 187–198. Berlin & New York: Peter Lang.

Prince, Alan and Paul Smolensky (1993). Optimality Theory: Constraint interaction in generative grammar. Rutgers University Center for Cognitive Science.

Rochemont, Michael S. (2013). Discourse new, F-marking, and normal stress. *Lingua*, 136:38–62.

Röhr, Christine and Stefan Baumann (2010). Prosodic marking of information status in German. In *Proceedings 5th International Conference on Speech Prosody*.

Rooth, Mats (1981). *Association with focus*. PhD thesis, University of Massachusetts.

Rooth, Mats (1992). A theory of focus interpretation. *Natural Language Semantics*, 1:75–116.

Schwarzschild, Roger (1999). Givenness, AvoidF and other constraints on the placement of accent. *Natural Language Semantics*, 7(2):141–177.

Selkirk, Elisabeth (1995). Sentence prosody: Intonation, stress and phrasing. In Goldsmith, John A., ed., *The handbook of phonological theory*, pp. 550–569. Cambridge / Oxford: Blackwell Publishers.

Selkirk, Elisabeth (2011). The syntax-phonology interface. In Goldsmith, John, Jason Riggle, and Alan Yu, eds, *The handbook of phonological theory, 2nd edition*. Oxford: Blackwell.

Sityaev, Dmitry and Jill House (2003). Phonetic and phonological correlates of broad, narrow and contrastive focus in English. In Solé, M. J., D. Recasens, and J. Romero, eds, *Proceedings of ICPhS-15*.

Surányi, Balázs, Shinichiro Ishihara, and Fabian Schubö (2012). Syntax-prosody mapping, topic-comment structure and stress-focus correspondence in Hungarian. In Elordieta, Gorka and Pilar Prieto, eds, *Prosody and meaning*, pp. 35–72. Berlin & Boston, MA: De Gruyter.

Szendrői, Kriszta (2012). Focus movement can be destressing, but it need not be. In Neeleman, Ad and Reiko Vermeulen, eds, *The Syntax of Topic, Focus, and Contrast: An interface-based approach*, pp. 189–225. De Gruyter Mouton.

Thiersch, Craig (1978). *Topics in German syntax*. PhD thesis, MIT, Cambridge, MA.

Truckenbrodt, Hubert (1995). *Phonological phrases: Their relation to syntax, focus, and prominence*. PhD thesis, Massachusetts Institute of Technology, Cambridge, MA.

Truckenbrodt, Hubert (2012). On the prosody of German wh-questions. In Elordieta, Gorka and Pilar Prieto, eds, *Prosody and meaning*, pp. 73–117. Berlin & Boston, MA: De Gruyter.

Truckenbrodt, Hubert (2019). Notes on stress reconstruction and syntactic reconstruction. In Krifka, Manfred and Mathias Schenner, eds, *Reconstruction effects in relative clauses*. Berlin: Akademie-Verlag.

Truckenbrodt, Hubert and Isabell Darcy (2010). Object clauses, movement, and phrasal stress. In Erteschik-Shir, Nomi and Lisa Rochman, eds, *The sound patterns of syntax*, pp. 189–216. Oxford: Oxford University Press.

Wagner, Michael (2005). *Prosody and recursion*. PhD thesis, MIT, Cambridge, MA.

Wagner, Michael (2012). Focus and givenness: A unified approach. In Kučerová, Ivona and Ad Neeleman, eds, *Contrasts and positions in information structure*, pp. 102–147. Cambridge: Cambridge University Press.

Wagner, Michael and Michael McAuliffe (2017). Three dimensions of sentence prosody and their (non-)interactions. *Proceedings of Interspeech 2017*.

Wierzba, Marta (2013). Subparts of contrastive topics and the syntax-information structure interface. In Boone, Enrico, Martin Kohlberger, and Maartje Schulpen, eds, *Proceedings of ConSOLE XX*.

Wierzba, Marta (2017). *Revisiting prosodic reconstruction: An interface-based approach to partial focus and topic fronting in German*. PhD thesis, Universität Potsdam, Potsdam.

Wierzba, Marta and Gisbert Fanselow (2020). Factors influencing the acceptability of object fronting in German. *The Journal of Comparative Germanic Linguistics*, 23(1):77–124.

Xu, Yi (2011). Post-focus compression: cross-linguistic distribution and historical origin. *Proceedings of The 17th International Congress of Phonetic Sciences*.

Johannes Heim and Martina Wiltschko
Interaction at the syntax–prosody interface

Abstract: The goal of this paper is to demonstrate the advantage of integrating sentence-final intonation into the syntactic spine. This addresses a gap in the literature first identified by Truckenbrodt (2012). Our case is built on the similarity of sentence-final particles and sentence-final intonation in Canadian English for Common Ground management. Some sentence final particles, such as Canadian *eh*, encode a request for confirmation of the speaker's belief. These particles contribute to Common Ground management in that they encode the speaker's commitment towards the proposition encoded in an utterance. In addition, their prosodic properties also contribute to Common Ground management by engaging the addressee to respond to the utterance. To model this observation, we assume two layers above CP which are responsible for these functions: GroundP and ResponseP (Wiltschko & Heim 2016; Wiltschko 2017). We show that this model can explain the prosodic variation of the sentence-final particle *eh* along with those of different sentence-final contours. With a syntactic integration of GroundP and ResponseP, we can better explain the distributional restrictions of sentence-final particles and their relation to the host clause than models without a syntactic integration of Common Ground managers. Furthermore, a unified analysis for sentence final-particles and sentence-final intonation allows for systematic cross-linguistic comparison between languages that appear to use different linguistic means for Common Ground management. Our analysis is grounded in a conversational model that assumes Common Ground to be the product of a dynamic and complex negotiation between the interlocutors (Brennan & Clark 1991; Farkas & Bruce 2010).

1 Introduction

For two (or more) interlocutors to reach agreement (even if it's agreement to disagree) can be a delicate act; but this act is what drives conversations. Accordingly, having a conversation entails the negotiation of Common Ground (CG; Stalnaker 1978). Canadian English employs a sentence-peripheral particle (SPP) *eh* which serves to moderate this act of negotiation. With the use of *eh*, the speaker (S) elicits confirmation from the addressee (A) about their belief. In Wiltschko & Heim (2016), we refer to this SPP and its equivalents in other languages as *confirmationals*. The following study of *eh* and its intonational profile shows that eliciting confirmation is quite nuanced. The dialogue in (1) exemplifies the prototypical function of requesting confirmation about the truth of a proposition (*p*). Here, a response is mandatory. The dialogue in (2) exemplifies a variant of *eh* that projects rather than elicits agreement. Here, a response is possible, but not expected. The dialogue in (3) exemplifies a function of a related, yet different nature. A response is not possible, unless A interrupts S (cf. Derek & Tagliamonte 2016 who provide corpus evidence for this generalization). In all three examples, sentence-final intonation (SFI) is indicated by arrows.[1]

(1) {John runs into his friend Mary who walks her new dog around the block.}
John: You have a new dog, eh↑?
Mary: Yes, I just got him last week.

(2) {Mary starts daydreaming about a trip to Hawaii, but she keeps coming back to the fact that this will be difficult with her latest addition to the household. John puts an end to her dreaming, and says:}
John: You have a new dog, eh↓.

(3) {Mary and Anna catch up over a drink after the summer break.}
A: So, I have a new dog, eh↗, and he just doesn't listen!

We note that the examples in (1) to (3) vary in distribution and in prosodic properties. (1) and (2) occur turn-finally; (3) occurs turn-medially. In Canadian English, (1) and (3) both occur with a rise – albeit of different shape[2] – while (2) occurs with a fall. *eh* in other varieties of English may have different prosodic properties. Incidentally, all three uses of SFI can occur without the SPP in the same contexts as above.

(4) {John runs into his friend Mary who walks her new dog around the block.}
John: You have a new dog↑?
Mary: Yes, I just got him last week.

---

1 We are thankful to Michael Rochemont for assisting us in designing the contexts in (1) to (3) to illustrate the differences in their contexts of use.
2 The rise represented by ↗ has a notably smaller pitch excursion than the rise represented by ↑. The former can be almost completely levelled. Support for this generalization comes from corpus data (Wiltschko et al. 2018) and a small-scale storyboard elicitation with several native speakers of Canadian English.

(5) {Mary starts daydreaming about a trip to Hawaii, but she keeps coming back to the fact that this will be difficult with her latest addition to the household. John puts an end to her dreaming, and says:}

John: You have a new dog↓.

(6) {Mary and Anna catch up over a drink after the summer break.}

Anna: So, I have a new dog↗, and he just doesn't listen!

Our goal here is to explore the differences between the three different contours in (1) to (3) and (4) to (6) with and without the SPP. We argue that the contribution of intonation and particles is complex. It can be decomposed into two components: Speaker COMMITMENT and Addressee ENGAGEMENT. This decomposition allows us to derive the similar functions of SPPs and SFI in the negotiation of agreement between interlocutors. We further propose that these functions are best modeled as part of an extended syntactic spine. Specifically, we propose that COMMITMENT associates with the syntactic position immediately above CP. CP is assumed to close-off propositional sentence structures (the grammar of truth) and to incorporate the descriptive content, i.e. the sentence radical (Lewis 1970; Davis 2011). The extension of the spine we explore here (the grammar of use) consists of GroundP and ResponseP (Wiltschko & Heim 2016; Wiltschko 2016). COMMITMENT is associated with GroundP whereas ENGAGEMENT is associated with ResponseP.

(7) The extended spine for the Grammar of use

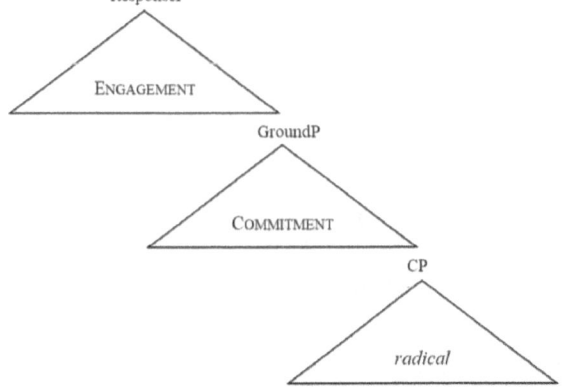

The syntactic integration of SFI and SPPs allows us to understand the complex relationship between SFI, SPPs and their host clauses. Furthermore, it allows us to decompose the contribution of SPPs and SFI into the two components that are necessary to arrive at an agreement between S and A. These components – COMMITMENT and ENGAGEMENT – drive our negotiation of CG and make it efficient.

The remainder of this paper is organized as follows. In Sect. 2, we propose that CG negotiation is best understood as a process where S presents an issue to be added to CG and also projects a response from A to make CG management more efficient. We refer to the two processes as COMMITMENT and ENGAGEMENT. In Sect. 3, we use these ingredients to explain the prosodic variation associated with the use of the SPP *eh*. In Sect. 4, we expand our proposal to SFI in the absence of SPPs. In Sect. 5, we show that a syntactic integration of CG modifiers has several advantages over approaches that ignore the modifiers in their formal analysis. In Sect. 6, we conclude.

2 The proposal: Modelling Common Ground management

In this section, we discuss and compare the functions of SPPs and SFI for the negotiation of CG. We begin with a discussion of the pragmatic aspects of CG management (Sect. 2.1), followed by a proposal how CG management can be modelled syntactically (Sect. 2.2).

2.1 The pragmatics of CG management

We follow Brennan & Clark (1991) in assuming that the negotiation of CG minimally includes two phases: presentation and acceptance (see also: Weigand 1991). However, we depart from their labels and use the terms *initiation* and *reaction* to reflect the fact that acceptance is not the only option for an interlocutor to react. In the initiation phase, S presents a proposition for negotiation; in the reaction phase, the erstwhile A indicates whether this proposition is accepted into the CG. From this point of view, let us reconsider the example in (1), repeated here as (8).

(8) {John runs into his friend Mary who walks her new dog around the block.}
    John: You have a new dog, eh↑?
    Mary: Yes, I just got him last week.

Here, John presents a proposition and – by employing the confirmational – puts it up for discussion. Mary's reaction – by employing a response particle – marks the proposition as accepted into the CG. In naturally occurring conversations, this process is not always as brief and straightforward (Clark & Brennan 1991). Acceptance is merely the unmarked option. For example, the initiation phase can be

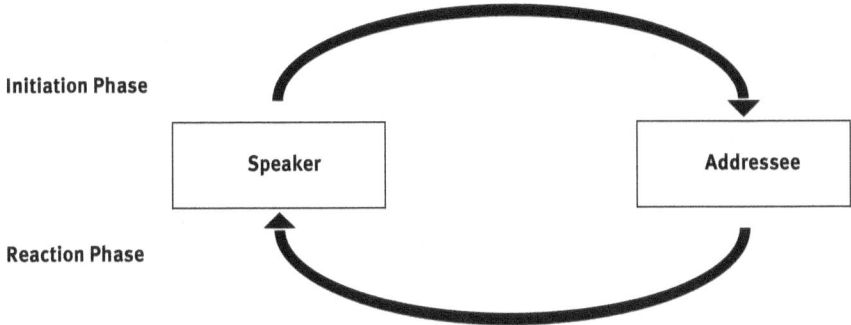

Fig. 1: Initiation and reaction phase

prolonged if the proposition requires further clarification. Similarly, the reaction phase can be prolonged if the interlocutors need to exchange arguments whether the proposition can enter the CG or not. Figure 1 visualizes these discourse moves as a process of going back and forth between S and A. What is crucial for our purpose is that each interlocutor must be assumed to hold an individual set of beliefs (Ground$_S$ and Ground$_A$). Propositions that are present in both grounds can be considered part of CG.

CG negotiation is still more complex than depicted in Fig. 1. In particular, we note that the request for acceptance is already projected by S. This is evident in (1) through the presence of the SPP. The particle *eh* does not only put up the proposition up for discussion; it also anticipates a positive response: S is biased toward the belief that the proposition is true. Specifically, John did not know about Mary's new dog before their encounter. Entering the conversation, he may assume that the dog she has with her is indeed her dog and hence that that she has a new dog. But he can only know for sure after Mary confirms, hence this is an instance of an uncertain Belief (Bel$_{uncert.}$). To capture the conversational properties of *eh*↑ and other CG modifiers, we adopt Thoma's (2016) notion of an *epistemicity matrix*. It summarizes the (publicly accessible) epistemic states that need to hold for the utterance to be well-formed. It separates S's and A's epistemic state, and it recognizes two different times: the time of the conversation (t_U), and a time prior to the conversation ($t_{>U}$). As we shall see, confirmationals may be sensitive to a difference in timing (i.e., it matters when relative to the time of the conversation the belief has been established; Burton & Wiltschko 2016). As summarized in Tab. 1, a felicitous context for the use of *eh* involves a new belief on behalf of S that the proposition is true. In addition, S has to have reasons to believe that A will be able to confirm this belief.

Auer (2002) takes projection to be a reason for the effectiveness of human com-

Tab. 1: Conversational properties of *eh*↑

	$t_{>u}$		t_u	
	S	A	S	A
—		Bel p	Bel$_{uncert}$ p	Bel p

munication. If S did not project agreement, conversation would be much more disfluent, making room for A to negotiate every statement of S. We therefore take acceptance to be the default response by A (Walker 1996). With the use of the SPP *eh*, S marks that he does not take acceptance to be the default; instead it marks that the proposition needs confirmation before it can enter CG. For propositions that require negotiation before they can enter the CG, we adopt Farkas & Bruce's (2010) concept of the *table*. The table can be viewed as a virtual platform for negotiation: S can put propositions on the table to request confirmation for her belief. Similarly, A can respond by putting other propositions on this table. This is a form of disagreement. Hence, the model in Fig. 2 needs to be expanded to include the table, as in Fig. 2. It illustrates that to negotiate CG, the interlocutors do not just hand over propositions; they are putting them up for discussion.

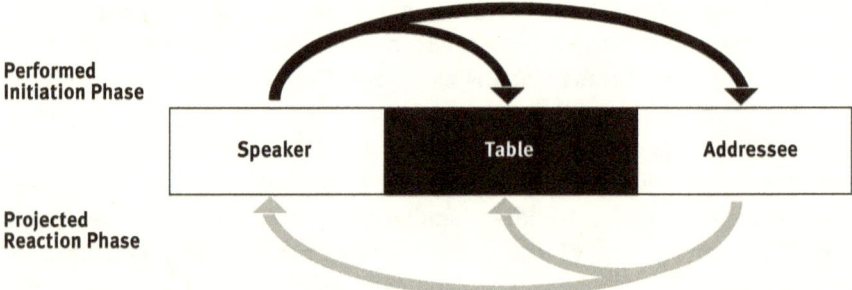

Fig. 2: Negotiating CG (abstract model)

According to the proposal we develop here, *eh*↑ is complex. In Wiltschko & Heim (2016), we propose that the SPP is combined with a call-on-A (Beyssade & Marandin 2007), which is encoded by rising intonation. We here argue that *eh* encodes COMMITMENT, and the contour encodes ENGAGEMENT. We show that both components (COMMITMENT and ENGAGEMENT) come in different degrees. The rise on *eh* encodes only one type of ENGAGEMENT, namely full ENGAGEMENT. Other degrees of ENGAGEMENT are encoded in different ways, as we will see in the discussion of the different variants of *eh* in Sect. 3.

2.2 The syntax of CG management

In the previous section, we proposed that COMMITMENT and ENGAGEMENT interact with each other (e.g., A is asked to engage with S's commitment to the proposition). In this section, we argue that their close relationship can be modelled syntactically. Assuming that CG management is syntactically encoded allows us to account for the fact that the conversational properties of *eh* depend on properties of its host clause. For example, if *eh* is hosted by a declarative clause, it is the declarative which contributes the propositional content of S's COMMITMENT. The rise on *eh* marks the expectation that A will provide that resolution. In contrast, *eh* cannot be used in the context of a (true) interrogative (though *eh* is compatible with rhetorical questions). This suggests that there is a tight connection between clause type (by hypothesis encoded in C), COMMITMENT (encoded in *Ground*) and ENGAGEMENT (encoded in Response). Specifically, we assume that this relation is a matter of syntactic selection. In other words, each of these functions is represented as a functional category in an extended spine as illustrated in (9).[3]

(9)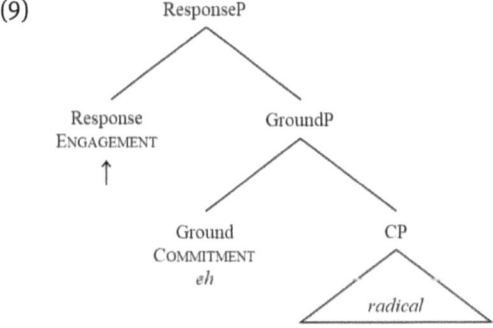

The syntactic integration of discourse-related components has its precedence in Ross's (1970) performative hypothesis, according to which the sentence radical is embedded in a *speech act structure*. On Ross' view, however, speech act structure is a type of propositional structure made up of the same ingredients as the sentence radical: it contains run-of-the mill lexical items (*I, tell, you*) and is assembled in the same way (Subject Verb Object). Contemporary analyses that postulate a dedicated speech act structure view this structure not as another layer of propositional structure but instead as an extension of the functional architecture

---

[3] For the derivation of the linear order, in which *eh* occurs sentence-finally, see Sect. 5. In brief, we assume a role-up operation after which the sentence radical ends up in the specifier position of ResponseP. There is evidence for the structure in (9) in languages that allow both sentence-initial and sentence-final particles (see Heim 2019b).

of the clause (Speas & Tenny 2003; Haegeman & Hill 2013; *inter alia*). The details of the syntactic configuration we propose here are based on the conceptualization of categories developed in Wiltschko (2014). According to this view, all categories are composed of a universal categorizer (see Fig. 3) with the following properties: i) it is transitive; ii) it relates two (abstract) arguments. The higher argument in the specifier is always pronominal; and iii) its head is intrinsically associated with an unvalued coincidence feature [*u*coin]. If the coincidence feature is positively valued (by an appropriate lexical item), then the category asserts that the two arguments coincide (e.g., present TENSE indicates that the reference time coincides with the utterance time). If the coincidence feature is negatively valued, then the category asserts that the two arguments do not coincide (e.g., past TENSE indicates that the reference time does not coincide with the utterance time).

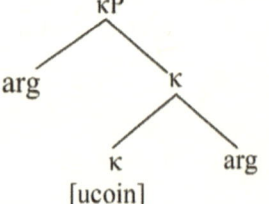

Fig. 3: Universal categories (Wiltschko 2014)

By hypothesis, the functional categories dedicated to CG management adhere to this scheme. The pronominal arguments can be linked to the interlocutors. For GroundP, the coincidence feature captures the relation between S and the proposition. For ResponseP, it captures the relation between A and the Ground$_S$. This is schematized in Fig. 4 below:

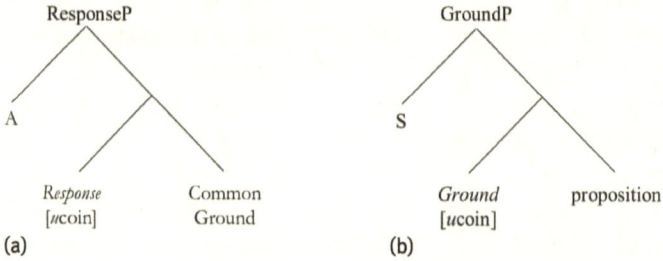

Fig. 4: Schematic configurations of ResponseP (a) and GroundP (b)

Our conversation model in Fig. 2 (see Sect. 2.1) allows for three possible locations of the proposition. It can be in the Ground$_{Spkr}$, in Ground$_A$, or under discussion (on our virtual table). Corresponding to the three locations, we assume three degrees of COMMITMENT and ENGAGEMENT. For each degree of COMMITMENT and ENGAGEMENT, there is a specific syntactic configuration in GroundP and ResponseP. The individual configuration depends on the valuation of [$u$coin]. In GroundP, a positive valuation corresponds to a belief in Ground$_{Spkr}$ ground that p is true. A negative valuation corresponds to a situation where S does not believe p. This is the case when S believes ¬p or when p is not at all part of S's set of beliefs. Hence it can encode disagreement or ignorance. The latter typically results in an expression of surprise. One property that differentiates between the grammar of truth and the grammar of use is that in the latter, but not the former, [$u$coin] may remain unvalued. Specifically, if features in the grammar of truth remain unvalued, then truth conditions cannot be assigned. However, this does not hold true for the grammar of use where the fact that a feature remains unvalued is interpretable. To see this, consider the example in (10). The use of *oh* indicates a change of (cognitive) state (James 1972, 1974; Heritage 1984, 1998; Schiffrin 1987; a. o.), in this case a new proposition enters the Ground$_{Spkr}$. This change of cognitive state is critical for the felicity of the SPP *huh*, which has a different context of use than *eh*.

(10) Oh, so you have a new dog, huh? I didn't know that.

In this context, the use of *huh* requests confirmation for a proposition that is not (yet) in the speaker's belief set. This is further corroborated by the fact that the follow up (*I didn't know that*) is well-formed. We thus assume, following Wiltschko (in prep.) that *huh* signals an unvalued coincidence feature in Ground$_S$. This is consistent with the fact that *huh* is incompatible with a proposition which the speaker must have first-hand knowledge of as in (11). People typically know whether they have a dog and therefore the use of *huh*, which signals the absence of p in the speaker's belief set is ill-formed.

(11) I have a new dog (#huh)?

Just as the coincidence feature in Ground$_S$ can remain unvalued, so can the coincidence feature in RespP. Here, it signals the absence of instructions for response and hence A may or may not respond. While by default S will continue, A can easily engage by interrupting the turn or by backchanneling. The different feature valuations for GroundP and ResponseP are summarized in Tab. 2.

Tab. 2: COMMITMENT and ENGAGEMENT and in GroundP and ResponseP

	Degree	Meaning	Projection	[coin]	Arguments
COMMITMENT	FULL	S believes p	GroundP	+	S, CP
	UNMARKED	S is agnostic about p		u	
	NO	S does not believe p		−	
ENGAGEMENT	FULL	S engages A	ResponseP	+	A, GrundP/CP
	UNMARKED	Engagement is possible[a]		u	
	NO	S engages nobody		−	

[a] A typical form of engagement would be backchanneling. No response is projected and the default is for S to continue the turn. Nevertheless, it is quite natural for A to nod, backchannel or even interject if (s)he does not follow.

3 Application: Decomposing SPPs

In this section, we show how the analysis introduced in the last section can account for the different uses of SPPs and SFI, respectively.

3.1 Rising *eh*

We begin our discussion of SPPs with the most frequent variant of *eh*, namely when it is realized with rising intonation. For an analysis of its conversational properties, consider again the example in (1), repeated below as (12).

(12) {John runs into his friend Mary who walks her new dog around the block.}
John: You have a new dog, eh↑?
Mary: Yes, I just got him last week.

Before John runs into Mary, there is a clear asymmetry in the belief set of the interlocutors. Mary knows about her new dog; John does not. The fact that Mary is walking a dog at the moment of their encounter suggests that she now has a dog. To exclude alternative explanations for the fact that Mary is walking a dog, John requests confirmation of his tentative belief. This is summarized in the epistemicity matrix in Tab. 1, repeated from Sect. 2.1 for convenience.

The use of *eh*↑ is felicitous, if S can commit partially to believing *p*, for lack of sufficient evidence. In our conversational model this means that S places the propo-

Tab. 1: Conversational properties of *eh*↑

	$t_{>U}$		t_U
S	A	S	A
—	Bel *p*	Bel$_{uncert}$ *p*	Bel *p*

sition on the table. Thus, *eh* marks the presence of an issue under negotiation on the table. In addition, S projects for A to respond in a way that resolves the issue: Hence, S fully engages A. The request for full ENGAGEMENT is only licensed if S can assume that A knows whether the proposition is true. For the example in (13), this is not a far-fetched assumption as typically we assume that people know whether they own the dog they walk.

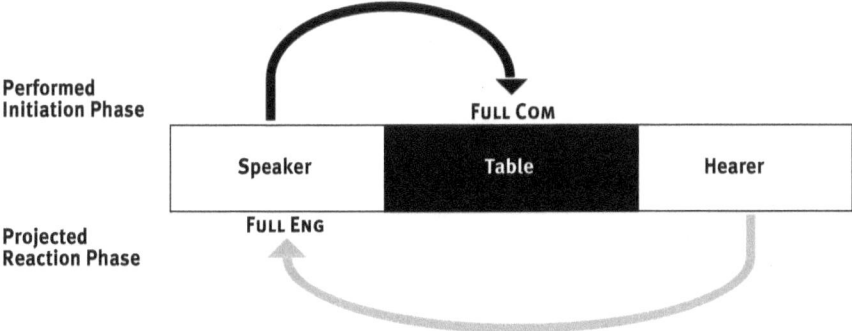

Fig. 5: Negotiating CG in the context of *eh*↑

As for the syntax of *eh*↑, we propose that the COMMITMENT is a consequence of a positive feature evaluation of [*u*coin] in GroundP, which marks the bias of S toward *p*. S encodes that *p* is in his ground, and hence that he believes *p*. We further assume that CP moves into the specifier of GroundP.[4] As for ResponseP, we argue that full ENGAGEMENT comes about via a positive evaluation of [*u*coin]. The utterance is thus asserted to be in A's Response set (hence A is expected to respond). We further assume that GroundP moves into the specifier of RespP. The derivation of (12) is illustrated in (13).

---

4 For the purpose of this paper we simply assume movement to derive the observed linear ordering (see also Haegeman & Hill 2013). An exploration of the motivation for this movement has to await future research.

(13)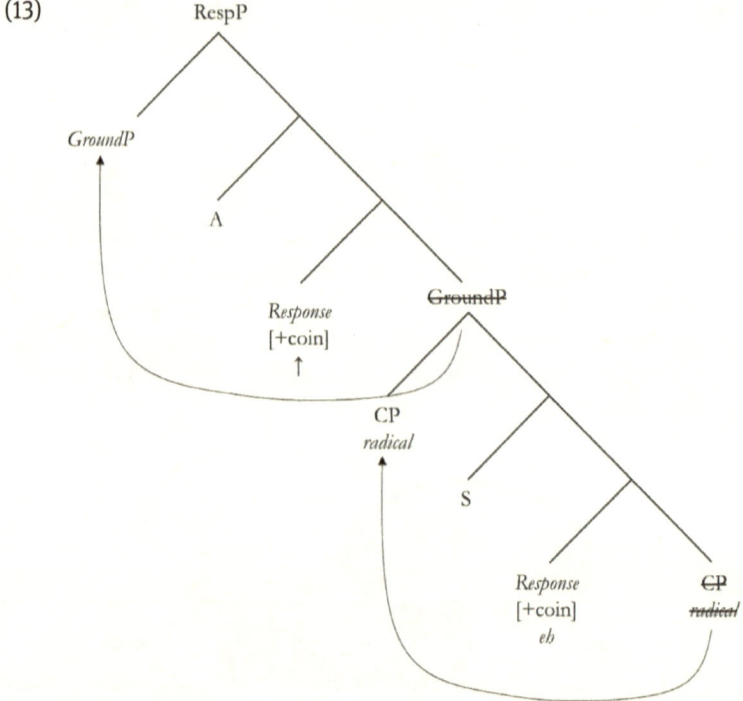

The final rise in *Response* associates with the rightmost overt constituent, namely *eh*.

3.2 Falling *eh*

Not all speakers of Canadian English use *eh* with falling intonation (*eh*↓).[5] The restricted use of *eh*↓ in Canadian English may be related to the fact that in this dialect its context of use is far more restricted than that of *eh*↑. To exemplify the conditions of use for *eh*↓, consider again example (2), repeated below as (14).

(14) {Mary starts daydreaming about a trip to Hawaii, but she keeps coming back to the fact that this will be difficult with her latest addition to the household. John puts an end to her dreaming, and says:}

John: You have a new dog, *eh*↓.

---

[5] The falling variant is the unmarked form of the SPP in New Zealand English (Meyerhoff 1994).

Here, *eh↓* is not used to request confirmation of S's belief that *p*. Rather, S and A both know that *p*. It is only that the deliberations of Mary intially do not reflect her knowledge of the truth of *p*. Given the epistemic states of the interlocutors – as summarized in Tab. 3 – *eh* is used in this context pretending that A does not know *p*.

Tab. 3: Conversational properties of *eh↓*

$t_{>u}$		t_u	
S	A	S	A
Bel *p*	(Bel *p*)	Bel *p*	Bel *p*

By decomposing the contribution of *eh↓* into two components (COMMITMENT and ENGAGEMENT), our model can account for the pragmatic differences between the variants of *eh*. The use of *eh* signals to A that there is an issue on the negotiation table. Negotiating the truth of *p* would be redundant given that both interlocutors in (14) know that Mary has a new dog. What is negotiated is not the truth, but the relevance of *p*. By choosing a fall over a rise, S does not engage A: no response to resolve the issue is required. Instead, S projects the relevance of his statement. The most likely response, if any, would be a confirmation of the relevance with a marker that indicates agreement (e.g. *oh, you're right*).

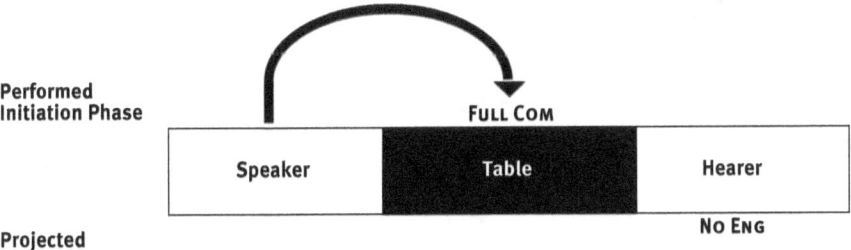

Fig. 6: Negotiating CG in the context of *eh↓*

In terms of the syntactic analysis, we propose that the two arguments in ResponseP are asserted not to coincide: the utterance is not placed into A's response set. The absence of a call-on-A to engage, we argue, is encoded by the falling intonation on *eh*. The configuration for GroundP, however, remains the same as for the SPP with a rise. This is illustrated in Fig. 6, where CP moves to the specifier left of S.

(15)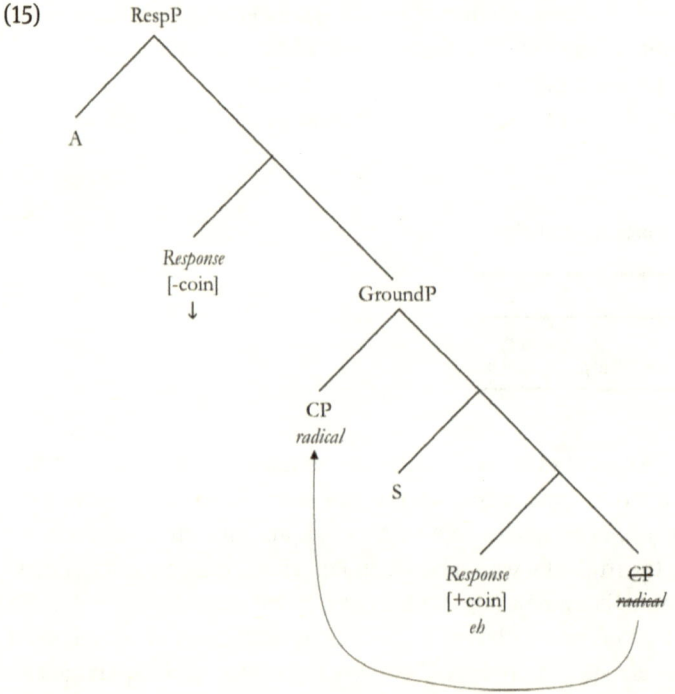

As before, the fall in *Response* associates with the rightmost overt constituent, i.e. CP.

3.3 Level *eh*

Next, we turn to the variant of *eh* which is realized with level intonation (*eh*↗). Under the term 'level intonation', we subsume contours that come with a slight rise or with a continuation of the preceding tone (Halliday 1967). The most notable difference between the context of use of *eh*↗ and the other variants we have discussed thus far is that S, not A has the authority over the truth of *p*: A is not (in any obvious way) a source for the truth of *p*. *eh*↗ is licensed where S believes *p* and assumes that *p* is plausible to A. For the sake of A, S tables *p* – with the intention to move on. Note that S holds the turn after uttering *eh*↗: the *eh* clause is followed by another statement. It follows that the contribution of the rise cannot be to project a response. If it did, S would have to give up her turn.

(16) {Mary and Anna catch up over a drink after the summer break.}
 Anna: So, I have a new dog, *eh*↗, and he just doesn't listen!

Following Avis (1972), Wiltschko & Heim (2016) refer to this variant of *eh* as the *narrative eh* because it is typically employed in narrative contexts. Table 4 summarizes the conversational properties of narrative *eh*:

Tab. 4: Conversational properties of *eh*↗

	$t_{>u}$		t_u	
	S	A	S	A
	Bel *p*	—	Bel *p*	—

eh↗ is employed when the negotiation is suspended. A is not expected to engage because S plans to continue. Nevertheless, S offers for A to intervene if what is presented requires clarification. Narrative *eh* signals that what is on the table is taken to be agreeable but will undergo further modification. The most appropriate response – if any – is backchanneling: S responds without engaging with *p* as backchanneling is merely a way to signal that A is listening (Gardner 2001).

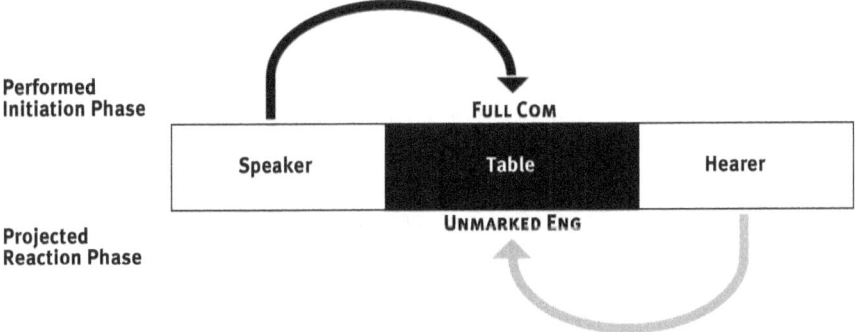

Fig. 7: Negotiating CG in the context of *eh*↗

The syntax of example (16) reflects the different use of the rise: it is employed to signal that engagement is possible but not necessary. [ucoin] in ResponseP remains unvalued. We further assume that GroundP moves to the specifier of ResponseP signalling that neither S nor A are asked to engage. At the prosodic level this corresponds to a notable difference in pitch excursion of the rise in narrative *eh* compared to confirmational *eh*.

(17)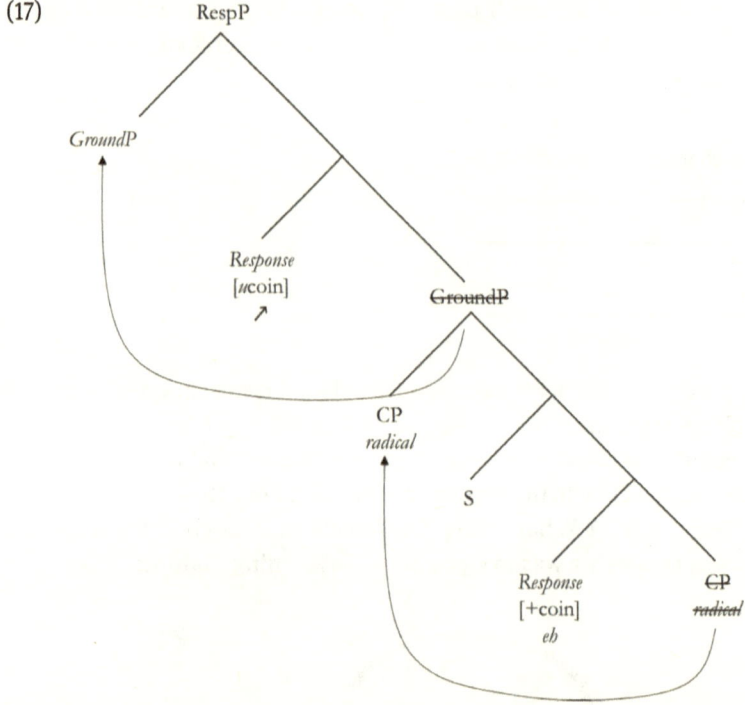

Note that the narrative function and the confirmational function of *eh* is not identical. While the valuation of GroundP is the same, the valuation of [*u*coin] in RespP is different, which in turn encodes a difference in the degree of ENGAGEMENT. In a narrative context, agreement is typically achieved by silence. The turn stays with S. By inviting A to backchannel, the confirmational function is still present in the narrative context of use. The confirmational function is more pronounced in combination with a full rise. Here, A is engaged fully – because S lacks evidence for her belief. We have therefore seen three different forms of negotiating CG. They differ first and foremost by the way S projects A's response. The degree of ENGAGEMENT is clearly marked by the contour. For *eh*↑, S engages A for a ratification of her belief. For *eh*↓, S does not engage A, because it is A who should know *p* in the first place. For narrative *eh*↗, S partially commits to *p*, puts it on the table to make sure that A follows, and plans to move on in the conversation. Table 5 summarizes the role of each variant of *eh* for the negotiation of CG.

Tab. 5: Interactive properties of *eh*

Variant	S($t_>$u)	A($t_>$u)	S(t_u)	A(t_u)	COMMITMENT	ENGAGEMENT
eh + ↑	—	Bel p	Bel$_{uncert}$ p	Bel p	FULL	FULL
eh + ↗	Bel p	—	Bel p	—	FULL	UNMARKED
eh + ↓	Bel p	(Bel p)	Bel p	Bel p	FULL	NO

4 Expansion: Decomposing SFI

In this section, we explore the relation between SFI and SPPs. We show that both fulfill similar functions in the negotiation of CG. We argue that this similarity in function derives from the fact that they have identical syntax. In particular, we can adopt the analysis for intonational properties of SPPs developed above and apply it to utterances without SPPs. We begin by demonstrating that the interactional properties of SFI can be captured by the same means as those that we needed for the description of the properties of SPPs. We then propose that COMMITMENT can be encoded independently of SPPs by means of the duration of the final contour. We also explore the question how SPPs like *eh* can contribute to a level of meaning that cannot be directly encoded with SFI.

Consider the examples in (18), which are the same as the ones discussed above, with the only difference that the SPPs are missing. Instead the SFI is realized on the clause itself. Example (18a) is typically referred to as a rising declarative (Gunlogson 2004). Analogously, we refer to example (18b) as a falling declarative. These examples will demonstrate how our model accounts for a number of different contours discussed in the literature. We can distinguish up to nine different functions of SFIs: each degree of COMMITMENT has three possible combinations with different degrees of ENGAGEMENT.

(18) {John runs into his friend Mary who walks her new dog around the block.}
 a. John: You have a new dog↑?
 b. John: You have a new dog↓.

We begin with a comparison of the licensing conditions for rising and falling declaratives. Both types of declaratives come with some degree of COMMITMENT. Gunlogson (2004, 2008) proposes that COMMITMENT can be associated with different interlocutors, depending on the SFI. In a falling declarative, S commits to p; in a rising declarative, S shifts the COMMITMENT to A. However, we argue that this is an over-simplification. It is both the Commitment and the call on the addressee that changes: The degree of COMMITMENT changes since the belief expressed is uncertain. Moreover, by requesting a response (i.e., full ENGAGEMENT) S indicates to A that he needs additional evidence that allows him to believe with certainty. So rather than shifting COMMITMENT, S projects a response from A that elicits confirmation of his bias. Table 6 lists the interactive properties of rising and falling declaratives.

Tab. 6: Interactive properties of rising and falling declaratives

Variant	$S(t_{>U})$	$A(t_{>U})$	$S(t_U)$	$A(t_U)$	COMMITMENT	ENGAGEMENT
Rising declarative	—	Bel p	Bel$_{uncert}$	Bel p	UNMARKED	FULL
Falling declarative	Bel p	—	Bel p	—	FULL	No

At the time prior to the utterance ($t_{>U}$) rising and falling declaratives have a strong asymmetry of knowledge: only S knows p in falling declaratives; only A knows p in rising declaratives. At the time of utterance (t_U), this changes because of the new information introduced at that point. Specific to example (18a), S has enough evidence to believing that p is true due to the presence of a dog that he did not know of before the encounter with his friend. The syntactic analysis for falling declaratives is provided in (19) with [+coin] in GroundP and [-coin] in ResponseP reflecting the pragmatic properties summarized in Tab. 6 above. The consequence of [-coin] in ResponseP is that the response set of A remains empty, so GroundP stays low. Hence, the fall in *Response* associates with GroundP, including the information about the duration of the fall.

(19)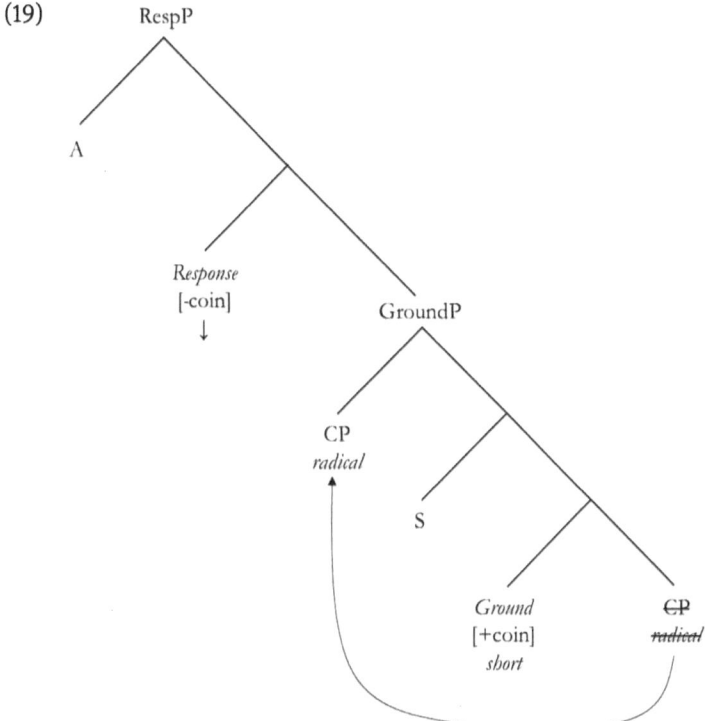

For rising declaratives and declaratives with *eh*↑, the degrees of ENGAGEMENT are the same, reflecting the identical shape of the final rise. What differs, however, is the degree of COMMITMENT – and as a consequence: the target of COMMITMENT. While a rising declarative targets *p*, *eh*↑ targets COMMITMENT:

Tab. 7: Interactive properties of rising declaratives and *eh* + ↑

Variant	$S(t_{>U})$	$A(t_{>U})$	$S(t_U)$	$A(t_U)$	COMMITMENT	ENGAGEMENT	TARGET
Rising declarative	–	Bel *p*	Bel$_{uncert}$ *p*	Bel *p*	UNMARKED	FULL	*p*
eh + ↑	–	Bel *p*	Bel *p*	Bel *p*	FULL	FULL	COM.

The fact that *eh* targets COMMITMENT is evident in contexts where S enters the conversation with a bias. A bias present at $t_{>U}$ is only compatible with *eh*, not with rising declaratives. This is shown in (20).

(20) {John notices a post of his friend Mary on Instagram where she holds a dog. Hours later, he runs into her walking that dog}.

a. *John: You have a new dog↑?

b. John: You have a new dog, eh↑?

The context in (20) is such that S already has some belief about the dog before the start of the conversation. John wants confirmation about his belief; not about the truth of *p*. Compare this with our previous example, repeated here in (21) where S enters the conversation without any previous knowledge of a dog. Here, both *eh* and the rising declarative are acceptable, because belief and truth both materialize at t_U.

(21) {John runs into his friend Mary who walks her new dog around the block.}

a. John: You have a new dog↑?

b. John: You have a new dog, eh↑?

We propose that the different targets of COMMITMENT in rising declaratives and declaratives including *eh*↑ correspond to a difference in syntactic configurations. Specifically, suppose CP moves to SpecRespP indicating that the proposition itself, rather than the belief that *p* is in the response set.

(22)

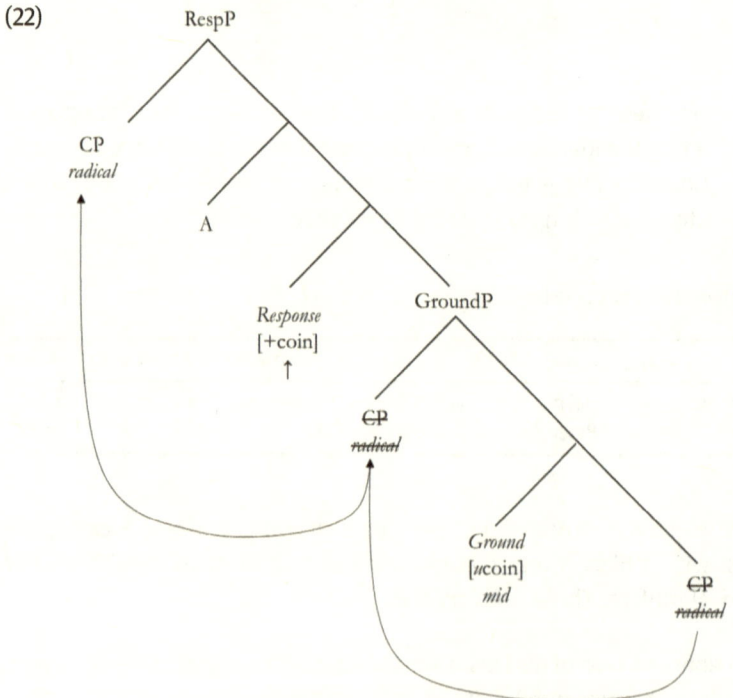

We have now seen that intonation has (unsurprisingly) similar effects independent of whether it associates with an SPP or with a clause without an SPP. On our analysis, this results from the assumption that SFI associates with the response structure of an articulated spine. It has the same function no matter whether the Grounding structure is or is not occupied by an SPP.

A remaining question arises, however, with regard to how the different degrees of COMMITMENT are encoded in the absence of a SPP. We propose that degree of COMMITMENT is encoded by means of the duration in which the contour unfolds (Heim, 2019a). That is, the longer the duration of the contour, the lower the degree of COMMITMENT. For Engagement, the different pitch excursions correspond to the three contour types discussed before: fall, rise and a modified/leveled rise.

Tab. 8: Architecture of negotiating CG

Type	Degree	[coin]	SFI
COM	FULL	+	short
	UNMARKED	u	mid
	No	–	long
ENGAGEMENT	FULL	+	high
	UNMARKED	u	mid
	No	–	low

For the constructions exemplified in (18), this means that the duration of the final contour will decrease from the rising declarative to the falling declarative. In other words, the degree of COMMITMENT correlates with the duration of the sentence-final contour. Below we illustrate the contours of a falling declarative and a rising declarative with the same lexical content produced by a native speaker of Canadian English. We see that the duration from the onset to the offset of the final movement is greater for falling declaratives than for rising declaratives, which corresponds with the increase of COMMITMENT (Fig. 8).

The duration of the rise on the last sillable in Fig. 8a is 277 ms; the duration of the fall in Fig. 8b is 231 ms. Hence, a the rising declarative that express some uncertainty is slightly longer than the falling declarative that expresses no uncertainty. A change in durations simply points to the speed in the change in fundamental frequency. The greater the duration, the less certain the speaker. Further support comes from Tomlinson & Fox Tree (2011) who report for Californian English that

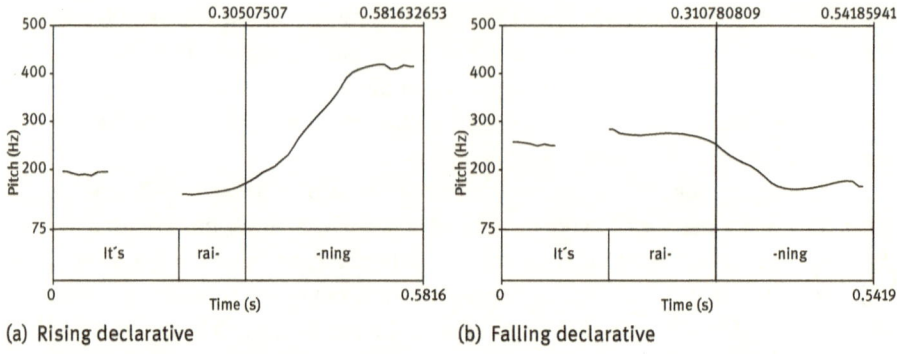

(a) Rising declarative (b) Falling declarative

Fig. 8: Contours encoding different degrees of COM

longer duration can negatively correlate with perceived expertise. We suggest that these findings correspond to what is generally known as hesitation. How this relates to the observations reported in Brinton & Brinton (2010) is presently unclear. They report that short falls encode attenuation and long rises express questioning.[6]

What we propose here for Canadian English is that COMMITMENT can be either encoded by SPPs or by the duration of SFI. SFI can be decomposed into pitch excursion and duration, which are the phonetic realizations of two intonational morphemes associated with the spine: COMMITMENT associates with *Ground*, while ENGAGEMENT associates with *Response*. Together these morphemes define the shape of the SFI. The compositional nature of the shape of the SFI proposed here differs from other analyses which seek to syntacticize SFI. Previous approaches associate meanings directly with level tones or tonal configurations. Davis (2011), for instance, proposes that Japenese *yo* is in complementary distribution with a rise. There is some similarity to our model, nevertheless, since *yo* can combine with a subsequent fall or rise. Davis assumes, however, that SFI is one single morpheme. If *yo* occupies the usual host for SFI, a higher projection serves as its host. Hence, *yo* can combine with either a rise or a fall. Trinh & Crnič (2011) also assume that rises and falls correspond to individual morphemes. These morphemes function as a [1st] and a [2nd] person inflection on an ASSERT operator on declaratives, which heads the sentence radical. [1st] person is encoded by a fall and [2nd] person is encoded by a rise. Both Davis (2011) and Trinh & Crnič (2011) relate the tonal configurations to speech-act functions or roles. A

---

[6] For a more detailed discussion of the encoding of COMMITMENT and possible differences between rises and falls, see Heim (2019a), which includes seome quantitative evidence.

different approach is taken by Truckenbrodt (2012) – both in terms of form and function. Adopting the autosegmental-metrical framework (Pierrehumbert 1980), Truckenbrodt proposes that a high pitch accent (H*) marks new information and that a high phrase accent (H-) marks questions. Hence, the form corresponds to individual tones, which may or may not coincide with SFI, and their function is associated with two different aspects of CG. Newness is a label that applies to the content of CG; questioning is a function that has only indirect consequences for the management of CG.

As for the syntactic integration of these tones, Truckenbrodt (2012) postulates that these morphemes are right-adjoined to a syntactic constituent, typically an unembedded sentence. The formal definitions of the two morphemes are given below.

(23) Let English have the intonational morphemes <H*, new_j> and <H-, $question_j$>, where j is an index of type proposition. Let these morphemes right-adjoin to a syntactic constituent α. Then (ignoring the phonology in the semantic interpretation):

a. $[[α <new_j>]]^{g,S,A}$ is defined as $[α]^{gSA}$ iff S is adding g(j) to the common ground of S and A.

b. $[[α <question_j>]]^{g,S,A}$ is defined as $[α]^{g,S,A}$ iff S is putting up g(j) for question

(Truckenbrodt 2012: 2051).

Proposing that intonational morphemes are right-adjoined is justified by assuming that these tones need to occur linearly after the syntactic constituent to have scope over it. This assumption seems mainly to be a consequence of the choice of the phonological framework. There is no syntactic motivation for associating right-adjunction (as opposed to left adjunction) with scoping. Independent of the nature of adjunction, however, we agree that a peripheral position seems the appropriate choice for a morpheme scoping over a proposition. Truckenbrodt (2012) leaves the host of these morphemes unspecified. In general, the precise formal details regarding the nature of the syntactic integration of intonation are left unspecified in most proposals, including Truckenbrodt's. One specific problem is that Truckenbrodt remains vague about the type of the syntactic constituent a tone adjoins to. Index j in (23) cannot be propositional in nature. Pitch and phrase accents frequently occur with constituents that are too small to be considered propositions.[7]

---

[7] The definitions in (23) also are also inconsistent form a phonological point of view. Truckenbrodt's (2012) account considers only accent and tones that are part of the "nuclear tune". This

Our proposal regarding the syntactic integration of SFI overcomes the shortcomings of previous accounts by associating prosodic properties with notions of CG modification. Specifically, we propose that the the prosodic information is hosted by two projections, GroundP and ResponseP, which directly relate a proposition to the future development of the Common Ground. By positing that SFI is hosted in a complex Speech Act structure above CP, we explain how SFI can serve to modify the CG. This mechanism provides the missing details for Truckenbrodt's (2012) proposal of the syntactic integration of intonational morphemes. Instead of stipulating right-adjunction, we propose movement of the radical into GroundP and the subsequent movement of GroundP into ResponseP. We follow Truckenbrodt, however, in assuming that syntax serves as a mediator between prosodic form and pragmatic function.

5 Evidence for the syntactic integration of Common Ground modifiers

To motivate the syntactic integration of SFI, we have thus far used the functional similarity of SPPs as a window into the formal properties of intonational morphemes. This was necessary since formal computations are impossible to trace for intonational morphemes. We review here two further arguments put forth in previous publications that suggest SPPs undergo the same syntactic computations that are present in the clause proper. We show that SPPs can be marked for agreement and are subject to word order constraints, and thus show a mirrored peripheral distribution. Both findings can be readily explained with the syntactic model proposed above. Moreover, this approach can also explain the distributional restrictions on *eh*.

In Wiltschko & Heim (2016), we report that Upper Austrian German has SPPs that show agreement with A. The SPP *goi*, a particle with similar pragmatic properties as Canadian *eh*, inflects for the formal 2nd person singular and for some speakers even for 2nd person plural. The data in (24) show that agreement is not marked for the arguments of the verb, which are 3rd person in (24a–c).

(24) a. *Ea hot an neichn Hund, goi*
         He has a new dog, conf.2informal

---

tune, which corresponds to our term of SFI, holds no specific status in the autosegmental-metrical tradition. Pitch accents are identical in function independent of whether they occur before or inside the nuclear tune (see esp. Pierrehumbert & Hirschberg 1990).

b. *Ea hot an neichn Hund, goi-ns*
   He has a new dog, conf-2formal

c. *Ea hot an neichn Hund, goi-ts*
   He has a new dog, conf-2pl

Addressee agreement as in (24) is not an isolated phenomenon. Hill (2007) reports vocative inflections and prefixes for so-called particles of address in Romanian, Bulgarian and Ubundu (cf. also Miyagawa 2017 for a recent account of allocutive agreement). We thus propose that CG modifiers are hosted in projections that are accessible to the checking mechanisms of φ features in the same way these features are checked inside the verbal domain. We can rule out the verbal domain since agreement is checked for third person here. The agreement mechanism must therfore be located higher. We propose that the 2nd person inflections are a result of agreement with A in GroundP. In the spirit of Trinh & Crnič's (2011) proposal, we can also extend this proposal to agreement of the interlocutors with SFI: The degree of ENGAGEMENT encoded by the pitch excursion reflects whether or not A is engaged to respond.

Another piece of evidence for the syntacticization of speech act properties stems from word order restrictions. For example, Haegeman & Hill (2013) report such restrictions for West-Flamish SPPs and vocatives. Independent of whether the particles occur sentence-finally or -initially, the vocative *Valère* follows the particle *né* or *wè*. The data in (25) suggests that the sequence of particle and vocative is impenetrable:

(25) a. Né Valère, men artikel is gereed (wè).

b. *Valère né, men article is gereed (wè).

c. (Né) Men artikel is gereed wè Valère.

d. *(Né) Men artikel is gereed Valère wè.

'(Here you are) my article is finished (you know)'

To account for these ordering restrictions, Haegeman & Hill (2013) propose a complex speech-act structure (similar to our grounding structure) that can host both the vocative and the SPP. The word order where both particle and vocative follow the sentence radical is derived by moving ForceP into the specifier of a complex speech act projection. The optional particle né in the sentence-initial position and the sentence-final particle wè mark the landing site:

(26) [saP1 [sa1 né][SAP1 [SA1 n̶é̶] [saP2 ForceP]] [sa2 wè] [SAP2 Valère [SA2 w̶è̶] [F̶o̶r̶c̶e̶P̶]]]]

We have adopted the idea of a roll-up operation to account for our own analysis of Canadian *eh* above.

Finally, a syntactic integration of CG modifiers such as presented here can explain some of the distributional restrictions attested. Consider the three contours in Fig. 9 that represent the prosodic information of the Falling declarative in (27a), the rising declarative in (27b), and the declarative containing *eh*↑ in (27c). Given the similarity of conversational properties of a rise with and without an SPP, we expect that the prosody of both declaratives should be similar in form:

(27) a. You have a new dog↓.
 b. You have new dog↑?
 c. You have a new dog, eh↑?

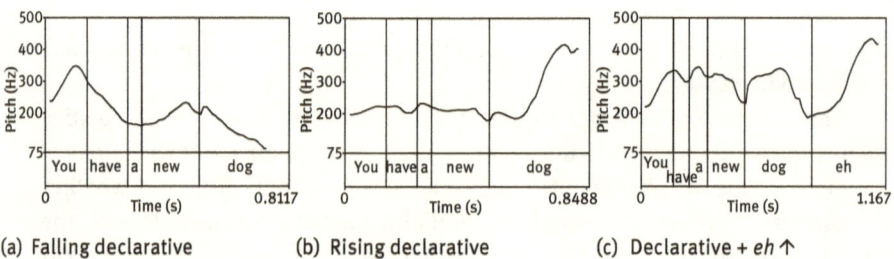

Fig. 9: Contours of three types of declaratives

The comparison of the contours in Fig. 9 shows two interesting patterns. Firstly, the rises of the rising declarative (Fig. 9b) and of the declarative with *eh*↑ (Fig. 9c) have a similar shape and pitch excursion. This is in line with our assumption that the two constructions share the same degree of COMMITMENT and ENGAGEMENT. Secondly, the falling declarative in Fig. 9a and the declarative with *eh*↑ in Fig. 9c have a similar contour leading up to the nuclear tune. The latter is particularly obvious when we compare them to the rising declarative in Fig. 9b. It appears that the declarative with *eh*↑ is better conceived as a falling declarative that occurs with a SPP which comes with a rise rather than a rising declarative that occurs with an SPP. Our syntactic analysis can explain the distributional pattern summarized in (28):

(28) a. Declarative + *eh* + ↑
 b. Declarative + ↑
 c. *Declarative + ↑ + *eh*

To account for the unacceptability of (28c), we simply need to assume that CP cannot move through the specifier of GroundP into the specifier of ResponseP if *eh* is present in *Ground*. This is a reasonable assumption since GroundP would otherwise contain *eh* without the propositional content in CP. In a rising declarative, S projects for A to engage with the proposition. In a declarative with *eh*↑ S projects for A to engage with both *eh* and the radical. A rising declarative with *eh* following is unacceptable since the intonational morpheme associates with the element in the response set (in the specifier of ResponseP).

6 Conclusion

The goal of this paper was to demonstrate that a syntactic integration of intonation is both possible and advantageous. An underlying assumption has been that syntax is well-equipped for mediating between the form and function of any type, hence ideal for incorporating prosodic and pragmatic information. This assumption allowed us to provide a uniform account of both SPPs and SFI with a small set of ingredients. We proposed that CG management is best understood as a negotiation between interlocutors that builds on the notions of COMMITMENT and ENGAGEMENT. The degree of both of these notions can be encoded by prosody alone or – to point directly to the need for negotiation – a combination of SPP and its prosodic properties.

An area that requires further research is the linearization process of CG modifiers. While the phenomena discussed in this paper all appear at the end of a sentence or phrase, cross-linguistic research suggests that these modifiers can also occur sentence-initially and -medially (Lam 2015; Heim et al. 2016; Thoma 2016). While sentence-initial and sentence-medial particles are well-attested, nuclear tunes typically occur at the end of prosodic phrases. This aspect complicates the relation of SPPs and SFI, unless we assume that even sentence-medial speech act particles are associated with heads in the grounding structure above CP (see Thoma 2016 for details). The pragmatic consequences of the linear order of modifiers and host-clauses seems also worth investigating. Associating the presence of CG modifiers in one or the other periphery with a specific pragmatic function may seem appealing (cf. Beeching & Detges 2014), but seems unlikely considering the overall distribution of CG modifiers (see Heim 2019b for a uniform treatment of SPPs).

References

Auer, Peter (2002). Projection in interaction and projection in grammar. *Text-Interdisciplinary journal for the study of discourse*, 25(1):7–36.
Avis, Walter S. (1972). So eh? is Canadian, eh? *Canadian Journal of Linguistics*, 17(2–3):89–104.
Beeching, Kate and Ulrich Detges (2014). *Discourse Functions at the Left and Right Periphery: Crosslinguistic Investigations of Language Use and Language Change*. Leiden: Brill.
Beyssade, Claire and Jean-Marie Marandin (2006). The speech act assignment problem revisited: Disentangling speaker's commitment from speaker's call on addressee. *Empirical issues in syntax and semantics*, 6:37–68.
Brinton, Laurel J. and Donna M. Brinton (2010). *The linguistic structure of modern English*. John Benjamins Publishing.
Burton, Strang and Martina Wiltschko (2016). The eh vs. geu problem. In Bakovic, E., ed., *A shortschrift for Alan Prince*.
Clark, Herbert H. and Susan E. Brennan (1991). Grounding in communication. *Perspectives on socially shared cognition*, 13:127–149.
Davis, Christopher M. (2011). *Constraining interpretation: Sentence final particles in Japanese*. Amherst: University of Massachusetts.
Denis, Derek and Sali A. Tagliamonte (2016). Innovation, right? Change, you know? Utterance-final tags in Canadian English. In Pichler, Heike, ed., *Discourse-Pragmatic Variation and Change in English: New Methods and Insights*, pp. 86–112. Cambridge: Cambridge University Press.
Farkas, Donka F. and Kim B. Bruce (2010). On reacting to assertions and polar questions. *Journal of Semantics*, 27(1):81–118.
Farkas, Donka F. and Floris Roelofsen (2017). Division of labor in the interpretation of declaratives and interrogatives. *Journal of Semantics*, 34(2):237–289.
Gardner, R. (2001). *When listeners talk: Response Tokens and Listener Stance*. Amsterdam: John Benjamins.
Gunlogson, Christine (2003). *True to form: Rising and falling declaratives as questions in English*. New York: Routledge.
Gunlogson, Christine (2008). A question of commitment. *Belgian Journal of Linguistics*, 22:101–136.
Haegeman, L. and V. Hill (2013). The syntacticization of discourse. In *Syntax and its limits*, pp. 370–390.
Halliday, Michael Alexander Kirkwood (1967). *Intonation and grammar in British English*. Berlin: de Gruyter.
Heim, Johannes (2019a). *Commitment and Engagement: The role of sentence-final intonation in deriving speech acts*. Ph. D. thesis, Department of Linguistics, UBC.
Heim, Johannes (2019b). Turn-peripheral management of Common Ground: A study of Swabian gell. *Journal of Pragmatics*, 141:130–146.
Heim, Johannes, Hermann Keupdjio, Zoe Wai-Man Lam, Adriana Osa-Gómez, Sonja Thoma, and Martina Wiltschko (2016). Intonation and particles as speech act modifiers: A syntactic analysis. *Studies in Chinese Linguistics*, 37:109–129.
Heritage, John (1984). A change-of-state token and aspects of its sequential placement. In Atkinson, J. Maxwell and John Heritage, eds, *Structures of Social Action: Studies in Conversation Analysis*, p. 299–345. Cambridge, U.K.: Cambridge University Press.

Heritage, John (1998). Oh-prefacing: A method of modifying agreement/disagreement. In Ford, Cecilia et al., eds, *The language of turn and sequence*. Oxford/New York: Oxford University Press.
James, Deborah (1972). Some aspects of the syntax and semantics of interjections. *Chicago Linguistic Society*, 8:162–172.
James, Deborah (1974). Another look at, say, some grammatical constraints on, oh, interjections and hesitations. *Chicago Linguistic Society*, 10:242–251.
Lam, Zoe W-M. (2015). A Complex ForceP for Speaker- and Addressee-oriented Discourse Particles in Cantonese. *Studies in Chinese Linguistics*, 35:61–80.
Meyerhoff, Mirjam (1994). Sounds pretty ethnic, eh? A pragmatic particle in New Zealand English. *Language in Society*, 23(3):367–388.
Ross, John (1967). *Constraints on Variables in Syntax*. Doctoral dissertation.
Speas, Peggy and Carol Tenny (2003). Configurational Properties of Point of View Roles. In DiSciullo, A., ed., *Asymmetry in Grammar*, pp. 315–343. Amsterdam: John Benjamins.
Stalnaker, Robert (1978). Assertion. In Cole, P., ed., *Syntax and Semantics 9: Pragmatics*, pp. 315–332. New York: Academic Press.
Thoma, Sonja. C. (2016). *Discourse particles and the syntax of discourse-evidence from Miesbach Bavarian*. Doctoral dissertation, University of British Columbia.
Tomlinson, Jr., John M. and Jean E. Fox Tree (2011). Listeners' comprehension of uptalk in spontaneous speech. *Cognition*, 119(1):58–69.
Walker, Marzlin. A. (1996). Inferring acceptance and rejection in dialog by default rules of inference. *Language and Speech*, 39(2–3):265–304.
Weigand, Edda (1991). The Dialogic Principle Revisited: Speech Acts and Mental States. In Stati, Sorin, Edda Weigand, and Franz Hundsnurscher, eds, *Dialoganalyse III. Referate der 3. Arbeitstagung Bologna 1990*, vol. 1, pp. 75–104, Tübingen. Niemeyer.
Wiltschko, Martina (2014). *The universal structure of categories. Towards a formal typology*. Cambridge: Cambridge University Press.
Wiltschko, Martina (2017). Ergative constellations in the structure of speech acts. In Coon, Jessica, Diane Massam, and Lisa deMena Travis, eds, *The Oxford Companion to Ergativity*. Oxford: Oxford University Press.
Wiltschko, Martina (in prep.). The grammar of interactional language. Ms. UBC.
Wiltschko, Martina and Johannes Heim (2016). The syntax of confirmationals. In Kaltenböck, G., E. Keiyer, and A. Lohrmann, eds, *Outside the Clause: Form and function of extra-clausal constituents*, pp. 305–340. Amsterdam: John Benjamins.
Zwicky, Arnold (1974). Hey, whatsyourname! In Galy, Michael La, Robert A. Fox, and Anthony Bruck, eds, *Papers from the Tenth Regional Meeting of the Chicago Linguistics Society*, pp. 787–801. Chicago: Chicago Linguistics Society.

E Jamieson
Syntacticizing intonation? Tag questions in Glasgow Scots

Abstract: This paper presents the results of a perception experiment investigating the acceptability of rising and falling intonation contours in a particular tag construction in Glasgow Scots. I show that intonation contour does not affect speakers' judgments of the acceptability of these tags, despite important roles for intonation in the acceptability of other constructions. I thus argue, contra Wiltschko & Heim (2016) and Wiltschko (2017), that the interpretation of intonation in these tags is pragmatic, and supports a modular conception of the relationship between syntax and intonation rather than the direct syntacticization of intonation in the left periphery.

1 Introduction

It is a standard description of English matrix interrogatives that they involve raising the auxiliary verb above the subject. However, the licensing or interpretation of the interrogative can often depend on its prosodic structure (Asher & Reese 2007; Banuazizi & Creswell 1999; Dehé 2017; Gussenhoven 2004; Han 2002; Hedberg, Sosa & Görgülü 2017; Ladd 1981; Pierrehumbert & Hirschberg 1990). In the realm of canonical tag questions[1], for example, Ladd (1981) and Asher & Reese (2007) point out that tag questions can either have falling or rising intonation, and can either be prosodically incorporated into their anchors, or have a separate nucleus[2]. The prosodic patterns identified depend on whether there is contextual evidence supporting the proposition *p*, which is presented in the anchor of the tag. Rising tags are used when *p* is being challenged, with rising intonation often argued to provide some sort of 'questioning' meaning to a construction (Farkas & Roelofsen 2017; Truckenbrodt 2012). Falling tags are used for more 'confirmational' contexts (Asher & Reese 2007; Ladd 1981). The idea that the intonation

---
[1] Following Sailor (2011), I used 'canonical tag questions' to refer to tag questions where there is agreement between the tag and the anchor (e.g. in terms of auxiliary verb, polarity and subject). I refer to invariant tags, such as *right* or *eh* as 'confirmational particles', following Wiltschko & Heim (2016).
[2] Prosodically incorporated tags always have rising intonation (Ladd 1981; Asher & Reese 2007). I do not discuss these in this paper.

affects interpretation has also been discussed for invariant tags ('confirmational particles') like *eh*, *right* and *huh* by Wiltschko & Heim (2016).

In this paper, I present the results of a perception experiment that tests speakers' acceptability of different intonation contours when using the particle *–int* in Glasgow Scots[3].

(1) He'll like that, w**int** he?

Despite appearing on the surface like a negation marker, Jamieson (2017) argues that *–int* is situated in the Call on Addressee (CoA) (Beyssade & Marandin 2006) position in the conversation domain in the left periphery (Wiltschko & Heim 2016), calling on the addressee to CHECK that the proposition is already in their set of beliefs. The tag is therefore not a true question and should not permit rising intonation on a traditional definition of the role of rising intonation. The results of the experiment presented here, however, show that final rise vs. fall intonation does not seem to play a role in how acceptable participants find the use of *–int*. Rather than taking rising intonation to mean that a proposition is 'up for question', then, I follow Gunlogson (2008) in considering the role of rising intonation to indicate *contingency*. Finally, I discuss how this pragmatic conceptualisation of the meaning of intonation should combine with the tag construction, looking firstly at whether syntactization in the left periphery is appropriate (Wiltschko 2017; Wiltschko & Heim 2016) but concluding that a more modular framework (e.g. Büring 2013; Jackendoff 2002; Nespor & Vogel 1986; Selkirk 1981, 1984; Zec & Inkelas 1990) is the best way to model the data presented in this paper.

Furthermore, the experimental design presented in this paper extends existing methodologies for dialect syntax (e.g. Barbiers & Bennis 2007) in an attempt to explore prosodic features of non-standard dialects without triggering the issues of Observer's Paradox (Labov 1972) that the 'interview method' for dialect syntax aims to reduce.

2 Background

2.1 Glasgow Scots *–int*

The variety of English spoken in Glasgow includes a particle, *–int*, which is available in a limited number of constructions with interrogative syntax: namely, tag

---

[3] In this paper, I use 'Glasgow Scots' to refer to the variety of English spoken in the Greater Glasgow area of Scotland.

questions, exclamatives and to some extent in polar rhetorical questions (Jamieson 2017). *–int* combines with the onset of the relevant auxiliary (Thoms, Adger, Heycock & Smith 2013) and looks on the surface like a negation marker.

(2) He was leaving, **wint** he?

(3) **Hint** she got an amazing wee voice! (Thoms et al. 2013:18)

(4) People widnae understand that, **wint** they no? (Jamieson 2017)

However, given its limited distribution, lack of negative function, and ability to co-occur with a lower negation marker in tag questions on negative anchors (see (5)), Jamieson (2017) argues that *–int* is not a marker of negation but a CHECK marker, formulated as in (i):

(i) $\lambda p.\forall w'.\forall w''[\text{EpiSpkr}(w)(w') \rightarrow (\text{EpiAdr}(w')(w'') \rightarrow p(w''))]$

The CHECK marker is not-at-issue content (Potts 2005) that operates on the at-issue content (a proposition, p) and effectively states that for every world w' in the speaker's epistemic set of worlds, then for every world w'' that is in the addressee's epistemic set in those w' worlds, p is in w'' – *the speaker believes that the addressee believes p.*

Jamieson (2017) argues, following the neo-performative confirmational syntax established in Wiltschko & Heim (2016), that *–int* should be situated in the Call on Addressee (CoA) projection in the ResponseP, above CP, shown in Fig. 1, with movement triggered by the Stray Affix Hypothesis (Lasnik 1981) rather than a Q feature on C. Wiltschko & Heim's (2016) syntax for confirmationals is designed to take into account the speaker/addressee relationship through Grounding and this CoA projection (see similar proposals from Speas & Tenny (2003) and Haegeman & Hill (2013)). CoA is modeled on Beyssade & Marandin's (2006) idea of 'calling on the addressee', where the speaker informs the addressee what they are expected to do with the proposition in order for the discourse to continue felicitously. For more details on this 'conversation domain' in the left periphery, see Wiltschko (2014, 2017) and Wiltschko & Heim (2016).

In all contexts where it is possible to use *–int*, the speaker is happy to take responsibility for p and thus to be the source (Gunlogson 2003) for p, as shown by the fact that in a situation where the addressee answers with *'I don't know'*, the speaker can themselves take full responsibility for p without requiring any input from the addressee. This is the same as a declarative, but unlike a question – even a matrix biased question (for more on biased questions see e.g. Romero & Han 2004). For full discussion of examples (5) and (6), see Jamieson (2018b).

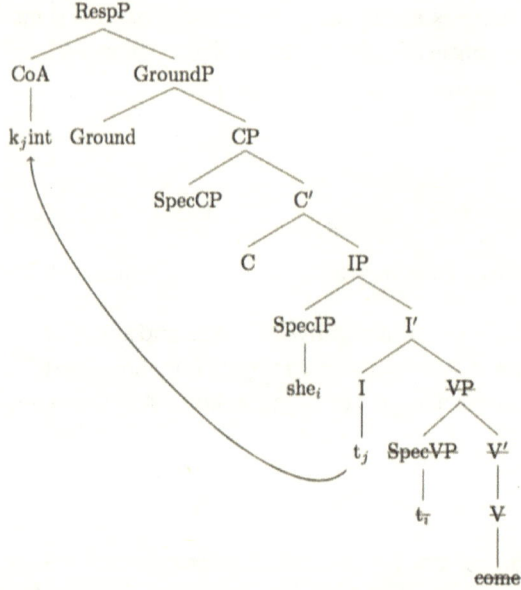

Fig. 1: Syntax for the tag *kint she* in the construction 'She can come, kint she?' in Glasgow Scots. Note that *–int* is in the CoA position, with the auxiliary verb raising due to the Stray Affix Hypothesis (Lasnik 1981).

(5) S: He can come, kint he? / He can come, can't he?
   A: I don't know.
   S: Well, he can.

(6) S: Can't he come? / *Kint he come?
   A: I don't know.
   S: #Well, he can.

Given that the speaker's commitment can hold even if the addressee informs the speaker that they do not have any knowledge of the truth of p (just like a declarative), and given that a straightforward declarative does not require any additional information or particles in the grounding domain (GroundP) (Wiltschko 2017), Jamieson concludes that the role of *–int* is purely about the relationship between the speaker and the addressee – in effect, 'calling on the addressee' to CHECK that p is part of their belief set and therefore situated in CoA. This is not the same as questioning or confirming, and crucially does not require a response. However, given that the speaker is making a statement about what they believe the addressee's beliefs to be, and given that one has the final say about their own belief state, there is some pressure on the addressee to respond.

It is interesting to consider how intonation interacts with these CHECK constructions, given the meanings for various intonation contours given in the literature (see Sect. 2.2 below). I explore this in the experiment below, looking specifically at tag question contexts, where both rising and falling intonation are possible (Dehé & Braun 2013), depending on evidential context (Ladd 1981). Specifically, I model evidential context following Sudo (2013).

Sudo presents various types of biased questions in English and Japanese, showing how epistemic beliefs and evidential biases affect the type of construction produced. For matrix biased questions in English, Sudo claims that speakers have an epistemic belief of *p*, and that the evidential context surrounding the interaction can either be *negative* or *neutral*. A *negative* evidential bias means that the context actively contradicts the speaker's existing belief of *p*, while a *neutral* evidential context neither supports nor provides evidence against that belief of *p*. Domaneschi, Romero, & Braun (2017) subsequently show that speakers do produce biased questions in these contexts in production tasks.

Tag questions are also licensed in the same contexts, though this is less explicitly discussed in the literature. However, Ladd's (1981) discussion of confirmational and questioning tag questions can be re-formulated in terms of these distinctions: Ladd's *confirmational* tags equate to the *neutral* evidential context (perhaps also including *positive* evidential contexts), while his *questioning* tags are referring to *negative* evidential contexts. See examples (10) and (11) below for examples of neutral and negative contexts which license tag questions and were used in the experimental materials.

2.2 The meanings of intonation in interrogatives and confirmationals[4]

It has long been argued that the intonation of English constructions with interrogative syntax can affect the meaning (Asher & Reese 2007; Banuazizi & Creswell 1999; Farkas & Roelofsen 2017; Gussenhoven 2004; Han 2002; Hedberg, Sosa, & Görgülü 2017; Ladd 1981; Pierrehumbert & Hirschberg 1990). In general, polar questions with rising intonation are presumed to be truly information seeking. Dehé (2017) finds that English speakers produce rising intonation (L*H-H%) in information seeking polar questions 78% of the time in experimental contexts, while Hedberg et al. (2017) found that low-rise nuclear contours (L*H-H%) were

---

[4] I will only discuss the intonation patterns of polar interrogatives in this paper: English *wh*-questions have different intonation patterns (Dehé 2017; Hedberg, Sosa & Görgülü 2017; Pierrehumbert & Hirschberg 1990), requiring separate study.

the 'unmarked', most common forms in their corpus study of American English and that in total, 90.5% of polar questions were rising.

Very generally, rising intonation is taken to encode that a proposition is 'up for question' (Truckenbrodt 2012:2039). This has also contributed to analyses of declarative questions like the example in (7), which intuitively has the meaning of questioning the proposition p: 'it is raining'[5]. Declaratives generally have falling intonation. Given that an example like (7) has standard declarative syntax, the obvious change that could be contributing to the change in meaning is the non-standard, rising intonation.

(7) It's ↗raining?

This idea of putting a proposition up for question via rising intonation has also been discussed with regard to confirmational particles like *right*, *huh* and 'Canadian *eh*' (Heim, Keupdjio, Lam, Osa-Gómez & Wiltschko 2014; Wiltschko & Heim 2016). Wiltschko & Heim (2016) argue that the interpretation of a particle like *eh* requires decomposition into two parts – the particle itself, *eh*, and its intonation. In order to act as a confirmational particle, they claim that *eh* must have rising intonation. An alternative *eh*, with non-rising intonation, acts as a 'narrative marker' that does not request a response. The authors take this as evidence that the two elements are operating independently, with only the *rising* intonation calling on the addressee to do something with the proposition – specifically, to confirm p.

There has been less discussion of the role(s) of non-rising intonation in polar interrogative type constructions: however, Dehé & Braun (2013) find falling intonation to be the most common intonation in their corpus study of English tag questions. Falling intonation is also found in Banuazizi & Creswell's (1999) corpus study of English rhetorical questions. Han (2002:202) claims that this falling intonation in a rhetorical question gives the interrogative 'the illocutionary force of an assertion' – however, she does not give any details for formalising this, and it is worth noting that polar rhetorical questions are most frequently produced with rising intonation (Dehé 2017).

Given these meanings posited for intonation, we might hypothesize that since the CHECK construction with –*int* is not a true question despite its surface appearance, it should not permit rising intonation. I test this in Sect. 3, below.

---

[5] I will return to Gunlogson's (2003, 2008) analysis of the role of intonation in rising declaratives in Sect. 4.2.1.

2.3 Other tags in Glasgow Scots

It is worth noting that as well as the *–int* particle in Glasgow Scots, there is another available tag question form: verb-subject-*no*, where *no* is the Scots negation marker equivalent to standard English *not*.

(8) He can come, can he no?

(9) She'll like that, will she no?

While constructions like these are possible in standard UK and US English varieties (with *not*), they are generally considered archaic or stilted (Bender 2001:73). However, this is the standard form for tags across Scots varieties (Brown & Millar 1980), and follows from the fact that *–nae* (the Scots negation marker equivalent to standard English *–n't*) is not available in interrogatives. Instead, Scots matrix interrogatives with negation use this verb-subject-*no* construction.

Brown & Millar (1980) state that these kinds of tags are not restricted to a 'confirmational' context i.e. they can be used where both rising and falling *–n't* tags can be used in standard English. Indeed, Jamieson (2017) finds that there is no effect of evidential context on Glasgow Scots speakers' ratings of verb-subject-*no* tag questions, with these tags equally acceptable regardless of whether the evidential context for the tag is negative or neutral.

Brown & Millar (1980:119) also claim that verb-subject-*no* tags always have rising intonation, regardless of context. Under the assumption that these are canonical tag questions – biased questions that have undergone VP-ellipsis (Sailor 2011) – these would thus be true questions, and would always put the underlying proposition up for question, in the framework of Truckenbrodt (2012) or Asher & Reese (2007).

In Glasgow Scots, then, there are two options for canonical tag constructions: *–int* and verb-subject-*no*. These are syntactically and semantically distinct. Verb-subject-*no* tags are syntactically and semantically questions, and are claimed to only have rising intonation. *–int* tags are semantically CHECK markers, with *–int* argued to be situated in CoA in ResponseP in the left periphery and rising intonation hypothesized to be unavailable. I will focus on *–int* in the results and analysis below, but will also present results for verb-subject-*no* tags for comparison.

3 Experiment

3.1 Design

The experiment was designed to vary rising and falling intonation contours, in neutral and negative evidential contexts in tag questions with *–int* and verb-subject-*no* (VSno).

Tab. 1: Experimental design: number of stimuli per context

	Neutral evidential context		Negative evidential context	
	–int	VSno	*–int*	VSno
Rising	4	4	4	4
Falling	4	4	4	4

20 speakers of Glasgow Scots split into two age groups (18–30 and 55+) judged 32 relevant examples as part of a larger experiment looking at the distribution of *–int*.

The methodology extended the 'interview method' for dialect syntax (Barbiers & Bennis 2007; Cornips & Jongenburger 2001; Thoms 2014) to also investigate prosody.

The interview method requires an interviewer to sit down with each participant in a location of their choosing – generally their home. The interviewer reads out a short context to each participant that sets a scene, followed by the example they want the participant to judge. The participant then gives a score to the example using a Likert scale (e.g. 1–5), and is encouraged to share the reasoning behind their judgments with the interviewer. This discussion is recorded.

The interview method is designed specifically to deal with the various issues of prestige and the Observer's Paradox (Labov 1972) that risk affecting the study of non-standard varieties. It is possible that as an academic and as (potentially) an outsider to the community, the researcher's presence will create a situation where speakers modify their behaviour or deny use of non-standard variants in order to seem more 'proper' (Adger & Trousdale 2007:267; Henry 1995:12). By designing a methodology that tries to make sure participants are in a situation they feel comfortable with *in their local community* i.e. where they would use their local variety (e.g. at their home, over a cup of tea), and that is as conversational as possible (chatting with the researcher, about contexts which are designed to be as natural as possible, encompassing everyday events in the community), the interview method aims to reduce the effects of the Observer's Paradox as far as possible – and has proven successful for a number of large scale dialect syntax projects such as the Syntactic Atlas of Dutch Dialects (SAND) and the Scots Syntax Atlas (SCOSYA).

Here, the methodology was adapted in order to be able to reliably control for intonation patterns. The interviewer still met with participants at a location of their choosing[6] and read out a short context to the participant in order to set the scene and establish the evidential contexts (e.g. (10) and (11)). However, instead of the interviewer reading out the example sentence to the participant, the participant pressed a button on a laptop and heard the relevant example, which was played using a programme built in PsychoPy (Pierce 2007). The examples were pre-recorded by a 33-year old male speaker of Glasgow Scots.

After hearing the example, participants then proceeded to judge it on a 1–5 Likert scale, with 1 described as 'terrible, nobody round here would say that' and 5 described as 'perfectly fine, I say that and I hear it around me'.

(10) A while ago, our friend Sarah told us she had been to Edinburgh Castle. You are trying to work out whether it is worth going to visit. You ask me, and I say 'you should ask Sarah'. You say:

🔊 Oh aye, she's been before, hint ↗she?

(11) We are organising a party. You are pretty sure our friend Yasamin will be able to make it. However, I say that Yasamin is really busy just now. You say:

🔊 She would make time, wint ↘she?

This adapted methodology attempted to combine the positive qualities of the interview method with the relevant features of experimental laboratory pragmatics, following e.g. Wochner, Schlegel, Dehé & Braun (2015) and Dehé (2017) who show that speakers in German (Wochner et al. 2015) as well as English and Icelandic (Dehé 2017) can distinguish between information seeking and rhetorical questions in examples that are identical in lexical and syntactic form, but vary in their prosody. Furthermore, Cruz-Ferriera (1989) develops a listening comprehension test for L2 speakers' intonation which relies on participants judging the meaning of sentences with varied intonation; Jiang (2005) successfully used this to explore understanding of question intonation with Cantonese and Mandarin L2 speakers

---

[6] Participants were told that the location had to be a) quiet and b) somewhere where the task would not be interrupted. The majority of participants chose to meet in their homes; five participants chose to meet in a local library, and one at their place of work.

of English. The methodology thus builds on these established results which show that speakers *can* reliably perceive intonational differences, and asks them to apply Likert scale judgments in a similar style task.

3.2 Results

Results for –*int* tags show no effect of intonation or interaction between evidence and intonation in either age group, as can be seen in Table 2. While for younger speakers, –*int* was rated significantly lower in negative evidential contexts than neutral evidential contexts, there was no difference in their judgments due to intonation. Older speakers also did not distinguish judgments based on intonation; however, neither did they distinguish their judgments based on evidential context – even when younger speakers did. I take this to be an effect of the methodology – older speakers are likely to be more permissive and 'overcompensate' for potential ongoing language change when asked to make sociolinguistic judgments (Carrera-Sabaté 2014; Drager 2011; Lawrence 2017), and so are less likely to observe subtle pragmatic or intonational distinctions when rating. –*int* may also be a more recent innovation, as is claimed in Macafee (2011), and thus more common with younger speakers. The most interesting results, therefore, are in the 18–30 group.

Tab. 2: Means and standard deviations for –*int* in neutral and negative evidential contexts with falling and rising intonation, by age group

	18–30				55+			
	NEUTRAL		NEGATIVE		NEUTRAL		NEGATIVE	
	mean	SD	mean	SD	mean	SD	mean	SD
FALL	4.55	0.749	4.03	1.112	4.68	0.656	4.68	0.846
RISE	4.69	0.468	4.03	1.307	4.65	0.770	4.55	0.749

In Table 3, the results for VSno tags are presented: again, there was no effect of intonation or interaction between evidence and intonation in either age group. For VSno tags, there was no effect of evidence, as discussed above.

I will focus on –*int* in the discussion below, considering firstly what the results here tell us about the meaning of intonation. I will then consider how intonation should be incorporated into the construction, and its potential syntacticization. The results for VSno tags are interesting, as it seems that Brown & Millar's (1980) claim about intonation does not hold. However, as I take VSno tags to be standard

Tab. 3: Means and standard deviations for VSno in neutral and negative evidential contexts with falling and rising intonation, by age group

	18–30				55+			
	NEUTRAL		NEGATIVE		NEUTRAL		NEGATIVE	
	mean	SD	mean	SD	mean	SD	mean	SD
FALL	3.83	1.238	3.95	1.260	4.40	0.982	4.43	0.958
RISE	3.85	1.329	3.90	1.317	4.50	0.906	4.20	1.159

VP-elided questions, they do not directly impact on the discussion of syntacticization in the left periphery and thus I will not discuss them in detail. Note, however, that the results for VSno tags will be accounted for in the discussion of the meaning of intonation.

4 Discussion

4.1 Interpreting the results

The first question that needs to be addressed is whether speakers were truly able to distinguish the rising and falling intonation patterns. Results from filler examples and speakers' comments suggest that they were able to hear differences based on prosody and incorporate these into their judgments.

Firstly, speakers judged filler examples of negative imperatives with 'subjects' above *don't* that had no intonation break. The addition of an intonation break between the 'subject' and *don't* means that the 'subject' is then interpreted as a vocative (Jensen 2003; Potsdam 1996; Zanuttini 2008).

(12) You don't leave yet!

Examples like (12), with no intonation break, were marked down with speakers commenting that there was not enough stress on the subject, or enough of a break between the subject and *don't*. This is a case where prosodic factors did seem to affect the results of the acceptability tasks.

Furthermore, when directly asked about intonation contours on *–int* examples, speakers did not indicate that rising intonation was unacceptable. It seems, from their comments, that there may be a *preference* for falling intonation. One younger male participant, for example, quoted below, accepted the rising intonation though he produced it himself with falling intonation:

GY01: I would expect to hear that all the time
INT: yeah
GY01: aye five
INT: ok ... even
GY01: the the 'hint'
INT: even yeah
GY01: 'hint' is like really really common I think
INT: mhm ... would you
GY01: more so than like 'dint'
INT: ok ok 'hint' more common ok ... emm would you expect to hear it in that way like that really sort of surprised like 'hint ↗they' kind of way
GY01: aye or like 'hint ↘ye'
INT: 'hint ↘ye' yeah
GY01: yeah
INT: ok

A different young male participant commented on three occasions that he wanted a tag question example with –*int* to have a more falling intonation – however, two of those examples already *had* falling intonation. It seems that this particular participant was alert to potential variation in intonation, but did not interpret any intonational cues in the stimuli.

Of course, it is not possible to know exactly what any one participant is basing their judgments on. However, these points seem to suggest that intonation *can* affect participants' judgments when the variation in intonation indicates a true syntactic distinction (e.g. subject vs. vocative) and thus affects the semantic interpretation. This has been shown to be true in other areas where prosodic boundaries help disambiguate ambiguous interpretations, for example of attachment, scope or parentheticals/appositives (e.g. Beach 1991; Carlson, Clifton & Frazier 2001; Gollrad, Sommerfeld & Kügler 2010; Hirschberg & Avesani 2000; Price, Ostendorf, Shattuck-Hufnagel & Fong 1991; Wagner & Crivellaro 2010; Warren, Schafer, Speer & White 2000).

Furthermore, when explicitly asked about intonation with regards to –*int*, participants gave answers indicating that they *did* hear intonation differences in the tag question examples, but still did not seem to treat the variation as important to their acceptance of the construction.

In the next section, I lay out the contribution that I believe intonation is making to the –*int* utterance (as well as the VSno tag), following and extending Gunlogson (2008). I then move on to discuss how we should conceptualise the incorporation of intonation with these tags. I will firstly consider whether intonation can be contained in a functional head in the an extended conversation domain in the left periphery as Wiltschko & Heim (2016) and Wiltschko (2017) do. This would fit with the syntactic analysis for the CHECK move provided in this framework by Jamieson (2017). However, I will conclude that it cannot, and that a modular framework is more appropriate. Under this analysis, intonation is still a 'unit of language' that contributes meaning, but it is not in the syntax.

4.2 Contribution of intonation

In Sect. 2.2 I laid out the general position in the literature that rising intonation has the meaning of introducing a question speech act. I follow these authors in arguing that the meaning of an utterance like *int it* or *right* can be decomposed into the meaning of its items and the meaning of its prosodic pattern. However, rather than following the likes of Truckenbrodt (2012) in stating that rising intonation puts a proposition *up for question*, I follow Gunlogson (2008) in arguing that the contribution of rising intonation is *contingency*[7]. The move toward understanding rising intonation as contingency rather than putting a proposition 'up for question' re-frames it as a more pragmatic meaning, rather than invoking a question speech act. This is a positive move, in light of the results above in which intonation did not affect speakers' comprehension of the speech act taking place – the meaning for them was clearly more flexible, and able to be influenced by context.

Regarding contingency, Gunlogson states that:

"A discourse move μ by an agent α is *contingent* on a discourse condition δ if:
a) δ does not obtain at the time of μ; and
b) It is inferable from the discourse context that the update effected by μ is to be retained only if δ obtains after the discourse move immediately succeeding μ."

(Gunlogson 2008:129)

So, to account for rising declaratives such as (7) (repeated as (13) below), Gunlogson argues that by using declarative word order, the speaker is expressing a commitment to *p*. However, the speaker is not able to be an independent source for the commitment, and thus they choose to defer to the addressee. To defer, they use rising intonation, which signals that the proposition they have put forward in the declarative will not be legitimised and added to the Common Ground (CG) *unless*

---

[7] I do not take a position on whether it is one particular part of the intonation contour that contributes the specific meaning of contingency, or whether it is the whole contour. Further research would be required to establish potential contributions of different individual tones and the relationship between them, as Pierrehumbert & Hirschberg (1990) and Truckenbrodt (2012) do.

the following discourse move from the addressee indicates that the addressee is willing to be the source of the commitment and thus that *p* should be added to CG.

(13) It's ↗raining?

The rising declarative in (13) is therefore only licensed a) when the speaker has *some* access to evidence regarding the truth of *p* (e.g. they are in an office with a window and have seen some specks of rain on it), but b) the speaker believes that the addressee has greater rights to know whether *p* is true (e.g. the addressee has just come in from outside, perhaps with an umbrella or a damp coat). Therefore, *p* (it is raining) will not be added to CG until the addressee confirms it should be.

Gunlogson distinguishes this semantic contribution of rising intonation from the contribution of interrogative word order in questions. While in declarative questions, the speaker is able to make a contingent commitment to *p* and requests the addressee become the independent source for the commitment, in a polar interrogative, the speaker indicates that they are not sure whether *p* or ¬*p* should hold, and that they believe the addressee is a potentially authoritative source for commitment to either *p* or ¬*p*. Gunlogson claims that it is this imbalance in authority that is brought about by word order signalling interrogativity – with rising intonation adding the contingency that the acceptance of *p* or ¬*p* is based on the addressee becoming a source for one or the other.

This contingency analysis accurately accounts for the Glasgow –*int* data. Recall the formulation for CHECK moves given in (i):

i. $\lambda p.\forall w'.\forall w''[\text{EpiSpkr}(w)(w') \rightarrow (\text{EpiAdr}(w')(w'') \rightarrow p(w''))]$

In CHECK moves, the speaker is the source for *p*, and is checking with the addressee that they also already believe *p*. Note that this is different from believing that *p* is in CG already – it is possible that it is[8], but it can also be something which is apparent from discourse-external evidence that the speaker wishes to make explicit in CG. ¬*p* thus does not need to enter the equation – the construction is purely about making a belief of *p* explicit for both participants. This accounts for the fact that CHECK moves are preferred in the situation where there is no negative counterevidence challenging *p*, though they are not *un*acceptable when there is negative counterevidence – the speaker is presumably just putting more stock in *p* being a shared belief between participants, rather than on the challenging evidence.

---

[8] Although *p* can already be in CG when a speaker produces a CHECK move, it cannot be currently active, or foregrounded, in CG.

It follows that contingency is not required with a CHECK move. As the speaker is the source for p, this indicates that they are willing to take responsibility for p in CG. However, the addition of contingency through rising intonation does not directly conflict with this position in terms of interpretability – although it might affect what is expected of the addressee, it does not affect the acceptability of the construction.

Furthermore, this accounts for the results in the VSno case. While the VSno cases are example of constructions with interrogative syntax, and thus do introduce the $p/\neg p$ uncertainty, the speaker has already committed to p in the declarative that is the anchor to the tag, and as we saw above in example (5), is able to revise their commitment to become the sole source if the addressee is not able to commit to p. The contribution of rising intonation to the tag, then, effectively requests an answer to the question, while with falling intonation, there is no longer an explicit contingency request.

Of course, both these outcomes make predictions about speakers' production. Firstly, they predict that non-rising intonation will be produced more often with *–int* constructions, and secondly they predict that rising intonation will be produced more often with VSno constructions. This is as Brown & Millar (1980) claimed for VSno constructions. However, further work would be required in order to establish whether or not this is actually the case.

Having established the contribution of intonation to the *–int* construction and supported the position that intonation does *not* contribute a full speech act meaning to a construction, we can now consider how intonation should combine with these tag constructions. I firstly consider the idea of syntacticizing an intonational morpheme in the conversation domain as proposed by Wiltschko & Heim (2016) and Wiltschko (2017); however, I show that for the *–int* construction, this analysis is not viable. I will then consider alternative, modular options, which I will argue are a better fit for the data.

4.3 The interaction between intonation and syntax

4.3.1 Syntactizing intonation?

In Sect. 2.1, I introduced Wiltschko & Heim's (2016) neo-performative speech act syntax, designed for confirmational particles. The authors argue that the meaning of confirmational particles like *eh* can be decomposed into two parts: the particle and its intonation. They further argue that the intonation (represented as /) is encoded in this 'conversation domain' as shown in Fig. 2.

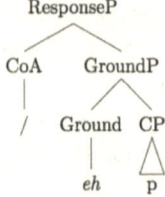

Fig. 2: The conversation domain showing the distribution of confirmational *eh*.

In this framework, the *eh* particle itself is situated in a GroundP projection. This encodes 'S's propositional attitude towards p' (Wiltschko & Heim 2016:27). Rising intonation, denoted as /, is situated in the CoA projection (Beyssade & Marandin 2006, see discussion above).

Wiltschko & Heim argue that intonation should be syntacticized in this way due to the relationship between intonational contours and speech acts (Trinh & Crnič 2011; Truckenbrodt 2012) – intonational contours can select for speech acts. Wiltschko and Heim argue that this happens as both are situated in the syntax. Furthermore, they show that there are languages in which the confirmational CoA and the attitudinal grounding can be contributed by two different particles.

(14) **kʉla** u ʉ Bʉ swə **a?**
      part 2.SG have dog new Q
      "You have a new dog, eh?"   (Medumba, Wiltschko & Heim 2016:26)

In the example in (14), *kʉla* marks the speaker's propositional attitude, and associated with the grounding layer (just as *eh* does). However, rather than signaling the request for confirmation through intonation, Medumba speakers signal this through an additional particle, *a*, which associates with the CoA projection. As the function carried out by particle *a* is carried out by intonation in English, the authors believe there should be a unified analysis that can account for the crosslinguistic contributions of both particles and intonation.

Recall that Jamieson (2017) argues that Glasgow Scots *–int* is in the CoA position. If Wiltschko & Heim (2016) are correct about the syntacticization of rising intonation in CoA, it should not be able to co-occur with the *–int* particle. However, as we saw in Sect. 3, whether or not there was rising intonation did not affect participants' acceptability of the *–int* tag. It thus cannot be the case that rising intonation can straightforwardly be in CoA, though some sort of recursive CoA could resolve this.

Wiltschko (2017) posits an ergative speech act structure that does just that, as shown in Fig. 3.

Wiltschko argues that for a confirmational particle like *huh*, the addressee (Adr) is externally merged in the RespSUBJ position. Rising intonation is situated

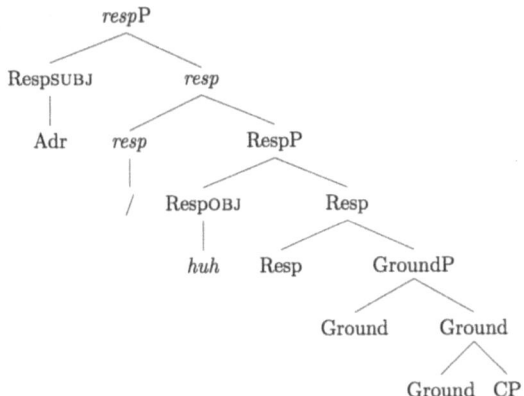

Fig. 3: The ergative speech act domain, as set out by Wiltschko (2017), showing the distribution of confirmational *huh*.

in *resp*, and *huh* marks out the proposition as the object for response, situated in RespOBJ.

Could this sort of ergative structure work for the Glasgow *–int* cases? It would perhaps be possible to argue that while Adr is still merged as an external argument in RespSUBJ, and intonation is still located as a unit in the head of *resp*P, *–int* is situated in the head of Resp.

This would be able to handle both CoAs in this neo-performative syntactic framework. It would also relate the *–int* tag to Wiltschko's analysis of polar interrogatives, which she posits as having Adr merged in RespSUBJ and rising intonation in the head of *resp* (like confirmationals), but with no particle in RespOBJ to mark out the object for response. *–int* tags would behave similarly, with Adr as the subject argument, intonation (whether rising or falling) marking contingency at the first layer of resp, and *–int* situated in the Resp head, closer to the proposition, where the auxiliary raises to.

However, this does not seem like a particularly satisfactory analysis. Firstly, in perception tasks, why do speakers ignore intonation when judging the acceptability of a construction? If the intonation is situated as a unit in the syntax just like *–int*, but contingency is not *required* in these constructions, why does intonation not affect participants' judgments of acceptability, while they do observe differences in acceptability between *–int* and VSno tags in negative evidential contexts (see Tables 2 and 3), or between tag questions and matrix biased questions in particular contexts (Jamieson 2018a)? In other words, participants do observe differences in acceptability when there are clear syntactic differences. Given that we saw that intonation could affect the acceptability of negative imperatives when it had clear syntactic consequences for the construction, if intonation was encoded in the syntax in the same way as –*int*, we would expect that there would be a preference for falling intonation in the acceptability judgments. This effect builds on research which has shown that the role of intonation contours in establishing speaker/addressee beliefs or speech acts has been shown to be strongly affected by contextual factors (Ladd 1978, 1980; Liberman & Sag 1974; Ward & Hirschberg 1985).

Secondly, this movement problem relates to what I believe is the wider issue with this analysis in relation to interrogative constructions more generally. The Wiltschko (2017) and Wiltschko & Heim (2016) analyses relate the intonation contour very strongly to the confirmational particle, and thus to the boundary tone. Syntacticizing intonation in this way does not take into account the importance of the whole intonation contour and the variation that can take place within it in establishing the meaning of a construction. For example, Dehé (2017) shows that prosodically, different combinations of boundary tones, nuclear accent placements and overall nuclear contour patterns contribute to speakers' interpretation of an interrogative as a rhetorical question – it is not as simple as saying that 'a rhetorical question has a falling intonation' (Han 2002:215) or even acknowledging the possibility of both final rise or fall in English rhetorical questions, as Banuazizi & Creswell (1999) do. It is difficult to see how Wiltschko's (2017) extension of the ergative framework to interrogatives, which simply posits Adr in RespSUBJ and rising intonation in *resp*, could be modified to take into account the apparent complexity of the relationship between intonation and meaning.

Therefore, I believe that, based on the evidence from this experiment as well as current ongoing research into the role of intonation in various types of interrogative clauses, the argument for syntacticizing intonation made by Wiltschko & Heim (2016) and Wiltschko (2017) cannot adequately account for the data from in –*int* tags. While I support the idea of having a speech act domain in the syntax, the perception data from tags presented in this paper, as well as the production data from other complex interrogative types does not support syntacticizing intonation in this domain. Below, I consider some alternative analyses for the Glasgow data.

4.3.2 Alternative approaches

In the literature, there have been many attempts at dealing with the relationship between syntax and prosody with respect to syntactic vs. prosodic constituency, ambiguity resolution, and discourse phenomena such as focus and topic – however, there have perhaps been fewer attempts to syntacticize phenomena that involve the whole intonation contour, such as speech acts, or expression of speaker attitudes. Two crucial exceptions are Pierrehumbert & Hirschberg (1990) and

Truckenbrodt (2012), who builds on Pierrehumbert & Hirschberg's compositional system.

Truckenbrodt (2012) argues various tones[9] have particular semantic meaning, by virtue of being 'intonational morphemes' which (in English, at least) right-adjoin to the syntactic structure prior to interpretation at LF. They are thus semantically interpreted in the same way as the rest of the syntactic structure.

For example, he posits that H- is an intonational morpheme, <H-, $question_j$>. This morpheme looks for a salient antecedent proposition that the speaker (S) is 'putting up for question', expecting an answer from the addressee (A).

(15)   [[p <H-, $question_j$>]]$^{g, S, A}$ = [[p]]$^{g, S, A}$ iff S is putting g(j) up for question
(Truckenbrodt 2012:13)

Crucially for his account, p needs to be interpreted *before* the intonational morphemes so as the antecedent nature of the proposition can be fulfilled.

Certainly, there are positive points to this analysis for the Glasgow data: if H- was redefined as making the acceptance of p contingent on the next discourse move, this would be able to capture the role of intonation posited by Gunlogson (2008), and its relationship to the proposition as a whole, while still contributing to LF interpretation. Rather than being syntactically incorporated with the proposition, intonation stands alone, but is still able to contribute meaning at LF. This reflects more possibilities for the meaning of the intonation contour, with meaning built up by contribution from different tones and patterns between them.

However, as Truckenbrodt himself states, H- is '... a primitive question indicating and question generating device that does not have the complexity to keep up with the semantics of interrogatives' (2012:12), and thus how exactly this formalisation would play out with the complex semantic and intonational patterns of interrogatives (e.g. Dehé 2017) remains to be seen.

While modelling tones as intonational morphemes which attach directly to the syntax is one possibility, a model which includes a separate prosodic domain which interfaces with syntax and semantics/pragmatics may in fact be a better fit for the data (e.g. Büring 2013; Jackendoff 2002; Nespor & Vogel 1986; Selkirk 1981, 1984; Zec & Inkelas 1990). Crucially, however the relationship between syntax and intonation is modelled, the intonation has to be able to select for a full proposition p (so as to be able to state that p is contingent on some δ). For example, in

---

9 Truckenbrodt is unsure about assigning meaning to all tones, discussing in particular L* and L-. This may weaken the idea of a compositional analysis, if there is no clear evidence for meaning for all tones. However, given the complexity of and variation included in prosodic contours, it may be that this evidence is simply yet to be established.

Büring's (2013) model, there are two separate domains, one containing the full set of well-formed syntactic structures and one containing the full set of well-formed prosodic structures. These domains are paired via mapping constraints to give well-formed pairs <synt,pros> which are input to LF. In order to have the correct interpretation of contingency, this must be an ordered pair in which *synt* is interpreted first.

With *–int*, then, the CHECK move would be input to LF from the syntax, and first interpreted as part of the syntactic structure at LF. Following the ordered pair, the intonation contour (whether rising or falling) would then contribute contingency (or lack thereof) with respect to CHECK(p). The ordered pair for *–int* with falling intonation would thus be as in (16).

(16)   < CHECK(p), p is not contingent on δ >

This is just one possible way to model the data – in general, though, I believe this sort of modular approach in which prosody and syntax can each contribute separately to semantics/pragmatics is most appropriate way to model the data. I leave the details of how to work this out for future research.

4.4 Consequences for confirmationals

Of course, moving away from an analysis like that of Wiltschko & Heim (2016) has consequences for the analysis of confirmational particles like *right*, *huh* and *eh*, which their framework is desgined to account for. However, I believe that confirmationals can be easily modelled – in a preferable way – in a more modular framework.

In Wiltschko & Heim's (2016) analysis, the confirmational particle itself serves to 'ground' p; in Wiltschko (2017) there is little semantic role for the particle itself except in 'picking out the object' for confirmation. These roles seem unnecessary, given that the speaker has just produced the relevant proposition for confirmation, and thus the 'object' is already salient in the discourse. In the modular analysis, the confirmational particle would need to be specified semantically for some kind of CONFIRMATION meaning, in a similar way to how CHECK was specified above for Glasgow Scots *–int*. Contingency (rising intonation) would play a bigger role in the interpretation of a CONFIRMATION tag particle which does not intuitively have such a strong preference for neutral evidential contexts as *–int* does (as seen in Table 2). I leave for future research how this confirmational meaning should be specified.

5 Conclusions

This paper presented the results of an experiment testing the hypothesis that Glasgow Scots particle *–int* could not co-occur with rising intonation. The results showed that participants did not judge examples with rising intonation any differently to examples with falling intonation. It does seem as though speakers could hear differences in intonation using the methodology developed here, as shown from evidence from other constructions, and from speaker comments about the acceptability of rising intonation in *–int* constructions. It seems as though while falling intonation may be preferred, rising intonation is also acceptable and does not affect a hearer's comprehension of the construction – something we would expect it to do, if it a) gave information about the speech act involved or b) was encoded in the syntax at the same level as the particle.

I followed Gunlogson (2008) in analysing the contribution of rising intonation as *contingency*, rather than the 'proposition up for question' approach of Truckenbrodt (2012) and Wiltschko & Heim (2016). While I maintained Wiltschko & Heim's underlying conceptualisation of the neo-performative 'conversation domain' in the left periphery, I argued that the fact that speakers do not consider either intonation contour as essential for judging the acceptability of the construction is evidence that it does not need to be treated as an element of the syntax, against the theory that Wiltschko & Heim (2016) and Wiltschko (2017) posit.

While I support Wiltschko & Heim's conjecture that the semantic contribution of the particle itself and the semantic/pragmatic contribution of the intonation to the overall meaning of the particle should be separated, I do not believe there is any reason to input intonation directly to the syntax. Instead, some sort of analysis where syntax and prosody separately contribute information to the semantics (e.g. Büring (2013) or Truckenbrodt (2012)) gives more flexibility and accuracy in capturing the complex relationships between intonation and syntax in questions and confirmationals.

Of course, a production study or the availability of corpus data would add valuable information to these results – I leave this for further research. What I have shown in this paper is that the difference between rising and falling intonation does not affect speakers' comprehension of canonical tag question constructions in Glasgow Scots, and thus any syntactic and semantic analysis of the construction will need to be consistent with this finding.

References

Adger, David and Graeme Trousdale (2007). Variation in English syntax: theoretical implications. *English Language and Linguistics*, 11(2):261–278.

Asher, Nicholas and Brian Reese (2007). Intonation and discourse: Biased questions. *Interdisciplinary Studies on Information Structure*, 8:1–38.

Banuazizi, Atissa and Cassandre Creswell (1999). Is that a real question? Final rises, final falls and discourse function in question intonation. In *Proceedings From the Annual Meeting of the Chicago Linguistic Society 35*, pp. 1–13.

Barbiers, Sjef and Hans Bennis (2007). The Syntactic Atlas of the Dutch Dialects: A discussion of choices in the SAND project. *Nordlyd*, 34:53–72.

Beach, Cheryl (1991). The interpretation of prosodic patterns at points of syntactic structure ambiguity: Evidence for cue trading relations. *Journal of Memory and Language*, 30(6):644–663.

Bender, Emily (2001). *Syntactic variation and linguistic competence*. PhD Thesis, Stanford University. Stanford.

Beyssade, Claire and Jean-Marie Marandin (2006). The speech act assignment problem revisited: Disentangling speaker's commitment from speaker's call on addressee. In Bonami, Oliver and Patricia Cabredo Hofherr, eds, *Empirical Issues in Formal Syntax and Semantics 6: Papers of CSSP 2005*, pp. 37–68.

Brown, Keith and Martin Millar (1980). Auxiliary verbs in Edinburgh speech. *Transactions of the Philological Society*, 78(1):81–133.

Büring, Daniel (2013). Syntax, information structure and prosody. In den Dikken, Marcel, ed., *The Cambridge Handbook of Generative Syntax*, pp. 860–896. Cambridge: Cambridge University Press.

Carlson, Katy, Charles Clifton, and Lyn Frazier (2001). Prosodic boundaries in adjunct attachment. *Journal of Memory and Language*, 45(1):55–81.

Carrera-Sabaté, Josefina (2014). Does meta-linguistic awareness play any role at the beginning of an ongoing sound change? The case of some vowel-ended verbs in Catalan. *Sociolinguistic Studies*, 8(2):193–221.

Cornips, Leonie and Willy Jongenburger (2001). Elicitation techniques in a Dutch syntactic dialect atlas project. In van der Wouden, Ton and Hans Broekhuis, eds, *Linguistics in the Netherlands 2001*, pp. 53–63. Amsterdam: John Benjamins.

Cruz-Ferriera, Madalena (1989). A test for non-native comprehension of intonation in English. *International Review of Applied Linguistics in Language Teaching*, 27(1):23–40.

Dehé, Nicole (2017). The prosody of rhetorical questions. Presentation at NELS 48, University of Iceland, 28th October.

Dehé, Nicole and Bettina Braun (2013). The prosody of question tags in English. *English Language and Linguistics*, 17:129–156.

Domaneschi, Filippo, Maribel Romero, and Bettina Braun (2017). Bias in polar questions: Evidence from English and German production experiments. *Glossa*, 2(1):23.

Drager, Katie (2011). Speaker age and vowel perception. *Language and Speech*, 54(1):99–121.

Farkas, Donka and Floris Roelofsen (2017). Division of labour in the interpretation of declaratives and interrogatives. *Journal of Semantics*, 34:237–289.

Gollrad, Anja, Esther Sommerfeld, and Frank Kügler (2010). Prosodic cue weighting in disambiguation: Case ambiguity in German. In *Proceedings of Speech Prosody 2010*.

Gunlogson, Christine (2003). *True to form: Rising and falling declaratives as questions in English*. New York: Routledge.
Gunlogson, Christine (2008). A question of commitment. *Belgian Journal of Linguistics*, 22:101–136.
Gussenhoven, Carlos (1983). *On the grammar and semantics of sentence accents*. Dordrecht: Foris.
Gussenhoven, Carlos (2004). *The phonology of tone and intonation*. Cambridge: Cambridge University Press.
Haegeman, Liliane and Virginia Hill (2013). The syntacticization of discourse. In Folli, Raffaella, Christina Sevdali, and Robert Truswell, eds, *Syntax and its limits*, pp. 370–390. Oxford: Oxford University Press.
Han, Chung-Hye (2002). Interpreting interrogatives as rhetorical questions. *Lingua*, 112(2):201–209.
Hedberg, Nancy, Juan M. Sosa, and Emra Görgülü. (2017). The meaning of intonation in yes-no questions in American English: A corpus study. *Corpus Linguistics and Linguistic Theory*, 13(2):1–48.
Heim, Johannes, Hermann Keupdjio, Zoe Wai-Man Lam, Adriana Osa-Gómez, and Martina Wiltschko (2014). How to do things with particles. In Teddiman, Laura, ed., *Proceedings of the 2014 Canadian Linguistic Association Conference*, pp. 1–15.
Henry, Alison (1995). *Belfast English and Standard English: Dialect variation and parameter setting*. Oxford: Oxford University Press.
Hirschberg, Julia and Cinzia Avesani (2000). Prosodic disambiguation in English and Italian. In Botinis, Antonis, ed., *Intonation: Analysis, modelling and technology*, pp. 87–95. Dordrecht: Kluwer.
Jackendoff, Ray (2002). *Foundations of language*. Oxford: Oxford University Press.
Jamieson, E. (2017). 'People widnae understand that, wint they no?': –*int* in Glasgow Scots. Presentation at the Linguistics Association of Great Britain Annual Meeting, University of Kent, 5th September.
Jamieson, E. (2018a). Experimental evidence for the contextual acceptability of biased questions and tag questions in English. In van Alem, Astrid, Anastasiia Ionova and Cora Pots, eds, *Proceedings of the 26th Conference of the Student Organization of Linguistics in Europe (ConSOLE XXVI)*, pp. 331–349, Leiden. Leiden University Centre for Linguistics.
Jamieson, E. (2018b). 'Negation' and CHECK moves in the Shetland dialect of Scots. In Hucklebridge, Sherry and Max Nelson, eds, *NELS 48: Proceedings of the Forty-Eighth Annual Meeting of the North East Linguistic Society*, pp. 67–80, Amherst. GLSA.
Jensen, Britta (2003). Syntax and semantics of imperative subjects. *Nordlyd*, 31(1):150–164.
Labov, William (1972). *Sociolinguistic patterns*. Philadelphia: University of Pennsylvania Press.
Ladd, Robert (1978). Stylized intonation. *Language*, 54:517–540.
Ladd, Robert (1980). *The structure of intonational meaning*. Bloomington: Indiana University Press.
Ladd, Robert (1981). A first look at the semantics and pragmatics of negative questions and tag questions. In *Proceedings From the Annual Meeting of the Chicago Linguistic Society 17*, pp. 164–173.
Lasnik, Howard (1981). Restricting the theory of transformations. In Hornstein, Norbert and David Lightfoot, eds, *Explanation in linguistics*, pp. 152–173. London: Longman.
Lawrence, Daniel (2017). The social perception of a sound change. *University of Pennsylvania Working Papers in Linguistics*, 23(1):111–120.

Liberman, Mark and Ivan Sag (1974). Prosodic form and discourse function. In *Proceedings From the Annual Meeting of the Chicago Linguistic Society 10*, pp. 416–427.
Macafee, Caroline (2011). Characteristics of non-standard grammar in Scotland. Ms. University of Aberdeen.
Merchant, Jason (2001). *The syntax of silence: Sluicing, islands and the theory of ellipsis*. Oxford: Oxford University Press.
Nespor, Marina and Irene Vogel (1986). *Prosodic Phonology*. Dordrecht: Foris.
Pierce, Jonathan (2007). PsychoPy – Psychophysics software in Python. *Journal of Neuroscience Methods*, 162(1–2):8–13.
Pierrehumbert, Janet and Julia Hirschberg (1990). The meaning of intonation contours in the interpretations of discourse. In Cohen, Philip, Jerry Morgan, and Martha Pollack, eds, *Intentions in communications*, pp. 271–311. Cambridge, MA: MIT Press.
Potsdam, Eric (1996). *Syntactic issues in the English imperative*. PhD Thesis, University of California, Santa Cruz.
Potts, Christopher (2005). *The logic of conventional implicatures*. Oxford: Oxford University Press.
Price, Patti J., Mari Ostendorf, Stefanie Shattuck-Hufnagel, and Cynthia Fong (1991). The use of prosody in syntactic disambiguation. *The Journal of the Acoustical Society of America*, 90(6):2956–2970.
Romero, Maribel and Chung-Hye Han (2004). On negative yes/no questions. *Linguistics and Philosophy*, 27(5):609–658.
Sailor, Craig (2011). Tagged for deletion: A typological approach to VP ellipsis in tag questions. Ms. UCLA.
Selkirk, Elizabeth (1981). On prosodic structure and its relation to syntactic structure. In Fretheim, Thorstein, ed., *Nordic Prosody II*, pp. 111–140. Trondheim: TAPIR.
Selkirk, Elizabeth (1984). *Phonology and syntax*. Cambridge, MA: MIT Press.
Speas, Peggy and Carol Tenny (2003). Configurational properies of point of view roles. In DiScullio, Anna-Maria, ed., *Asymmetry of grammar: Syntax and semantics*, pp. 315–344. Amsterdam: John Benjamins.
Sudo, Yasutada (2013). Biased polar questions in English and Japanese. In Gutzmann, Daniel and Hans-Martin Gärtner, eds, *Beyond expressives: Explorations in use-conditional meaning*, pp. 275–296. Leiden: Brill.
Thoms, Gary (2014). Report for "Refining the questionnaire method of judgment data collection: a Buckie pilot study" pilot project. Ms. University of Glasgow.
Thoms, Gary, David Adger, Caroline Heycock, and Jennifer Smith (2013). Remarks on negation in varieties of Scots. Presented at the Cambridge Workshop on English Dialects, University of Cambridge, 6th November.
Trinh, Tue and Luka Crnič. (2011). On the rise and fall of declaratives. In Reich, Ingo, Eva Horch and Dennis Pauly, eds, *Proceedings of Sinn und Bedeutung 15*, pp. 1–16, Saarbrücken. Unviersaar/Saarland University Press.
Truckenbrodt, Hubert (2012). Semantics of intonation. In Maienborn, Claudia, Klaus von Heusinger, and Paul Portner, eds, *Semantics: An international handbook of natural language meaning*, p. 2039–2069. Berlin/Boston: de Gruyter.
Wagner, Michael and Serena Crivellaro (2010). Relative prosodic boundary strength and prior bias in disambiguation. In *Proceedings of Speech Prosody 2010*. Available at: http://speechprosody2010.illinois.edu/papers/100238.pdf.

Ward, Gregory and Julia Hirschberg (1985). Implicating uncertainty: The pragmatics of fall-rise intonation. *Language*, 61(4):747–776.
Warren, Paul, Amy Schafer, Shari Speer, and S. David White (2000). Prosodic resolution of prepositional phrase ambiguity in ambiguous and unambiguous situations. *UCLA Working Papers in Linguistics*, 99:5–33.
Wiltschko, Martina. (2014). *The universal structure of categories: Towards a formal typology.* Cambridge: Cambridge University Press.
Wiltschko, Martina (2017). Ergative constellations in the structure of speech acts. In Coon, Jessica, Diane Massam, and Lisa Travis, eds, *The Oxford Handbook of Ergativity*, pp. 419–446. Oxford: Oxford University Press.
Wiltschko, Martina and Johannes Heim (2016). The syntax of confirmationals: A neo-performative analysis. In Kaltenböck, Gunther, Evelien Keizer, and Arne Lohmann, eds, *Outside the clause: Form and function of extra-clausal constituents*, pp. 303–340. Amsterdam: John Benjamins.
Wochner, Daniela, Jana Schlegel, Nicole Dehé, and Bettina Braun (2015). The prosodic marking of rhetorical questions in German. In *Interspeech 2015*, pp. 987–991.
Zanuttini, Raffaella (2008). Encoding the addressee in the syntax: evidence from English imperative subjects. *Natural Language and Linguistic Theory*, 26(1):185–218.
Zec, Draga and Sharon Inkelas (1990). Prosodically constrained syntax. In Zec, Draga and Sharon Inkelas, eds, *The phonology-syntax connection*, pp. 365–378. Chicago: University of Chicago Press.

Hisao Tokizaki and Jiro Inaba
A prosodic constraint on prenominal modification

Abstract: In this paper, we argue that the word order patterns of the prenominal modification structures across languages are regulated by the universal prosodic constraint we propose; No Prosodic Boundary (NPB) bans the structure in which a modifier and the modified head is separated by a prosodic boundary (i.e. * ... M ... / ... H ...). Together with the bare mapping algorithm proposed in Tokizaki (1999, 2008a), according to which syntactic brackets (both right and left) are interpreted as prosodic boundaries (/), our proposal accounts for the contrast between *a [sleeping [on the sofa]] baby vs. ein [[in München] wohnhafter] Künstler, without recourse to such syntactic constraints as head final filter or head adjacency condition. Our analysis can also be extended to prenominal modification structures in Russian and phrasal compounds in languages such as English or German. If our analysis is on the right track, it enables us to account for phenomena pertaining to word order by way of constraints operating outside the narrow syntactic component, thus contributing to one of the minimalist theses that syntax is universal, only hierarchically organized without linear information.

1 Introduction

The word order of nouns and their modifiers in noun phrases is different among the languages of the world. Head nouns precede or follow their modifiers (e.g. *un livre difficile* (French) vs. *a difficult* book (English)). In this chapter, we focus on prenominal modifiers and investigate the word order within them. They may be head-initial (e.g. [gotovyi *na vse*] *student* 'a student ready for anything' (Russian)) or head-final (*ein* [*in München* wohnhafter] *Künstler* 'an artist living in München' (German)).

In generative syntax, the head adjacency condition has been proposed in order to explain the unacceptability of head-final noun phrases containing a head-initial modifier phrase (e.g. *a [sleeping on the sofa] baby (Grosu & Horvath 2006; Haider 2004, 2010; Emonds 1976; van Riemsdijk 1998, cf. the Head Final Filter (Williams 1982), the Final-Over-Final Constraint (Biberauer et al. 2014; Sheehan 2017)). We argue that the head adjacency condition and similar conditions on linear order cannot be tenable as a syntactic condition in the minimalist program, which assumes that linear order is determined at Externalization, not in syntax.

In Sect. 2, we discuss the head adjacency condition and its conceptual and empirical problems concerning phrasal compounds in Germanic languages and head-initial prenominal modifiers in East Slavic languages and Greek. In Sect. 3, we propose a prosodic constraint on prenominal modification, which states that prenominal modifiers cannot be separated from the head by prosodic boundaries. Section 4 concludes the discussion.*

2 The head adjacency condition and its problems

2.1 The head adjacency condition

It has been argued that in a number of languages, the head of a prenominal modifier must be adjacent to the head noun (van Riemsdijk 1998:672; Grosu & Horvath 2006:474; Haider 2004, 2010; Escribano 2004, 2005).[1]

(1) English
    a. a [*sleeping baby*]
    b. *a [[*sleeping* on the sofa] *baby*]
    c. a *baby* [*sleeping* on the sofa]

(2) German
    a. ein [[in München *wohnhafter*] *Künstler*]
        a   in München living   artist
    b. *ein [[*wohnhafter* in München] *Künstler*]
        a   living   in München artist

---

* We would like to thank Gerrit Kentner, Joost Kremmer, Yoshihito Dobashi, Kuniya Nasukawa and the anonymous reviewers for their invaluable comments and suggestions. We are also grateful to Go Hikita for Russian data. Thanks also go to the participants of the DGfS workshop 2017. This work was supported by KAKENHI 15H03213.
1 English has *tough* adjectives, which are head-initial prenominal modifier phrases, as illustrated in (i) (Nanni 1978, 1980; Sadler & Arnold 1994; Escribano 2005).
(i)   a.   a [difficult to please] child
         b.   a [hard to pronounce] name
Nanni argues that these phrases are complex predicates.

(3) Dutch (van Riemsdijk 1998: 672)

    a. de [op zijn zoon *trotse*] *vader*
        the of his son proud father

    b. *de [*trotse* op zijn zoon] *vader*
        the proud of his son father

(4) Hungarian (Grosu & Horvath 2006:474)

    a. [[*Elégedetlen* (*a fizetésükkel)] munkások] nem dolgoznak
        dissatisfied the salary-their-with workers-Nom not work-3PL
        jól.
        well

    b. [[A fizetésükkel *elégedetlen*] munkások] nem dolgoznak
        the salary-their-with dissatisfied workers-Nom not work-3Pl
        jól.
        well

    'Workers dissatisfied with their pay don't work well.'

(5) French (Abeillé & Godard 2000:339)

    a. une [*longue* (*de 2 metres)] *table*
        a long of 2 meters table

    b. une *table* [*longue* de 2 metres]
        a table long of 2 meters

    'a long table' / 'a table 2 meters long'

In the acceptable noun phrases (e.g. (3a)) the head of the noun phrase (*vader*) is adjacent to the head of the modifier phrase (*trotse*). In the unacceptable noun phrases (e.g. (3b)) the head of the noun phrase is separated from the head of the modifier phrase by the intervening complement (*op zijn zoon*). Thus, the head adjacency condition successfully explains the word order in the modifier phrases shown above.

Some constraints on linear order have been proposed, which are similar to the head adjacency condition: the Head Final Filter for NPs (*[$_{NP}$ [$_{XP}$ X YP] N]) (Williams 1982), and the Final-Over-Final Constraint (FOFC) banning *[$_{βP}$ [$_{αP}$ α γP] β] (Biberauer et al. 2014; Sheehan 2017). Also related is the Early Immediate Constituent (EIC) analysis by Hawkins (1994, 2001), which predicts preference for head adjacency. Our arguments against the head adjacency condition also apply to these alternative ideas that are based on linear order.

2.2 Conceptual problems of the head adjacency condition

The head-to-head adjacency condition is not tenable in the minimalist framework, which assumes no linear order in syntactic derivation (cf. Chomsky 2012). Uriagereka (1999) uses the metaphor of a Calder's mobile in explaining the linearization of a syntactic hierarchical structure: a Calder's mobile has hierarchical structure but no linear order when it is in the air (i.e. in the syntactic component); in the metaphor, linear order comes when the mobile is laid on the ground. The linear order of a structure's constituents is decided by externalization to the sensory-motor system (see Tokizaki 2018 for further discussion).

There is no conceptual reason why the head of a modifier and the modified head must be adjacent in principle. One might argue that the head adjacency condition is necessary in order for the syntactic feature of one head to check a feature of another head which it c-commands or is c-commanded by. However, if we assume that feature-agreement takes place on the basis of the c-command relation (cf. Chomsky 2000), the adjacency in the linear order of heads is not necessary. In other words, a head can agree with another head in its c-commanding domain irrespective of the adjacency.

One might want to assume the head adjacency condition in the phonology or at the syntax-phonology interface (the PF-interface). However, head adjacency cannot be an output condition in phonology because there is nothing wrong phonologically in violations of head adjacency. Head adjacency is not like the Obligatory Contour Principle, which bans a sequence of the same phonological features, e.g. the same tones (Goldsmith 1976).

One might also argue that language processing has some cost if a head is not adjacent to its related head (cf. Early Immediate Constituent by Hawkins 1994, 2001, Dependency Locality by Gibson 2000). However, we do not know where these parsing constraints are located in the minimalist program of linguistic theory. Thus, head adjacency has conceptual problems in the current theory of generative linguistics.

2.3 Empirical problems of the head adjacency condition

The head adjacency condition has empirical problems as well as conceptual problems. The condition wrongly rules out phrasal compounds in Germanic languages and noun phrases containing head-initial modifiers in East Slavic languages and Greek. First, let us look at the phrasal compounds in English and German shown in (6) and (7) (cf. Lieber (1992: 11) for phrasal compounds in Dutch and Afrikaans).

(6) a. [[*over*-[the-fence]] *gossip*]
   b. a [[*connect*-[the-dots]] *puzzle*]

(7) a. der ['*Fit*-[statt- fett']]- *Bürowettbewerb* (German)
       the fit-   over- fat   office-contest
       'the fit-over-fat office contest'
   b. der [[*Zwischen*-[den- Zeilen]]-*Widerstand*
       'the between- the- lines opposition'   (Wiese 1996a)

In these phrasal compounds (e.g. (6a)), the head of the phrasal modifier (*over*) is not adjacent to the noun head of the phrasal compound (*gossip*).

Second, the head adjacency condition wrongly rules out head-initial modifiers in East Slavic languages (e.g. Russian and Bulgarian) and Greek (cf. Cinque 2010:46).

(8) Russian
   a. [*polnaja* solnca]   *komnata*
      full   sun.GEN   room
      'a room full of sunlight'   (Babby 1975:25)
   b. [*gotovyi* na vse]   *student*
      ready   on anything student
      '(the) student ready for anything'   (Babby 1975:25)
   c. [*dovol'nyi* vyborami]   *prezident*
      satisfied   elections-Instr president
      'the president satisfied with the elections'   (Bailyn 1994:25)

(9) Bulgarian (Tasseva-Kurktchicva 2005: 285)
    [mnogo *gord-iyat* səs svoe-to dete] *basta*
    very   proud-the   with Self-the child father
    'the father very proud of his child'

(10) Greek (Androutsopoulou 1995: 24)[2]
     i [*perifani* ja to   jo tis] (i) *mitera*
        the proud   of the son her the mother
     'the mother proud of her son'

---

[2] Sheehan (2017:140) points out that the Greek example in (10) is slightly marginal for some speakers.

The complement of the modifier head can be a Case-marked noun (phrase) (e.g. *solnca* in (8a)) or a prepositional phrase (e.g. *na vse* in (8b)). These structures violate the head adjacency condition, the Head Final Filter and the Final-Over-Final Constraint (if Sheehan's (2017) argument that HFF is reducible to FOFC is on the right track).[3]

These languages contrast with the languages with head-final prenominal modifiers, including Germanic, West Slavic and literary Italian (cf. Cinque 2010: 45).

(11) a. German (Fanselow 1986,343)
 die [dem   Mann *treue*]   *Frau*
 the the-Dat man faithful woman
 'the woman faithful to her husband'

 b. Swedish (Platzack 1982a,b)
 en [mig *motbjudande*] *tanke*
 a   me repulsive   thought
 'a thought repulsive to me'

 c. Literary Italian (cf. Cinque 1994:93 n. 12)
 l'a [noi piu *invisa*]   *sete* di potere
 the to-us more displeasing thirst of power
 'the thirst for power more hated by us'

The typology of word order in prenominal modifiers distinguishes two groups of languages with respect to head directionality (head-initial/head-final) (cf. Cinque 2010:127; Siewierska & Uhlifova 1998:135–136). The languages in the first group place complements after the prenominal adjective (or adjectival participle).

---

[3] The head of prenominal modifier phrases agrees with the modified head noun in languages with head-initial prenominal modifiers, such as Russian, as well as in languages with head-final prenominal modifiers, such as German. The fact that the head of the modifier phrase is not adjacent to the head of the noun phrase in Russian shows that the adjacency of heads is not a necessary condition for agreement.

(i) a. ein [$_{AP}$ [$_{PP}$ in München] *wohnhafter*] *Künstler*
 b. eine [$_{AP}$ [$_{PP}$ in München] *wohnhafte*] *Künstlerin*

(ii) a. [*gotovyi* [na vse]] *student* (Russian)
 b. [*gotovaja* na vse] *devuška*
   '(the) ready-for-anything girl'   (Babby 1975:26)

(12) Head-initial modifier phrase: [A Compl] N
   a. East Slavic: Russian, Bulgarian, Macedonian, Polish, Ukrainian
   b. Greek

The languages in the second group place complements before the prenominal adjective (or adjectival participle).

(13) Head-final modifier phrase: [Compl A] N
   a. West Slavic: Czech, Slovak, Sorbian, Bosnian/Croatian/Serbian, Slovene
   b. Germanic other than English: German, Dutch, Swedish
   c. literary Italian

Siewierska & Uhlífova (1998:135–136) observe that the West Slavic languages in (13a) obligatorily place complements before the prenominal adjective.

Note that Russian allows a variety of word orders for a noun and its modifier, as shown in (14).

(14) a. *student [gotovyi [na vse]]*
       student ready   for anything
   b. [[**na vse**]   *gotovyi*] *student* (emphatic focus)
       for anything ready   student
   c. *student* [[na vse]   *gotovyi*] (poetic)
       student for anything ready

(14a) is another unmarked order of postnominal modification like English; (14b) is possible when the complement of the modifier head is emphasized; (14c) is also possible and sounds rather poetic according to a native speaker of Russian. The variation in word order is an important point for our discussion. We will return to this in Sect. 3.4.

Note also that Grosu & Horvath (2006:475) observe that Russian can violate HFF only as long as the contained phrases are not exceedingly heavy. (15a) is acceptable while (15b) is unacceptable or marginal.

(15) a. [*polnaja* solnca] *komnata*
       full   sun-Gen room
       'room full of sunlight'

b. ??[*nesoglasnyj* [na to, čtoby ego vodili za nos s
nonagreeing.Nom on that Comp him.Acc make-a-fool from
pervogo dnja sovmestnoj žizni,]] *molodoj suprug*
first day common life young spouse
'young spouse unwilling to be made a fool of from their first day of life together'

Bivon (1971:78) also notes that in Russian the order of the head noun and the phrasal modifier ('submodifier' in Bivon's terminology) is influenced by the complexity of the submodifier. He observes that "[t]he simpler the structure of the submodifier, the likelier it is to precede the head; the more complex the structure of the submodifier, the likelier it is to follow the head." He also observes that the order is influenced by the type of text as well: "[t]he more formal the text, the likelier it is for a complex submodifier to precede the head; the more popular the text, the likelier it is for a complex submodifier to follow the head." This stylistic factor will be discussed in Sect. 3 below.

To summarize Sect. 2, the head adjacency condition has both conceptual and empirical problems. In the next section, we will investigate another idea about constraints on prenominal modification in terms of the syntax-phonology interface.

3 Prosodic constraint on prenominal modification

3.1 No prosodic boundary condition (NPB)

In this section, we propose the following constraint on modifiers and the head, which is dubbed the No Prosodic Boundary condition (NPB).

(16) A modifier and the head it modifies cannot be separated by a prosodic boundary: *..M.. / ..H..

We take the prosodic boundaries here to be derived from syntactic boundaries between constituents, as we argue in Sect. 3.2.

The prosodic constraint (16) is different from the head adjacency condition and other constraints on linear order between heads, such as HFF, EIC and FOFC, in that NPB refers to the phonological distance between a modifier (phrase) and the modified head, and not between the head of a modifier (phrase) and the modified head.

The intuition behind this prosodic constraint is that a modifier (phrase) should be close enough to the modified head phonologically. The phonological closeness between a head and the modifier helps hearers to build a constituent (i.e. an NP) consisting of a noun and its modifier. In this sense, the NPB condition is a guideline for easy parsing. The violation of NPB is unacceptable because it makes it more difficult for hearers to process a phrasal modifier plus noun sequence as an NP, because of the prosodic boundary between them.

This proposal suggests that linearization or externalization can be constrained by a processing factor. This possibility requires us to reconsider the interface(s) of syntax and the output conditions at the articulatory-perceptual system (A-P) and the conceptual-intentional system (C-I). However, we will not consider the details of this here. In the next section, we discuss how to formalize the phonological closeness between a head and its modifier.

3.2 Bare mapping from syntax to phonology

In this section, we argue that the intuition about the strength of prosodic boundaries can be captured in terms of the bare mapping from syntactic structure onto phonological representation proposed in Tokizaki (1999, 2008a). The bare mapping is formalized as in (17).

(17)   Interpret a syntactic bracket ([or]) as a prosodic boundary (/) at PF.

This rule converts syntactic brackets into prosodic boundaries at the syntax-PF interface as illustrated in (18) and (19).

(18)   [[white lions] [live [in [South Africa]]]]

(19)   // white lions // live / in / South Africa ////

The representation in (19) shows the basic juncture between words. Tokizaki (1999, 2008a) also proposes a deletion rule for prosodic boundaries as formulated in (20), which makes various levels of prosodic phrases.

(20)   Delete a number (n) of prosodic boundaries between words to make prosodic phrases.

If we apply the deletion rule with $n = 1$ and $n = 2$, we get (21a) and (21b).

(21)   a.   / white lions / live in South Africa /// (Delete one /)
       b.   white lions live in South Africa // (Delete two /s)

We can argue that the representation (21a) corresponds to phonological phrases while (21b) corresponds to an intonational phrase (cf. Tokizaki 2008a).

Now let us apply these rules to the modifier constructions in the languages we have seen so far. In the case of phrasal modifiers in English, we have the paradigm shown in (22) to (23).

(22) a. a [baby [sleeping [on [the sofa]]]]
 b. *a [[sleeping [on [the sofa]]] baby]

(23) a. a / baby / sleeping / on / the sofa ////
 b. a // sleeping / on / the sofa /// baby /

If we delete one prosodic boundary between words, the resulting representations are (24).

(24) a. a baby sleeping on the sofa
 b. *a / sleeping on the sofa // baby

The modifier phrase is separated from the head noun in the unacceptable order (24b), but not in the acceptable order (24a).

In the case of German, prenominal modifiers are acceptable if they have head-final order as in (25a) but not if they have head-initial order as in (25b).

(25) a. ein [[[in München] wohnhafter] Künstler]
     a   in München   living   artist
 b. *ein [[wohnhafter [in München]] Künstler]

The mapping rule (17) applied to (25) gives (26).

(26) a. ein /// in München / wohnhafter / Künstler /
 b. ein // wohnhafter / in München // Künstler /

If we delete one prosodic boundary between words with the rule (20), the resulting representations are (27).

(27) a. ein // in München wohnhafter Künstler /
 b. *ein / wohnhafter in München / Künstler /

The modifier phrase is separated from the head noun in the unacceptable order (27b), but not in the acceptable order (27a).⁴

Our bare mapping hypothesis has advantages over other theories such as the edge-based theory (Selkirk 1986) and the match theory (Selkirk 2011). The edge-based theory would predict a prosodic boundary between AP and the head N in (25a) because German counts the right-edge of XP as the relevant prosodic boundary (cf. Truckenbrodt 2005). In order to explain the difference in acceptability between (25a) and (25b), the edge-based theory would have to resort to such syntactic constraints as the head-adjacency condition (cf. Sect. 2). Besides the various problems of the syntactic constraint that we have already pointed out, our analysis is to be preferred in that it only makes use of an output condition applied in phonology. This approach conforms to the minimalist idea of linguistic theory (cf. Chomsky 1995 et seq.).

Thus, assuming bare mapping, the NPB condition correctly predicts the acceptability of word order in modifier constructions in English and German. The difference between English and German is that English modifier phrases are head-initial while German modifiers can be head-final. A head-final (i.e. left-branching) modifier phrase in German ([[*in München*] *wohnhafter*]) has only one bracket (hence only one prosodic boundary) on its right edge in the basic representation.

Here one might wonder why German phrasal modifiers can be prenominal and head-final (e.g. (25a) *ein* [[*in München*] *wohnhafter*] *Künstler*) while English ones cannot be (e.g. *an* [[*in London*] *living*] *artist*). We argue that word-stress location correlates with head-directionality in the world's languages. German, which has left-hand word-stress (stem-initial stress (Wurzel 1980; Inaba & Tokizaki 2018)), may have head-final noun phrases and head-final modifiers within them, as in (25a), as well as head-initial noun phrases with head-initial PPs and relative clauses (N-PP/CP).⁵ Romance languages, which have right-edge stress (stress

---

4 The boundaries between *ein* and *in* in (27a) may not be interpreted as a prosodic boundary because of the clitic nature of articles and prepositions. For the prosodic nature of function words, see Selkirk (1984:343ff), Chomsky & Halle (1968:366ff) and Lahiri & Plank (2010). Also, Wagner (2005) and Kentner & Féry (2013) argue that left edges are, in general, not tonally marked in German (cf. Tokizaki 2008b for the asymmetry of boundary strength in left-branching and right-branching structures). We thank the anonymous reviewer, Gerrit Kentner and Yoshihito Dobashi for bringing our attention to these points.

5 Researchers are not unanimous as to word-stress location in German (Domahs et al. 2014). Jessen (1999), Féry (1998) and Wiese (1996b) observe that the word-stress location in modern German is right-oriented (antepenult, penult or ultimate). We rather follow the idea that German still preserves Germanic stem-initial stress (especially in native words (Wurzel 1980:302; Benware 1980:299, 1987:113; Féry 1986:28)), which often corresponds to penult or antepenult stress in a short word consisting of two or three syllables (cf. Lahiri et al. 1999; Inaba & Tokizaki 2018).

on the penultimate or ultimate syllable of a word (Goedemans & van der Hulst 2005)), generally have head-initial NPs and head-initial modifiers within them (cf. (5b) for a French example). English is in between Germanic and Romance: some phrases (e.g. DP, PP and VP) are head-initial while some constituents (e.g. compound words) are head-final. Goedemans & van der Hulst (2005) classify the English stress system as right-oriented stress (antepenult, penult or ultimate), which is the same system as other Germanic languages. However, English has historically been influenced by French, which has right-edge stress (penultimate or ultimate) (Dell 1984; Tranel 1987; van Oostendorp 1995; Roca 1999; Goedemans & van der Hulst 2005; cf. Féry 2001 for the view that French does not have lexical stress; cf. Hayes 1995:24 for the view that rules of destressing may eliminate word stresses on the surface at the phrase level in French and Italian; cf. Halle & Keyser 1971 and Minkova 2007 for Germanic Stress Rule and Romance Stress Rule).

3.3 Phrasal compounds and prosodic boundaries

Next, let us consider phrasal compounds in English and German, which are acceptable in spite of the violation of the head adjacency condition. A phrasal compound is different from a noun phrase containing a modifier phrase in that the whole category is a word rather than a phrase. If we assume the No Phrase Constraint (Botha 1980), which states that words do not contain syntactic phrases, the phrasal modifier in a phrasal compound is a word (cf. the Lexical Integrity Hypothesis (Lieber & Scalise 2006)). Also, the wordhood of phrasal modifiers in phrasal compounds can be seen in their orthography: the constituents of phrasal modifiers in phrasal compounds are often tied together with hyphens (e.g. *over-the-fence gossip*). Thus, we argue that phrasal modifiers in phrasal compounds do not have internal boundaries.[6] Then, their representations are not (28)–(29), but (30)–(31).

(28) a. [$_N$ [$_{PP}$ over-[$_{DP}$ the-fence]] gossip]

　　 b. a [$_N$ [$_{VP}$ connect-[$_{DP}$ the-dots]] puzzle]

(29) a. der [$_N$ [$_{AP}$ 'Fit-[$_{PP}$ statt- fett]']- Bürowettbewerb]
　　　　 the　　　　　fit-　　over- fat　　office-contest

　　 b. der [$_N$ [$_{PP}$ Zwischen- [$_{DP}$ den- Zeilen]]- Widerstand
　　　　 the　　　　 between-　　the- lines　　opposition

---

6 This does not mean that there is no structure in a compound. If the head adjacency constraint applies also in word-internal structures, data such as (28)–(29) still remain counter-examples.

(30) a. [_N_ [_X_ over-the-fence] gossip]
    b. a [_N_ [_X_ connect-the-dots] puzzle]

(31) a. der [_N_ [_X_ 'Fit-statt-fett']-Bürowettbewerb]
    b. der [_N_ [_X_ Zwischen-den-Zeilen]-Widerstand]

In (30) and (31), X is used for the label of the 'phrasal' modifier because its status is a word and not a phrase XP. The category X can be N, P, V or A, but this is not relevant to our discussion here. (30) and (31) are mapped onto (32) and (33) by bare mapping.

(32) a. // over-the-fence / gossip /
    b. a // connect-the-dots / puzzle

(33) a. der // 'Fit-statt-fett'/-Bürowettbewerb /
    b. der // Zwischen-den-Zeilen/-Widerstand /

The boundary deletion rule with $n = 1$ applies to (32) and (33) to give (34) and (35).

(34) a. / over-the-fence gossip
    b. a / connect-the-dots puzzle

(35) a. der / 'Fit-statt-fett'-Bürowettbewerb
    b. der / Zwischen-den-Zeilen-Widerstand

These representations show that there is no prosodic boundary between the noun head and its 'phrasal' modifier in a phrasal compound. Since phrasal compounds in English and German do not violate NPB, this analysis correctly predicts that phrasal compounds are acceptable.

Our analysis also predicts that phrasal compounds are possible even if the modifier phrase is rather long, because a phrasal modifier has at most one boundary on its left or right edge. This prediction is in fact borne out. The modifier can be as long as a sentence, as shown in the examples (36).

(36) a. der Aber-da-hört-sich-doch-gleich-alles-auf-Blick
       'the but-this-puts-a-stop-to-everything look'   (Wiese 1996a: 184)
    b. "Learn what is there and don't question it" attitude   (Trips 2012)

Note that in some phrasal compounds in English and German, a number of orthographical means are used to mark phrasal modifiers in phrasal compounds: hyphens, italics, capitals and quotation marks (" " or ' '), as shown in (37) (cf. Trips 2012).

(37) a. And what about the Polluter Must Pay Argument?
   b. the 'we-know-best' philosophy
   c. the *Small is Beautiful* brigade
   d. the Small is Beautiful brigade

These orthographical means help readers to correctly parse phrasal compounds into a phrasal modifier and a modified head. If there are no orthographical marks, readers might wrongly parse phrasal compounds as shown in (38) and (39).

(38) a. ?the we know best philosophy
   b. #the [we [know [best [philosophy]]]]

(39) a. ?the small is beautiful brigade
   b. #[the small] [is beautiful brigade]

Thus, these orthographical means for demarcating the 'phrasal' modifier in a phrasal compound are necessary in written text, where there is no prosodic information about the constituency of phrasal compounds. It is interesting to investigate the prosody of phrasal compounds in the world's languages, but we will leave this matter for further study (cf. Tokizaki 2017 for the prosody of Japanese phrasal compounds).

3.4 Russian and NPB

Now let us reconsider the observation by Grosu & Horvath (2006:475) that Russian can violate the Head Final Filter (or the head adjacency condition) only as long as the contained phrases are not exceedingly heavy (cf. Bivon 1971). If we compare a simple phrasal modifier in (40a) and a complex one in (41a), it is clear that the numbers of boundaries between the modifier and the head noun are quite different, as shown in (40b) and (41b), which are the results of bare mapping from (40a) and (41a).

(40) a. [[polnaja solnca] komnata]
       full   sun-Gen room
       'room full of sunlight'
   b. // polnaja solnca / komnata /

(41) a. ??[[nesoglasnyj   [na to]], [čtoby [[ego   [vodili za nos]]
         nonagreeing.Nom   on that Comp   him.Acc make-a-fool
         [s   [[pervogo dnja] [sovmestnoj žizni]]]],] [molodoj suprug]]
         from first   day   common   life   young   spouse
         'young spouse unwilling to be made a fool of from their first day of life together'
   b. // nesoglasnyj / na to //, / čtoby // ego / vodili za nos /// s // pervogo dnja // sovmestnoj žizni /////,/ molodoj suprug //

If we delete one boundary between words in these examples (40b) and (41b), the resulting representations show that a complex phrasal modifier is separated from the head noun ((*molodoj*) suprug) in (42b) while a simple modifier is not in (42a).

(42) a. / polnaja solnca komnata
    b. / nesoglasnyj na to /, / čtoby / ego vodili za nos // s / pervogo dnja / sovmestnoj žizni ////,/ molodoj suprug /

Thus, we can ascribe the difference in acceptability between simple and complex phrasal modifiers to the number of boundaries between the modifier and the head noun.[7,8]

---

[7] We still need to explain why Russian allows a head-initial prenominal modifier to consist of more than one word while German does not.

(i) a. [gotovy [na vse]]   student
        ready   for anything student
    b. [serdityj [na [ves'   mir]]] muzykant
        angry   at whole   world musician
        'a musician angry at the whole world'   Bailyn (2012:71)

(ii) *ein [wohnhafter [in München]] Künstler

We assume that Russian has right-hand stress in words and phrases (cf. Lavitskaya & Kabak 2014), which allows head-initial prenominal modifier phrases. The stress pattern is determined prior to NPB. In German, which has left-hand stress, a head-initial modifier is not acceptable in the prenominal position because of NPB, as in (ii). Note that an adjectival phrase with a PP-complement may be head-initial as well as head-final in predicative use, as shown in (iii).

(iii) a. Eric ist [[auf die Kinder] *stolz*]
          Eric is of the child   proud
          'Eric is proud of his children.'
     b.   Eric ist [*stolz* [auf die Kinder]]

This fact shows that (ii) is unacceptable not because it has right-hand stress (on *München*) but because it violates NPB.

[8] Another difference between Russian and German could be that Russian shows more overt agreement between adjectives and noun than German. If this is the case, the overt agreement

The length-sensitivity of Russian prenominal modifiers contrasts with the length-insensitivity of the prenominal modifiers in head-final languages such as Japanese.

(43) a. [[konki-no   kekka-ni] manzoku-siteiru] senshu
        this-season-Gen result-Dat satisfied-is   player
     '(a) player who is satisfied with this season's result'

   b. [[[jibun-de   setteishita] pasuwaado-o] wasureta] hito
        oneself-by set   password-Acc forgot   person
     '(a) person who forgot the password that (s)he set by himself/herself'

These noun phrases are mapped onto the phonological representation in (44).

(44) a. // konki-no kekka-ni / manzoku-siteiru / senshu

   b. /// jibun-de setteishita / pasuwaado-o / wasureta / hito

In these examples, the head noun (*senshu* and *hito*) is separated from the modifier phrase by only one boundary, which can be easily deleted by the boundary deletion rule (20). Thus, consistently head-final languages, which have head-final modifiers, do not have the length effect seen in languages with head-initial modifiers, such as Russian.

Another point relevant here is the observation by Bivon (1971:78) who notes that prenominal modifiers in Russian are formal as well as simple. The difference between formal style and informal style generally accords with the difference between written text and spoken form. Written texts basically have no phonological information, other than orthographical emphasis such as capitalization. In other words, the prosodic constraint NPB has less effect on written text than on spoken form. Thus, a number of boundaries between a prenominal modifier and the head noun, which violate NPB (e.g. [*polnaja solnca*] *komnata* (40)), are not critical for the acceptability of a noun phrase, especially in written texts. Then, the prosodic analysis presented here correctly captures the style difference of prenominal modifiers, which remains a mystery in a syntactic analysis presented in terms of the head adjacency condition.[9]

---

could be another factor in allowing violation of NPB in Russian: the overt agreement shows the modification relation between the modifier and the head noun in spite of the prosodic boundary. We thank Gerrit Kentner for bringing our attention to this point.

9 We agree with Fodor (2002), who argues that one silently reads texts with specific prosody in order to disambiguate the meaning. The point here is that written/formal texts are less affected by the prosodic constraint than spoken/informal texts. We thank the anonymous reviewer for calling our attention to this point.

4 Conclusion

We have argued that the word order in prenominal modifiers is determined by the universal prosodic constraint No Prosodic Boundary (NPB). It was argued that constraints on linear order such as the head-to-head adjacency condition, the Head Final Filter and the Final-Over-Final Constraint, which have conceptual and empirical problems, should be replaced by NPB at the syntax-PF interface. The result of this study shows that we can pursue the minimalist program that assumes no linear order in syntax.

References

Abeillé, Anne and Danièle Godard (2000). French word order and lexical weight. In Borsley, Robert D., ed., *The nature and function of syntactic categories*, pp. 325–360. San Diego: Academic Press.
Androutsopoulou, Antonia (1995). The licensing of adjectival modification. In Camacho, José, Lina Choueiri, and Maki Watanabe, eds, *Proceedings of the 14th West Coast Conference on Formal Linguistics (WCCFL) 14*, pp. 17–31, Stanford. CSLI Publications.
Babby, Leonard Harvey (1975). *A transformational grammar of Russian adjectives*. The Hague: De Gruyter Mouton.
Bailyn, John Frederick (1994). The syntax and semantics of Russian long and short adjectives: An X'-theoretic account. In Toman, Jindřich, ed., *Formal approaches to Slavic linguistics: The Ann Arbor meeting: Functional categories in Slavic syntax*, pp. 1–30, Ann Arbor, MI.
Bailyn, John Frederick (2012). *The syntax of Russian*. Cambridge: Cambridge University Press.
Benware, Wilbur A. (1980). Zum Fremdwortakzent im Deutschen. *Zeitschrift für Dialektologie und Linguistik*, 47:289–312.
Benware, Wilbur A. (1987). Accent variation in German nominal compounds of the type (A (B C)). *Linguistische Berichte*, 108:102–127.
Biberauer, Theresa, Anders Holmberg, and Ian Roberts (2014). A syntactic universal and its consequences. *Linguistic Inquiry*, 45:169–225.
Bivon, Roy (1971). *Element order. (Studies in the Modern Russian Language 7)*. Cambridge: Cambridge University Press.
Botha, Rudolph P. (1980). Word-based morphology and synthetic compounding. *Stellenbosch Papers in Linguistics* 5. doi:10.5774/5-0-117.
Chomsky, Noam (1995). *The minimalist program*. Cambridge, MA: MIT Press.
Chomsky, Noam (2000). Minimalist inquiries: The framework. In Martin, R., D. Michaels, and J. Uriagereka, eds, *Step by step: Essays on minimalist syntax in honor of Howard Lasnik*, pp. 89–155. Cambridge, MA: The MIT Press.
Chomsky, Noam (2012). *The science of language: Interviews with James McGilvray*. Cambridge: Cambridge University Press.
Chomsky, Noam and Morris Halle (1968). *The sound pattern of English*. New York: Harper & Row.

Cinque, Guglielmo (1994). On the evidence of partial N-movement in the Romance DP. In Cinque, Guglielmo, Jan Koster, Jean-Yves Pollock, Luigi Rizzi, and Raffaella Zanuttini, eds, *Paths towards universal grammar: Studies in honor of Richard S. Kayne*, pp. 85–110. Washington, D.C: Georgetown University Press.

Cinque, Guglielmo (2010). *The syntax of adjectives: A comparative study*. Cambridge, MA: MIT Press.

Dell, François (1984). L'accentuation dans les phrases en français. In Dell, F., D Hurst, and J. R. Vergnaud, eds, *Forme sonore du langage*, pp. 65–122. Paris: Hermann.

Emonds, Joseph (1976). *A transformational approach to English syntax*. New York: Academic Press.

Escribano, José Luis González (2004). Head-final effects and the nature of modification. *Journal of Linguistics*, 40:1–43.

Escribano, José Luis González (2005). Discontinuous APs in English. *Linguistics*, 43:563–610.

Fanselow, Gisbert (1986). On the sentential nature of prenominal adjectives in German. *Folia Linguistica*, 20:341–380.

Fodor, Janet D. (2002). Prosodic disambiguation in silent reading. In Hirotani, Masako, ed., *Proceedings of the North East Linguistic Society (NELS) 32*, pp. 113–132, Amherst. GSLA. University of Massachusetts.

Féry, Caroline (1986). Metrische Phonologie und Wortakzent im Deutschen. *Studium Linguistik*, 20:16–43.

Féry, Caroline (1998). German word stress in Optimality Theory. *Journal of Comparative Germanic Linguistics*, 2:101–142.

Féry, Caroline (2001). Focus and Phrasing in French. In Féry, Caroline and Wolfgang Sternefeld, eds, *Audiatur Vox Sapientiae. A Festschrift for Arnim von Stechow*, pp. 153–181. Berlin: Akademie-Verlag.

Gibson, Edward (2000). The dependency locality theory: A distance-based theory of linguistic complexity. In Marantz, Alec P., Yasushi Miyashita, and Wayne O'Neil, eds, *Image, language, brain*, pp. 95–126. Cambridge, MA: MIT Press.

Goedemans, Rob and Harry van der Hulst (2005). Weight-sensitive stress. In Haspelmath, Martin, Matthew S. Dryer, David Gil, and Bernard Comrie, eds, *The world atlas of language structures*, pp. 66–69. Oxford: Oxford University Press.

Goldsmith, John (1976). *Autosegmental phonology*. Cambridge, MA: MIT dissertation.

Grosu, Alexander and Julia Horvath (2006). Reply to Bhatt and Pancheva's "Late merger of degree clauses": The irrelevance of (non)conservativity. *Linguistic Inquiry*, 37:457–483.

Haider, Hubert (2004). Pre- and postverbial adverbals in OV and VO. *Lingua*, 114(6):779–807.

Haider, Hubert (2010). *The syntax of German*. Cambridge: Cambridge University Press.

Halle, Morris and Samuel J. Keyser (1971). *English stress: Its form, its growth, and its role in verse*. New York: Harper & Row.

Hawkins, John. A. (1994). *A performance theory of order and constituency*. Cambridge: Cambridge University Press.

Hawkins, John A. (2001). Why are categories adjacent? *Journal of Linguistics*, 37:1–34.

Inaba, Jiro and Hisao Tokizaki (2018). Head parameters and word stress in German. In Tokizaki, Hisao, ed., *Phonological Externalization*, vol. 3, pp. 85–101. Sapporo University.

Jessen, Michael (1999). German. In van der Hulst., Harry, ed., *Word Prosodic Systems in the Languages of Europe*, pp. 515–544. Berlin/New York: Mouton de Gruyter.

Kentner, Gerrit and Caroline Féry (2013). A new approach to prosodic grouping. *The Linguistic Review*, 30:277–311.

Lahiri, Aditi and Frans Plank (2010). Phonological phrasing in Germanic: The judgement of history, confirmed through experiment. *Transactions of the Philological Society*, 108:370–398.

Lahiri, Aditi, Tomas Riad, and Haike Jacobs (1999). Diachronic prosody. In van der Hulst, Harry, ed., *Word prosodic systems in the languages of Europe*, pp. 335–422. Berlin/New York: Mouton de Gruyter.

Lavitskaya, Yulia and Barış Kabak (2014). Phonological default in the lexical stress system of Russian: Evidence from noun declension. *Lingua*, 150:363–385.

Lieber, Rochelle (1992). *Deconstructing morphology*. Chicago: The University of Chicago Press.

Lieber, Rochelle and Sergio Scalise (2006). The lexical integrity hypothesis in a new theoretical universe. *Lingue e Linguaggio*, 5:7–32.

Minkova, Donka (2007). The Forms of Speech. In Brown, Peter, ed., *A Companion to Medieval English Literature and Culture: C.1350–C.1500*, pp. 159–175. Malden, MA: Blackwell.

Nanni, Deborah Linett (1978). *The easy class of adjectives in English*. Amherst, MA: University of Massachusetts.

Nanni, Deborah Linett (1980). Adjectives in English: attribution and predication. *Lingua*, 18:1–34.

van Oostendorp, Mark (1995). *Vowel Quality and Phonological Projection*. dissertation, Tilburg University.

Platzack, Christer (1982a). Transitive adjectives in Old and Modern Swedish. In Ahlqvist, Anders, ed., *Papers from the 5th International Conference on Historical Linguistics*, pp. 273–282. Amsterdam: Benjamins.

Platzack, Christer (1982b). Transitive adjectives in Swedish: A phenomenon with implications for the theory of abstract Case. *Linguistic Review*, 2:39–56.

van Riemsdijk, Henk (1998). Head movement and adjacency. *Natural language and linguistic theory*, 16:633–678.

Roca, Iggy M. (1999). Stress in the Romance languages. In van der Hulst, Harry, ed., *Word prosodic systems in the languages of Europe*, pp. 659–811. Berlin/New York: Mouton de Gruyter.

Sadler, Louisa and Douglas J. Arnold (1994). Prenominal adjectives and the phrasal/lexical distinction. *Journal of Linguistics*, 30:187–226.

Selkirk, Elisabeth (1984). *Phonology and syntax: the relation between sound and structure*. Cambridge, MA: MIT Press.

Selkirk, Elisabeth (1986). On derived domains in sentence phonology. *Phonology Yearbook*, 3:371–405.

Selkirk, Elisabeth (2011). The syntax-phonology interface. In Goldsmith, John, Jason Riggle, and Alan Yu, eds, *The Handbook of Phonological Theory*, pp. 435–484. Oxford: Blackwell: 2nd edn.

Sheehan, Michelle (2017). The Final-over-final condition and the head-final filter. In Sheehan, Michelle, Theresa Biberauer, Ian Roberts, and Anders Holmberg, eds, *The final-over-final condition: A syntactic universal*, pp. 121–149. Cambridge, MA: MIT Press.

Siewierska, Anna and Ludmila Uhlířová. (1998). An overview of word order in Slavic languages. In Siewierska, Anna, ed., *Constituent order in the languages of Europe*, pp. 105–149. Berlin/New York: Mouton de Gruyter.

Tasseva-Kurktchieva, Mila (2005). Possessives, theta roles, and the internal structure of Bulgarian DPs. In Arnaudova, Olga, Wayles Browne, Maria Luisa Rivero, and Danijela Stojanović, eds, *Proceedings of FASL (Formal Approaches to Slavic Linguistics) 12: The Ottawa meeting*, pp. 251–269, Ann Arbor, MI. Michigan Slavic Publications.

Tokizaki, Hisao (1999). Prosodic phrasing and bare phrase structure. In *Proceedings of the North East Linguistic Society (NELS) 29, vol. 1*, pp. 381–395.

Tokizaki, Hisao (2008a). *Syntactic structure and silence*. Tokyo: Hituzi Syobo.

Tokizaki, Hisao (2008b). Symmetry and asymmetry in the syntax-phonology interface. *Phonological Studies*, 11:123–130.

Tokizaki, Hisao (2017). Prosody and branching direction of phrasal compounds. In *Proceedings of the annual meeting of Linguistic Society of America, Volume 2, 21*, pp. 1–10.

Tokizaki, Hisao (2018). Externalization, stress and word order. In *Proceedings of Sophia University Linguistic Society No. 32*, pp. 18–34.

Tranel, Bernald (1987). *The sounds of French: An introduction*. Cambridge: Cambridge University Press.

Trips, Carola (2012). Empirical and theoretical aspects of phrasal compounds: Against the 'syntax explains it all' attitude. In Ralli, Angela, Geert Booij, Sergio Scalise, and Athanasios Karasimos, eds, *Online proceedings of the eighth Mediterranean morphology meeting*, pp. 322–346, Patras. University of Patras.

Truckenbrodt, Hubert (2005). A short report on intonation phrase boundaries in German. *Linguistische Berichte*, 203:273–296.

Uriagereka, Juan (1999). Multiple spell out. In Epstein, Samuel David and Norbert Hornstein, eds, *Working minimalism*, pp. 251–282. Cambridge, MA: MIT Press.

Wagner, Michael (2005). *Prosody and recursion*. Cambridge, MA: MIT, dissertation.

Wiese, Richard (1996a). Phrasal compounds and the theory of word syntax. *Linguistic Inquiry*, 27:183–193.

Wiese, Richard (1996b). *The phonology of German*. Oxford: Clarendon Press.

Williams, Edwin S. (1982). The NP cycle. *Linguistic Inquiry*, 13:277–295.

Wurzel, Wolfgang Ullrich (1980). Der deutsche Wortakzent: Fakten – Regeln – Prinzipien. *Zeitschrift für Germanistik*, 1(3):299–318.

Volker Struckmeier
Cartography cannot express scrambling restrictions – but interface-driven relational approaches can

Abstract: In this paper, a non-standard point of view is taken with regard to the syntactic implementation of scrambling in German: The standard view on this phenomenon seems to be that information structural (IS) functional heads, arranged above vP, trigger movements of DPs, PPs, etc., which are themselves equipped with a corresponding feature specification. In this paper, a different approach is taken: It is argued that restrictions hold mostly in the mapping of syntactic structures to the semantic and phonological interfaces – and IS features do not figure in these interface restrictions. Instead, restrictions over the prosodic, syntactic, and semantic relations, established as the outcomes of a derivation, restrict scrambling. This treatment, it will be shown, is theoretically and empirically preferable, and cannot be restated in cartographic terms.

In this paper, a strong stance is taken against syntacto-centric descriptions of German scrambling generally and against cartographic approaches to the issue specifically. Scrambling in German has mostly received cartographic treatments in the past. In these analyses, scrambling is generally barred, unless it is enforced by syntactic trigger features (but see Bayer & Kornfilt 1994; Fanselow 2001, 2003, 2006; Neeleman & Reinhart 1998 for different approaches). The alleged scrambling trigger features are almost always information structural in nature: *Topic* features (cf., e.g., Meinunger 2000; Frey 2004) or *anti-focus* features (Abraham & Molnarfi 2001; Molnarfi 2002, 2004) cause obligatory syntactic movements of XPs specified for topic or anti-focus features, respectively, in a given discourse context.

The current paper criticizes these approaches and provides an alternative treatment: In Sect. 1, recent developments regarding the 'trigger' nature of the features allegedly driving scrambling movements are compiled from the literature. The upshot of Sect. 1 is that there is no empirical or theoretical basis to assume that IS trigger features cause scrambling.

Section 2 then goes on to discuss another phenomenon, which is well-established empirically, but received very little theoretical attention: Foci, it has long been recognized (cf. already Lenerz 1977) are reluctant to scramble. However, given empirical results presented in Sect. 2, there can be no general restriction against the scrambling of focussed phrases: Focussed phrases can in fact scramble, given certain semantic constellations (Sect. 2.1): German is a *scope-transparent* language (Frey 1993; Bobaljik 2002; Bobaljik & Wurmbrand 2012). The reluctance of foci to scramble, experimental data show, simply does not hold in cases where word order changes are required in order to obtain a certain scope reading for a scrambled argument. Thus, what Sect. 2.1 shows is that Lenerz' cautious original generalization was on the right track empirically: The scrambling of foci is a marked option – but a possible one, given marked contexts. This subsection also shows that cartographic analyses that would bar the scrambling of focussed phrases categorically, are empirically inadequate.

Syntactic analyses could, however, try and implement the semantically driven movement of quantified phrases as feature-driven (cf., e.g., Hinterhölzl 2006 for one proposal along these lines). However, in Sect. 2.2 we show that such a move would not remove all the problems associated with a general ban against focus movement: As it turns out, the scrambling of foci is possible even without any associated semantic changes – as long as the resulting word order can receive a phonologically inconspicuous stress contour. This, of course, puts the restriction on scrambling in a domain that is not well-suited to a syntactic treatment, since core syntax is generally taken to be oblivious to the phonological properties of structures. Also, since core syntax cannot *look ahead* to PF, there is no way that syntactic operations could allow for certain phonological outcomes, while preempting others.

Section 3 discusses the empirical findings from Sect. 2. Cartographic analyses did not have to prevent the scrambling of foci: Given the trigger logic they employ, they predicted that foci would never be able to scramble anyway, as long as no movement triggering head targetted them. Contrary to these implementations, then, the findings from Sect. 2 show that cartographic analyses were wrong to bar foci from scrambling in general. Given the results from Sect. 2.2, specifically, it seems very hard to describe the scrambling potential of focussed phrases without recourse to questions of phonological stress placement. Since stress placement is, however, handled in a different component of the grammar, this paper argues, in sum, that cartographic analyses are incapable of representing both the *triggers* of scrambling (via topic or anti-focus heads), as well as the relevant *restrictions* on scrambling (given the findings of this paper).

Since an implementation by functional cartographic positions seems constitutionally incapable of predicting the phenomena under discussion with any degree of accuracy, an alternative approach is outlined in Sect. 4: A treatment that assesses scrambling cases on the basis of phonological (linear, e.g., prosodic) as well as syntactic (i.e., structural) and semantic (structural) *relations* (rather than functional *positions*) seems positioned much better to represent and explain the various phenomena at hand.

1 Information structural heads do not trigger scrambling movements

In the wake of Lenerz' (1977) findings, many syntactic analyses sought to capture his generalisations in generative terms. However, developments in the theoretical framework of generative grammar conspired against a direct representation of Lenerz' findings: Initally, government-and-binding approaches offered relatively well-suited theoretical tools to emulate Lenerz' findings: For example, it should have been possible to consider scrambling as an instance of unrestricted *move-a*: Given the (untriggered) definition of this operation, the possibility for relatively free word orders was certainly implementable in this framework. In addition, filters, commonly employed over outputs of syntactic operations, could have been defined to capture the information-structural restrictions Lenerz points out. While some problems (e.g., how to translate Lenerz' predominantly linear statements into corresponding structural requirements) were given, an approach via (untriggered) move-alpha still appeared quite congenial to Lenerz' generalization. With the onset of triggered movement operations, however, the picture changed: Given that movement operations were considered as last resort operations, applicable only when enforced by feature triggers, later generative frameworks became less well-suited for the representation of restrictions over the outcomes of scrambling movements – and in turn, the established restrictions had to be re-captured as movement-triggering features. These attempts often adopted the same technical format: Information structural (IS) features were posited, in order to represent that some elements, but not others, in a clause, were able to scramble. For, e.g., topics, a well-established approach was to install [topic] features on target positions, which consequently attracted topic-marked XPs to their specifiers in (what I call) the *left middle field* (e.g., Frey 2004):

1. [$_{CP}$ XP V$_{+fin}$ [$_{TP}$ [$_{TopP}$ DPs$_{-Foc/+Top}$ Top^0 [(particles) [$_{vP}$ DPs$_{\pm Foc, -Top}$]] (V$_{-fin}$)]]]
           left middle field   *right middle field*

However, note that these approaches essentially turned the older assumptions on their heads: Lenerz (1977) had essentially assumed that word orders were a) relatively free, and b) only more or less *marked*. In near-complete contradistinction, trigger approaches tend to predict that, given a certain context, some word orders are strictly enforced by syntactic operations – and other word orders should be ungrammatical, since they fail to carry out these obligatory movement operations. In other words, cartographic analyses likened scrambling movements to phenomena like, e.g., English subject movements. This, however, has always been a dubious movement empirically, since judgments (a/b versus c/d) differ, e.g.:

2. a. [$_{TP}$ Peter has not [$_{VP}$ ~~Peter~~ eaten his cake]].
    b. *[$_{TP}$ ___ has not [$_{VP}$ Peter eaten his cake]]

    What happened to the teacher yesterday?

    c. Gestern hat Peter dem Lehrer wohl ~~Peter dem Lehrer~~ Geld geliehen.
        yesterday has P. to-the teacher MP   money lent
    d.(?)Gestern hat Peter _____ wohl ~~Peter~~ dem Lehrer Geld geliehen.
        yesterday has P.   MP   to-the teacher money lent
    'Yesterday, Peter lent the teacher money, apparently.'

In short, the mechanisms invoked by cartography (obligatory, syntactic operations) never seemed to actually fit the phenomenon (soft preferences, in discourse contexts) all that well.[1] Therefore, triggered movements drew criticism: Bayer & Kornfilt (1994), e.g., argue that the observable word order variations are not caused by movement, but by variable base orders in the language – because the optionality of the word order changes basically does not seem to support a movement analysis. Fanselow (2001, 2003, 2006) points out that the alleged syntactic movements simply do not behave empirically like other movement operations do: Failure to move, e.g., a topicalized element never result in the hard and fast crashes that characterize established types of movement operations. The assessment that scrambling was mostly optional (if sometimes preferred) was also (explicitly or implicitly) reached by, e.g., Büring 2001; Müller 2001; Haider & Rosengren 1998 and many others.

Struckmeier (2014, 2017) agrees with these assessments and points out that the trigger features that supposedly enforce scrambling movements were never made clear enough in the first place: Instead, scrambling analyses can be mostly sorted into two kinds, but both are unsatisfactory for different reasons: Either, the alleged movement trigger is defined so hazily that, in fact, no real predictions can be made about which elements are predicted to move after all: If it is not objectively clear what constitutes, say, a topic that allegedly moves, then it is not clear

---

[1] Some proposals have tried to address the optionality of scrambling, cf. e.g. Hinterhölzl 2006. However, for reasons I discuss in Struckmeier 2017, I do not think that these more or less isolated proposals do the phenomenon justice. The argument cannot be repeated here, for reasons of space.

which elements in which contexts will, in fact, move. The same problem occurred, *mutatis mutandis*, for various other notions of scrambling triggers. Struckmeier argues that these theories cannot be accepted as scientific theories a priori: They fail basic requirements for precision in their predictions – and, accordingly, it is not clear how they would be falsified. Theories of this type, I maintain here, basically warrant no scientific discussion, given their definitions.

However, on the other hand, there are very well-executed proposals which indeed do define movement triggers properly (e.g., Meinunger 2000; Frey 2004; Abraham & Molnarfi 2001). However, the empirically attested optionality of scrambling movement disqualifies these authors' well-defined features from being the features actually needed: In general, the predictions they make can be shown to be too harsh to be empirically tenable. While many predictions do turn out alright, there are too many significant counter-examples that turn out differently from the predictions of the theories – to the point that they constitute clear counter-examples to the theory (see Struckmeier 2014, 2017 for various relevant cases). The proposals that defined their movement triggers clearly, then, fail not despite of, but because of their precision, I argue: There are certainly many extremely interesting discussions and very many interesting empirical points to be found in these publications.The precision and explicitness with which the triggering features are defined open up these accounts for criticism and falsification – and the proposals are therefore of immense scientific value as a matter of course. However, in view of the facts, I believe that the predictions of these proposals fail to hold up empirically.

Logically, cartographic analyses also never seemed to go beyond the description of scrambling phenomena – since they are only representation devices which would yield only circular 'explanations' even if they were true: Why, after all, would cartographers posit a Top projection above modal particles? Because topics move there. Why, then, would topics move above modal particles? Because a topic position is posited there. Note that 'explanations' of this type cannot answer even the most basic questions as to the justification of target positions: Why, for example, is the Top position posited exactly where it is posited – rather than anywhere else?[2]

---

[2] One reviewer notes that the same criticism would apply to many other movement triggers, specifically the EPP of T, as well. I agree with that assessment, which is why no EPP is assumed in my analyses of scrambling (Struckmeier 2017). I would also like to alert the reader to the general discussion of the problems (or potential uses) of formal features, specifiers, and the like, in Chomsky 2013; Ott & Šimík 2017, etc.

Note that relational explanations, as advocated here (as in Struckmeier 2017), are very different theoretically, since cartographic trigger heads, by definition, bundle movement inducing features with features that identify the elements to be moved.

The relational approach, on the other hand, states restrictions and constraints on derivational outcomes, which apply generally. These relations thus constitute valid generalizations in their own right (if stated correctly), and are therefore not stipulative in the same way a cartographic trigger head is. Note that cartographic heads are assumed to be stored in the lexicon, but often receive no phonological matrix and are thus virtually impossible to be detected by a child during language acquisition. Cartographic proposals try to counter these issues with a second stipulation, i.e. that the assumed heads are universally available, as a part of the innate language faculty. This, of course, raises questions (insurmountable, I believe) as to the evolvability of a language faculty with such complex lexical equipment. Note, in addition, that lexical items are precisely *not* considered to be included (at least not in any great detail, beyond the most abstract of feature inventories, etc.) in conceptions of an innate language faculty, even by proponents of such innatist conceptions. In sum, cartography has to adopt stances on both language acquisition and language evolution that are, to say the least, not widely shared in the field.

The bundling of properties stipulated for cartographic trigger heads is not replicated in the relational approaches advocated here: To discuss a relevant example, suppose that QPs can scramble for a semantic effect (to avail themselves of new scopes). Also, binders can scramble (to avail themselves of new binding options). In a relational approach, no syntactic stipulations beyond the duality of semantics are required, and the movements are expected to arise as a matter of course. Also, no artificial restrictions need to be imposed to state that scope-driven movements are restricted to QPs, and binding-driven movements are restricted to elements that will actually serve as binders in the resulting structures: These restrictions follow from the lexical nature of the scrambled arguments, and the structural relations that follow from syntactic mergers in derivations. Both of these pieces of information are read off at the semantic interface as a matter of course – to yield the compositional semantic interpretation of the structures in standard ways. Consequently, no special stipulations are needed for the interfaces of core syntax, either, given the relational approach to semantic scrambling. Cartographic proposals, on the other hand, would have to assume one triggering head that addresses either some scopal property (to drive the movement of QPs), and another triggering head that targets some kind of referential, binding-relevant property (to trigger the movement of binders). These heads, of course, are nothing but construction-specific restatements of the fact that binders and scope-bearing elements can move. Further difficulties arise for cross-linguistic comparisons, e.g. in view of the fact that the same construction-specific triggering heads are unavailable in even closely related languages, say English. Attempts to generalize across these cases to overcome the construction-specific nature of dedicated heads would arguably fail: E.g., to assume that Case features are attracted by the semantically active target head would *under*generate structures, since adverbial phrases in German can scramble, too (Frey & Pittner 1998, 1999 and much subsequent literature), but arguably have no Case features in any meaningful sense of the term. The proposal to target Case features would also *over*generate structures, since DPs which will not serve as binders (for instance, because there is simply no bindee in the structure) would scramble still, because they, too, have the targetted Case feature and should consequently be able to move. On the other hand, to check on the semantic effect of Case-driven movements, to make the movements conditional on those effects, would constitute a case of *look-ahead* (to the semantic interface) if implemented in core syntax – unwanted under current standard assumptions. Relational approaches, on the other hand, have no corresponding issues: Since no movements are implemented via triggering heads, no construction-specific stipulations are made for lexical (!) "trigger items" in the first place. In their stead, general restrictions are stated, which are precisely *hard* to restate as constructions, given their relational nature. If, for example, a binder-bindee relation can be established at the semantic interface, this comes down to independent lexical properties of the binder (whatever establishes autonomous referential capacity), independent lexical properties of the bindee (whatever causes referential dependancy), and the structural relations that independently hold between the two items (which are not lexically stored entities to begin with).

In sum, relational proposals have no comparable difficulties to clearly explain interesting structural phenomena. For cartography, no similarly simple solutions present themselves. Rather than having to guess what such solutions could potentially look like, we can point out here that it is incumbent on proponents of cartography to state how construction-specific stipulations can be avoided to capture these phenomena, and to show how predictions too coarse-grained to hold much empirical conviction can be avoided, too. To the best of my knowledge, no such worked-out proposals exist for semantically driven movements, despite some efforts to address various scrambling factors (cf., e.g., the proposal by Hinterhölzl 2006, an interesting attempt to implement these aspects against the backdrop of cartographic assumptions).

Furthermore, the treatment of *asemantic* word order changes is radically different between the relational analysis advocated in this paper, compared to the available cartographic literature: Asemantic movements can be addressed by cartographic proposals most easily by just assuming yet *more* features for the attracting heads: For scope and binding, e.g., target specifiers can simply be stipulated to be A' positions, and thus semantically opaque for scope and binding purposes. In my analysis, on the other hand, asemantic word order changes follow from the size of the moved phrases: Elements that are *contained* in a larger phrase that moves cannot scope or bind out of that larger phrase as a matter of course, given just the most general assumptions on structural inclusion.

In sum, it can be argued that cartographic representations have very significant problems to represent accurately – let alone explain – the relevant *causes* of German scrambling. As the next section points out, cartographic solutions are, in addition, also incapable of representing the relevant *restrictions* known to hold for scrambling.

2 On scrambling foci: Theoretical assumptions and empirical findings

At least since Lenerz (1977), it has been a long-standing assumption that foci are reluctant to scramble. It is probably fair to say that this generalization is the most robust restriction known for scrambling in the literature. Lenerz' observations have often been taken (by functionally-minded proposals) to support the view that focus-background structures are expressed via word order. Other interpretations assumed that prosodic factors (that favour late main stress placements in a sentence) are behind the generalization (cf., e.g. Büring 2001; Müller 2001). It has also been shown that restrictions on scrambling foci are, in fact, empirically real, given the right empirical procedures (cf., e.g., Keller 2000).

An open question is, however, how to represent the generalization (whatever it may turn out to be, precisely) in a theoretical framework. Given their all-or-nothing stance on syntactically enforced movements (outlined in Sect. 1 above), it may not come as a surprise that cartographic analyses predicted mostly that foci should be categorically incapable of scrambling: Given that no target positions are posited that would attract a focussed phrase in the German middle field, and given that movement depends strictly on the presence of such a trigger mechanism in cartographic analyses, focussed phrases were predicted not to scramble at all. Note, in addition, that cartographic analyses could not (and still cannot) take a softer stance on the issue: Adding a focus position in, e.g., the left middle field, would open up the possibility for scrambling foci basically without restriction. Given such a position, the scrambling of foci would have been predicted to be possible across the board (as with the scrambling of topics or anti-foci)! The empirical truth (that foci scramble only under marked conditions) is basically inexpressible through triggered movements, as far as I can see. Since foci are known to be reluctant to scramble, cartographic approaches were therefore happy to represent this reluctance in a (somewhat rough-around-the-edges) way, by excluding the option for the scrambling of focussed materials altogether.

In the following two subsections, however, experimental data are presented that directly contradict the prediction that foci can never scramble. In other words, we support Lenerz' original wording again, according to which the scrambling of foci is *marked*, i.e. depends on conditions that less restricted cases of scrambling do not have to meet. Given the right conditions, however, foci can (and do) scramble in German: The scrambling cases discussed in 2.1., for example, are driven by semantic factors: Since German uses word order to signal widescope readings, this requirement for scope transparency can be pitted against the restrictions on scrambling foci. As it turns out, foci not only can, but preferably should move, if semantic transparency requires them to. Since cartographic analyses could try and replicated scope-driven movements as feature-triggered movements (cf., e.g. Hinterhölzl 2006[3]), an additional finding is presented in Sect. 2.2: Even without a clear-cut semantic trigger (as in 2.1), foci can in fact scramble, if the resulting word order is phonologically inconspicuous. These word order changes, note, go straight against cartographic assumptions, since the relevant examples constitute very clear cases of scrambling syntactically: The movements of the focussed phrases are designed to cross syntactic boundary elements that are located very high in the syntactic structure, *specifically* given cartographic assumptions.

2.1 Scrambling foci is possible, given semantic incentives

In this experiment, participants listened to short monologues spoken by a female voice.[4] In her monologues, all-quantified direct objects are consistently scrambled

---

[3] Note that these proposals rely on the assumption that scope features can somehow be *assigned* to elements in a clause. This is problematic, given *inclusiveness* – and does not make relational assessments superfluous, either. Furthermore, I maintain that the approach does not do justice to the different scenarios in which scopes are expressed overtly, or obscured, by surface word orders. If syntax relates PF to LF representations, then syntax is the wrong place a priori to explain *mis*matches between these interfaces (cf. Struckmeier 2017 for a complete argument in this regard).

[4] The recordings were made by Christine Röhr, at the *Institut für Phonetik* of the *University of Cologne*. I thank Christine whole-heartedly for her great help with these stimuli.

to the left of sentence-level negation and a particle in some (tested) sentences. Given that the crossing of these elements clearly places them outside their unmarked base positions (which follows negation and particles), we assume that these experimental sentences allow us to test whether the scrambling of foci is indeed categorically barred – or possible, given the right (experimental/ linguistic) conditions.

Participants. 24 students from the University of Cologne participated in this experiment for monetary compensation (EUR 4). All participants were native speakers of German and reported normal or corrected-to-normal vision.

Materials. Experimental monologues consisted of a context, followed by a test sentence. All the test sentences employed the very same word order, with an all-quantified direct object scrambled across a negation and a particle, as in, e.g.:

3. Dann würden sie [alle$_\forall$ Patienten]$_{QP}$ nicht$_{Neg}$ mehr$_{Part}$ ~~sie alle Patienten~~
   then would they   all patients   not anymore
   heilen.
   heal
   'Under those circumstances, they would not heal any patients anymore.' ($\forall\neg$)

Since all test sentences employed this general word order pattern, and all required the all-quantifier to outscope the negation semantically, differences in ratings between the conditions cannot be caused by word order or semantic differences. Rather, the contexts of the test sentences were manipulated, which resulted in a different focus assignment (and concomitant stress placement) in the test sentences: In the *all stress* condition, the all-quantified object was the sole focus of the test sentence. Consequently, given the stress rules of German, these QPs received the sentential main stress, as in 4a). In the *neg stress* condition, on the other hand, the sentential negation receives the main stress, since it is contrastively focussed, given the context, as in 4b):[5]

4. a. At the moment, doctors heal about 80 percent of patients. If they gave them less money for drugs, however, then there would be SOMe patients they would NOT heal. If, on the other hand, you gave the doctors no funding at all...

---

[5] Note that the stimuli were presented in German. We present the contexts in English here, to save space required for glosses and translations.

    ... dann würden sie [ALLe Patienten]_Focus nicht mehr heilen.
        then   would   they   all   patients   not anymore heal
    'then, they would not heal any patients anymore.' (∀¬)   (*all stress*)

b. At the moment, doctors heal many patients. If they gave them more money for drugs, they would probably even heal ALL patients. However, if they gave them no funding at all...

    ... dann würden sie   alle Patienten [NICHT]_Focus mehr heilen.
        then   would   they   all   patients   not   anymore heal
    'then, they would not heal any patients anymore.' (∀¬)   (*neg stress*)

In addition to the 14 experimental monologues, we created 14 monologues whose final sentence was fully felicitous and additional 14 monologues whose final sentence was nonsense. We opted for these kind of fillers to provide the two ends of the rating scale, with our fully felicitous monologues on the *absolute appropriate* end and the nonsense monologues on the *not appropriate at all* end. All materials were presented aurally over headphones.

Procedure. At the beginning of each trial, a prompt appeared onscreen asking participants to press the left button of the mouse to hear a small monologue by the female speaker. Another button-press then triggered the presentation of a monologue after a delay of 500 ms. Participants were instructed to carefully listen to the monologue, as they would be asked to judge how appropriate they thought the last sentence of these monologues was, given the preceding context. Participants were encouraged to base their judgments on syntactic (*Was the grammar appropriate?*), semantic (*Did the speaker use the correct words and did her monologue make sense altogether?*), and/or intonational properties (*Did the monologue sound normal?*). 500 ms after a monologue ended, a rating scale, ranging from 1 for *not appropriate at all* to 7 for *absolute appropriate*, was presented on the computer screen. Participants made their judgment by clicking on a particular rating score of the presented scale. 500 ms after participants provided their rating, a prompt was presented asking them to continue with the next monologue.

Prior to the main experiment, participants received four practice trials to familiarize themselves with the task. Feedback was provided throughout the practice session but not during the main experiment.

Results and Discussion. Mean rating scores and standard deviations for experiment 1 are presented in Table 1 in (5). Monologues with final nonsense sentences were judged to be very inappropriate. Monologues with fully felicitous final sentences received very high scores. Regarding the experimental conditions, target sentences of the *all stress* condition received a high rating score. More interestingly, target sentences of the *neg stress* condition were rated to be as appropriate as sentences of the *all stress* condition. To test for statistical reliability, we conducted generalized mixed effects regression models with rating scores as dependent and condition (*all stress* vs. *neg stress* sentences) as independent variable. In the first model, we included our filler materials (felicitous vs. non-sense sentences) as two additional levels in condition. Condition was sum-coded and random intercepts were included for participants and items. We also included random slopes for participants and items.

5. **Tab. 1:** Mean rating scores and standard deviations for experiment 1

Condition:	felicitous	nonsense	all stress	neg stress
Score:	5.63 (1.65)	1.93 (1.38)	5.01 (1.95)	4.80 (1.60)

Notes. Mean rating scores for responses can range from 1 for *not appropriate at all* to 7 for *absolutely appropriate*; Standard deviations are provided in parentheses; Materials were presented visually as texts in Experiment 1 and aurally over headphones in Experiment 2.

As expected, the model revealed that *nonsense* target sentences were significantly less appropriate than *felicitous*, $b = -2.93$, $SE = 0.13$, $z = 22.59$, $p < .001$, *all stress*, $b = 1.34$, $SE = 0.09$, $z = 14.36$, $p < .001$, and *neg stress* sentences, $b = 0.88$, $SE = 0.12$, $z = 7.41$, $p < .001$. As a crucial test of the hypothesis that the scrambling of foci is possible given semantic incentives, we fitted a new model that only included rating scores of the *all stress* and *neg stress* conditions. Results of this model clearly indicate that, in line with our predictions, there was *no* reliable difference between the two kinds of final sentence presentation, $b = 0.21$, $SE = 0.17$, $z = 1.22$, $p = .222$. Thus, the data obtained in this experiment provide good evidence that the scrambling of foci is indeed possible – or, minimally, not more restricted than is the scrambling of unfocussed arguments: On the contrary, while the scrambled foci in the *all stress* condition were rated as insignificantly better than sentences in the *neg stress* condition, the insignificance of the difference warrants no further conclusions regarding scrambling triggers or restriction, I believe.

2.2 Scrambling foci is possible even without semantic triggers!

As we have seen in 2.1, foci can scramble, if required to do so. However, an even more general question arises: Could it be that the scrambling of foci is, in fact, only restricted to the degree that its outcome goes against prosodic preferences? Recall that some theoretical proposals saw prosody as the driving factor behind scrambling movements. These movements would occur, the authors argue, in order to improve the overall prosody of clauses: Scrambling, in this view, would move unstressed elements away from the right edge of the clause, so that stressed elements (foci) would end up closer to the right edge as a result– a prosodically preferred outcome. However, of course, foci could still end up at *some* distance from the right edge in other cases: Indirect objects, e.g., precede direct objects in the base order. Thus, focussed indirect objects are often not found at the very right edge of sentences, even in *un*marked orders. Given that the base order is defined as the least marked order, some 'distance' of main stress-bearing elements to the right sentence edge seems clearly acceptable. However, if prosodically non-optimal outcomes are obviously acceptable here, how categorical a prosodic restriction can be imposed over scrambling outputs at all? Could it be that scrambling movements that do not lead to strikingly problematic outcomes prosodically are not categorically restricted?

In order to establish more precisely what kind of restriction is entailed by Lenerz' restrictions of focus scrambling, an experiment was conducted: In his examples, Lenerz uses mostly questions containing a single wh-word as the contexts for sentences with scrambled foci. However, in this way, he does not make clear the distinction that we now want to make: If focussed arguments and adjuncts are reluctant to scramble – does this restriction hold for discourse-new elements, or does it apply to prosodically stressed elements? Since the arguments and adjuncts targeted by the wh-words in Lenerz' question contexts are the only discourse-new elements in the answer sentences, they receive stress as a matter of course. Thus, discursive and prosodic categories are not kept apart in Lenerz' examples.[6]

Suppose that the restrictions on scrambling foci are, say, restrictions on placing a sentence's main stress too far away from the end of the sentence (cf., e.g., Büring 2001; Müller 2001). In a generative framework, then, this would make the pertinent restrictions hard to phrase as syntactic restrictions. In core syntax, questions of stress placement are simply undecided (and undecidable), given that another component of the grammatical architecture (the mapping to PF), not syntax, is concerned with the computation of these properties. However, syntax also

---

[6] An anonymous reviewer worries that this statement could be construed as a criticism of Lenerz' findings or method. On the one hand, I insist that Lenerz' use of single-wh question contexts does not help differentiate between the various discourse and prosodic constellations at issue here. On the other hand, note that this paper shows how the very cautious wordings (i.e., the markedness logic) Lenerz employs for scrambling restrictions are much closer to the empirical truth than the brute-force trigger logic of cartography.

cannot *look ahead* to the phonological mapping, in order to preemptively arrange syntactic objects in such a way as to avoid prosodic problems. Restrictions over scrambling stressed elements, in other words, would argue for a relatively unrestricted syntactic array of word order options – and the restrictions imposed by stress would be placed outside the realm of syntax proper, in a separate module that maps syntactic structures onto phonological representations. This is, e.g., the notion essentially taken by Struckmeier (2014, 2017). Quite clearly, this is not at all the kind of prediction that cartographic analyses would typically make, given the heavy restrictions they place on the availability of movement operations: Cartographic analyses, while not incapable of delegating decisions to the PF mapping, generally impose syntactic restrictions in order to describe word order patterns. In addition, and crucially, cartographic frameworks use syntactic features to enforce core syntactic movement operations. Given this approach, free movement operations are to be avoided in general: Not only would they take away the theoretical necessity for movement triggers, and triggers would seem redundant, but free movements would also completely obscure the triggered movements empirically: Given any word order change, it would be near-impossible to argue that that word order change was tied to a syntactic trigger feature – rather than to an instance of free movement (even of identical elements, with the very same feature specifications, in identical contexts, etc.). Prosodically driven word order changes would thus be problematic operations to cartographic approaches, to say the least.

If, on the other hand, discourse-new elements are reluctant to scramble (and prosody only follows from IS constellations indirectly), the situation is problematic for syntactic analyses, too: Of course, we can devise features (like [F], cf. Schwarzschild 1999) and label syntactic structural objects for them. If these features are taken to constitute *bona fide* syntactic features, we could also allow for them to trigger syntactic operations – or, in the case of the [F] feature, bar elements from some operations, such as scrambling movements.[7] However, questions arise in current theorizing as to the precise mechanisms that would actually label syntactic objects as 'discourse-new', in technical terms. With regard to all other currently standard syntactic features, the basic assumption of *inclusiveness* (Chomsky 2000) states that features can only appear in a derivation if they come part and parcel of the feature specifications of lexical items that occur in that derivation. For obvious reasons, now, the same solution cannot be applied to discourse features: Given the very nature of (context-independently defined) lexemes as the

---

[7] Note, however, that even for *triggered* movements, there typically do not exist features that make elements *un*available for triggered operations. While it is easy to imagine solutions that stipulate such mechanisms, it is also clear that operation-bleeding features have no real tradition in generative syntax, and thus cannot be stipulated without a very thorough argument.

basic elements stored in the lexicon, it is entirely unclear how lexical items could ever be labelled for discourse properties. Note, additionally, that it is often not individual lexical items that can be assumed to be topics, foci, etc., but rather more complex syntactic objects, which are not lexical items in the first place, but constructed of many lexical items. However, these complex syntactic objects have no status as lexically stored elements by definition. How, to give but one example, a complex DP (formed of various lexical items, such as D, N, attributive constructions etc.) could be labelled as discourse-old in technical terms, is therefore anybody's guess. Note, however, that it is often precisely these complete descriptions semantically achieved by complex DPs that can be shown to be discourse-old, as e.g. in:

6. I saw a picture of a great physicist the other day.
   [The inventor of the theory of generalized relativity].$_F$ looked unamused.

No individual lexical item present in the DP "the inventor of the theory of generalized relativity" is, technically, given in the situation (because, amongst other things, 'physicists' are no subset of 'inventors'). However, with the mention of "great physicist" in the preceding clause, the overall DP is (as witnessed, e.g., by the use of the definite article *the inventor of...*). We submit, therefore, that neither a purely discourse-related, nor a prosodic definition of focus would be particularly well-suited for syntactic approaches to scrambling.

The experiment attempted to disentangle the prosodic and discourse-related aspects of the category of focus: Participants had to judge sentences involving scrambled elements that were either stressed, but discourse-old (a prosodically defined group of arguments), or else elements that were discourse-new, but not stressed (a discursively defined group of arguments), or else elements that were unstressed and discourse-old (a group of quintessential non-foci under anybody's definition). We originally predicted that stress placements, but not discourse status would restrict the possibility for scrambling. To our surprise, the experiments shows that bans on scrambling cannot be defined over any of the categories just pointed out, given cartographic standards of what counts as scrambling in the first place.

Participants. 25 students at the University of Cologne participated in this experiment for monetary compensation (EUR 4). All participants were native speakers of German and reported normal or corrected-to-normal vision.

Materials. The experimental dialogues consisted of a question context, and an answer, which was tested for discourse coherence. The contexts were manipulated, and defined either one argument, or else two arguments from the tested answer sentences as discourse-new. Given the stress placement rules of German, however, only one of these arguments could receive the sentences' main stress. Thus, in some conditions, e.g., the indirect object and the direct object were discourse-new elements – but only the unscrambled direct object received sentence-level main stress. The indirect objects, in turn then, constituted discourse-new, but *unstressed* arguments. In other conditions, only the indirect objects were targeted by a (single) wh-question context. In these conditions, the indirect objects were both discourse-new, as well as bearers of sentence-level main stress. In the third condition, the wh-question context introduced a set of alternatives, from which the indirect object was then chosen in the answer. Therefore, the indirect object did receive stress, but was not discourse-new.

To present examples of the conditions themselves, unstressed and given indirect objects are predicted to be good scrambling items by most available theories, since they are not focussed under most definitions of the term *focus*. In the *unstressed-given* condition, scrambled elements are given by the question and remain unstressed in the answer, as in:

6. Q: Every year, Peter gives the pope something as a present.
       What about this year? What does he give to the pope this time?

   A: Er schenkt [dem Papst]$_{\text{-new, -stress}}$ wohl die neueste BIBelausgabe.
       he gifts   to-the pope   MP   the newest bible.edition
       'He apparently gives the newest bible edition to the pope as a present.'

The *unstressed-given* condition was mainly chosen to ensure that the placement of an indirect object to the left of a modal particle is possible for our subjects at all. Given what we know about German word order, no problems were predicted (nor encountered, see below), which was intended to show that the placement of the indirect object preceding the modal particle as such was not penalized by our participants.

In the other experimental conditions, arguments were focussed in the different ways outlined above: In the *unstressed-new* condition, scrambled indirect objects were not given by the context, but rather asked for by the wh-question context. This is commonly taken to constitute the discourse definition of focus (cf., e,g. Büring 2006; Schwarzschild 1999). However, given the stress rules of German, the scrambled indirect object remained unstressed, since the following direct object, too, was not given and also targeted by the question under discussion. Suppose, now, that the purpose of scrambling is construed to place argument and adjunct phrases according to their discourse status (in order to express discourse status via word order). Under this assumption, the scrambling even of unstressed discourse-new indirect objects is predicted to be impossible (or not the preferred option, minimally). The answer sentences from *unstressed-new* condition should therefore receive poor ratings, for example the answer in the following discourse:

7. Q: Peter gives a present every year to somebody he does not know. What about this year? What does he give to who?

   A: Er schenkt dem Papst$_{+new,-stress}$ wohl die neueste BIBELausgabe$_{+stress, +new}$.

If, on the other hand, the ban on scrambling is restricted to stressed phrases, then the answer sentences from the next condition, *stressed-given*, should receive poor ratings:

8. Q: Every year, Peter gives a new bible to either the pope, or his local priest. What about this year? Does he give the bible to the pope, or to his priest?

   A: Er schenkt dem PAPST$_{-new, +stress}$ wohl die neueste Bibelausgabe.

Since the indirect object is the target of the question under discussion (and formally, the argument corresponding to the only wh-word in Q), it receives sentential main stress. However, given that the indirect object is mentioned *verbatim* in the question, it does not qualify as a discourse-new element, given standard assumptions (cf., e.g. Schwarzschild 1999, Büring 2006).[8] Note also that the larger verbal argument projection that includes the indirect object as well as the predicate (forming a discourse-new constituent) is not the target of the scrambling movement here: The indirect object as such is given in the context – and is still the element that scrambles (alone).[9]

In addition to the 20 experimental monologues, we created 20 monologues whose final sentence was fully felicitous and additional 20 monologues whose

---

[8] An anonymous reviewer claims that these elements would always constitute contrastive topics, at least if they occur in combination with in-situ foci. I whole-heartedly disagree with this assessment, based on the definitions of (multiple) foci and contrastive topics in Büring (2015, 1997), which I assume here. The scrambled elements are clearly no contrastive topics. Any easy way for cartographers to disregard the observations presented here as irrelevant to the question of focus scrambling is consequently barred under my definitions.

[9] An anonymous reviewer criticizes that the type of focus constitutes a *selective focus* rather than an *information focus*. I agree that these subtypes of foci can be distinguished. However, note that the definitions of focus employed by me base on Schwarzschild (1999), and discourse-givenness and prosodic marking are consequentially disentangled. Note also that alternative ways of arriving at discourse-old, but stressed phrases (e.g. contrastive foci) are arguably less well suited for the task at hand. Therefore, given the purposes of the experiment at hand, I maintain that the discourse-old, stressed phrases used are not only suitable, but even the best choice.

final sentence was nonsense. We opted for these kind of fillers to provide the two ends of the rating scale, with our fully felicitous monologues on the absolutely-appropriate end and the non-sense monologues on the absolutely-inappropriate end. All materials were presented aurally over headphones.

Procedure. At the beginning of each trial, a prompt appeared onscreen asking participants to press the left button of the mouse to hear a small monologue constituting the context of the tested sentence. All contexts ended in a certain type of question, in accordance with the conditions outlined above. Another button-press triggered the presentation of the tested answer sentences with a delay of 500 ms. Participants were instructed to carefully listen, as they would be asked to judge how appropriate they thought the last sentence of these monologues was in context of the preceding two sentences. The participants were encouraged to base their judgments on syntactic (*Was the grammar appropriate?*), semantic (*Did the answer make sense altogether?*), and/or intonational properties (*Did the answer sound natural?*). 500 ms after a monologue ended, a rating scale, ranging from 1 for not appropriate at all to 7 for absolute appropriate, was presented on the computer screen. Participants made their judgment by clicking on a particular rating score of the presented scale. 500 ms after participants provided their rating, a prompt was presented asking them to continue with the next monologue.

Prior to the main experiment, participants received four practice trials to familiarize themselves with the task. Feedback was provided throughout the practice session but not during the main experiment.

Results and Discussion. Mean rating scores along with their standard deviations for this experiment are presented in Table 2. As can be seen (and as expected), materials with final non-sense sentences were judged to be not acceptable at all, eliciting the lowest scores. In contrast, test items with fully felicitous final sentences were rated as highly acceptable, eliciting the highest scores. Interestingly, Table 2 also reveals marginal differences at best in ratings between the three experimental scrambling conditions of interest here. To test for statistical reliability, we again fitted a generalized mixed effects model with rating scores as dependent variable and condition (felicitous, non-sense, unstressed-new, unstressed-given, stressed-given) as independent variable. Condition was sum-coded and random intercepts were included for participants and items. We also included random slopes for Condition for both participants and items. However, because the model failed to converge with these slopes, they were removed from the final model.

9. **Tab. 2:** Acceptability of different types of scrambled arguments

Conditions:	felicitous	nonsense	unstressed-new	unstressed-given	stressed-given
Score	6.42 (1.04)	1.83 (1.22)	5.24 (1.59)	5.33 (1.68)	5.68 (1.26)

Notes. Mean rating scores and standard deviations (in parentheses) for acceptability rating in Experiment 3.

When we used the fully felicitous condition as reference level in the model, the model revealed that the four remaining conditions received significantly lower scores, all $zs > 2$, all $ps < .05$. In the same vein, when we used the non-sense condition as reference level, the model again showed that all other conditions reliably differed from this non-sense condition, all $zs > 3$, all $ps > .001$. More critically, however, when we directly compared only the experimental conditions (*unstressed-new*, *unstressed-given*, and *stressed-given*), with *unstressed-given* as reference, we found no significant differences between the different ratings. Neither *unstressed-new*, $b = -0.02$, $SE = 0.06$, $z = -0.30$, $p = .761$, nor *stressed-given*, $b = 0.07$, $SE = 0.06$, $z = 1.18$, $p = .237$, were rated as significantly poorer materials than materials of the condition *unstressed-given*.

While it is important to keep in mind that no strong conclusions should be based on the statistically insignificant differences between the experimental conditions, it is equally important that these (null) results are nonetheless incompatible with the predictions to be derived from cartographic analyses: Despite the fact that a relatively long scrambling movement is assumed by cartography (crossing even the highest member of the adverbial cascade, according to Coniglio 2006, 2007), the data do not show this movement to be restricted. The findings are, however, in accordance with the model proposed here, which assumes that the relatively modest shift of scrambled elements over a single, unstressed, monosyllabic element should not be harshly penalized.

The experimental sentences were carefully designed as to avoid confounding factors that have often plagued scrambling-related experiments: First of all, all tested answer sentences employed the same word order (indirect object > modal particle > direct object). The sentences differed only in their stress pattern and the discourse context they were presented in, but crucially not in their basic word order. Therefore, no general (dis-) preferences for word orders could cause any differences in judgments between the conditions. In addition, note that this particular word order of answer sentences was chosen, since it reflects, of all things, the base order of German. Therefore, no penalty should be incurred because experimental subjects would deem the resulting linear word order unnatural per se:

The base order, on the contrary, is defined as the word order that issues the least general restrictions on discourse contexts (cf., e.g., Lenerz 1977; Höhle 1982, and much subsequent literature).

The scrambling operation carried out only took the indirect object across a modal particle contained in the answer sentences. Because indirect objects were chosen as the scrambled elements, the base order of arguments (and only these) was maintained (while the scrambling of direct objects across indirect objects and modal particles would not have maintained the base order of arguments). Furthermore, indirect objects are known to scramble relatively easily (cf. Musan 2002). Therefore, it was not expected that general restrictions on the scrambling of indirect objects should cause poor ratings across the experimental conditions, either.

These results suggest that neither stressed, but discourse-old indirect objects, nor discourse-new but unstressed indirect objects show any restriction for the scrambling across the modal particle:
- *Unstressed-given* argument scrambling was judged highly, at 5.33 out of 7, as predicted: unstressed, given arguments are expected to scramble in most scrambling theories.[10]
- However, the scrambling of *unstressed-new* arguments, at 5.24 out of 7 is not significantly worse than the scrambling of *unstressed-given* arguments. This goes against the assumption that the discourse status of argument phrases can be held responsible for the restriction on scrambling foci: Discourse-new arguments can, in scenarios like these, scramble across modal particles.
- The scrambling of *stressed-given* arguments, at 5.68 out of 7 is (obviously) also not worse than the other experimental conditions (but also not significantly better). This, then, runs contrary to the assumption that stressed phrases are somehow exempt from syntactic movement: Stressed phrases can scramble across modal particles.[11]

---

[10] Note, however, that these elements were in no way set up to constitute topics. Therefore, at least for analyses that employ topic features as syntactic movement triggers, the word order change is not exactly expected. However, scrambling analyses that employ anti-focus features as movement triggers would predict the outcome for the *unstressed-given* condition straightforwardly (but fail to predict the outcome of the *stressed-given* condition, see below).

[11] Anti-focus triggers (Abraham & Molnarfi, Molnarfi 2002, 2004) would not predict such a rating for what is, in essence, a scrambled focus (not: *anti*-focus), in their definition. Given that they will not want to allow both foci and anti-foci (i.e., every logically possible object) to scramble, this finding is problematic for them.

These results are particularly problematic for cartographic approaches: The scrambling of the indirect object crosses the modal particle in the tested sentences. Modal particles, however, are the highest member of the adverbial cascade in cartographic analyses (cf., e.g., Zimmermann 2004; Coniglio 2006, 2007). In non-cartographic analyses, they are likewise taken to be placed above all adverbial elements (cf., e.g. Struckmeier 2014). In any event, the scrambling of the indirect object should therefore register as a syntactic movement to a very high syntactic position in the middle field, according to cartographic tenets: It is precisely the crossing of 'boundary stone' elements (such as modal particles) that defines 'height' in the cartographic approach after all. Therefore, the results were entirely unpredicted for cartographic approaches: Given the boundary stone metaphor, the movement is doubtlessly a clear case of scrambling. However, given the empirical results, a well-known restriction on scrambling does not appear to hold at all, in these cases.

However, under a non-cartographic approach to syntax, the scrambling cases may well turn out to be unproblematic, e.g. in relational approaches to syntax. Note that modal particles in German do not take part in morpho-syntactic relations: They do not agree with other elements, do not (as particles) receive any other morphological markings, and in general do not seem to interact with other arguments and phrases morpho-syntactically at all. Given these empirical facts about modal particles, relational approaches to syntax could well conclude that modal particles are more or less unrestricted in terms of their relations vis-a-vis the scrambled indirect objects: In approaches such as these, no 'boundary stone' metaphor is employed. Therefore, no question of 'absolute height' is implied in the assessment of syntactic structures. Rather, the crossing of a modal particle is predicted not to be a 'long' movement to a 'high' position, crossing multiple (phonologically empty) functional heads and their (equally empty) specifiers. It is, on the contrary, a relatively inconspicuous morpho-syntactic change: It crosses only a morpho-syntactically inert element, the modal particle, which enters into no particularly note-worthy relations with the moving object at all.[12] Note, on the other hand, that the base order of arguments was maintained across all experimental conditions. Thus, no restrictions that would penalize the scrambling across other arguments could be invoked. Recall that Lenerz' ban on scrambling foci predicts those cases of scrambling to be marked. However, the current examples, in relational approaches to word order, would constitute no counter examples. In sum, then, relational approaches to scrambling would not predict that the

---

[12] Note, however, that modal particles may interact with C elements, cf., e.g. Struckmeier 2014.

word order change effected in the experimental conditions would necessarily be penalized – the correct prediction, as we have seen.

Last but not least, the experimental setup was also designed to make the scrambling cases relatively inconspicuous in terms of the resulting prosodic relations: Since the modal particles used were all only one syllable long (as most modal particles are), the effect of the scrambling in all scenarios does not weigh too heavily in terms of prosodic violations: If, say, a stressed element was indeed moved further away from the sentences' ends, it only moved 'left' by one syllable. Therefore, if the ban on scrambling foci is taken to register in terms of dispreferred prosodical outcomes, the prediction would be that the mild change of stress placement (one additional syllable away from the sentence end) should not register as a dramatic violation. This, too, seems to fit the empirical results quite nicely.

In sum, it seems possible to see the experimental results as support for theories that employ (syntactic and/or prosodic) relations for the formulation of restrictions. Theories that define target positions for scrambled arguments, and trigger features that attract the scrambled arguments, are not supported at all by our results.

3 Discussion of empirical results and their consequences for cartography

The empirical results presented above support two important conclusions: Firstly, cartographic analyses prove to be too harsh in their empirical predictions: For topicality (or anti-focus) as syntactic trigger features, recent works have called into question their empirical viability already (Fanselow 2001, 2003, 2006; Struckmeier 2014, 2017). For the necessary restrictions on foci, this paper has shown that cartographic approaches may not have a chance to represent what is arguably empirically true: Given certain marked scenarios, there are no restrictions on scrambling foci: As the experimental results have shown, scrambled foci can be judged highly, given the right contexts. However, as also outlined above, cartographic analyses cannot resort to the addition of additional focus positions in the functional clausal cascade: The addition of such (stipulated) devices would essentially predict that foci should always be able to move, contrary to the established literature on the topic (cf., again, Keller 2000; Büring 2001). In either case, cartography turns out to be constitutionally incapable of representing the preference for the non-scrambling of foci in unmarked contexts (but cf. Sect. 2.1 for the limits of that preference) and, at the same time, maintain the option to allow for scrambling in those contexts where it is available, as a marked option.

Proponents of cartographic approaches will, no doubt, try and argue that target positions for scrambled foci can be devised more cleverly. One approach could, for example, claim that there are focus positions in the middle field, for focussed arguments and adjuncts to scramble – but that the phonological spellout of the focus movements is then computed at PF: For example, a sole focus (e.g. in the contexts used by Lenerz 1977) would receive main stress, and so would the last discourse-new phrase in a multiple-focus sentence. Therefore, one could be tempted to tie the spellout position of a moved focus to the prosodic question of stress placement on PF: Stressed foci spell out low, whereas unstressed foci optionally spell out high (or low). Whereas this approach may suffice to represent the stress phenomena pointed out above, it does not represent correctly the fact that German is, after all, a scope-transparent language: Note that it is precisely the low spellout of a moved QP that is barred by scope transparency: German, unlike, say, English, has no quantifier raising. However, allowing for low spellouts of moved QPs would implement exactly the configuration that QR achieves:

10. [~~QP~~ ... Neg ... [... QP ...]]

In other words, allowing for a PF solution for scrambled foci would predict that foci are exempt from scope transparency. To the best of my knowledge, this observation has not been argued anywhere – and it certainly fails to hold for the central cases, such as the ones we discussed above:

11. Q: How many patients would the doctors not heal?

   A: Die würden wohl nicht mehr [ALLe Patienten]$_F$ heilen (... #also keinen)
   they would part not anymore all patients heal   (... #so none)
   'They would not heal all patients anymore (... #so no patients at all)'

Therefore, syntactically driven scrambling analyses cannot use the mapping to the phonological interface as the trash bin for all the optional and preferred vs. dispreferred movements that their syntactic theory fails to represent accurately: Since the phonological component is not involved in semantic computations (by assumption), any such theoretical move would deny German scrambling its semantic transparency, contrary to the empirical facts. I submit, therefore, that there may be no way for a cartographic analysis to represent the empirical findings we have presented above.

In the meantime, I would like to present an alternative to syntactic cartographies which is able to handle the data without further ado: a relational approach to syntax that leaves actual work for the interfaces to do.

4 An alternative approach: relational, interface-oriented architectures

Rather than syntactify every prosodic, information structural, scopal or binding phenomenon found in languages, we should assign the interfaces of core syntax to syntax-external systems of the grammatical architecture some function. Unlike in the heyday of cartography, current syntactic approaches often take this route in order to achieve current aims in syntactic theorizing:

- The move unburdens core syntax of linguistic phenomena that are patently not syntactic. Core syntax therefore handles syntactic phenomena, and nothing else.
- The interface to the semantic component handles semantically relevant phenomena, such as scopal, binding, and information structural aspects of "meaning" (in a wide sense of that word), so that semantics is now, in fact, run by the semantic component, not pre-empted by syntax.
- The interface to the phonological component of the grammar is now in charge of linguistic phenomena that were never syntactic to begin with, such as stress assignment, and the placement of certain intonational contours. No syntactified "prosody features" are tolerated anymore.
- The overall architecture could be called "subtractive" in that no individual system issues *all* restrictions (unlike in syntactified approaches like cartography, where syntax determines the workings of passive interfaces). Rather, requirements from individual sub-components of the overall grammatical architecture stack up. The resulting grammar is at once simpler than syntactocentric approaches (which need to 'syntactify' non-syntactic notions), as well as empirically more nuanced (since restrictions can be stated in terms of the subsystems most capable of handling them). Not surprisingly, given the extra detail resolution afforded by this approach, it can capture the empirical phenomena we pointed out correctly and in great detail, unlike cartographic approaches, which required enormous syntactic machinery – and still never got the facts right even then.
- The new approach also fares significantly better with regard to questions of language acquisition and language evolution. These aspects of language used to impose restrictions on formulable cognitively realistic grammars. I argue that they should, in fact, remain in place, if syntactic research wants to be seen and heard outside of an ever-smaller circle of people who like to stipulate baroque feature-driven solutions without any regard to their cognitive plausibility.

These points will now be taken up in turn.

Syntactically, if there is one single thing that the operation Merge readily supplies, it is structural relations. In fact, the relations Merge construes between merged syntactic objects may well be the *only* thing that core syntax adds to the feature specifications introduced by the lexical items that merge in the course of derivations (cf. the notion of *inclusiveness*). These relations also come 'for free', as it were, part and parcel of the order in which Merge operations apply to lexical items. Since Merge is a binary operation, *some* ordering always comes for free (as soon as more than two syntactic objects are merged, the norm for actual sentences in actual languages). Thus, it seems fair to say that structural relations are predicted on conceptually necessary grounds. If current aims of syntactic theorizing are on the right track at all, then we should all consider (in fact: hope) that structural relations should prove integral to the workings of core syntax – alongside the feature specifications of merged lexical items, of course.

The same thing cannot be said about cartographic technology: Nowhere in current syntax does it state that complex cascades of functional heads should exist, with each head equipped with a strict selection for a sister node, and attracting formal features to predict the specifiers of the functional heads deterministically in addition. Cartography, thus, has absolutely no special status in current syntactic thinking. On the contrary, it requires massive lexical stipulations (about the set of functional heads that build the cascade) even to start working. Given just the most basic assumptions about theory building, cartographic approaches would have to justify this massive complexity by yielding equally massive empirical advantages. As we have already seen above, this promise is not only not met (at least not by any currently available cartographic theory) – rather, the predictions of cartographic approaches to German scrambling fail to hold almost completely. Theoretically speaking, then, cartographic syntax seems somewhat old-fashioned, and empirically speaking, downright problematic.

Relational approaches to syntax are nothing new: Some general points about structural relations have long been at the center of some types of syntactic research. Binding and scopal relations, it was found, are based on hierarchical relations, not on linear ones. Thus, I propose that the fact that Merge provides hierarchical relations (with linearization being delegated to the phonological interface) should be included in our attempts to model syntactic phenomena more generally: Relations cannot only help to explain scope and binding phenomena, they can more generally be employed to judge the outcomes of syntactic derivations in more (maybe: all) cases. Restrictions based on syntactic relations can operate much less deterministically than cartographic derivations, as we will see below.

With regard to scrambling in German, the fact that movements can take place at all in the syntax should not be surprising, given free Merge (the standard structure-building operation as of today): If external Merge is free (a position mostly uncontested in the literature), then so is internal Merge, without any further ado. The question then is not how to trigger movements – which are implemented by free (internal) Merge – but how to restrict the outcomes of these applications of Merge. Not anything goes, of course. With regard to the issue at hand here, I will shortly summarize the findings by Struckmeier (2014, 2017) on scrambling in German:

- Semantically transparent scrambling (i.e. scrambling that causes effects to the meaning of the sentences at hand) can be implemented with the most basic assumptions currently available.
- Semantically intransparent scrambling (i.e. scrambling that either has no effect on the meaning of a sentence, or even fails to have effects on meaning that would prima facie be expected to occur) requires us to assume that syntax is not driven by the interface to the semantic component exclusively, but has to produce outcomes that are, in addition, acceptable to the interface to the phonological component as well.

The following paragraphs will illustrate these two kinds of scrambling in turn.

As long as the outcome of internal Merge operations are legible to the semantic interface, applications of Merge are legitimate. Semantically transparent instances of scrambling can be readily explained as the outcome of a semantically licensed Merge.

12. a. ... weil ein Arzt nicht [$_{vP}$ ~~ein Arzt~~ [$_{VP}$ alle Patienten heilt]]

    b. ... weil ein Arzt alle Patienten nicht [$_{vP}$ ~~ein Arzt~~ [$_{VP}$ ~~alle Patienten~~ heilt]]

13. a. ??... weil er einander$_i$ [alle Gäste]$_i$ vorgestellt hat

    b. ... weil er [alle Gäste]$_i$ einander$_i$ ~~[alle Gäste]~~$_i$ vorgestellt hat

Recall from the experiments above that German seems to have no (English-style) QR, and changes in surface orders can (but do not have to) reflect semantic effects (as in 12). These types of Merge operations thus relate to different relational outcomes of applications of Merge. The effects at the interface to the semantic component license Merge applications as in (12). Likewise, the scrambled structure in (13b) avails the sentence of a bound reading for the reciprocal pronoun, which is not (easily, or at all) available in (13a). Applications of Merge of this type are also licensed by their semantic effect: The interface to the semantic component understands to interpret the newly merged structure. No known issues therefore arise with derivations that employ semantically transparent applications of free Merge. Stipulations regarding the workings of syntactic operations that would actively *cause* such issues can, of course, be made (in order to try and thwart the relational proposal), but these stipulations would be faced with an enormous empirical burden of proof.

Both scopal orderings and binding configurations are inherently relational: They state how scope-bearing elements can be interpreted, given certain syntactic relations *between* such elements. No individual scope-bearing element needs to be equipped with movement features, and it seems positively counterproductive to envision heads that would attract wide-scope elements: There are countless structural configurations in which a wide scope element can, in fact, scope over a lower element. Thus, to stipulate potential target positions for wide-scope elements would serve as a *reductio ad absurdum* of cartographic attempts.[13]

Likewise, binding configurations consider the relations between (potential) binders and (potential) bindees. No binding-relevant element comes with movement features, or any specific distribution in a clause – as long as *some* binding constellation can be found as required. Again, the number of binding configurations in a language like German are legion (and, may I add, very hard to pin down). Again, no cartographic solution seems at hand, and none has been proposed for binding, to the best of my knowledge.

In sum, then, syntactic phenomena exist for which feature-driven movement solutions seem unavailable. Relational accounts for these phenomena, however, have been proposed many times in the literature. With regard to the specifics of scope and binding in German scrambling scenarios, I would like to refer the reader to Struckmeier (2014, 2017) for a more complete discussion of the way that structural relations should matter in the discussion of scrambling. The proposal made here agrees with Struckmeier (2014, 2017) that we should expand the notion of relational output configurations to include other types of syntactic operations, such as scrambling outcomes.

---

13 Consider, for instance, the following – completely fictitious – cascade for wide-scope elements (WS):

   [$_{TP}$ der Arzt [$_{WS1}$ (alle Patienten) WS$_1$ [$_{MP1}$ (MP$_1$) MP^0 [$_{WS2}$ (alle Patienten) WS$_2$ [$_{MP2}$ (MP$_2$) [$_{WS3}$ (alle Patienten) WS$_3$...]]]]]] ...

and so on, for every adverbial, argument, negation element, or what have you that happens to merge in the course of the derivation.

Merge that is not semantically licensed, on the other hand, cannot receive a semantic relational explanation. Other configurations that may turn out to be relevant for syntactic derivations may not be *semantically* relevant relations in syntax – but they base on *structural* relations, still: Following (again) Struckmeier (2017), I will now show, in a short summary, that the mapping to the phonological component can likewise issue requirements that syntactic derivations have to meet for convergence.

The *Final-over-Final Constraint* (*FOFC*) posits that no syntactic head can be linearized as head-final if the label of that head dominates another head which is linearized as non-final (Biberauer et al 2010a; 2010b; Biberauer & Sheehan 2010). Given that Merge is a free option in core syntax, the FOFC can, however, be overridden by merging conflicting structures at structurally higher positions. For German, this constraint has proven problematic, since modal particles (MPs) seem to position in exactly the kind of configuration that the FOFC disallows:

14. [$_{TP}$ ... [$_{MP}$ MP [$_{vP}$ ...]] T]

T, according to standard assumptions, is a head-final element in German. MPs, on the other hand, precede the vP, causing the FOFC-violating structure in (14). Struckmeier (2017) however argues that the movement of vP (recall: freely available via internal Merge) creates a new configuration as in:

15. [$_{TP}$ [$_{vP}$ ...] ... [$_{MP}$ MP [$_{vP}$ ...]] T]

In this configuration, vP neither precedes nor follows the MP, and it is neither higher nor lower, being a discontinuous element (cf., again, Struckmeier 2017 for the complete argument). Thus, the FOFC violation is avoided for this stretch of the German clause structure, iff vP moves obligatorily to a position that caNn be called SpecTP.[14]

Note now that the vP contains all arguments, non-finite verbs as well as adverbials. It is certainly no coincidence that precisely these elements can scramble – whereas, e.g., MPs and finite verbs, which are not included in vP, cannot. Struckmeier proposes to consider these asemantic cases of movements as spellout phenomena, concerning elements that are contained inside the vP copy in SpecTP.

---

[14] Note that "subjects", nominative DPs, agents etc. all need not move anywhere in German, completely unlike in English. Thus, SpecTP is not a "subject" position, and not related to nominative/ phi-feature Agree operations, let alone theta role assignments.

Note that for this arrangement to work, no element inside the vP itself has to have any incentive to move. They are simply taken across MPs by the movement of the larger vP that contains them:

16. [$_{TP}$ [$_{vP}$ ein Arzt alle Patienten ~~heilt~~]... [$_{MP}$ ja [nicht [$_{vP}$ ein Arzt alle Patienten ~~heilt~~]] heilt$_T$]]

As for the spellout of the arguments[15], Struckmeier argues that prosodic requirements can cause a "leftward" spellout of an argument, which is, however, not structurally "high". For example, a strict prosodic requirement of German seems to be that (contrastive) rise contours must come to precede fall contours (e.g. focus exponents) wherever the two co-occur in a sentence. For the structure just derived, this would yield the following spellout:

17. [$_{TP}$ [$_{vP}$ ein Arzt /ALLe Patienten ~~heilt~~] ja NICHT$_F$ [$_{vP}$ ~~ein Arzt alle Patienten heilt~~] heilt$_T$]

These structures have been associated with a "focus reversal of scope reversal" effect (e.g., Jacobs 1996, 1997; Büring 1997; Krifka 1998). In the analysis provided by Struckmeier, no scope reversal occured in the first place: The QP contained in the vP is not in a structural configuration to scope over the negation! While the QP does in fact precede the negation, it is contained inside the vP so deeply that no wide scope of QP over the negation is expected – nor does it occur.[16] In this way, the connection between certain prosodic markings and certain semantic readings can be explained: Prosodic requirements (such as rises preceding falls) can cause specific spellouts of syntactic structures which have the required semantic readings without further stipulations. Prosody, it seems, can override the semantic transparency otherwise attested for German scopal phenomena. In exactly the same way, potential binders can end up preceding potentiel bindees, without a concomitant binding effect. Note that the r-expression *Peter* can bind the possessive (in accordance with binding principle a) and be unbound itself (in accordance with principle c):

---

15 Also, adverbials, set aside here. Cf. Struckmeier 2014 for a more detailed description.
16 Note also that contrastive rise can occur on elements that are embedded inside argument phrases – so it does not seem as though these elements require any structural 'scope' in terms of hierarchically "high" positions, cf.: *Gestern hat [der Mann, [von dem Peter sagt [dass er geFÄHRlich ist]]] uns beDROHT. Und [der Mann, [von dem Peter sagt [dass er /HARMlos ist]]] hat uns geRETTet.*

18. weil...

   a. [~~vP~~ ~~nur P.~~ seine_i /SCHUHe ~~vergessen~~] ja [vP nur PETer_i ~~seine S.~~ vergessen] hat

   b. [vP nur P. seine_i SCHUHe vergessen] ja [vP nur PETer_i ~~seine Schuhe vergessen~~] hat

In addition, the mapping to the phonological component can only issue preferences which seem hard to reformulate in syntactic terms: It has long been noted (ever since Lenerz 1977) that foci are reluctant to scramble. However, our experimental results show that the subjects in our experiments, at least, do not penalize scrambled foci when the results or prosodically inconspicuous – e.g., when the scrambling of even a stressed focus exponent does not cause large-scale prosodic changes. If, as we have seen, focus exponents scramble only across a single-syllable modal particle, a soft preference for late focus exponents is obviously not massively violated, explaining the experimental findings. Note, specifically, that focus exponence is, in fact, quite often affected by, e.g. the phonological length of focus exponents. It cannot come as a surprise, therefore, that the preference for late main stress placement in fact cannot be stated in harsh, or even absolute terms.[17]

Conversely, semantic transparency requirements can override prosodic preferences, as with the cases of semantically licensed scrambling of foci discussed above (e.g. in Sect. 2.1). Recall now that syntax has traditionally been considered as the representation of aspects that feed *both* the meaning and form components – i.e. the component that represents the way that the two interfaces *relate to each other*. We therefore arrive at a situation where syntax-centered approaches (cartography being a prominent one amongst those) fail for a conceptual reason, too: Scrambling can be driven by prosodic requirements, to the detriment of semantic transparency. Conversely, scrambling can be driven by semantic requirements, to the detriment of prosodic preferences. Syntax, quite obviously, is precisely the *wrong* component of our overall grammatical architecture to state *mis*matches, given standard assumptions. We would therefore have to conclude that stating the ordering requirements at separate interfaces (each of which oblivious to the preferences of the other) seems more convincing. This, of course, is exactly what an interface-driven approach does.

---

[17] Consider, again, only a single example, where adding to the phonological length of the focus exponent phrase makes the main stress seem to shift 'leftwards' – with absolutely no penalty incurred by adding 3 unstressed syllables: *Q: Who did Peter kiss? – A: Peter hat Marie BROCK(meierle) geküsst.*

Last, but not least, a relational approach to word order in German would remove a theory-internal tension that has been felt by many: Cartography places trigger features in fixed positions which, by virtue of their complement selection, are ordered vis-a-vis other functional projections in the cascade. In effect, then, target positions had an *absolute* and *fixed* place in syntactic structures. However, notions like (*relativized*) *minimality* never operated over absolute positions, but were relational by nature: In order for some element to interact with another element, there should be no intervening element between them (of the same type, for relativized minimality). Defining syntactic operations over relational output constellations just seems more congenial to the notion of (*relativized*) *minimality* than functional cascades ever did.

The relational approach, on the other hand, can integrate minimality effects quite congenially, and avail itself of a larger number of scrambling factors, given that relations can be syntactic, or prosodic, or semantic in nature. Recall now that the scrambling of foci was, in fact, recognized as a marked option by Lenerz. Given that the scrambling of foci for reasons of scope transparency is definitely possible, it seems that scope transparency requirements are one way of defining what factors can cause the marked option. Likewise, prosodic requirements can cause marked types of scrambling. The relational approach therefore avails syntactic theory of exactly the ways of explaining the syntactic options German requires – whereas cartographic proposals are empirically problematic and conceptually unattractive at virtually every step of the way.

More experimental data are certainly required to support further (or falsify) the relational approach. To the degree that experimental data are available (cf. the experiments above as well as, e.g., Keller 2000 for an investigation of German scrambling that fits the relational approach perfectly), the results seem promising – but I would not want to argue that they are conclusive at this point (needless to say). Still, the interface to the phonological component may be able to handle certain (only apparently) 'syntactic' issues with aplomb.

Leaving behind questions of the formulation of the grammar as such, we are now in a position to evaluate the ways in which the competing analyses fare with regard as to how the grammar links up to the problems of language acquisition and language evolution.

A relational approach, I claim, has at least two advantages over a cartographic one: First of all, many properties can be delegated to the interfaces of core syntax and to other components of the architecture of grammar, as we have seen:

- Questions of stress placement are simply left unresolved (in fact, are never addressed) by core syntax, and the pertinent prosodic restrictions are computed where such computations arguably belong: in the mapping to the phonological component. Properties of the phonological component can be readily observed by a child learner – unlike syntactic properties, which face poverty of stimulus-related issues.
- Likewise, questions of scopal interpretations and binding options do not have to be assessed by syntax – they should be assessed in the semantic component. Semantics has been argued by many to be universal across languages, removing those aspects of scopal and binding properties which can in fact be regarded as universal from the set of properties the learner has to acquire in the first place.
- Furthermore, relational approaches can avoid the opposite solution, required by cartographic analyses: To syntactify every notion that seemed to matter for word order in German (as well as comparable phenomena in other languages). Not only does this allow us to keep syntax 'uncontaminated' of these notions (as Fanselow 2006 puts it) – rather, syntactified properties always seemed to replicate something syntax-internally that was duplicated in other components of the grammar anyway. Therefore, to remove these features from syntax proper is to avoid architectural redundancy as well as a particularly dubious aspect of syntax. At the same time, these properties form no problems for syntactic acquisition anymore, simply because they are not stated in the (itself unobservable) workings of core syntax.

In fact then, not only theoretical elegance is at stake with regard to cartographic approaches to syntax – but rather, the feasibility of a cognitively plausible theory of syntax: Language acquisition has been recognized as a central body of restrictions that help differentiate feasible syntactic theories from cognitively unrealistic ones. Cartography, I believe, does extremely poorly with regard to questions of acquisition, as I will outline in the following.

By its definition, cartography employs an unchanging cascade of functional projections: Every head selects for its sister and specifier. Note, however, that many of the heads stipulated in this manner have no phonological matrix in many languages. To give but one example here discussed above, cartographic analyses have to assume that modal particles in German have to be situated in the specifier of a modal particle-attracting head (cf. Coniglio 2006, 2007) for various reasons (which Coniglio points out in detail). There are at least two issues with this assumption from a language acquisition point of view: Firstly, modal particles never project complex phrases. For all intents and purposes, they must look to a language-learning child just like heads would, since no other element ever joins a modal particle "phrase". Furthermore, the functional head that attracts the phrase that looks like a head to its specifier, is itself never visible for any modal particle in German. Likewise, modal particles cannot undergo phrasal movement, nor do they have phrasal pro-forms (or any proforms), nor can they be addressed by a question-under-discussion (a common test for *Satzglied-* and hence phrase status in German). How, then, is a child ever to know that the modal particle-attracting invisible head exists, and furthermore that the modal particle itself (which looks exactly like a head, because it is one) is not the head of the projection? Catch-22 situations of this type are positively commonplace for cartography. Note, for example, that the cartographic trigger heads allegedly responsible for scrambling (Topic, Antifocus, and what have you), are universally characterized by extremely ephemeral meaning contributions – which, in fact, are so hard to pin down that no commonly accepted notion of these (alleged) linguistic categories is at hand for linguistic theory. Also, the heads have no phonological matrix in German (and beyond). Furthermore, the movement to these positions is, as we have seen, not obligatory, so the presence of the scrambling trigger head cannot be observed indirectly by the language learner based on (surface-) syntactic effects. In sum, then, cartographic scrambling heads have no form or meaning effects that could be detected by children in the first place. Thus, these heads could not be learned in principle (let alone in practice). The assumption mostly taken by cartographic proposals is, consequently, that the cascade of functional heads is simply innate, as a part of universal grammar. Note that this approach inflates UG quite substantially, placing a burden of proof on the proposal that, to the best of my knowledge, cartography never attempted to meet: Nothing really gets explained by this stipulation. It only serves to sweep the language acquisition issue that cartography obviously faces under the rug.

Given the now common question of language evolution, however, the cartographic UG stipulation refuses to stay under the rug: We are told, in effect, that homo sapiens at some point was subject to a genetic mutation (the only possible change in species, if we subscribe to Darwinism), such that mutant member of the species came to know a number of aspects of structure, amongst which we would need to find statements such as:
- There is a modal particle-attracting head in sentences, even if this head is not phonologically implemented.
- This modal-particle head has to be structurally higher than a negation head.
- There may be various topic positions in a clause, but only ever one vP.

Note that, according the cartographic stipulation of a UG (i.e.: human-universal) cascade, no humans currently exist which have no innate cascade of function heads (since the cascade is, allegedly, part of the genetic endowment of modern-day homo sapiens). This is begging the question, however: How precisely could the functional head cascade have improved the fitness of a specimen of early homo sapiens carrying the required mutations? Sadly, no explanations come to mind that are not utterly silly. Quite on the contrary, said mutations raise the question how some random mutation should even have such (language-) specific, high-level, cognitive, abstract effects in the first place? However, some genetic/ evolutionary explanation must hold in order for the cartographic stipulation of an innate cascade of functional heads to receive any kind of explanation at all.

Note that current syntactic thinking revolves centrally about these questions. Pointing out that biological claims (which stipulations about UG entail) are in need of biological explanations is not at all polemic – it is a requirement for thinking about syntax not as a plaything for theoreticians, but as an actual cognitive endowment of actual, living creatures. I do not for a second want to imply that proponents of cartographic syntax theories in fact want to ignore the rules of scientific discourse here – but for the time being, their theory is simply stated without even a shred of (biological/ genetic as well as properly linguistic) evidence.

Finally, then, theories that can be stipulated without evidence can be rejected without evidence, the old adage goes. The cartographic claim of the UG status of the functional head cascade is in dire need of evidence, I submit: Both linguistically (in the harshness of its predictions) as well as biologically (in its vast assumptions about the human genome), the current status quo of cartographic theories is tenuous at best.

5 Conclusion

Removing cartographic machinery should be a primary objective for syntactic theorizing:
- Cartographic trigger heads, by their definition, make very harsh predictions as to the obligatoriness of movements. In many cases, these predictions are not met by the actually empirical data. Cartography, in other words, often fails to deliver nuanced descriptions of the facts.
- Furthermore, the cartographic trigger logic is circular as an explanatory device in any event: Instead of explaining why certain elements move to certain positions, feature-attraction is simply used to restate that they do. Why certain elements are affected (but not others), and why the position that attracts

them is positioned in the way it is (and not anywhere else, really), is never explained clearly. To adapt a beautiful wording by Samuels (if somewhat off topic meaning-wise): "While perhaps on some level all logic is ultimately circular, this is a very small circle." (2015: 166).
- Instead of trigger features, this article proposes to regard the outcome of (free) Merge operations as potential inputs to the semantic and phonological interfaces. Core syntactic restrictions, needless to say, exist. However, they are stated not in terms of feature-attraction mechanisms (a lexical, and construction-specific stipulation), but as far-reaching constraints on relations in structures which Merge elegantly supplies. In this way, I hope, a program for a non-circular syntax can be made out – if only in the sketchiest of outlines.
- The interfaces in interface-oriented approaches have actual work to do. Since non-syntactic phenomena in a language are not syntactified, phonological properties will have to be handled by (the mapping to) the phonological component. Meaning properties, likewise, are handled by the semantic component.
- Given that core syntax is near-impossible for children to observe during their language acquisition process, the interface-driven approach eases the difficulties associated with the acquisition of syntax: only very general mechanisms are posited to matter in syntax, mostly related to restrictions imposed by the operation Merge.
- These general mechanisms are, furthermore, exactly of the type that are currently debated as the *faculty of language in the narrow sense*, embedding the human faculty of language in the context of general cognition and its potential biological genesis.

In sum, then, although relational, interface-driven approaches to syntax have not been developed in great detail here, I would like to submit that the advantages these attempts could potentially offer should warrant giving them a chance at demonstrating their worth.

References

Abraham, Werner and László Molnárfi (2001). German clause structure under discourse functional weight: Focus and antifocus. In Abraham, Werner and Jan-Wouter Zwart, eds, *Issues in Formal German(ic) Typology*, pp. 1–43. Amsterdam/Philadelphia: John Benjamins.

Bayer, Josef and Jaklin Kornfilt (1994). Against Scrambling as an Instance of Move-α. In Corver, Norbert and Henk van Riemsdijk, eds, *Studies on Scrambling: Movement and Non-*

Movement Approaches to Free Word Order-Phenomena, pp. 17–60. Berlin/New York: Mouton de Gruyter.

Biberauer, Maria Theresa, Anders Holmberg, and Ian Gareth Roberts (2010a). A syntactic universal and its consequences. *Linguistic Inquiry*, 45:169–225.

Biberauer, Maria Theresa, Glenda Newton, and Michelle Sheehan (2010b). Impossible changes and impossible borrowings: The Final-over-Final Constraint. In Breitbarth, Anne, Christopher Lucas, Sheila Watts, and David Willis, eds, *Continuity and change in grammars*, pp. 35–60. Amsterdam/Philadelphia: John Benjamins.

Biberauer, Maria Theresa and Michelle Sheehan (2010). Disharmony, antisymmetry, and the Final-over-Final Constraint. In Uribe-Etxebarria, Myriam and Vidal Valmala, eds, *Ways of structure building*, pp. 206–244. Oxford: Oxford University Press.

Bobaljik, Jonathan (2002). A-chains at the PF-interface: Copies and ‚covert' movement'. *Natural Language and Linguistic Theory*, 20(2):197–267.

Bobaljik, Jonathan and Susi Wurmbrand (2012). Word Order and Scope: Transparent Interfaces and the 3/4 Signature. *Linguistic Inquiry*, 43:371–421.

Büring, Daniel (1997). *The meaning of topic and focus: the 59th Street bridge accent*. London: Routledge.

Büring, Daniel (2001). Let's phrase it: Focus, Word Order, and Prosodic Phrasing in German Double Object Constructions. In Müller, Gereon and Wolfgang Sternefeld, eds, *Competition in Syntax*, pp. 68–105. Berlin/New York: Mouton de Gruyter.

Büring, Daniel (2006). Intonation und Informationsstruktur. In Blühdorn, Hardarik, Eva Breindl, and Ulrich H. Waßner, eds, *Text – Verstehen: Grammatik und darüber hinaus*, pp. 144–163. Berlin/New York: Walter de Gruyter.

Büring, Daniel (2015). (Contrastive) Topics. In Féry, Caroline and Shinchiro Ishihara, eds, *The Oxford Handbook of Information Structure*. online edition doi:10.1093/oxfordhb/9780199642670.013.002.

Chomsky, Noam (2000). Minimalist inquiries: the framework. In Martin, Roger, David Michaels, and Juan Uriagereka, eds, *Step by Step: Essays on Minimalist Syntax in Honor of Howard Lasnik*, pp. 89–155. Cambridge, MA: MIT Press.

Chomsky, Noam (2013). Problems of Projection. *Lingua*, 130:33–49.

Coniglio, Marco (2006). German Modal Particles in the Functional Structure of IP. *University of Venice Working Papers in Linguistics*, 16:57–95.

Coniglio, Marco (2007). German Modal Particles in Root and Embedded Clauses. In *University of Venice Working Papers in Linguistics 17*, pp. 109–141.

Fanselow, Gisbert (2001). Features, Theta-Roles, and Free Constituent Order. *Linguistic Inquiry*, 32:405–437.

Fanselow, Gisbert (2003). Free Constituent Order: A Minimalist Interface Account. In Werner Abraham and László Molnárfi (eds.) *Optionality in Syntax and Discourse Structure: Aspects of Word Order Variation in (West) Germanic and other Languages. Folia Linguistica*, 37(1–2):191–231.

Fanselow, Gisbert (2006). On Pure Syntax (Uncontaminated by Information Structure). In Brandt, Patrick and Eric Fuß, eds, *Form, Structure, and Grammar: A Festschrift to Günther Grewendorf on Occasion of His 60th Birthday*, pp. 137–157. Berlin: Akademie Verlag.

Frey, Werner (1993). *Syntaktische Bedingungen für die semantische Interpretation*. Berlin: Akademieverlag.

Frey, Werner (2004). A Medial Topic Position for German. *Linguistische Berichte*, 198:153–190.

Frey, Werner and Karin Pitney (1998). Zur Positionierung der Adverbiale im deutschen Mittelfeld. *Linguistische Berichte*, 176:489–534.

Frey, Werner and Karin Pittner (1999). Adverbialpositionen im deutsch-englischen Vergleich. In Doherty, M., ed., *Sprachspezifische Aspekte der Informationsverteilung*, pp. 14–41. Berlin: Akademie-Verlag.

Haider, Hubert and Inger Rosengren (1998). Scrambling. *Sprache & Pragmatik*, 49:1–104.

Hinterhölzl, Roland (2006). *Scrambling, Remnant Movement, and Restructuring in West Germanic*. Oxford: Oxford University Press.

Höhle, Tilman (1982). Explikation für ‚normale Betonung' und ‚normale Wortstellung'. In Abraham, Werner, ed., *Satzglieder im Deutschen: Vorschläge zu ihrer syntaktischen, semantischen und pragmatischen Fundierung*, pp. 75–153. Tübingen: Gunter Narr.

Jacobs, Joachim (1996). Bemerkungen zur I-Topikalisierung. *Sprache & Pragmatik*, 41:1–48.

Jacobs, Joachim (1997). I-Topikalisierung. *Linguistische Berichte*, 168:91–133.

Keller, Frank (2000). *Gradience in Grammar: Experimental and Computational Aspects of Degrees of Grammaticality*. PhD thesis, University of Edinburgh.

Krifka, Manfred (1998). Scope inversion under the Rise–Fall Contour in German. *Linguistic Inquiry*, 29(1):75–112.

Lenerz, Jürgen (1977). *Zur Abfolge nominaler Satzglieder im Deutschen*. Tübingen: Gunter Narr.

Meinunger, André (2000). *Syntactic Aspects of Topic and Comment*. Amsterdam/Philadelphia, PA: John Benjamins.

Molnárfi, László (2002). Focus and antifocus in modern Afrikaans and West Germanic. *Linguistics*, 40:1107–1160.

Molnárfi, László (2004). On Scrambling as defocusing in German and West Germanic. In Breitbarth, Anne and Henk van Riemsdijk, eds, *Triggers*, pp. 231–386. Berlin/New York: Mouton de Gruyter.

Müller, Gereon (2001). Order Preservation, Parallel Movement, and the Emergence of the Unmarked. In Legendre, Géraldine, Jane Grimshaw, and Sten Vikner, eds, *Optimality-Theoretic Syntax*, pp. 279–313. Cambridge, MA: MIT Press.

Musan, Renat (2002). Informationsstrukturelle Dimensionen im Deutschen. *Zeitschrift für Germanistische Linguistik*, 30:198–221.

Neeleman, Ad and Tanya Reinhart (1998). Scrambling and the PF Interface. In Butt, Miriam and Wilhelm Geuder, eds, *The Projection of Arguments: Lexical and Compositional Factors*, pp. 309–353. Stanford: CSLI Publications.

Ott, Dennis and Radek Šimík, eds (2017). *What drives syntactic computation?* Special collection, *Glossa*. http://www.glossa-journal.org/collections/special/syntactic-computation/.

Samuels, Bridget D. (2015). Biolinguistics in phonology: a prospectus. *Phonological Studies*, 18:161–171.

Schwarzschild, Roger (1999). GIVENness, AvoidF and Other Constraints on the Placement of Accent. *Natural Language Semantics*, 7:141–177.

Struckmeier, Volker (2014). *Syntax und Prosodie von Scrambling-Bewegungen im Deutschen: Zur komplexen Architektur grammatischer Beschreibungen*. Berlin: Akademie Verlag.

Struckmeier, Volker (2017). Against information structure heads: A relational analysis of German scrambling. *Glossa*, 2(1):1–29.

Zimmermann, Malte (2004). Zum Wohl: Diskurspartikeln als Satztypmodifikatoren. *Linguistische Berichte*, 199:253–286.

Joost Kremers
Head movement as a syntax-phonology interface phenomenon

1 Introduction

Head movement has been a staple of derivational approaches to generative grammar at least since analyses such as those by Travis (1984); Baker (1985); Pollock (1989) established it as a useful theoretical analytical device. However, it has not gone unnoticed that head movement is also problematic for several reasons. As a result, a number of alternative analyses has been proposed (see Dékány 2018 for a recent overview).

Some of these alternative analyses deal with head movement (or at least some forms of head movement, see below) post-syntactically. While the details vary, the claim is generally that (some) head movement operations do not take place in syntax proper but rather in the component that readies a syntactic structure for phonology.

In this paper, I would like to go one step further and claim that some forms of head movements (in particular those that involve syntactic word formation) are triggered by phonological properties of the elements involved. Unlike proposals such as those by e.g., Platzack (2013), who adds a phonological diacritic to syntactic heads, introducing information into the syntactic structure that is not needed for syntax itself, I argue that there is no need whatsoever for any special marking on syntactic heads. Nor is it necessary to introduce special features into the phonological structure that exist solely to solve a syntactic problem.

The phonological features that I assume are well-established in the literature on phonology and the syntax-phonology interface: prosodic domain boundaries,[1] and autosegmental phonology (Goldsmith 1976 and much subsequent work). In essence, I argue that what we commonly call affixes are in fact prosodic morphemes (cf. McCarthy & Prince 1990) and that it is this property that results in their observed behaviour.

---

[1] Scheer (2008) argues that prosodic domains are what he calls "diacritics", technical devices that do not reflect actual properties of the relevant phenomena, and should be abandoned. Scheer only accepts prosodic boundaries, not the domains that they are thought to define. The current proposal, as far as I can tell, does not need prosodic domains; it can be formulated in terms of boundaries.

https://doi.org/10.1515/9783110650532-011

2 Some problems with head movement

Head movement is the theoretical term used to describe phenomena whereby the head of a phrase appears to move from its base position to some other position in the structure (clause, noun phrase), while leaving behind (or *stranding*) its dependent elements (arguments, adjuncts). A typical case is the well-known verb-second movement in many Germanic languages (Dutch, German, Frisian, Scandinavian languages), remnants of which exist in English as well:

(1) Marie schrijft vandaag nog het artikel af.   *Dutch*
     Marie writes today   still the article off
     'Marie will finish the article today.'

In (1), the finite verb *schrijft* appears in second position, while the particle *af*, which forms part of the lexeme *afschrijven* 'to finish writing' and the direct object *het artikel* 'the article' are in clause-final position. There are several arguments supporting the assumption that the finite verb has moved from the clause-final position: firstly, the particle *af* is part of the lexeme. Secondly, there are structures (specifically, embedded clauses and clauses in which the main verb is non-finite) in which the main verb appears clause-finally as well, together with the particle and the direct object, as demonstrated in (2):

(2) a. dat Marie vandaag nog het artikel afschrijft.
       that Marie today   still the article off-writes
       'that Marie will finish the article today.'

    b. Marie gaat vandaag nog het artikel afschrijven.
       Marie goes today   still the article off-write.INF
       'Marie is going to finish the article today.'

In contrast, there are no structures in which the finite verb, the particle and the direct object obligatorily (and simultaneously) appear clause-initially, cf. (3)[2]:

(3) *Het artikel afschrijft Marie vandaag nog.
      the article off-writes Marie today   still

---

[2] The direct object can appear clause-initially, but it can do so independently of the main verb, e.g., when the main verb is non-finite. The particle can marginally appear clause-initially with the verb, but only under exclusion of the direct object and usually only with special (emphatic/contrastive) intonation, e.g., ?*AF schrijft zij het artikel*. See Müller (2002) for discussion of similar German examples.

These data strongly suggest that the finite verb *schrijft* has a clause-final base position and that under specific circumstances, it obligatorily moves to the second position in the clause, stranding the other elements in the phrase it projects.

Crucially, since work done in the eighties, head movement is also thought to be involved in the formation of complex word forms, especially complex verb forms in a process that is sometimes called *roll-up movement*. Pollock's (1989) analysis of French verb forms is a typical example of this kind of analysis:

(4) a. Marie **ne parl-er-ait** pas *French*
Marie NEG speak-COND-3SG NEG
'Marie would not speak.'

b.

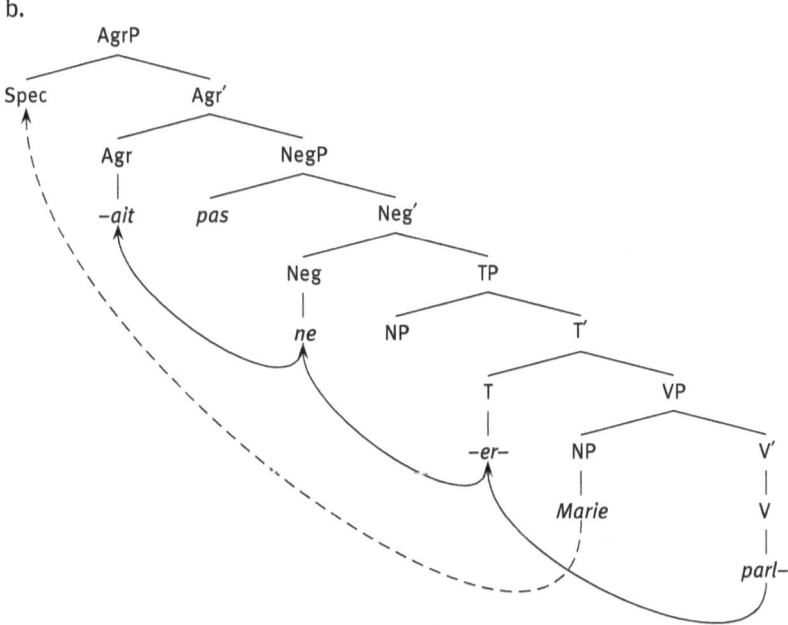

In Pollock's analysis, the complex word form *ne parlerait* 'would not speak' is formed by moving the stem *parl* to the next higher head T, then to Neg, and finally to Agr. On the way, the stem picks up the affixes *er, ne* and *ait*.

As pointed out by Rizzi & Roberts (1989) and more recently by Harizanov & Gribanova (2019), the two examples discussed here, verb-second movement and roll-up movement, actually have quite different properties and should be analysed separately. Verb-second movement is an example of *head substitution*, where the moved head essentially replaces the head in the target position. The target head in such cases is phonologically empty, although it usually contributes certain morphosyntactic features.

Roll-up movement is an example of *head adjunction*, where the target head is phonologically not null. The result of such a movement is that the moved head and the target head are phonologically combined. Technically, this is usually analysed as a form of adjunction: the moved head and the target head form a complex structure which acts syntactically as a single, complex head:

(5)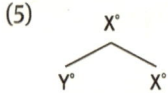

The structure in (5) illustrates some of the theoretical problems that head movement, and especially head adjunction, raises. In Minimalist theories, movement is essentially an instance of the operation Merge, which joins two elements into a new, larger structure. In the case of movement, one of the elements originates as a constituent of the other element.

Since Merge can only combine two elements at the root, the moved element can only target the root of the tree: movement must extend the tree. This assumption is formalized by Chomsky (1993, 22–23) as the Extension Condition. In the case of head adjunction, the Extension Condition is violated, however. The target of the movement must be a head, but a head cannot dominate any other material, so it cannot be the root of the tree. If it were, it would not be a head.

Another problem for head adjunction is the structure of the resulting complex head. Chomsky (1993) adopts an approach to phrase structure, called *bare phrase structure*, in which typical phrase structure notions such as *head* and *phrase* are defined configurationally. In this approach, a head is a simplex element, one that is not composed of two smaller elements. This means that the structure in (5) cannot actually exist: in bare phrase structure, there is no such thing as a "complex head".[3]

Depending on the exact theoretical implementation, these problems do not affect head substitution, as Harizanov & Gribanova (2019) also note. With head substitution, the moved head is remerged with the root of the tree and no complex head is formed. For this reason, Harizanov & Gribanova, who develop an analysis of head movement within the framework of Distributed Morphology (DM),

---

[3] Bare phrase structure would be compatible with a theory that assumes a separate morphology module, meaning that a head could be complex in morphology but simplex in syntax. Current minimalist theories generally assume that morphology is part of syntax, however, and the current paper is premised on that assumption: if morphology were a separate module of grammar, head adjunction would not exist and the current discussion would be meaningless.

argue that head substitution is a purely syntactic process, while head adjunction is a post-syntactic, morphological process. For this to work, however, Harizanov & Gribanova need to assume that syntactic heads are endowed with a morphological feature M. If M has the value [M:−], the head is adjoined post-syntactically to the next lower head (through a process that is known in Distributed Morphology as *Lowering*). Similarly, a value of [M:+] triggers adjunction to the next higher head (through the upward counterpart of Lowering, which Harizanov & Gribanova call *Raising*).

This feature is problematic, however, because it is lexical in nature but actually exists on syntactic heads. In DM, morphological operations are defined on syntactic heads.[4] That is, DM assumes that when morphological operations take place, the heads in the structure are not endowed with phonological features yet (cf. Halle & Marantz 1993). For this reason, operations that appear to involve the actual morpho-phonological forms of words (or Vocabulary Items, in DM terms), are actually defined on the underlying syntactic heads.

This is hardly a desirable state of affairs. Word-forming head movement (i.e., head adjunction) crucially involves the morpho-phonological form of the heads involved. Ideally, one would like to say that Raising or Lowering takes place because of the morpho-phonological form of the relevant head: if T is expressed as a suffix (e.g., *-ed* for past tense in English), Raising or Lowering should take place. However, DM does not offer any way of doing so. In DM the operations that effectuate this type of word formation must be defined on syntactic heads, which by definition lack any morphological form.

The idea behind this separation of syntactic heads and morpho-phonological forms (Vocabulary Items in DM's terminology), is that the morpho-phonological form of a word has no effect on its syntactic behaviour. However, while this may be true for *core* syntactic behaviour, it is not true for morphological behaviour.

To give an example, in German, some prepositions can incorporate a following definite determiner. For example, the preposition *zu* 'to' can combine with the determiner *der* (DAT.SG.f) to form *zur*, and with *dem* (DAT.SG.m) to form *zum*. Similarly, the preposition *in* 'in' can combine with *das* (ACC.SG.n) to form *ins*. Syntactically, in most minimalist models and indeed in DM, any combination of preposition + determiner is simply represented as [P [D …]], no distinction is made between *zu der* and *in das* in the syntactic structure. Only when Vocabulary Insertion takes place can these two be distinguished.

---

[4] Note that although in DM morphological operations are ordered after syntax proper, the structures they operate on are purely syntactic, so the idea that there is no separate morphology module is maintained.

The problem is that there are clear morphological restrictions on which combinations of P+D can fuse in this manner. Crucially, there are combinations that could fuse from a phonotactic point of view, but for some reason simply do not. One particular example is the combination of *zu* with the determiner *den* (DAT.pl). Following the pattern of *zu+der* and *zu+dem*, one might expect that *zu+den* can fuse to *zun*, which would be phonotactically acceptable. However, *zu+den* does not fuse in this manner.

The same problem arises in the verbal domain. In German, a present tense T head would require movement of V to *v* and T, because the present tense marker is an ending on the verb stem. A future tense T head does not require V movement, however, because it is realised as the auxiliary verb *werden*, which is not affixal in nature. Similarly, in English, an indicative present tense 3sg T head, morpho-phonologically the ending -*s*, lowers onto the verb, but modal T heads (i.e., auxiliary verbs such as *may, can, will*, etc.) do not. In both cases, the question of whether to raise/lower or not depends on the morpho-phonological form of one of the heads involved.

An analysis of word-building head movement must therefore take the actual morpho-phonological forms of the relevant heads into account. A DM model, such as the one proposed by Harizanov & Gribanova, is not able to do this and is therefore forced to assume that the relevant feature, here the feature M, is part of syntax. But this amounts to distinguishing between different heads of the same category (i.e., different P heads, different D heads, etc.) on purely lexical grounds, something that runs counter to DM's basic assumptions.

The proposal that I outline here takes a different approach: I assume that it is the phonological form of an element that determines how it is combined with other elements. In short, whether an element is a suffix or not is only relevant to phonology, not to syntax. As will become clear below, this does not mean that all lexical features can be abolished: we still need features to distinguish, say, irregular verbs from regular verbs. These features can be implemented as selectional features, however, of the kind that exist in abundance in syntax. Unlike the [M:±] feature that Harizanov & Gribanova propose, which marks what a head does morphologically, selectional features describe with which kinds of elements a particular head can be combined with.

3 A phonological approach

3.1 English -*ing*

In order to solve the issue that head movement presents us with, I propose to encode the affixal nature of a head in its phonological form. The English gerund suffix -*ing* can be represented as in (6), for example:[5]

(6) $\begin{bmatrix} \text{SEM} & \text{GERUND} \\ \text{SYN} & [\text{N, SG}, u\text{V}] \\ \text{PHON} & \text{ŋ}|_\omega \end{bmatrix}$

The semantics of -*ing* is simply represented as GERUND, without any further details.[6] Relevant to the present discussion are the syntactic and phonological representations. Syntactically, a gerund is a singular noun, as indicated by the features [N, sg],[7] and it has the phonological form /ɪŋ/. The phonological form, however, specifies something more: it contains a prosodic *alignment* requirement. The symbol |ω represents a prosodic word boundary. The phonological form in (6) says that the form /ɪŋ/ must be right-aligned in the prosodic word (more precisely, that it appears at a right p-word boundary). This essentially states that -*ing* is a suffix.

Alignment requirements are a common feature of syntax-phonology mapping theories (see, for example, Truckenbrodt (2007)). They are also required in the analysis of phonological features that function as morphological affixes, cf. Akinlabi (1996, 2011), since the relevant features are usually associated with either the right or left edge of a (prosodic) word. Extending this notion to segmental affixes is a small and logical step. We do not need to adopt substantial new phonological mechanisms for it.

Thus, the fact that -*ing* is a suffix is encoded as part of the phonological form, it is not part of the (morpho)syntax. While Harizanov & Gribanova (2019) require a syntactic feature M to encode whether a syntactic head is an affix or not, the

---

[5] The representation is somewhat reminiscent of HPSG-style analyses, but for the current proposal, this is not relevant. (6) is only supposed to capture the intuition that an affix such as -*ing* is an association of a particular syntactic head with a particular phonological form and a particular semantic meaning.
[6] In fact, I will leave out the semantic representation in most examples below.
[7] [uV] is a selectional feature: -*ing* selects a verbal projection as its complement. I ignore the discussion whether the -*ing* suffix is really a gerund suffix or simply a suffix expressing some form of non-finiteness common to both the gerund and the present participle (cf. Yoon 1996).

current proposal allows us to state this information as part of the phonological form of a head.

In Abney's (1987) analysis of English gerunds, -*ing* can attach to V or to VP. Attachment to V yields an N° head that projects to an NP and governs an *of*-PP and a prenominal possessor, as in (7a). When -*ing* attaches to the VP, the gerund assigns accusative case to the internal argument. Since the external argument is assigned case outside the VP, however, it is still realised as a prenominal possessor, as in (7b). This follows from the fact that after attachment of -*ing*, the VP is converted into an NP and nominative case assignment is no longer possible:

(7) a. John's singing of the Marseillaise

b. John's singing the Marseillaise

I assume that Abney's analysis is essentially correct, even though the details would have to be reassessed in light of current syntactic theory. Considering the case of -*ing* attaching to VP, we can follow Abney's idea that attachment of -*ing* to VP converts it into an NP:

(8)

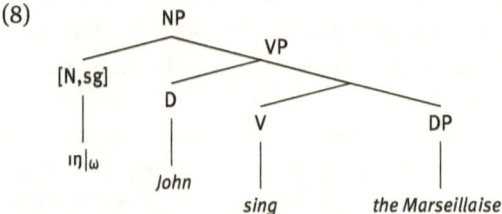

This tree illustrates the problem that head movement was intended to solve. The verb *sing* and the suffix -*ing* are not adjacent and can therefore not be pronounced together as a single prosodic word. Moving V to the suffix (and subsequent movement of *John* to obtain the correct word order) solves this issue, but raises the problems discussed in the previous section (plus the additional problem why the subject *John* would move).

In addition, there is another question that has no easy answer. In Minimalist theories, it is generally assumed that movement can only take place if there is a trigger. In essence, there must be some syntactic feature that must be checked, either on the moved element or on the target, or on both. In the current example (and indeed in many examples of word-building head movement), there is no obvious syntactic trigger. From a syntactic point of view, the tree in (8) is fine: there is no head with unvalued/unchecked features, so there should be no reason for any kind of movement. The same is true for semantics: there is no semantic reason to move *sing*. The semantics of the structure can basically be read off the syntactic tree in (8).

In fact, it appears that the only module that requires that *sing* and *-ing* are combined is phonology: the forms [sɪŋ] and [ɪŋ] are combined to form the prosodic word [sɪŋɪŋ]. Mapping the tree in (8) onto a phonological string yields (9):

(9) ing John sing the Marseillaise

We may assume that this structure violates a prosodic well-formedness condition given the prosodic alignment condition on the affix. *-ing* itself is not able to constitute a prosodic word, but it needs to be right-aligned to one. As a result, the structure is ruled out.

The solution to this problem cannot be something along the lines of Agbayani & Golston's (2010) proposal of *phonological movement*, which essentially amounts to an operation in which an element is swapped with an adjacent element in order to meet some phonological requirement. Even if we were to adopt this notion, it would put *-ing* on *John*, not on *sing*, since in Agbayani & Golston's proposal, phonological movement can only swap adjacent elements. It is not possible to move an element over a longer distance.

3.2 Arabic deverbal nouns

I nonetheless assume that phonology has a decisive role in the formation of *singing*. To see how, it is useful to first look at another example: the gerund construction in Arabic.[8] Arabic has a so-called *masdar* construction, which is a construction centered on a deverbal noun (called *maṣdar* in Arabic), and which behaves much like the English gerund construction (cf. Fassi Fehri 1993; Kremers 2003 for discussion).

Consider the following examples (taken from Fassi Fehri 1993). The relevant masdar form is *(i)ntiqād* (here in bold face):

(10) a. ʔaqlaqa-nī   **-ntiqād-u**   -l-rajul-i   -l-mašrūʕ-a
         annoy.3sg.m-1sg.OBJ criticising-NOM DEF-man-GEN DEF-project-ACC
         'The man's criticising the project annoyed me.'

---

[8] I use the term Arabic here to refer to the standard written variety, often called (Modern) Standard Arabic, or *Fuṣḥa*.

b. ʔaqlaqa-nī **-ntiqād-u** -l-rajul-i li
annoy.3sg.m-1sg.OBJ criticising-NOM DEF-man-GEN to
-l-mašrūʕ-i
DEF-project-GEN

'The man's criticising of the project annoyed me.'

The masdar form takes a genitive subject *al-rajul* 'the man', which is a postnominal genitive, since Arabic does not have prenominal genitives or possessors. The object, here *al-mašrūʕ* 'the project', can be licensed either by accusative case or by using the preposition *li*.[9] As argued by Fassi Fehri, Abney's (1987) analysis of gerunds carries over to masdars without significant modifications.

I focus here on the construction in which the masdar assigns accusative to its object, i.e., the equivalent of Abney's Acc-*ing* construction, but the relevant argument holds for the masdar+*li* construction (the equivalent of Abney's Poss-*ing*) as well, since it is the masdar form itself that is relevant. According to McCarthy & Prince (1990), the masdar form contains four morphemes:

(11)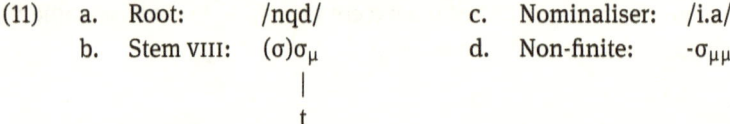

Roots in Arabic generally consist of three consonants (sometimes two or four) and are always category-neutral. They need a stem-forming affix to turn them into a nominal, verbal or adjectival stem. In the current case, the stem affix is (11b), which is a syllabic structure consisting of two syllables (σ). The first is an extrametrical syllable, which in this case only contains a consonant position. The consonant that comes to occupy this position is syllabified in a post-lexical phonological process. The second syllable of the stem marker is a full, short syllable and has a segment /t/ associated with its onset position.[10]

This stem marker turns the root *nqd* into a verb. Two additional derivational morphemes turn this verb into a deverbal noun: a non-finiteness marker, which consists of a long syllable (as indicated by the double mora subscript), and a nominaliser, consisting of the two vowels /i.a/. The dot indicates that the two vowels obligatorily belong to two different syllables.[11]

---

[9] Furthermore, if the subject is not present, it can be licensed by genitive case.
[10] Arabic has up to fifteen different verb stem markers, which are numbered I-XV in Western grammars of Arabic. The stem marker in (11b) is the marker for stem VIII.
[11] Note that in Kremers (2012a) I argue that the nominaliser and non-finiteness morpheme are actually just one single morpheme. McCarthy & Prince (1990) recognise these as two separate

Because the verbal stem can still govern accusative case, we must assume, following Abney, that the masdar structure is syntactic and that the nominaliser is merged higher than the VP. The structure I propose in Kremers (2017) is the following:

(12)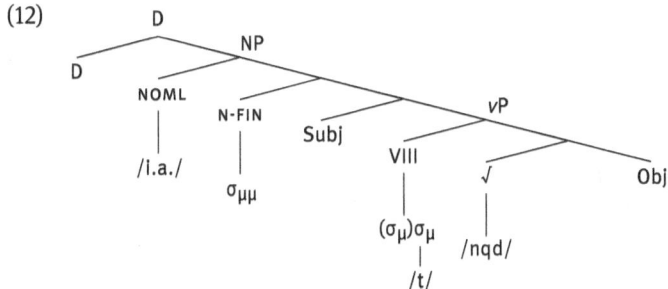

I assume that the stem marker is actually a little v head and that the object is merged with the root (although it is licensed by v, as per standard minimalist assumptions). Since v also introduces the subject, it is merged here before the nominaliser.

The details of the structural analysis are not crucial to the point at hand, therefore I will not dwell on these. The important point here is that however one constructs the tree, the root, stem marker and nominaliser morphemes do not form a distinct subtree and are not adjacent in the linear structure resulting from (12), which, given that Arabic is consistently head-initial, would be (13):

(13)   D NOML Subj vIII √ Obj

The traditional solution to problems of this kind is of course head movement. If we assume that the root moves to the stem marker and on to the nominaliser, the heads would end up in a distinct subtree, making it possible for the relevant morphemes to be composed into a single word form.

However, these movement operations constitute head-adjunction, meaning that they suffer from all the problems associated with it. In this case, however, there is no real need to resort to head movement. The relevant morphemes are

---

morphemes, arguing that the non-finiteness marker also occurs in some participles, based on the fact that they also have a long vowel. However, most participle forms lack a long vowel, and not all masdar forms have one, therefore (and for theoretical reasons not discussed here, see Kremers 2012a for details), I assume that there is no separate non-finiteness morpheme. For the discussion at hand this issue is not relevant.

prosodic morphemes and the way they are composed into a coherent phonological form is fairly well understood. Basically, the stem marker and the non-finiteness morpheme create a syllabic template, into which the segments are inserted:

(14)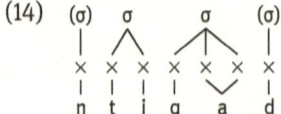

The first two syllables in (14) come from the stem marker. The first syllable, as mentioned above, is in parentheses because it is extrametrical. The third syllable in (14) is a long syllable and is provided by the non-finiteness morpheme. The non-finiteness morpheme is marked as a suffix in (11), therefore it is placed after the stem marker. The final syllable, which is also in parentheses, is added by default, because all Arabic word stems end in an extrametrical (non-morphemic) syllable, which provides solely an onset position.[12]

The segments in (14) are provided by the root, the stem marker and the nominaliser. These are positioned in the template from left to right, according to the common principle of Left-to-Right Association, with the exception of the final root consonant, which is always associated with the final (non-morphemic) extrametrical syllable. The first root consonant is associated with the initial extrametrical syllable, which provides a coda position. Since the onset position of the second syllable is lexically specified as /t/, the second root consonant cannot occupy it. The second syllable, being short, also does not have a coda position, which means that the second root consonant is associated with the onset position of the third syllable. This is a long syllable, which mean that it could in principle provide a coda for another consonant, but the only remaining consonant is the third root consonant /d/, which, as just mentioned, is obligatorily associated with the final syllable.

The vowels are also associated with the template from left to right. The first vowel in the nominaliser, /i/, is associated with the nucleus of the second syllable, since the first syllable is extrametrical and lacks a nucleus position. The second vowel /a/ is associated with the nucleus of the third syllable. Since this syllable provides another position, the vowel spreads, resulting in a long vowel.

---

[12] Most words receive an additional suffix consisting of (at least) a short vowel: case endings in nouns, verbal mood endings for verbs. The consonant in the onset position is then syllabified with this vowel.

Crucially, the composition of this form involves only phonological principles. There is no need to refer to the syntactic structure in order to describe it. However, we do need to make sure that phonology "knows" it needs to combine these four formatives into a single phonologically coherent structure. If we forego the option of head adjunction, however, the syntactic structure does not provide this information. In syntax, the four relevant morphemes are not in a distinct subtree, which by standard assumptions means that they are not adjacent in the linear structure (cf. e.g., Partee et al.'s 1993 Nontangling Condition).

Note, however, that the phonological structure is more complex than a simple linear alignment of morphemes. The structure is layered, in the sense of Goldsmith's (1976) Autosegmental Phonology, consisting of at least a syllabic and a segmental tier. The elements on each individual tier are linearly ordered, but the tiers are stacked on top of each other, so to speak, and the elements on each tier are associated with the elements on the tiers above and below.

To understand how exactly the information that these four morphemes should be combined into a single form reaches the phonological system, we need to consider how syntactic structures are mapped onto phonological structures. This involves mapping syntactic constituents onto prosodic constituents (cf. Selkirk 1981; Nespor & Vogel 2007; Truckenbrodt 1995, and related work),[13] but it also involves another aspect that is usually considered part of morphology: the mapping of individual heads onto phonological forms. As I discuss in Kremers (2012b, 2015), a grammar model that incorporates *bare phrase structure* (Chomsky 1995) and some variant of Beard's (1988) Separation Hypothesis[14] cannot draw a clear line between syntax and morphology. There is a large 'grey area' of structures that are partially syntactic and partially morphological and that benefit from a unified analysis.[15]

If there is no clearly defined distinction between syntax and morphology, the principles that map morphological structures onto phonology apply in syntax as well. Ackema & Neeleman (2004) define two such principles that are crucial to the present proposal:[16]

---

13 Note that there are different views, see, e.g., Scheer (2008). For present purposes, this discussion is not relevant, however.
14 Cf. *Late Insertion* in Distributed Morphology, (Halle & Marantz 1993)
15 Furthermore, In Kremers (2015), I argue that the intuitive distinction between syntax and morphology is essentially one of perception: syntactic structures that are mapped onto syllables and prosodic words are considered "morphological", while structures mapped onto phonological or intonational phrases are considered "syntactic".
16 See also Sadock (1991). Note that Ackema & Neeleman actually propose a third principle, *Quantitative Correspondence*, which is not relevant to the present discussion.

(15) a. *Linear Correspondence*:
If a node A is structurally external to B, then Φ(A) is linearly external to Φ(B).

b. *Input Correspondence*:
If A selects (a projection of) B, Φ(A) selects Φ(B)

Φ describes the function that maps syntactic structures onto phonological structures. As such, Φ(A) is the phonological material associated with the syntactic structure A. Note that A does not have to be a head, it can also be a larger syntactic structure. Similarly, Φ(A) does not have to be a prosodic word, it can be any piece of phonological structure, including prosodic structure.

Although Ackema & Neeleman propose these principles as *morphological* principles, they are equally applicable to syntax. Linear Correspondence is essentially a variant of Partee et al.'s (1993) Nontangling Condition. It states that two sister nodes are adjacent in the linear structure. In other words, if Φ(A) = «x» and Φ(B) = «abc» and A and B are sisters, then Φ([AB]) may be «xabc» or «abcx», but not «axbc» or «abxc», because A is structurally external to everything that B dominates.

Input Correspondence states that if a head A selects B in syntax, Φ(A) will take Φ(B) as its phonological host. Crucially, this also happens when A merges not with B directly but with a *projection* of B (i.e., BP). In Ackema & Neeleman's proposal, Input Correspondence only applies when Linear Correspondence can also apply, but as I argue in Kremers (2012b), this changes when prosodic morphology is involved. To see why, consider the following tree, where the syntactic heads are in upper case and their associated phonological material in lower case:

(16)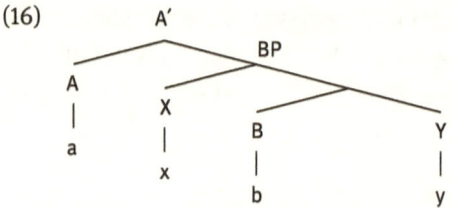

Since A is structurally outside BP, Linear Correspondence requires that Φ(A) appears to the left or the right of Φ(BP), which consists of the string «xby». What I argue in Kremers (2012b) is that if Φ(A) is an autosegment, it can take Φ(B) as its phonological host, even though such a constellation would appear to violate Linear Correspondence, because «a» is external to «xby». However, in such a case, Linear Correspondence does not apply (or applies vacuously), because Φ(A) and Φ(BP) are not realised on the same tier and therefore no linear order is defined between them. This, then, allows Input Correspondence to require that Φ(A) be associated with Φ(B).

Now consider again the structure of the Arabic verbal noun in (12), repeated here:

(12)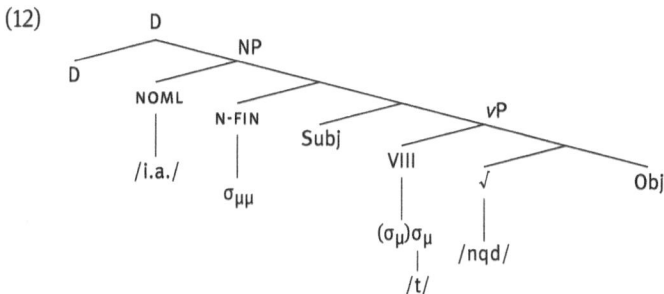

Here, the stem marker selects the root, which means that Input Correspondence requires that Φ(VIII) takes Φ(√) as its host. Similarly, the non-finiteness marker selects ν (i.e., the stem VIII marker) and the nominaliser in turn selects the projection of the non-finiteness marker. Input Correspondence therefore ensures that all of these morphemes are realised together in a single form.

Obviously, this is only part of the story. Input Correspondence may be responsible for ensuring that the four morphemes are combined, but it has nothing to say about the final position of the resulting word form in the linear string. If this were any other language, we would be tempted to say that the position of the word stem in the tree determines the linear position of the word form.

In Arabic, things are a bit more complex, however. The actual lexical meaning of the verb underlying the verbal noun arises only when the stem marker is merged. The root *n-q-d* together with the stem VIII marker yields *intaqada* 'to criticise', but the same root with the stem IV marker yields the verb *ʔanqada* 'to pay in cash'. Note, however, that the stem marker and the root together do not yield a pronounceable form. Only when combined with the nominaliser and the non-finiteness marker can the form be pronounced.

The word order facts clearly show that the form *intiqād* must be pronounced in a position above the subject: as can be seen in the examples in (10), *intiqād* is the first element in the noun phrase it heads. The construction in which *intiqād* appears in (10) is a typical Semitic genitive construction, in which the head noun appears in a special morphological form called the *construct state*. In (Standard) Arabic, this form is characterised by the absence of definiteness marking.[17] Vari-

---

[17] In other Semitic languages, the formal changes may be larger, e.g., Hebrew *bayit* 'house' becomes *bēt* in the construct state.

ous analyses of the construct state assume that the head noun moves to D or a functional projection below D, often labelled Poss (cf., e.g., Fassi Fehri 1999; Ritter 1991; Siloni 1997; Kremers 2003), a movement that is also often assumed to take place in other languages (see, e.g., Longobardi 1994, 1996 for Romance). This not only explains the special morphological form, but also the position of the head noun: D being the first head in the noun phrase, nothing can precede the head noun after it has moved to D.

This movement of N to D or Poss is a case of head substitution, since the target is phonologically null: D is realised as *al-* in definite, non-construct state nouns,[18] but in the genitive construction there is no reflex of D on the head noun. However, these facts do not really help us to determine in which position the four morphemes comprising the deverbal noun are pronounced. We essentially have two options: we may assume that it is the position of the morpheme that yields a phonologically licit form, or it may simply be the highest head position in the structure. The data discussed here do not provide a definitive answer to this question.

The important point for now is that head adjunction is implausible as a mechanism for the construction of the Arabic deverbal noun. Head adjunction could in principle bring the heads together into a distinct subtree, but cannot account for the way they are combined. Adjunction essentially provides two options: left adjunction and right adjunction.[19] It should be clear that adjunction, neither right nor left, can account for the complex morpho-phonological structure of the *masdar*. Therefore, given that phonology must play a role, and given that head adjunction is problematic for independent reasons, the most sensible conclusion is that head movement is not involved in the construction of the Arabic deverbal noun. The only remaining question we need to answer is what factors determine where the resulting form is pronounced.

3.3 *-ing* as a prosodic morpheme

In Sect. 3.1, we arrived at the question why the tree in (8), repeated here, does not yield the word order *ing John sing the Marseillaise*:

---

[18] Note that in Standard Arabic, indefinite nouns are usually marked with a suffix *-n*.
[19] In fact, minimalist models nowadays generally assume that adjunction is always to the left, so right adjunction would not even be an option.

(8)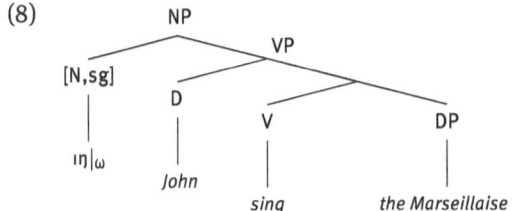

We can now formulate an answer to this question: the phonological representation of -ing as ɪŋ|ω, i.e., as a phonological syllable with a prosodic alignment requirement, means that we can treat it as a prosodic morpheme.[20] This in turn means that it is not mapped (directly) onto the segmental tier in phonology but rather on a separate tier that must be associated with the segmental tier. As such, the initial linearisation just involves *John*, *sing* and *the Marseillaise*, but not the suffix *-ing*. Input Correspondence determines that it must be associated with the head of the projection it heads, which is *sing*. Given that *-ing* has a right-alignment requirement, it is construed as a suffix, yielding *singing*.

Note that the placement of the full form *singing* in this example differs from what we might expect on the basis of the Arabic example in the previous section. The Arabic deverbal noun is placed in the position of its highest morpheme, *singing* on the other hand is placed in the position of its stem. This means that we can rule out the option that it is the highest morpheme in the structure that determines the position in the linear string. The most viable option at the moment seems to be that once a phonologically licit form has been created, it is mapped onto the segmental tier. Any further formatives that Input Correspondence associates with the form must be realised there. In the case of the English gerund, the verb stem without *-ing* constitutes a licit form, hence the suffix appears to be lowered onto the stem. In the case of the Arabic deverbal noun, no licit form is created until all morphemes are merged into the structure, therefore the deverbal noun is pronounced in the position of its highest head, the nominaliser.

Claiming that *-ing* is a prosodic morpheme and therefore mapped onto a separate tier in phonology may seem at odds with the fact that it contains two segments. Note, however, that the tiers in an autosegmental analysis are phonological in nature, not phonetic. They are part of the grammar of a language and adapt to its logic. It is not uncommon, for example, to distinguish between a vocalic and a consonantal tier in analyses of Arabic. It is also important to keep in mind that the segmental tier is not fundamentally different from any other tier. Rather, the fundamental tier to which all segmental and non-segmental phonolo-

---

20 Despite the fact that it contains two segments, a matter I will discuss shortly.

gical material needs to be linked is the timing tier, i.e., a tier of timing slots usually represented by a series of × signs.

What this means is that the mapping from syntactic structure to phonological string does not linearise the segments directly. The linear ordering is determined in phonology, and things such as linearisation parameters (or Kayne's 1994 LCA) and Ackema & Neeleman's Linear Correspondence (or the Nontangling Condition) are merely factors in this process.

4 Verbal complexes

Harizanov & Gribanova (2019) discuss verb complexes in four different languages: French, English, Russian and Danish. The reason for looking at these specific languages is that they show that *amalgamation* (in Harizanov & Gribanova's terms) of the various morphemes that make up the verb form is not related to the position of the tree in which the verb ends up. In French, for example, the (finite) verb moves to a high position (assumed to be T), as seen by the fact that it precedes (temporal) adverbials, as in (17):

(17) a. Astérix mangeait souvent du sanglier.
       Asterix eat.3.IMPF often   of boar
       'Asterix often ate boar.'

   b. *Astérix souvent mangeait du sanglier.
       Asterix often   eat.3.IMPF of boar

The adverb *souvent* appears after the finite verb, it cannot appear before it. This contrasts with English, where the adverbial must appear before the verb:

(18) a. Asterix often ate boar.

   b. *Asterix ate often boar.

The underlying idea, already expressed by Pollock (1989), is that the clausal skeleton and the hierarchical position of the adverbial are identical in both languages. The difference is traditionally explained by the assumption that in French, the finite verb moves to T, while in English it stays in V or, in more recent analyses, moves no higher than little *v*.

In Russian, placement of adverbs and quantifiers shows that the verb is in a low position, as well:

(19) a. Ivan   často ubiraet   (*často) komnatu.
       Ivan.NOM often cleans.3SG (*often) room.ACC
       'Ivan often cleans his room.'

   b. My   vse čitaem   (*vse)   gazetu.
       we.NOM all read.1PL newspaper.ACC
       'We all read the newspaper.'   (Gribanova 2917, 1095)

Harizanov & Gribanova (2019) argue that the verb in Russian is higher than V and in fact moves to Neg. Note that the negation *ne* in Russian is phonologically part of the verb, even though it is orthographically separated:

(20) ne za- bol'- e-   va-   la.
     NEG PFX- hurt- THEME- 2IMPF- PST.sg.f
     'She was not falling ill.'

In Danish, adverb placement also shows that the verb remains low:

(21) a. Jeg spurgte hvorfor Peter **ofte** havde læst den.
        I   asked   why   Peter often had   read it.
        'I asked why Peter had often read it.'

   b. *Jeg spurgte hvorfor Peter havde **ofte** læst den.
        I   asked   why   Peter had   often read it.   (Vikner 1995, 145)

Danish being a verb-second language, the relevant order can best be observed in subclauses, in which the finite verb does not move to C. As (21) shows, the adverb *ofte* 'often' must precede the finite verb *havde* 'had', indicating that the verb is in a low position. In fact, for reasons not discussed here, Harizanov & Gribanova assume that in Danish, the verb actually remains in V.

The schema in (22) indicates the position of V in the four languages discussed by Harizanov & Gribanova:

(22)
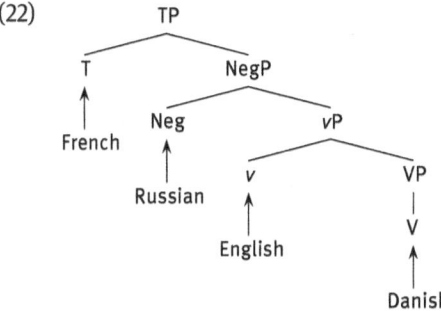

Crucially, however, all four languages show reflexes of the highest head T on the verb: each language marks (at least) past tense with verbal suffixes. Under a traditional analysis, this means that V must move to T. Since this does not appear to happen in at least three of the four languages, Harizanov & Gribanova argue that morphological composition cannot be the result of head movement, a conclusion that I concur with.

Under the current proposal, the analysis is relatively straightforward: the tense suffix is still a reflex of the T head, but, being a suffix, it is a prosodic morpheme. The English suffix *-ed* can serve as an example. Its phonological form is similar to the phonological form of *-ing*, discussed above:

(23) əd$|_\omega$

Given this form, the placement of the suffix is determined by Input Correspondence: Since T selects Neg, $\Phi(T)$ must combine with $\Phi(Neg)$. Assuming that $\Phi(Neg)$ is empty in English (the element '*not*' being in Spec,NegP), Input Correspondence targets the head selected by Neg, which is *v*. On the assumption that in English, V does indeed move to *v* by substitution, we can account for the fact that the suffix *-ed* ends up on V without having to assume V-to-T movement.

4.1 The position of phonological composition

The analysis seems to work well for English, but it does of course raise an important question concerning the position of phonological composition. The issue is that we have two or more syntactic heads that are not structurally adjacent (specifiers intervene), which are combined by the mechanism described into a single phonological form. Given that they are not adjacent, where in the linear string does the resulting word form end up? It seems reasonable to assume that the word form should end up in a position that corresponds to one of the heads in the structure, but it is not immediately clear which head that would be. Intuitively, one is tempted to say that it should be the head that constitutes the stem of the word, which is the lexical head, V in the cases under discussion.

The question is not so simple, however: there are at least two problems with this idea. The first problem involves the position of the verb in the four languages discussed in the previous section, French, English, Russian and Danish. Of these languages, Harizanov & Gribanova argue, only Danish has the verb in the V° position. In the other languages, V seems to have moved. While this may not be immediately obvious for Russian and English, in French the verb's pre-adverbial position clearly indicates that it is in a high position. This suggests that it is not necessarily the position of the lexical V° head that determines where the phonological form is composed.

The second problem was discussed earlier: the deverbal noun in Arabic has a triconsonantal root at its base. The lexical meaning of the verb underlying the noun is obtained when this root is augmented with a stem marker. The resulting form, however, is still not a word stem and is, in fact, phonologically still incomplete (i.e., it cannot be pronounced). Only when the non-finiteness marker and the nominaliser are added is the word stem complete and pronounceable.

It is beyond the scope of this article to resolve this issue: more empirical research is needed to determine the options and possibilities that exist in this domain. Here, I will only point out some options and further questions that they raise.

Both the French and Arabic data make clear that it is not simply the position of the lexical head that determines the position of the composed word form. The Arabic data suggest that the word form may be placed in the position where a pronounceable form is created: the deverbal noun is phrase-initial and we may assume it is in the position of the nominaliser, preceding all other heads in the structure. The same cannot be said of the French data, however. Consider again the example in (17), repeated here:

(17) a. Astérix mangeait souvent du sanglier.
       Asterix eat.3.IMPF often   of boar
       'Asterix often ate boar.'

   b. *Astérix souvent mangeait du sanglier.
       Asterix often   eat.3.IMPF of boar

The conjugated verb here is *mangeait* 'ate'. Its stem is *mange* /mɑ̃ʒ/, which is a phonotactically licit word form in French.[21] One possibility is that V does indeed move in French, just not through head adjunction but rather through head substitution. This could actually be a solution for the Arabic verbal noun as well, if we assume, as discussed above Sect. 3.2, that the nominaliser moves to D°. However, this would raise the question to which head V° in French actually moves. It is assumed here that the inflectional ending on the French verb is a reflex of T°, and since the ending is non-nil in most cases, V-movement to T cannot be a case of head substitution. If head adjunction is not a possibility, another option would be to argue that V moves to a position directly below T, but this would in turn raise other questions: which head is it that V moves to and why does it move there?

---

21 In fact, /mɑ̃ʒ/ is the conjugated form in the singular and third person plural forms of the present tense, given that these forms have a null ending.

Alternatively, one may assume that it is not V that moves to T but T that moves to C. That constellation would actually match the Arabic case to some extent: the highest morph involved in the complex word form (T in the French clause and the nominalising N in Arabic deverbal nouns) moves through head substitution and as a result the entire word form is placed in that head's target position. In the French case, however, this would require a plausible argument that the verb is actually in C, not in T, which, to my knowledge, has never been made.

Summarising, based on the limited data presented in this paper it is unfortunately not possible to provide a satisfying answer to the question where a complex word form composed of multiple non-adjacent morphs is positioned in the linear string. More data should shed more light on this question.

4.2 Other T heads

The discussion so far centred on T heads that are affixal. It is insightful to consider other kinds of T heads as well. First, let us consider the case where T is occupied by an auxiliary verb. In English, auxiliary verbs precede both negation and adverbs, and they should obviously not be combined with V:

(24)   John **does** not often kiss Mary.

This is easily accounted for: the form *does* /dʌz/ is a full prosodic word and does not have a prosodic alignment requirement (i.e., it is not an affix). This means that its placement is not governed by Input Correspondence but rather by Linear Correspondence, which puts *does* where traditional analyses would put it: after the subject (its specifier) and before Neg (its complement). The fact that *does* and *not* usually fuse to a single form (either [dʌznt] or [dəznɒt]) is a phonological matter that is not conditioned by syntax in any way. It occurs because both words are functional and therefore have a tendency to be phonologically reduced, and because they are adjacent.

Another interesting question concerns irregular tense forms, which lack the *-ed* ending. Consider the following example:

(25)   John never wrote a book.

The past tense form *wrote* is positioned like any finite full verb: it follows *never*, which means it occupies *v*. In a traditional analysis, which assumes (possibly covert) head movement of V to T or lowering of T to V, V and T combine in syntax, so that mapping the T+V complex on an irregular form such as *wrote* is straightforward. Similarly, in a Distributed Morphology approach, the assumption that T and V are combined in a post-syntactic, morphological process before

Vocabulary Insertion means that Vocabulary Insertion can select a Vocabulary Item that realises both T and V.

In the current approach, however, it is the *phonological* form of T that ensures that it is combined with V. This means that compared to the traditional (or DM) approach, the order of operations is reversed: after selecting a V head with the semantics of ⟦write⟧ and a T head with the feature [+past], the traditional analysis first combines the two heads and then selects the phonological forms. In the current approach, the phonological forms are selected *before* the two are combined.[22] This means that we cannot rely on the syntactic proximity of T and V to ensure that the form *wrote* is selected.

The actual problem here, however, is not the way Φ(T) and Φ(V) are combined. If we analyse *wrote* as a rote form, it follows that Φ(T) is phonologically null, which means there is nothing to combine. If Φ(T) is some ablaut feature, it is an autosegment and will be combined with Φ(V) in a way similar to the suffix *-ed*. This means that once we have mapped T and V onto their correct phonological forms, combining them is not problematic. The actual problem is ensuring that T is mapped onto the empty string (or the ablaut feature) in the presence of the verb *write*.

Note that this is a morphological fact about English, it cannot be reduced to phonology and it cannot be derived regularly from some syntactic feature. Since there is no morphological module (as in lexical morphology and similar models), nor a specific set of post-syntactic, morphological operations (as in Distributed Morphology) we are forced to deal with this fact in syntax. That is, we must adopt the assumption that the V head that is mapped onto a phonological form *wrote* has an additional feature that ensures that a silent T is selected.

Technically, this can be implemented in several ways. A minimalist analysis could assume a selectional feature on T that matches the relevant feature on V. Projections in between T and V (at least *v*), would have to be endowed with the same feature to ensure that T can actually match V. Alternatively, some sort of feature percolation could be assumed, as was occasionally done in Government & Binding theory, or more generally in HPSG with the Head Feature Principle.

What is important to note, however, is that the relation between an irregular verb such as *write* and the T head that this verb must combine with does not differ in any significant way from the relation between other types of T heads that select specific forms of the verb. For example, if T is realised by the auxiliary *have*, V has to be in the past participle form; if T is realised by a modal verb, V has to be in the

---

22 Or, more precisely, the syntactic heads are not combined at all. Only the phonological forms that they are mapped onto are combined.

infinitive form, etc. In such cases, there is a dependency between the T head and the form of the verb that we must account for in syntax in some way or other. The dependency between a [+past] T is not realised phonologically (i.e., $\Phi(T) = \emptyset$) and a V head that represents an irregular verb (i.e., a verb form that explicitly marks past tense), is the same: T and V depend on each other.

The main difference is that the combination of an auxiliary with its dependent full verb makes a specific semantic contribution (passive, progressive aspect, etc.). This is obviously not the case for an irregular verb combined with a phonologically null T head: semantically it does not differ from a regular past tense verb. But whichever method we use to model the dependency between a past participle form of V and the auxiliary *to have*, or between the gerund form of V and the auxiliary *to be*, we can use the same method to model the dependency between an irregular past tense form of V and a phonologically null T.

This means that the current approach does not need a special-purpose morphological feature such as the M-feature that Harizanov & Gribanova (2019) propose, which behaves quite differently from the other features on syntactic heads. Basically, syntactic features restrict the syntactic contexts in which a head can appear: a noun with an accusative case feature cannot appear in subject position; a verb with a [+finite] feature cannot appear in a non-finite context, etc. Harizanov & Gribanova's M-feature does not function in this way and as such it is a qualitatively different kind of feature. The feature that distinguishes an irregular verb from a regular one as described here is not. It simply restricts the syntactic contexts in which the verb can appear to those in which T is phonologically null and endowed with [+past].

Obviously, having a syntactic feature to mark irregular verbs runs somewhat counter to the intuitive idea of what syntax should be: a description of the ordering and dependence relations between words with all word-specific properties abstracted away. However, if we subscribe to the view that there is no strict distinction between syntax and morphology, which is a common assumption in minimalist models and a specific argument behind Distributed Morphology ("syntax all the way down"), this is not a valid argument. It is a well-known fact that there are purely morphological phenomena that cannot be reduced to syntax, semantics or phonology (e.g., Aronoff 1994; Maiden 2004) and if there is no distinction between morphology and syntax, such phenomena need to be modelled with syntactic features.[23]

---

[23] One well-known example is Maiden's (2004) so-called 'N-pattern', an inflectional pattern in Romance verbs. Maiden shows that this is an abstract pattern that cannot be reduced to se-

5 Conclusions

The main argument of the current paper is that word-forming head movement (head adjunction) is not a syntactic phenomenon. Rather, the observations that lead us to assume head movement are better described in terms of their phonological structure. A syntactic head A is mapped onto a phonological element that has a prosodic alignment requirement and is therefore treated by the phonological system as an autosegment. It is associated with a prosodic word; as a result of this association it is attached to it. The prosodic word in question corresponds to the syntactic head B that A selects in syntax. As a result, A appears as an affix on B, or more precisely, Φ(A) appears as an affix on Φ(B).

Since A and B may be separated by overt material (specifically, the specifier of B), it may appear that B has moved to A (and the specifier has moved further up) or that A has been lowered onto B. Neither type of movement is necessary, however, because being an autosegment, the position of Φ(A) in the linear string is determined by the element with which it is associated, which is Φ(B). Neither A nor B therefore needs to move in syntax.

The proposal has the advantage that we can abandon the notion of word-forming head movement (i.e., head adjunction), which is a problematic notion for a number of reasons, as has often been pointed out in the literature. It also allows us to account for morphological effects by separating them into a phonological and a syntactic part and thus to truly eliminate morphology as a module of the grammar without losing the ability to express morphological generalisations.

Obviously, several open questions remain. Besides the obvious question whether it is truly possible to handle all morphological phenomena in the manner proposed here, the main question is where exactly a prosodic word that is construed by associating one or more autosegments with it is positioned in the linear string. The limited data presented in this paper suggests that it is not (necessarily) the position of the (lexical) root of the word in question. If this is not the case, it could be that the word is placed in the linear string at the position where a licit phonological word can be construed. In the case of Arabic deverbal nouns discussed in Sect. 3.2, this would be the highest head involved in the formation of the deverbal noun, which would be the nominaliser. Alternatively, it is possible that the nominaliser moves (through head substitution) to D and that this movement is what ensures that the entire word form is realised in the D position. Which of these two options is correct is a matter for future research.

---

mantics, syntax or phonology. In Kremers (2014) I discuss a way in which such phenomena can be modelled in syntax.

References

Abney, Steven (1987). *The English Noun Phrase in its Sentential Aspect*. Phd thesis, Massachusetts Institute of Technology (MIT). MIT Working Papers in Linguistics.
Ackema, Peter and Ad Neeleman (2004). *Beyond Morphology: Interface Conditions on Word Formation*. Oxford: Oxford University Press.
Agbayani, Brian and Chris Golston (2010). Phonological Movement in Classical Greek. *Language*, 86:133–167.
Akinlabi, Akinbiyi (1996). Featural Affixation. *Journal of Linguistics*, 32(2):239–289.
Akinlabi, Akinbiyi (2011). Featural Affixes. In Van Oostendorp et al. (2011), pp. 1945–1971.
Aronoff, Mark (1994). *Morphology by Itself: Stems and Inflectional Classes*. Cambridge MA: MIT Press.
Baker, Mark (1985). The Mirror Principle and Morphosyntactic Explanation. *LI*, 16(3):373–415.
Beard, Robert (1988). On the Separation of Derivation from Morphology: Toward a Lexeme / Morpheme-Based Morphology. *Quaderni di Semantica*, 9:3–59.
Cheng, Lisa Lai-Shen and Norbert Corver, eds (2013). *Diagnosing Syntax*. Oxford: Oxford University Press. doi:10.1093/acprof:oso/9780199602490.001.0001.
Chomsky, Noam (1993). The Minimalist Program. In Hale & Keyser (1993), pp. 1–52.
Chomsky, Noam (1995). *The Minimalist Program*. Cambridge MA: MIT Press.
De Lacy, Paul, ed. (2007). *The Cambridge Handbook of Phonology*. Cambridge: Cambridge University Press.
Dehé, Nicole, Ray Jackendoff, Andrew McIntyre, and Silke Urban, eds (2002). *Verb-Particle Explorations*. Berlin/New York: Mouton de Gruyter.
Dékány, Éva (2018). Approaches to head movement: a critical assessment. *Glossa*, 3(1):1–43. doi:10.5334/gjgl.316.
Eid, Mushira and John McCarthy, eds (1990). *Perspectives on Arabic Linguistics II*. vol. 72 of *Current Issues in Linguistic Theory*. Amsterdam/Philadelphia: John Benjamins.
Fassi Fehri, Abdelkader (1993). *Issues in the Structure of Arabic Clauses and Words*. vol. 29 of *Studies in Natural Language and Linguistic Theory*. Dordrecht: Kluwer Academic Publishers.
Fassi Fehri, Abdelkader (1999). Arabic Modifying Adjectives and DP Structures. *Studia Linguistica*, 53(2):105–154.
Goldsmith, John (1976). *Autosegmental Phonology*. Phd thesis, Cambridge MA: MIT Press.
Gribanova, Vera (2917). Head Movement and Ellipsis in the Expression of Russian Polarity Focus. *Natural Language and Linguistic Theory*, 35(4):1079–1121.
Hale, Kenneth and Samuel Jay Keyser, eds (1993). *The View from Building 20: Essays in Linguistics in Honor of Sylvain Bromberger*. vol. 24 of *Current Studies in Linguistics*. Cambridge MA: MIT Press.
Halle, Morris and Alec Marantz (1993). Distributed Morphology. In Hale & Keyser (1993), chapter 3, pp. 111–176.
Harizanov, Boris and Vera Gribanova (2019). Whither Head Movement? *Natural Language and Linguistic Theory*.
Hartmann, Jutta, Veronika Hegedűs, and Henk van Riemsdijk, eds (2008). *Sounds of Silence: Empty Elements in Syntax and Phonology*. Amsterdam: Elsevier.
Kayne, Richard S. (1994). *The Antisymmetry of Syntax*. Cambridge MA: MIT Press.

Kremers, Joost (2003). *The Noun Phrase in Arabic: A Minimalist Approach*. Phd thesis, University of Nijmegen. LOT Dissertation Series 79.
Kremers, Joost (2012a). Arabic Verbal Nouns as Phonological Head Movement. In Iordăchioaia, Gianina, ed., *Proceedings of JeNom 4*, vol. 9 of *Working Papers of the SFB 732* Incremental Specification in Context, pp. 73–96. Stuttgart University.
Kremers, Joost (2012b). The Syntax of Simultaneity. *Lingua*, 122(9):979–1003. doi:10.1016/j.lingua.2012.03.008.
Kremers, Joost (2014). The Selection of Marked Exponents in a Parallel Grammar. *Lingue e Linguaggio*, 2014(1):103–125. doi:10.1418/77002.
Kremers, Joost (2015). Morphology is in the Eye of the Beholder. *Linguistische Berichte*, 243:246–294.
Kremers, Joost (2017). *Prosodic Syntax*. Postdoctoral thesis, University of Göttingen. *Habilitationsschrift*.
Longobardi, Giuseppe (1994). Reference and Proper Names: A Theory of N-Movement in Syntax and Logical Form. *LI*, 25(4):609–665.
Longobardi, Giuseppe (1996). The Syntax of N-Raising: A Minimalist Theory. *OTS Working Papers*, 96(5).
Maiden, Martin (2004). When Lexemes Become Allomorphs – On the Genesis of Suppletion. *Folia Linguistica*, 38(3–4):227–256. doi:10.1515/flin.2004.38.3-4.227.
McCarthy, John and Alan Prince (1990). Prosodic Morphology and Templatic Morphology. In Eid & McCarthy (1990), pp. 1–54.
Müller, Stefan (2002). Syntax or Morphology: German Particle Verbs Revisited. In Dehé et al. (2002), pp. 119–139.
Nespor, Marina and Irene Vogel (2007). *Prosodic Phonology*. Dordrecht: Foris.
Partee, Barbara, Alice ter Meulen, and Robert Wall (1993). *Mathematical Methods in Linguistics*. Dordrecht: Kluwer.
Platzack, Christer (2013). Head Movement as a Phonological Operation. In Cheng & Corver (2013). doi:2210.1093/acprof:oso/9780199602490.003.0002.
Pollock, Jean-Yves (1989). Verb Movement, Universal Grammar and the Structure of IP. *Linguistic Inquiry*, 20(3):365–424.
Ritter, Elizabeth (1991). Two Functional Categories in Noun Phrases: Evidence from Modern Hebrew. In Rothstein, Susan D., ed., *Perspectives on Phrase Structure: Heads and Licensing*, vol. 25 of *Syntax and Semantics*, pp. 37–62. San Diego: Academic Press.
Rizzi, Luigi and Ian G. Roberts (1989). Complex Inversion in French. *Probus*, 1:1–30.
Sadock, Jerrold M. (1991). *Autolexical Syntax*. Chicago: University of Chicago Press.
Scheer, Tobias (2008). Why the Prosodic Hierarchy Is a Diacritic and Why the Interface Must Be Direct. In Hartmann et al. (2008), pp. 145–192.
Selkirk, Elisabeth (1981). On Prosodic Structure and its Relation to Syntactic Structure. In Fretheim, Thorstein, ed., *Nordic Prosody II*, pp. 111–140. Trondheim: Tapir.
Siloni, Tal (1997). *Noun Phrases and Nominalizations: The Syntax of DP*. vol. 40 of *Studies in Natural Language and Linguistic Theory*. Dordrecht: Kluwer Academic Publishers.
Travis, Lisa (1984). *Parameters and Effects of Word Order Variation*. Phd thesis, MIT.
Truckenbrodt, Hubert (1995). *Phonological Phrases: Their Relation to Syntax, Focus and Prominence*. Phd thesis, Cambridge, MA: The MIT Press.
Truckenbrodt, Hubert (2007). The Syntax-Phonology Interface. In De Lacy (2007), pp. 435–456.
Van Oostendorp, Marc, Colin J. Ewen, Elizabeth V. Hume, and Keren Rice, eds (2011). *The Blackwell Companion to Phonology*. Malden, MA: Wiley-Blackwell.

Vikner, Sten (1995). *Verb Movement and Expletive Subjects in the Germanic Languages*. Oxford: Oxford University Press.

Yoon, James (1996). Nominal Gerund Phrases in English as Phrasal Zero Derivations. *Linguistics*, 34:329–356.

Index

accent
- phrase accent / phrasal accent 88, 211
- pitch accent 20, 25, 37, 43, 55, 88, 161, 165, 169, 170, 176–178, 183, 211, 212

accent/accentuation 5, 6, 11, 19, 20, 43, 120–122, 125, 131, 132, 134–136, 149, 150, 165, 170, 174

adverb 120, 123, 126, 128, 137, 138, 143, 144, 157

alignment 180, 184, 309, 311, 315, 319, 324, 327

Arabic 311–314, 317–319, 323, 324, 327

architecture of grammar 160, 169, 180

bare mapping 253, 255, 257, 258
bare NP comparative 121, 125, 131, 136, 142
bare NP ellipsis 120, 123, 127, 131, 132, 136, 146–150
belief 189, 193, 194, 197, 198, 201, 204, 206, 208, 222, 223, 232
binding 267, 270, 272, 288, 289, 291, 293, 296
boundary 54, 55, 132, 180, 303
- intonational phrase boundary / IntP boundary 3, 8
- phonological (phrase) boundary 57–59, 62–64, 71–80
- prosodic boundary 3–5, 56, 77, 246, 252–257, 260, 303
boundary stone (metaphor) 285
boundary tone 55, 88, 89, 91, 96, 98, 100, 132, 236
branching 5, 255
Bulgarian 249, 251

Call on (the) addressee 194, 206
Canadian English 189, 190, 200, 209, 210
Cartography 268, 270, 271, 277, 283, 286–289, 294–298
CHECK marker 221, 225
commitment 191, 192, 194, 195, 197–199, 201, 205–210, 214, 215, 222, 231–233

common ground (CG) 189, 191–194, 199, 201, 203–205, 209, 211, 231–233
- management 192, 195, 196, 211, 215
Compound Stress Rule (CSR) 20, 22
comprehension (experiment) 52–54, 57, 58, 66, 70, 71, 73, 75, 76, 79, 80, 103–106, 113
compression / (post-focal) compression 169, 174, 177, 180, 184
confirmational/confirmationals 189, 192, 193, 200, 203, 204, 219, 221, 223–225, 233–236, 238, 239
constituent size 4
contingency 220, 231–233, 235, 238, 239
contour / (intonational) contour 180, 183, 191, 194, 202, 204, 205, 209, 210, 214, 266
contrast 120–125, 127, 128, 131, 134, 135, 140, 142–148, 179
contrastive stress 19
contrastive topic 183, 184
conversation domain 220, 221, 231, 233, 234, 239
corpus 120, 121, 123, 125, 126, 128, 136–140, 142, 147–150
c-structure 65, 66, 69, 104, 105, 107–111

Danish 320–322
deaccentuation / (post-nuclear/post-focal) deaccentuation 159, 160, 162, 169, 173–175, 177
declarative 195, 205–210, 214, 215
default focus 121, 136, 149
disambiguation 87, 97, 104, 105, 114
Distributed Morphology 306, 307, 315, 324–326
duration 58, 61, 63, 67, 74, 75, 205, 206, 209, 210
Dutch 304

East Slavic 246, 248, 249, 251
ellipsis 120
embedding 1, 4, 5

https://doi.org/10.1515/9783110650532-012

Index

engagement 191, 192, 194, 195, 197–199, 201, 203–205, 207, 209, 213–215
English 3, 5, 7, 8, 10, 12, 122, 125, 126, 128, 129, 133, 137, 148, 149, 267, 271, 274, 287, 290, 292, 304, 307–309
Extension Condition 306

falling contour 200, 208–210, 293
Finnish 39, 40, 45
focus 52, 87–89, 120–125, 131, 136, 148–150, 159–164, 265, 266, 272, 274, 277, 279–281, 284, 286, 287, 293, 294
French 305, 320, 322–324
frequency 120, 121, 125, 126, 136, 138, 139, 141, 149, 150, 157
functional head 285, 289, 296–298

gapping 124, 127, 130–132
German/Germanic 3, 5, 9–13, 40, 52–54, 58, 60, 71, 80, 124, 159–163, 165–167, 169, 170, 212, 245, 246, 248, 250, 254–257, 265, 266, 271–274, 279, 280, 283, 285, 287, 289–293, 295–297, 304, 307, 308
gerund 309
givenness 52, 159, 169–171, 173, 175–180, 184, 185
Glasgow Scots 220, 222, 225–227, 234, 238, 239
Greek 246, 248, 249, 251

head 55, 245
head adjacency 245–250, 252, 256, 258, 260, 261
head adjunction 306, 307, 315, 318, 323, 327
head directionality 250
head movement 303–310, 313, 318, 322, 324, 327
head substitution 305, 306, 318, 323, 324, 327
head-final 245, 250, 251, 254–256, 259, 260
head-initial 245, 246, 248–251, 254–256, 259, 260
Heavy-NP Shift 7
Hindi 86–89, 91, 92, 94, 111

indirect reference 2
information structure 159, 164, 169, 176, 179, 183, 265, 267, 288

informativity 21, 25
initiation 192, 193
Input Correspondence 316, 317, 319, 322, 324
interface / syntax-prosody interface / syntax-phonology interface 1, 3, 5, 11, 12, 265, 270, 271, 273, 287, 288, 290, 294, 295, 299
interrogative 92, 195, 219, 220, 223, 224, 232, 233, 236

Japanese 258, 260

left periphery 165, 166, 220, 221, 225, 229, 231, 239
Lexical Functional Grammar (LFG) 52, 56, 65, 67, 77, 80, 103
LH contour (rise / rise contour) 88, 89, 91, 97, 99, 100, 103, 112
Linear Correspondence 316, 320, 324

masdar 311–313, 318
match theory 51, 52, 55, 69
metrical 160, 169, 171
metrical grid 28
metrical stress 19
minimalist program 245, 248, 261

negotiation (negotiate/negotiating) 189, 191–195, 199, 201, 203
No Prosodic Boundary condition (NPB) 252
Nuclear Stress Rule (NSR) 17, 20, 22, 35, 163

object fronting 159–161, 169, 171, 172, 174, 175
Optimality Theory 159, 163
OT-constraint (constraint / OT-like constraint) 77–79, 164, 171, 185

parallel model (of grammar) 168
parallelism 120, 127–132, 134–136, 143–150, 154
perceived stress 21, 22, 27–31, 34–36, 40–43
perception (experiment) 58, 87, 97, 100, 170, 177, 183, 220, 235, 236
PF / PF-interface 248
phonological phrase head 173, 174, 176
phonology 177, 182, 303, 308, 309, 311, 315, 318–320, 325–327

phrasal compound 249, 256–258
phrasal modifier 249, 252, 253, 256–259
phrasal stress 19, 39, 40, 161, 163, 166, 170–173
pitch 190, 203, 209, 210
pitch accent 161, 165, 169–171, 174–178, 183
pitch register 174, 175
polar question 86, 87, 89–91, 93, 94, 97, 104, 109, 111
post-focal compression / post-nuclear compression 169, 174, 177, 180, 184
post-nuclear/post-focal deaccentuation 159, 160, 162, 169, 173–175, 177
prenominal modification 246, 252
processing 120–127, 131, 136, 147–150
production (experiment) 52–54, 57, 58, 66, 70–73, 75, 79, 80, 87, 97, 100, 103, 112, 113, 170, 183
prominence / prosodic prominence 17–20, 25, 27, 28, 38, 42, 43, 93, 94, 161, 163, 165
prosodic head 180
prosodic phrase boundary / prosodic boundary / phrase boundary 246, 252–257, 260
prosodic reconstruction 166, 167, 172, 184
prosody / prosodic structure 159, 164, 214, 215
prosody-syntax interface 94, 105, 108, 109, 112
pseudogapping 120, 126, 139, 141, 144, 146–148
p-structure / p-diagram 65–67, 69–78, 80, 105, 106, 108, 109

reaction 192, 193
relation 271
rise / rising (rise contour / LH contour) 88, 89, 91, 97, 99, 100, 103, 112, 190, 194, 195, 200–204, 207, 209, 210, 214
roll-up movement 305
Romance 255, 256
Russian 245, 246, 249–252, 258–260, 320–322

scope 266, 270, 272, 273, 287, 289, 291, 293, 295
scrambling 265–274, 276, 277, 279–287, 289–291, 294, 295, 297
sentence-final intonation 190–192, 198, 205, 206, 209–213, 215
serial model (of grammar) 160, 168, 176, 180, 181, 183, 185
Slavic/ West Slavic /East Slavic 246, 248–251
speaker variability 53, 54, 62, 64, 77, 78
stress 18–22, 55, 56, 59, 67, 68, 71, 122, 266, 272, 274, 276, 277, 279–281, 283, 286–288, 294, 296
– contrastive stress 19
– meaningful stress 18, 26, 27, 29, 35
– mechanical stress 19, 21–23, 26, 27, 29, 30, 32–35, 37, 40, 42, 43
– perceived stress 21, 22, 27–31, 34–36, 40–43
– phrasal stress 19, 39, 40, 161, 163, 166, 170–173
– sentence stress 18–20, 22–24, 26, 38, 39, 43, 159–171, 173, 178, 179, 184
– word stress 256
stress ambiguity / stress ambiguous 24
stress hierarchy 36, 37, 39
StressXP/Stress-XP 5, 6, 55
syntactic ambiguity 55, 57, 59, 65, 75, 79–81
syntactic integration 191, 192, 195, 211, 212, 214, 215
syntactic phrasing 53, 57, 69, 71, 75, 77, 80
syntax 1–3, 5, 7–13, 165, 166, 168, 169, 175, 179, 180, 185, 195, 199, 203, 205, 212, 215, 245, 253, 261, 266, 270, 273, 277, 278, 285, 287–290, 292, 294–296, 298, 299, 303, 306–308
syntax-phonology interface 248, 252, 303
syntax-prosody interface 1, 3, 5, 11, 12, 103

tag question 223, 225, 230, 239
topic 52, 53, 58, 68, 265–269, 284, 286, 297, 299
transfer of structure 67, 69–71, 73, 75, 80, 106, 108, 109, 112
transfer of vocabulary 67, 69–71, 75, 80, 109
trigger / trigger feature 265–268, 270–273, 277, 278, 286, 290, 295, 297–299

Urdu 86–89, 91, 92, 94, 97, 98, 100, 101, 104, 111, 113

VP ellipsis 120, 123, 124, 126, 130, 132, 136, 139–150

West Slavic 250, 251
wh-constituent question 86, 87, 89, 91, 97, 101, 102, 112, 113
word order 2, 160, 162, 165, 167, 178, 184, 212, 213, 245, 247, 250, 251, 255, 261, 310, 317, 318

www.ingramcontent.com/pod-product-compliance
Lightning Source LLC
Chambersburg PA
CBHW030521230426
43665CB00010B/709